Of Light and Struggle

POWER, POLITICS, AND THE WORLD

Series editors: Christopher R. W. Dietrich,
Jennifer Mittelstadt, and Russell Rickford

Power, Politics, and the World showcases new stories
in the fields of the history of U.S. foreign relations,
international history, and transnational history. The
series is motivated by a desire to pose innovative
questions of power and hierarchy to the history of
the United States and the world. Books published in
the series examine a wide range of actors on local,
national, and global scales, exploring how they
imagined, enacted, or resisted political, cultural,
social, economic, legal, and military authority.

A complete list of books in the series
is available from the publisher.

OF LIGHT AND STRUGGLE

Social Justice, Human Rights,
and Accountability in Uruguay

Debbie Sharnak

PENN

UNIVERSITY OF PENNSYLVANIA PRESS

PHILADELPHIA

Published by
University of Pennsylvania Press
Philadelphia, Pennsylvania 19104-4112
www.upenn.edu/pennpress

Printed in the United States of America on acid-free paper
10 9 8 7 6 5 4 3 2 1

Hardcover ISBN: 978-1-5128-2424-7
eBook ISBN: 978-1-5128-2425-4

A Cataloging-in-Publication record is
available from the Library of Congress

For Diane and Larry Sharnak

Found in the Archivo General de la Universidad, undated, and handwritten on a piece of loose-leaf paper, this is a selection of a poem written by "Gabriel" to mathematician José Luis Massera in 1984, after Massera's release from years of imprisonment.

Here we await you:
Me and my dreams
Here we await you.
Together we'll go
down paths
of light and struggle
to our destiny.
Our hearts slung over our shoulders
and in our hands
the vibrant flag.
The flag of red,
of blood.
The flag that seeks
to erase hunger forever.
The flag that seeks
to extinguish wars.
The flag that illuminates the future,
the unyielding.
And if we must fight
we will be by her side.
We will form the brigade
of all that is new
to combat violence
and tyrants.
You, I, and the flag
will overcome
because we are
life
and joy.
Because we are
freedom and reason.
Because we are
hope and desire.
Because we are
the certainty of tomorrow.

CONTENTS

ABBREVIATIONS

ABA	American Bar Association
AW	Americas Watch
AI	Amnesty International
ACSU	Asociación Cultural y Social del Uruguay
ASCEEP	Asociación de Estudiantes de la Enseñanza Pública
CAT	Campaign for the Abolition of Torture
CELS	Centro de Estudios Legales y Sociales
CIESU	Centro de Informaciones y Estudios de Uruguay
CDM	Coalition for a Democratic Majority
CNPR	National Pro-Referendum Commission
CPJ	Committee to Protect Journalists
CALA	Community Action on Latin America
COSENA	Consejo de Seguridad
CONAPRO	Concertación Nacional Programática
CNT	Convención Nacional de Trabajadores
CDU	Convergencia Democrática Uruguaya
CBI	Corriente Batllista Independiente
DINARP	Dirección Nacional de Relaciones Públicas
FEUU	Federación de Estudiantes Universitarios del Uruguay
FMS	Foreign Military Sales
FA	Frente Amplio
FER	Frente Estudiantil Revolucionario
GA	General Assembly
GRECMU	Grupo de Estudios sobre la Condición de la Mujer en Uruguay
GRISUR	Grupo de Información Sobre Uruguay
GDP	Gross Domestic Product
ISI	Import Substitution Industrialization
IELSUR	Instituto de Estudios Legales y Sociales

ICTJ	International Center for Transitional Justice
ICJ	International Commission of Jurists
IMF	International Monetary Fund
IDI	Izquierda Democrática Independiente
LGBT	Lesbian, Gay, Bisexual, Transgender
MLN-T	Movimiento de Liberación Nacional-Tupamaros
OAS	Organization of American States
OLAS	Organization of Latin American Solidarity
PCU	Partido Comunista de Uruguay
PST	Partido Socialista de los Trabajadores
PIT	Plenario Intersindical de Trabajadores
PRM	Policy Review Memorandum
SERPAJ	Servicio Paz y Justicia
SIJAU	Secretariado Internacional de Juristas por la Amnistía en Uruguay
SCJ	Supreme Court of Justice
UDHR	Universal Declaration of Human Rights
UJC	Brigada Líber Arce de la Juventud Comunista
UN	United Nations
USAID	United States Agency for International Development
UdelaR	Universidad de la República
WOLA	Washington Office on Latin America
WCC	World Council of Churches

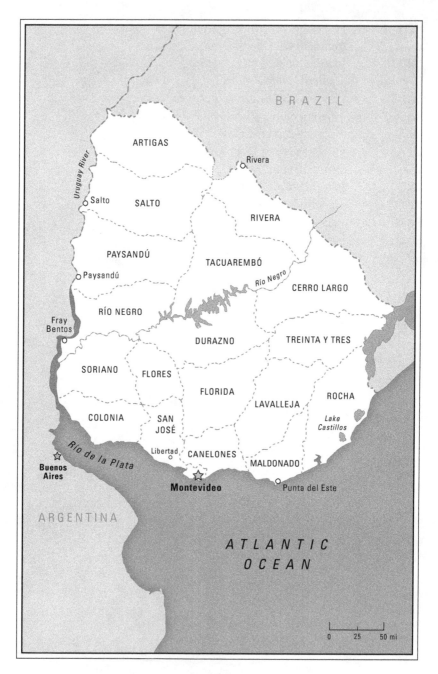

Figure 1: Map of Uruguay. Cartography by Erin Greb.

Figure 2: Map of Uruguay in South America. Cartography by Erin Greb.

Introduction

On March 14, 1985, the last political prisoners in Uruguay were released from *Penal de Libertad* and *Punta de Rieles*, the two most notoriously harsh prisons that operated during the country's military dictatorship. The date fell exactly two weeks after Julio María Sanguinetti took the oath of office as the country's first elected civilian president in twelve years. Marking another milestone in the transition back to democratic rule, families received the former prisoners with broad smiles and warm embraces. For some of these men and women, their only contact with loved ones for over a decade had been through a tiny window in the glass partition that separated prisoners from visitors—and that was when the military even permitted these sporadic visits to take place.[1] Almost all of the newly released people had been tortured, subjected to long periods of solitary confinement, unceasingly harassed by prison guards, and forbidden from reading newspapers or communicating with other prisoners. The former prisoners' gaunt bodies bore evidence of these hardships, made visible on that day through sunken cheeks and, for the men, closely shaved heads.[2]

This inhumane treatment of political prisoners was one of the multitude of ways that Uruguay's dictatorship operated between 1973 and 1985. After enjoying strong democratic traditions for most of the twentieth century, the government employed increasingly repressive measures against perceived subversives beginning in the late 1960s until the elected president closed Parliament and handed governing authority to the military on June 27, 1973. With this newfound power, the military exerted its authority through widespread political imprisonment, eventually jailing nearly one in every fifty people, the highest rate of political incarceration in the world.[3] Hundreds more were "disappeared"—kidnapped by state agents and never heard from again. Many of those fortunate enough to remain outside the regime's prisons nonetheless endured government monitoring and harassment, as well as the effects of the government's harsh neoliberal economic policies. Fear became pervasive throughout the country.[4] Indeed, more than 10 percent of the population fled these conditions, eventually totaling somewhere between 300,000 and 400,000 exiles from a nation of just over three million people. To the famed Uruguayan writer Eduardo Galeano, it appeared "everyone was imprisoned . . . even if the jails seemed to hold only a few thousand. . . . Invisible hoods covered the rest as well, condemned to isolation and incommunication, even if they were spared the torture."[5]

After this prolonged and harsh dictatorship, 1985 marked a momentous transition back to civilian government. Yet, both individuals and the country had to work out how to move forward into a new period of tenuous democratic rule. Just a few months after the release of the last prisoners, one student newspaper, *Estudiante Libre*, asked a seemingly simple question that cut to the core of the issues the nation faced: "What are human rights now?"[6]

Answers to that question changed over time. During the dictatorship, a transnational movement of victim groups, student associations, unions, and political parties, as well as international human rights organizations, foreign governments, and philanthropic institutions, emerged and defined human rights primarily as freedom from torture, political imprisonment, and disappearances. For them, that definition was a strategic means to fight against the most repressive modes of the military regime. After the dictatorship, some students wondered whether human rights would continue to be defined in this narrow way—although human rights now also encompassed a continuation of the fight to seek justice for these crimes. Upon the return to civilian rule, the students who wrote this article were part of a growing population that asked whether the language of human rights would be expanded and mobilized to include much broader social and economic claims about what a reconstituted democratic rule might entail, including for example, the human rights to fair salaries, educational reform, and improved working conditions. Unions, political parties, and student groups increasingly made these arguments in the new political environment and were joined by emerging new social movements that utilized a human rights discourse to advocate for Afro-Uruguayan, lesbian, gay, bisexual, transgender (LGBT), and women's rights.[7]

Indeed, Uruguay's long process of transition back to democracy in the 1980s both reflected and influenced heated national and international debates about what constituted human rights. The students' ostensibly straightforward question spoke to a larger and more contentious current in global and international history about contested visions of rights, and how these ideas changed as individuals and societies struggled with violence and democracy. By looking at this pivotal period in Uruguayan history, this book suggests that discussions occurring in places from activists' living rooms to bureaucratic halls of power about the small country on the Río de la Plata had global implications about the limits and possibilities of human rights well beyond Uruguay's shores. At the root of these inquiries lies a story about how and why the concept of human rights shifted between a mechanism to challenge state oppression and a tool that could be utilized in diverse ways for substantive social change. These are the transformations that this book will explore.

*   *   *

Human rights' universality is what makes the concept so appealing to activists and theorists alike, but it is also what has made it so difficult to define. For decades, historians have attempted to ground the concept in key historical moments to understand how and when it first was used as an organizing force.[8] The results have varied widely. Whereas some scholars trace the beginning of a human rights discourse back to eighteenth-century enlightenment ideas around the American and French Revolutions, others look to the 1940s, with the creation of the Universal Declaration of Human Rights (UDHR) and the flurry of activity following the atrocities of World War II. They see human rights as a response to those horrors.[9] More recently, some scholars have connected the modern birth of human rights to decolonization, while others link it to the death of socialism and the search for new utopias in the 1960s or 1970s.[10]

Many Latin American scholars locate the emergence of human rights as a prominent political language in the rise of repression in the Southern Cone in the 1960s and 1970s.[11] Starting with the onset of Brazil's dictatorship in 1964, it took only a decade for every government in the region to fall to military rule, leading to a coordinated military coalition against perceived subversives called Operation Condor. The process through which a human rights language gained urgency occurred in large part as a response to the staggering abuses perpetrated by these governments. Widespread human rights violations motivated transnational movements, multilateral institutions, individuals, and a range of foreign policy makers to take action against these practices. While the UDHR had enumerated rights that ranged from freedom of religion to equal pay and the right to an education, activists responded to the repressive dictatorships by adapting and narrowing these varied ideas of human rights circulating globally to respond to specific and targeted conditions across the region that largely included the right to be free from torture, political imprisonment, and disappearances.[12]

Despite this coherence during the height of the repressive dictatorships, across the Southern Cone these ideas of human rights did not remain static. The language of rights had a much longer local cultural and political history in the region that predated the dictatorships and included the invocation of rights to protect a range of social and economic conditions. Indeed, this tradition influenced how activists articulated and employed a rights discourse, at first to respond to the abuses of their governments, and then, especially after the fall of these dictatorships, to confront challenges in their newly reconstituted democracies. The content and contours of their human rights categories were not fixed; rather, they changed over time, both shaping and being shaped by the political contexts in which activists constructed them. Human rights language ultimately proved fluid, capable of addressing and reflecting the needs of society as different concepts gained salience and meaning at distinct points in time. As historian Alison Bruey explains, what emerged out of these debates in the Southern Cone was "an image of human rights as a constantly changing, historically and contextually contingent set of ideas about how people should treat one another, especially in the context of relationships between states and those living within their jurisdictions."[13]

Perhaps most notable is that at particular moments during the struggle against authoritarianism in the Southern Cone, the language of human rights took on fundamentally different, and at times conflicting, meanings. In societies with changing problems, human rights histories reveal a tale of debates, disagreements, and struggles. In exploring the intersection between activists, transnational movements, and governments at the center of these discussions during the late Cold War, this book examines the process of when and how divergent actors utilized a human rights discourse to imagine, describe, and advocate for their projects. It examines how politicians, unionists, and students articulated expansive social justice visions, how activists employed human rights to combat repression, how the military attempted to co-opt the language for its own purposes, and eventually how broader debates about human rights transformed the fight over citizenship in renewed democratic societies. As anthropologist Winifred Tate has argued, "Different social actors can use [a human rights] frame to advance profoundly different ideological projects."[14] This was certainly true in Uruguay.

Uruguay is a particularly compelling case for the study of the international history of human rights. Previously, in both regional and global narratives exploring the history of human rights, Uruguay was frequently left out.[15] Mostly, this is due to its size—it is a country of only three million people wedged between its more powerful neighbors, Argentina and Brazil. As historian Eric Zolov has noted, even within the historical profession, Uruguay often constitutes "a periphery within the periphery that is Latin America."[16] Nevertheless, Uruguay played a prominent if paradoxical role in the dynamic international human rights regime of the late Cold War. For one, its small size and relative strategic unimportance made it an ideal place for transnational activists and U.S. foreign policy makers to test new tactics and policies, which in turn made Uruguay a prime battlefield for the advancement of the new global movement for human rights. For example, when Amnesty International (AI) moved away from its individual-based approach, which emphasized freeing specific prisoners of conscience, and decided to wage its first-ever country-wide campaign against torture and political imprisonment, it chose Uruguay to unveil its new strategic shift. Uruguay also drew considerable attention as a prime testing ground for U.S. president Jimmy Carter's human rights–focused administration, which was the first U.S. administration to have such a focus in its foreign policy. In addition, activists in Uruguay eventually organized a diverse, domestic human rights movement—one that scored a major victory in 1980 when the military attempted to rubber-stamp an expansion of their power with a constitutional referendum. Through advocacy around the limited invocation of human rights, they defeated the military's initiative at the ballot box, helping spur the beginning of a transition back to civilian government, which finally succeeded in 1985.

Though the combination of international interest and domestic activism gave Uruguayan human rights prominence on the global stage, the country did not follow regional patterns in its transition back to democratic rule. By the late 1980s, as other Southern Cone countries began to challenge the norms of impunity regarding state violence by pioneering accountability mechanisms such as trials and truth commissions, Uruguayans moved in the opposite direction.[17] When the government passed a 1986 amnesty law for members of the military, civil society groups who sought to build on the strength of earlier human rights mobilization organized to overturn it in the hope of pursuing justice for the military's human rights abuses. Yet, when the possibility of repealing the law came before voters in 1989, organizing efforts fell short. Amnesty for the military withstood the popular referendum, and impunity took hold. Many activists described this defeat as "devastating."[18] The perceived failure also served to undermine the assumption that as human rights gained momentum internationally, local political cultures would align with the larger trend. Uruguay seemed to move in the opposite direction—from an international trailblazer for human rights to one of the only countries in the region to fail to engage in any accountability mechanisms for the military's crimes in those initial transitional years. The seeming contradictions of these intersecting narratives raise questions about how divergent political actors defined human rights at particularly significant junctures—and how these meanings paralleled or conflicted with intramovement battles, national political concerns, transnational movements, and larger international bureaucracies.

*   *   *

To understand how these shifts occurred, this book looks at each phase of Uruguay's long military rule, charting the various visions and invocations of human rights discourse at the national and international levels. First, it examines the years leading up to the formal establishment of a dictatorship, exposing the diverse voices and social justice ideals that sought solutions to the country's economic decline and political deadlock. Then, it explains how during military rule in the 1970s, transnational human rights groups, Uruguayan exiles, and the Carter administration largely understood human rights as defined by freedom from political imprisonment, torture, and disappearances—the most prominent tools of the Uruguayan dictatorship. Even as groups struggled and failed to create a cohesive transnational coalition, this minimalist definition proved remarkably consistent as the central component of groups' claims across both borders and electoral divides. It was a strategic and galvanizing definition. By the 1980s, however, even this veneer of coherence broke apart as activists began to envision and implement a much broader vision of human rights that also included social and economic rights.

Many of these seemingly new movements, however, were not really new at all. Instead, they emerged from two important sources. First, these groups had their roots in the social justice activism of the 1960s, which had been suppressed during the dictatorship. Second, while a broad transnational organizing effort had been waged on behalf of a narrow conception of human rights, many marginalized groups that had suffered particular forms of repression had been left out of the emerging definitions of human rights. In the transitional period, they organized new groups and launched movements for inclusion in the new democratic environment that utilized a more capacious human rights rhetoric to advocate for women's, Afro-Uruguayans', and gay rights.

By recovering the connection between the pre-dictatorship articulations of a just Uruguayan society and the human rights language of the transitional period, this book shows how a more expansive language helped give new force to a set of ideas that were nonetheless deeply rooted in the period before the 1973 coup. Continuity remained important in another way too. During the transitional decade, groups did not abandon the 1970s vision of human rights for which they had fought so hard. In fact, during the 1980s labor unions, political parties, and student organizations were often crucial partners for human rights groups looking to hold the dictatorship accountable for its crimes. However, during the fight for a return to civilian government, domestic actors grappled with both the physical violence of military rule and the continual structural violence of neoliberal policies. The narrow language that had defined the country's struggle against the military's violations had created tenuous, temporary alliances. Many allies to the groups fighting for accountability, therefore, shifted their energies to focus on other pressing concerns such as recovered visions of workers' rights and student power, and the rights of long-marginalized groups. In the process of applying human rights discourse to these movements, activists for social and economic rights fractured the minimalist human rights discourse of the 1970s.

As a more expansive human rights language became a powerful tool for various projects in the reestablished democracy, it ultimately had the contradictory effect of diverting attention and resources from the fight for justice regarding the dictatorship's crimes. Compounding the dispersed domestic efforts was a reduced interest from foreign governments and transnational groups. Some turned their efforts to other "hot" zones around the world, especially the conflicts in Central America, while others, if still engaged in Uruguay, often offered resources for different human rights goals, unrelated to accountability projects. In this sense, the Uruguayan human rights movement did not completely fail in the 1989 referendum against the amnesty law so much as it revealed the ways that the concept of human rights had shifted and expanded in practice. In the end, human rights in Uruguay evolved into a mechanism to debate national identity and values, notions of citizenship, and the very meaning of democracy at a crucial transitional moment in the country's history.

Studying this process is part of a new history of human rights that goes beyond the intense debates about origins in the field. Indeed, the case of Uruguay points to some of the ambiguity and limits in historians' discussion of origins. In the country, there is a long history of rights claims that predated the 1940s and impacted both global rights discourse and the local utilization of the term. For example, the country's earliest conception as a modern nation-state stems from a set of collective and individual rights first granted under President José Batlle y Ordoñez in the early twentieth century. Uruguay was also a major contributor to the founding of the United Nations (UN) and advocated for human rights norms to be integrated into the global organization by, for example, making arguments for an early International Bill of Rights. Thus, Uruguay's early engagement with human rights does not fit seamlessly within either the 1940s or the 1970s dominant framework. This study is not interested so much in an origins moment as in understanding the processes through which activists employed and defined human rights at key junctures, and how language and politics shifted over time as a result of tensions and convergence between national, regional, and global dynamics. By exploring the relationship between all three levels of analysis, this study uncovers the messy and contingent process through which human rights became a powerful discourse for social change, and thus contributes to a new method for exploring the history of human rights.

In addition to moving beyond historiographical discussions of human rights origins, this book is the first study that explores Uruguay's experience with dictatorship through an examination of the competing rights visions across the globe. In the past two decades, scholars such as Vania Markarian, Marisa Ruiz, Diego Sempol, and Ana Laura de Giorgi, among others, have written important histories of specific groups that worked on Uruguayan human rights at key moments.[19] Rather than focus on one rights movement or organization that advocated for human rights—such as exiles, families of the disappeared, LGBT activists, or women—this book takes a wide view of the human rights landscape, both within the country and from abroad. It explores the fluid and interwoven dynamics among these groups domestically, as well as how they influenced and were influenced by global and transnational forces. To do this, it charts how local movements impact international events, which are then refracted back into local struggles.

This study also reintegrates Uruguay into histories of transitional justice that tend to omit the country from early analyses of the field. Narratives about the history of transitional justice often start with the Latin America transitions during the 1980s.[20] The remarkable fall of military dictatorships in Argentina, Brazil, Uruguay, and Chile in the 1980s prompted serious conversations about how justice and peace would fit into the newly recon-stituted democratic governments, and subsequently spurred a new field of inquiry around what eventually came to be known as transitional justice. Uruguay, however, was an outlier in how it dealt with these questions. The 1989 democratic vote that failed to repeal the amnesty law served in many ways to silence the conversation on justice in the nation for years. Unlike most of its regional counterparts, Uruguay's new democratic government failed to employ any of what are now understood as transitional justice mechanisms. There were no trials, no official truth commissions, and no memorialization. Since early studies of transitional justice connected these accountability tools with the immediate period of democratic transition, Uruguay was largely absent from studies about the global history of transitional justice until the early twenty-first century.[21]

Outliers, however, tell interesting stories. Uruguay poses a challenge to what has been written about the global justice movement from the perspec-tive of the Southern Cone. This book explores the discussions in Uruguay about the country's attempt to provide accountability in the immediate after-math of the transition and, in doing so, raises questions about whether to pri-oritize justice or social and economic rights that still exist in the field today. It re-centers Uruguay as an important country for which to explore initial transitional justice debates and the enduring battles for accountability. Exam-ining this period of Uruguayan and global history reveals how contingency and human agency—as well as ideas, beliefs, and experiences—help explain the success or failure of justice initiatives in particular historical cases. For Uruguay, it also helps illuminate how the lack of transitional justice mea-sures related to broader and more diverse human rights concerns.[22] It offers a paradoxical conclusion that suggests that the success of an expanded human rights movement in some ways weakened the initial engagement with transi-tional justice mechanisms because other concerns took priority.

Reexamining these dynamics of the transition offers important lessons. The analysis proposes, first, a reorientation of how one understands the diver-sity among regional actors, encouraging scholars to think about the trade-offs involved in divergent rights movements and the legitimacy of certain types of amnesty as a tool of transition. Second, in disaggregating rights prioriti-zation among diverse actors, it also offers an initial explanation of why, even decades later, Uruguayans continue to grapple with the implementation of justice initiatives. The dominant justice narrative about the slow, inexorable

buildup of justice at the international level is at odds with Uruguay's more circuitous path and domestic conversations over national reconciliation, which
have included a debate over the role of justice in achieving human rights and
democracy.[23] Unpacking these differences is an important project because
it provides a more layered history that reveals alternative pathways and the
variety of activists' goals. The oft-forgotten case of Uruguay reminds us that
human rights is a history of fits and starts, not a *longue durée*.

*   *   *

Of Light and Struggle engages with the fields of human rights, transnational social movements, and transitional justice by bringing Uruguay into
the broader imperative of incorporating Latin America more seriously into
global and international histories. The dividing line between global and international history is thin, and the terms are often used interchangeably as a
means of transcending conventional national divisions to look at parallels
and entanglements in the modern world.[24] Global histories tend to focus
more on connection, integration, and dependence across societies, whereas
international histories often align more closely with the interactive process
of diplomatic relationships between national governments and other kinds
of transnational political actors.[25] Yet, both fields have often "overlooked"
Latin America. As historians such as Aldo Marchesi, Tanya Harmer, Alberto
Martín Álvarez, Matthew Brown, and others have noted, the omission is stark
for no shortage of reasons—ranging from Latin American national teaching
traditions, financial and resource scarcity for global research, and the priv-
ileging of "triumphant" actors from Anglophone countries.[26] Yet, as these
scholars and an emerging body of research explain, local ideas and movements within Latin America shaped and challenged global narratives about
rights, activism, and accountability. The book looks to bridge both international and global historical approaches by charting the iterative process of
how ideas flowed both to and from Uruguay during the late Cold War.

    If Uruguay is at the periphery of the periphery, placing it at the center
has distinct benefits. It also requires an inclusive methodology. *Of Light and
Struggle* draws from a broad array of documents from within Uruguay and
around the globe. It utilizes public reports, records of legislative debates,
and local and international newspapers. It analyzes national and university
archives, as well as domestic and transnational nongovernmental organization
(NGO) materials, some that were widely distributed for advocacy purposes

and others that had been confidential internal memos; some found in public archives and others found by combing through personal papers or disorganized file cabinets and closets that organizations granted me access to. The book also utilizes more traditional sources from diplomatic archives in Uruguay, the United States, and England, politicians' and bureaucrats' personal papers, as well as correspondence between government officials and human rights groups. Published primary sources as well as material from the UN archives, Organization of American States reports, and philanthropic organizations such as the Ford Foundation and the Rockefeller Foundation also contribute to illuminating global dynamics during this period. I also conducted more than two dozen oral history interviews with activists, politicians, embassy officials, and NGO campaigners. These sources are drawn primarily from Uruguay and the United States, but also from key archives in Argentina, Mexico, England, Geneva, and Amsterdam.[27] In this way, this book uses a wide range of original sources from around the globe, while also building on theoretical works and other case studies that explore the mutually constitutive process of human rights formation between local and global forces.[28]

While this study is instructive in terms of charting actors' engagement with human rights and accountability at these various scales, the story follows a roughly chronological order, beginning with the deepening political crisis of the 1960s. Chapter 1 follows the breakdown of the Uruguayan political system, examining the various and disparate political visions that dominated the pre-dictatorship landscape in response to economic calamity and political deadlock. Looking beyond the Tupamaros, this chapter analyzes how labor unions, political parties, and student movements imagined alternative political ideas and utilized a collective rights language. It argues that these visions stemmed from Uruguay's long history of rights talk, and studies the divergent ideas of which rights took precedence and laid the groundwork for later fault lines.

Chapter 2 explores how these groups' broader social justice ideas changed in the 1970s, when survival during the dictatorship became the main concern. Many individuals in these groups fled abroad during the decade due to the repressive nature of Uruguay's dictatorship. International groups and exiles often invoked a very specific and strategic set of rights focused on addressing the repressive conditions in Uruguay, particularly torture, political imprisonment, and forced disappearances. This discursive unity, after such divergent visions in the 1960s, placed a moral imperative around countering a repressive state that had ripped apart so many lives. The disparate social justice visions and grandiose claims for revolution of the 1960s still existed in some spheres, but they were often subsumed by minimalist calls for stopping certain violations. This chapter also explores how the narrowing of human rights concerns of the period developed at the expense of addressing other violations. Most especially, the experiences of diverse citizens were ignored: Afro-Uruguayans, who were displaced at high rates by the dictatorship; LGBT individuals, who were targeted in specific, horrific ways during torture sessions; and Jews, who were singled out for their perceived association with communism. These cases offer a wider view of the compromises involved during the emergence of transnational human rights advocacy, and help us understand how activists focused their efforts narrowly to achieve international attention, but left out particularly vulnerable groups in the process.

Chapter 3 traces the U.S. government's response to targeted advocacy by activists who were seeking an ally in the fight against the Uruguayan military regime. As such, it explores the slow adoption of human rights in U.S. foreign policy during the "long 1970s" from Richard Nixon's administration to Jimmy Carter's. It argues that Carter's assertive pursuit of a human rights–based agenda in Uruguay constituted a fundamental departure from his predecessors' policies, in large part because he had little to lose diplomatically in relations with the small Southern Cone nation. As such, it charts how local embassy officials implemented a change in policy. However, this focused pressure on the regime did not stem solely from congressional pressure or Carter's intrinsic moral vision. Rather, it followed the transnational human rights movement's efforts to define the problem in Uruguay narrowly, as one committed to stopping torture and ensuring that Uruguayans had a right to be free from governmental violation of the integrity of the person. Far from having human rights originate in the Carter presidency and gain credibility around the globe, this chapter uses the lens of U.S. foreign policy with Uruguay to show how resistant and then reactive U.S. foreign policy was to one of the most pressing issues of the day. It also reveals how Uruguay, as a small country, offered the opportunity to test out a new policy direction for larger administrative priorities.

Chapter 4 explores the human rights environment that surrounded the 1980 plebiscite. Against incredible odds, Uruguayans voted against the military's proposed constitution, which would have given the military government permanent and more sizeable control in the country. While observers and activists from abroad regularly invoked human rights when discussing the plebiscite, the domestic opposition to the military's project rarely relied on human rights language. In a revealing moment for the mutability of human rights language, it was actually the military that more regularly tried to justify their project by redefining human rights in ways that focused on the shield of state sovereignty and sought to refute the global movement's critiques. In this way, the plebiscite demonstrates the political and ideological nature of the emerging global human rights language that could be bent, interpreted, and deployed by divergent and, at times, competing groups that ranged from international NGOs to state actors and opposition organizers.

Chapter 5 examines the domestic, regional, and international human rights dynamics during the country's push for transition from 1981 to 1984, placing particular emphasis on the influence of other Latin American human rights groups within Uruguay's burgeoning human rights landscape. This includes positive results, such as the emergence of a domestic human rights movement and the rebirth of civil society, and more ominous repercussions, such as the military's subsequent crackdowns to try to maintain power. It argues that the hopefulness following the plebiscite proved essential to restarting a domestic human rights movement, but the military's retrench-ment also exposed fissures among various social actors over what human rights would mean in a return to democracy. These challenges influenced the possibilities for which human rights promises would be feasible in the future. This nonlinear negotiation process ultimately exposed both the power and the limits of various levels of activism.

Chapter 6 focuses on the period between the democratic elections in late 1984 and the passage of the country's 1986 amnesty law, which blocked the possibility of trials for human rights violations during the dictatorship. This chapter analyzes claims that trace the amnesty law to the Naval Club Pact in 1984, when prominent political parties and the military agreed to hold elections. Rather than locate amnesty for the military's crimes in those secret negotiations, it shows that the question of justice was indeed hotly debated at various levels of society, from President Sanguinetti to the more radical Left. Yet at the same time, justice was often not the main concern. Many of the strongest allies in the pre-election period paid less attention to issues of accountability as other important projects of reconstituting democracy took center stage. Activists focused on reasserting many tenets of their 1960s social justice visions that had been subsumed during the direct battles against the dictatorship, while politicians proved unreliable allies in debates over truth and justice in Parliament.[29] Examining these disparate groups raises ques-tions about the shifting human rights terrain not only among leftist activists but also among political actors in the complex interplay involved in debates over a broader human rights discourse, transitional justice, and access to power.

Finally, Chapter 7 explores the role of human rights in the campaign to overturn the amnesty law. While many leftist groups had not focused on justice concerns during the first twenty months of democratic rule, the amnesty law set into motion a renewed coherence of purpose among these groups. Ironically, and perhaps paradoxically, the referendum to overturn the protection of human rights abusers centered on a campaign that ended up ignoring those very violations. The debate focused instead on broader claims to democracy. Combined with the difficult domestic and international conditions, the movement to overturn the amnesty law failed at the ballot box. The chapter also explores where human rights became more prevalent: in the language to address the nation's social and economic rights. Although many groups rallied around the referendum efforts, both new and reconstituted civil society groups did not focus solely on issues concerned with justice and accountability. As the referendum battle dragged on for years, the rise of other domestic challenges displayed a continued effort to define human rights more broadly than had been done during the 1970s. As revealed in other cases, "justice" for human rights violations is frequently not a top concern in the immediate aftermath of repressive periods.[30]

Uruguay's experience in the 1980s and after points to both the continued dispersal of the meaning of the term "human rights" within civil society and the competing social concerns beyond a justice framework to address past abuses. The conclusion traces these new social movements and transitional justice concerns into the twenty-first century, highlighting the enduring legacies of these movements and rights debates from the long transitional decade.

Together, these chapters reframe the development of human rights discourse and offer two additional perspectives about the concept of human rights and dictatorship more broadly. First, Uruguay's decline into dictatorship and its difficult transitional period back to democratic rule challenge easy categorizations of dictatorship and democracy.[31] As opposed to Chile's dramatic coup in September 1973, there was no such obvious moment that one can trace to the exact date a dictatorship was installed in Uruguay. Many look to Congress's closure as the beginning of the *auto-golpe* in June 1973. However, the Uruguayan people had experienced years of the government's draconian methods in combating communism. In addition, the 1971 election has often been viewed as unfairly won by Juan María Bordaberry.

The confusion over when the dictatorship began is evident even in debates about the amnesty law, where arguments raged over whether the law should protect violations beginning in 1968 or 1973—demonstrating just how difficult a project it is to identify the start of dictatorship and repression in a period marked by violent continuities. Similarly, in the return to democratic rule, the elections in 1984 proscribed hundreds of candidates and jailed the opposition's main opponent, Wilson Ferreira, for the course of the electoral period. These practices often cast doubt on the true democratic nature of Julio María Sanguinetti's first term in office. The difficult descent into dictatorship and fierce battles to reemerge in democratic rule expose the unclear dichotomy between democracy and dictatorship and the problems of periodization. As historian G. M. Trevelyan once wrote, "Unlike dates, periods are not facts. They are retrospective conceptions that we form about past events, useful to focus discussion, but very often leading historical thought astray."[32] Accordingly, the longer periodization of the book takes these subtle temporal boundaries into account, expanding the chronology of Uruguay's undemocratic experience. This book does not seek to place new exact boundaries around the period of dictatorship, but rather expose the fluidity and unclear delineation around dichotomies of dictatorship and democracy, and the rights violations that spanned well before and after the traditionally understood period of dictatorship.

Additionally, this book considers how human rights can act as both a cohesive mechanism and an exclusionary tool in social struggles. When examining the 1970s human rights consensus as defined by torture, political imprisonment, and disappearances, the narrow invocation of the term contributed to concerted international pressure and transnational cooperation to change conditions on the ground for Uruguayans. It also helped forge alliances between various groups that held contested ideas about the future of the country that were evident during the country's descent into dictatorship in the mid-1960s and early 1970s. At the same time that these groups organized around a specific definition of human rights, the minimalist classification created a hierarchy of claims that put a limited set of rights on the agenda and excluded others. Mainly, historically marginalized groups such as Afro-Uruguayans, LGBT people, and Jews suffered a different sort of repression from the military government on the basis of these identities. These violations were not part of the burgeoning global lexicon of human rights, and thus these groups' plights received little to no acknowledgment.

Subsequently, these violations have often been written out of the history of the dictatorship period in Uruguay.

This tendency speaks to the broader ways that discrimination based on gender, identity, race, and religion has often been ignored as a prevailing problem in Uruguay's "homogenous" culture, as well as the way that social exclusion operates even within rights movements. As a corrective, this book discusses the suffering that these groups experienced during the dictatorship, and the emergence of issue-specific social movements in the post-dictatorship period that sought to expand a rights narrative to address their lived experience in the not-always-tolerant Uruguay. This account questions Uruguay's exceptionalist narrative of being a nation deeply committed to its social progressive traditions as the oft-described "Switzerland of South America," and exposes the difficult process of a country grappling with nationalist narratives versus the lived experience of many of its citizens. In this way, this story is as much about the shifts and changes in a discourse as it is about silences in society and in the archives when charting the emergence of a new global language.

*   *   *

Of Light and Struggle explores the winding and at times enigmatic path of human rights during three decades through the lens of Uruguay and global history. At its core, this book is a history of rights, as well as a history of humans. It is the human cost and struggles that give human rights their particular meanings. This is a story of individuals who suffered under repressive rule and risked everything to fight for ideals of social justice. It is a story of the strengths and limits of international solidarities. And it is a story of the difficult choices people make over which battles are worth fighting.

This book's title, *Of Light and Struggle*—"de luz y de lucha"—comes from a poem written to the world-famous Marxist mathematician José Luis Massera upon his release from prison in March 1984 after many years in jail at the hands of the military.[33] While notes on impressive letterhead poured in from around the world in solidarity with his newly regained freedom, there was one written on a torn-out piece of loose-leaf paper, undated, and signed only as "Gabriel." In it, Gabriel wrote of the inspiration Massera provided for those suffering throughout the difficult years of dictatorship and the long march that it would take to overcome these abuses. When Gabriel wrote the poem in early 1984, there was still no assurance of an end to the military rule. Gabriel's optimism, fear, and deep pain over the future of the country are all evident in his poetic words. His modest letter is demonstrative of the stories of how everyday Uruguayans struggled in a local context over what it meant to fight for a better future, paralleling a larger struggle in the global arena over human rights that characterized this period of Uruguayan history and has continued to play out ever since.

CHAPTER 1

Rights and Social Justice in
the Pre-Dictatorship Period

In 1969, seven members of the MLN-T stole $220,000 from a casino in the popular beach town of Punta del Este.[1] At the time, it was the biggest robbery in Uruguayan history. Even before the Tupamaros claimed credit for the episode, the Uruguayan newspaper, *El País*, guessed the MLN-T was responsible because of the way the heist had been carried out: the robbers used impeccable fake identification cards, treated the employees and other bystanders respectfully, and disappeared from the scene without a trace.[2] No one was hurt, despite several men carrying submachine guns. After the Tupamaros acknowledged responsibility, they returned some of the money to casino workers to compensate for lost wages. The group committed to take only from the bourgeois, who acquired property "through the exploitation of workers," to fund their revolution against the unjust Uruguayan state.[3]

The Tupamaros burst into the Uruguayan political milieu in the years leading up to this attack and gained a reputation for similar spectacles, which were aimed at humiliating the government and garnering attention for their cause. Admiration for this type of revolutionary idealism extended beyond the shores of Uruguay. For example, instead of condemning the attack, *Time* magazine called the Tupamaros "Robin Hood Guerrillas" for taking from the rich and giving to the poor.[4]

The Tupamaros' unique antics, and how they tied their activities to their politics, made them famous throughout the region and the world.[5] During the 1960s, the group captured many people's imaginations as "passionate, committed, and most of all, hip revolutionaries capable of outsmarting the police and the increasingly authoritarian Uruguayan government."[6] In many ways, this romanticism is understandable; the Tupamaros' dramatic acts were based on adapting Ernesto "Che" Guevara's own idealized *foquismo* to an urban setting.[7] Their vision of overthrowing a repressive government, similar to what Che and Fidel had done in Cuba, was reflected in their creative measures like the casino robbery. During a period of economic and political crisis, these stunts appealed to a frustrated citizenry.

In addition to dominating headlines in the late 1960s and early 1970s, the Tupamaros have also been a focus in many histories of the pre-dictatorship period.[8] One reason why is because of the attention-grabbing methods the Tupamaros employed and the fact that they provided an inspirational model to rebels and dissenters around the world. The military regime, moreover, justified its increasingly harsh measures against the population as a response to the Tupamaros, even long after they were defeated.[9] Despite the debunking of the "two demons" theory, many studies of Uruguay's path to dictatorship still focus on the MLN-T and the military's reasoning for taking power as a response to the group.[10]

In spite of the Tupamaros' dominance in existing scholarship, the pre-dictatorship era should be understood as a period of broader societal contestation. Beyond the Tupamaros, various groups and voices emerged during the tumultuous 1960s in response to economic calamity and the government's use of increasingly repressive measures. These included labor unions, student activists, and political parties, which collectively imagined and battled for their own visions of a better future. Their ideas varied considerably from those of the Tupamaros. However, rarely did any of these groups explicitly invoke the term "human rights" when discussing political possibilities. Instead, groups more often referred to social justice visions, replete with a wide range of social and economic rights, in these debates. These strands of collective rights existed in Uruguayan politics long before the Tupamaros announced their urban campaign against the Uruguayan state and were often derived more from Uruguay's own national traditions than from an international language of human rights.

Looking beyond the well-documented endeavors of the Tupamaros, this chapter explores the disparate social justice projects that characterized Uruguay's pre-dictatorship landscape. It examines what diverse social groups advocated for during this period, particularly as their aims intersected with both international movements and long-held ideas in Uruguayan history.[11] These transnational and local connections are essential. Many of these domestic groups linked and identified with the various organizations that dominated the 1960s at a regional and global level, such as unions, student movements, and the Communist Party. Yet, placing the 1960s in a longer view of Uruguayan history also spotlights the country's rich democratic and social welfare history and the ways that this self-image influenced expectations of rights and dreams of a better future.

Tracing this trajectory, this chapter begins by exploring the historical roots of Uruguay's unique democratic traditions and influence on the international establishment of human rights. It places these ideals in the context of the country's gradual descent into dictatorship, which undermined decades of stable governance. In contrast to the sudden and dramatic coup in Chile, Uruguay's breakdown proceeded in a slower, escalating manner amid social, political, and economic difficulties. Against this backdrop, this chapter then addresses the Tupamaros' emergence, main political platform, and relationship to a rights discourse. The following section explores the "minor utopian" visions of the workers' union, the student movement, and a new leftist political coalition, the Frente Amplio (Broad Front), to paint a more complex landscape of the voices of protest and rights in the 1960s in Uruguay.[12] Finally, it reviews some of the few explicit pre-dictatorship uses of the term "human rights." How actors employed the term in this moment exposes key fault lines in debates about the contested nature of the term "human rights" in the context of Uruguay's democratic breakdown.

While there were fissures both within individual groups as well as between them, this chapter provides an overview of some alternative political ideas during this period that extended beyond the Tupamaros.[13] It explores other groups' expansive and fluid visions of rights, before the actual language of human rights became ubiquitous, and places a rights discourse within a longer trajectory of Uruguayan history. Yet, while noting broad articulations of rights, the chapter underscores a general dearth of women's rights concerns from these core groups, even as women's participation increased. In many of these movements, male-dominated leadership subordinated women's rights to what it perceived as larger goals.

Thus, while highlighting historiographically underrepresented groups, this chapter explores these alternative ideas amid a deteriorating narrative of Uruguayan exceptionalism. The conditions throughout the 1960s caused many groups to doubt the efficacy of Uruguay's democracy, opening space to reimagine what rights should be protected. The various social justice concepts that emerged, many based in ideas of collective rights, set the backdrop for the changed discourse of the post-dictatorship human rights visions in the 1980s. Although these ideas shifted thirteen years later, and came to include women's rights, many stem from this tumultuous period.

The Social Welfare State and Its Breakdown

Few history or travel books about Uruguay fail to mention its reputation as the "Switzerland of South America."[14] Uruguay acquired this label in the first half of the twentieth century because of the country's high literacy rates, advanced health care system, political democracy, and perceived European racial makeup. This image, as *un país de excepción* or model country, remained a pervasive and influential ideal during Uruguay's struggles in the 1960s and sharply impacted various groups' social justice claims.[15]

These exceptionalist ideas began to take hold when José Batlle y Ordóñez held the presidency from 1903 to 1907 and again from 1911 to 1915.[16] Batlle oversaw the development of a centralized state that protected its citizens, and his ideology has remained dominant in the nation ever since. Batlle's presidency witnessed tremendous changes, including high rates of immigration from Europe to Montevideo.[17] Batlle framed his political vision around the importance of an interventionist state that sought to provide essential services for an expanding citizenry, enhance the general welfare, and ensure international sovereignty for the nation. To achieve this, Batlle enacted legislation that secured economic and social rights. Among other measures, it created an urban minimum wage, social security, educational opportunities, labor rights such as an eight-hour workday, progressive taxation, advances for women, and secularization. Batlle had the financial capacity to enact these bold social and political experiments on the back of a strong economy, mainly a robust export market in Europe for items such as beef, wool, and leather.[18]

Batlle also implemented policies that advanced the rights of historically disadvantaged peoples. For example, most Latin American nations in the early twentieth century lacked robust protection or legal codes to further equality for women.[19] Batlle, however, opened up space for the advancement of women's rights in areas such as divorce, sexuality, and public health.[20] Batlle permitted girls to attend school to get the same education as men as early as 1912, and he laid the foundation for granting female suffrage, which ultimately, alongside strong advocacy from domestic feminist groups, led to Uruguay becoming the first nation in Latin America to allow women to vote.

Batlle's policies helped Uruguay flourish during his presidencies and for decades afterward. The resulting prosperity had two major repercussions for the nation's development. First, it helped consolidate an unstable political system into a centralized state. The Colorados and Blancos, the two political groups that had dominated Uruguay since independence, shifted from warring factions to traditional parties that focused their actions on the political process and governmental activities. This two-party system lasted until the 1970s and was relatively stable compared to many of the nation's regional neighbors, which experienced regular upheaval.[21] Second, his presidency created certain expectations that the government would enact policies to protect disadvantaged societal sectors such as workers, immigrants, religious minorities, and women. Historian Milton Vanger argues that Batlle's presidency, in addition to implementing social policies, also initiated mass politics, which enfranchised vast portions of the population and looked after the marginalized sectors in society.[22] Batlle's presidency, therefore, established a national identity based on a strong set of rights guaranteed by the state, and raised citizens' expectations about the government's role in society.[23]

Indeed, for the first half of the twentieth century, Uruguay implemented a strong social welfare system that continued or extended many of these early principles. On the backs of the same strong export economy, the state offered its citizens a vast web of social rights unique to Uruguay. These achievements included, among others, health care—particularly for infectious/contagious diseases, mental health, and maternal infant programs—protection of workers' rights, rent freezes and subsidies, guaranteed pensions for senior citizens, and free schooling through the university level that produced literacy rates above 95 percent. Thus, through much of the 1950s, Uruguay maintained strong democratic traditions, a stable two-party system, and a unique, albeit imperfect, array of social and economic rights.[24]

Internationally, the nation also argued for the importance of guaranteeing social and economic rights during the original discussions surrounding the development of international human rights norms.[25] Various scholars have illustrated that Latin American nations were among the first to promote international protection for human rights, demonstrated by the drafting of the American Declaration of the Rights and Duties of Man before even the UDHR was passed in the UN General Assembly. Using this experience working on the Americas version, Laitn American delegates also had a strong presence during the negotiations over the writing of the UDHR.[26]

Uruguayan delegates were prominent members of this group and played a large role in advocating for human rights to be a bigger part of the UN's core mission. They proposed that the promotion of human rights be listed among the purposes of the organization. Further, Uruguayan Foreign Minister Alberto Rodríguez Larreta submitted a draft proposal to include a Declaration of Rights in the UN Charter rather than produce one as a separate document. He sought for nations to be expelled from the organization should they fail to follow these standards.[27] Although many of the Uruguayans' suggestions were not adopted, undergirding these proposals was a unique international promotion of rights that Uruguayans also sought to protect at home. Uruguayan delegates at the conference proclaimed that to "safeguard peace and security, fundamental human rights should be internationally declared and internationally protected."[28]

Uruguayan officials at the UN continued to promote these principles in the early years of the organization as well. In 1951, for example, they proposed a plan for the creation of an Attorney-General for human rights. The proposal sought to embed the Covenant on Civil and Political Rights into the central functioning of the UN, rather than proceed through a lengthy treaty ratification process.[29] While these proposals were not approved, they highlight Uruguay's leadership within international forums at the beginning of the postwar international emergence of human rights. This commitment continued throughout the 1950s. In the first years of the UN Commission on Human Rights, Uruguay was reelected to serve on the commission after successfully pitching the country as "having always been very enthusiastic and devoted to the noble task of international cooperation," with a "special concern in social legislation and its constant interest in the matter."[30] Eduardo Jiménez de Aréchaga, Uruguay's representative to the Inter-American Commission on Human Rights, also played a huge role in operationalizing the body to protect human rights in the region.[31] Thus, in these early years, Uruguay promoted stability, democracy, and rights domestically, and championed the codification of these rights at a regional and international level.

While maintaining a strong international presence, by the late 1950s Uruguay faced domestic challenges as its robust economy began to falter. These financial challenges exposed critical fault lines and structural crises in the economic, political, and social realms that propelled a reevaluation of the relationship between citizens and their government. It also prompted a fundamental rethinking and renewed emphasis on the idea of rights from within the country—although what rights and how they were defined remained up for debate. The economic collapse occurred, in part, because exports, which had been the bedrock of Uruguay's economy, declined precipitously. Uruguay followed the region's attempts to adjust by adopting an import substitution industrialization (ISI) model, erecting high tariffs and encouraging domestic manufacturing. Throughout the region, and particularly in the small country of Uruguay, this model failed to take off and only plunged Uruguay deeper into financial calamity. By 1964, the nation's economic outlook reached crisis proportions. The growth rate fell to almost zero and inflation hit between 40 and 50 percent with a growing budget deficit. Wool exports, traditionally Uruguay's strongest commodity, were being priced out of the market.[32] Uruguay's commitment to its social welfare program relied on a strong economy. The changing economic climate threatened these rights and values that took root at the start of the century.

The government struggled to adapt to the new reality as the shortcomings of the political system surfaced. A U.S. report about Uruguay during this period explained that the government was proving "indecisive" and "virtually leaderless" in the face of changes.[33] Part of Uruguay's leadership deficit reflected the very structure of the government instituted by the constitution of 1952, which placed the executive within a "collegiate" model of a nine-person governing board. Six members of this group represented the largest political party and the other three were from the second-most popular political party. With nine people attempting to run the government from different parties, no individual provided the leadership necessary to cope with the predicament.[34]

Officials also struggled to respond to the economic crisis when so many Uruguayans understood their education, health, and pension benefits as essential rights, guaranteed in the social contract since the era of Batlle. In many ways, it produced a crisis of Uruguayan national identity.[35] Abroad, officials took notice. For example, the Assistant Secretary of State for Inter-American Affairs, Thomas Mann, told President Lyndon Johnson in July 1964 that Uruguay was "just in a hell of a mess because they can't manage their affairs very well."[36] Faltering social services generated "increasing disillusionment within all sectors of Uruguay." [37] Editors of popular leftist paper *Marcha* wrote that the government "is delinquent, and more than delinquent, deceitful. . . . It did not fix any problems that it promised to solve. It aggravated them, complicated them, and made them worse."[38] Even the United States began to worry about "a coup in 'model' Uruguay" which officials believed would "have many repercussions throughout the hemisphere."[39] After the

1959 Cuban Revolution, U.S. officials increasingly feared another country "falling" to communism and began paying more attention to Uruguay.

The Uruguayan government first responded through reform of its political structure. A one-man presidential system replaced the nine-person National Council of Government. After national elections, President Óscar Diego Gestido of the Colorado Party assumed office on March 1, 1967. Gestido's presidency began with high hopes. He was a retired army general who had directed the nation's airline and the railway system, held a reputation for honesty, and possessed strong administrative skills.[40] These qualities, however, were not enough to reverse the situation; conditions continued to deteriorate. Gestido could not "grapple effectively" with the economic calamity, which included spiraling inflation, a budget imbalance, and serious damage to the agricultural sector caused by inclement weather.[41]

Further, President Gestido proved indecisive and politically unsavvy as politicians argued over how to address the domestic situation. By June 1967, Gestido's poor political administration reached an apex. The leader of the largest faction of the Colorado Party criticized Gestido on his management of the economy. The president reacted by excluding the faction from his government. He formed a new government which represented only a minority of the party and reversed his administration's economic policy. While the government's intraparty battles raged, Uruguayans responded to governmental ineptitude by protesting the country's poor management and deteriorating conditions. In 1967 alone, Uruguayans from various sectors went on strike more than seven hundred times.[42]

Gestido's attempts to handle the growing crisis came to an abrupt and unexpected end. He had a heart attack and died on December 6, 1967.[43] Consequently, Vice President Jorge Pacheco Areco assumed the presidency. Pacheco had been a newspaperman in the conservative wing of the Colorado Party and was directly involved in politics for only four years before becoming vice president.[44] Under his leadership, political tensions accelerated.[45] While Gestido attempted to quiet dissent of his administration, Pacheco ordered to silence it by invoking Cold War tropes. For example, less than a week after assuming office, Pacheco shut down the Socialist Party's newspaper, El Sol, and the independent leftist paper Época; the editors for these leftist publications were also jailed. In addition, Pacheco also outlawed the Socialist Party and several other smaller anarchist and leftist groups for supposed subversive activity and intent to destroy the regime, linked to these groups' involvement with the Organization of Latin American Solidarity (OLAS).[46]

Pacheco's measures further alienated many Uruguayans. In *Marcha*, editors began warning of an impending dictatorship.[47] A popular joke in Uruguay proliferated when Uruguayans explained their situation as if they had "voted for Eisenhower and got Nixon," meaning that they had voted for a well-liked former general and ended up with a staunch anti-communist willing to take extreme measures.[48] Leftists responded to Pacheco's ascension by calling him "Paco Arecho"; they believed that because of the Uruguayan president's actions, he did not deserve the inclusion of the acclaimed icon "Che" in his name.[49]

The erosion of civil liberties and civilian control in the country proceeded.[50] Unlike the more dramatic democratic collapses in Brazil in 1964 and Chile in 1973, Uruguay had a much slower progression toward complete military rule. The government instituted various "states of sieges" and "prompt security measures," which progressively limited liberties and broadened governmental power in response, it claimed, to the Tupamaros and to the militant labor movement. Pacheco interpreted the Tupamaros' militancy and union strikes to be part of a broader web of subversive leftist networks to which he had to respond with force.[51] Consequently, the military gradually increased its political role in the country.[52] For example, on June 13, 1968, the government invoked its emergency power under the *Medidas Prontas de Seguridad*, or the "Prompt Security Measures." The decree granted Pacheco increased power and suspended all civil liberties on the basis that the nation's very survival was at risk. He argued that the government needed to implement these measures to protect the country from "enemies of the Republic."[53] Torture became an accepted police practice during his presidency as both social mobilization and harsh repression increased.[54]

While Batllismo had ushered in an impressive period of growth and stability in the first half of the twentieth century, it became an impediment to progress in the 1960s. Because the country's political parties were centralized, there was little access to the political system outside of them. This dynamic, which stabilized the country at the turn of the century, proved to be problematic in the 1960s because it precluded alternative avenues for participatory democracy, denying Uruguayans the chance to air grievances or advocate for change outside of the two-party system. This led many in Uruguay, particularly on the Left, to attempt to make their voices heard by alternative methods. As political scientist Martin Weinstein explains, Batllismo created a way to contain conflict in the first half of the century that made politics more open, plural, and democratic than previous national models. By the 1960s, however, that model became an impediment to change and reform. The system was unable to respond creatively to major societal shifts or check the military's power grab.[55] While it alone does not explain the breakdown of democracy, the two-party system's limits played a part in its collapse.

Under increasing pressure and violence by the military and police, Uruguayans grew more frustrated with the situation. Groups across the political spectrum all advocated for the need to address the governmental deadlock and economic crisis. However, what that looked like, and what rights should be guaranteed in a different political future, diverged, at times, quite dramatically.

The Left Responds

Historically, Uruguay's democracy included a tradition of respect for individual freedoms and all political ideologies, including Trotskyites and anarchists. Historian Aldo Marchesi argues that this political openness made Montevideo "a thriving intellectual scene" and a "dynamic climate." In the 1960s, numerous bookstores and publications made Uruguay a place for the Left to imagine a new political future in the midst of national crisis.[56] While the Tupamaros remain the most prominent symbol for discontent, groups from the Communist Party to a vibrant student movement articulated numerous and sometimes clashing visions, which in turn articulated rights frameworks for moving beyond the political deadlock of the period.

The Tupamaros

The Tupamaros began as a splinter group primarily from Uruguay's Socialist Party, drawing initial membership from the country's Communist Party and other smaller left-wing groups as well. Breaking from the country's "old Left," the Tupamaros believed their forbearers had failed to change society through their manifestos and electoral strategies. Frustrated with the national gridlock, they saw no option except for armed action.[57] Influenced by the Cuban Revolution, the Tupamaros worked hard to develop tactics that would raise consciousness and result in minimal bloodshed, but maximize embarrassment to authorities, to radicalize a deeply troubled Uruguayan polity. They endorsed a violent and confrontational means of political expression to challenge the increasingly repressive government.[58] The group's first official meeting took place in 1962, evolving into a more prominent presence by January 1966.[59]

Unlike other revolutionary movements in this period, the Tupamaros tended to be more open in their ideological criteria for membership in hopes of attracting all who aspired to change the political deadlock. Their language emphasized a fight "for liberty, independence, bread, and land," while welcoming those who wanted to work for an "Uruguay without repression."[60] The group explicitly challenged "ism" ideologies. Instead, they called for absolute equality between the government and those that it ruled. With an openness in rhetoric and low ideological bar for entry, the Tupamaros began to grow in size as discontent increased throughout the 1960s.[61]

In one of their only known manifestos, the Tupamaros outlined the broad contours of their beliefs. It declared that the Tupamaros were

> the armed political organization of students, workers, clerks, farm
> hands, intellectuals, and the unemployed. That is to say it represents
> all the exploited and those forced into poverty by your "order" whose
> very basis is injustice . . . the problems of the country will find a
> solution when the land is in the hands of all and not just a few privi-
> leged people; when it produces the wealth it is capable of producing
> and this wealth is shared among the people; when the land feeds
> the poorest people . . . when monopoly capital is expropriated from
> banking, industry and commerce and these three key sectors of the
> economy are placed at the service of the workers and all the people;
> when the shameful ties that bind us to foreign exploitation are
> broken and we can pursue a national and truly independent foreign
> policy; and when the theoretical right of every person to education,
> housing, health and work has become a reality.[62]

This document explained a more just vision that the Tupamaros imagined for Uruguay. It imagined an ideal that overcame imperialism through armed conflict and was rooted in a future with enumerated rights to education, housing, health, and work in line with Uruguay's social welfare tradition.[63] The Tupamaros also supported women's roles in the organization, rhetori-cally promoting equality within a revolutionary context and offering women some prominent roles in guerrilla actions, though these ideas were subordi-nated to the larger ideals.[64] Women's rights and a "gendered transformation of society" were rarely considered critical aspects of the revolutionary struggle.[65]

Women, however, made up a relatively high number of combatants, and the Tupamaros' ranks continued to swell as they conducted more publicity-generating actions.[66] For example, the group carried out their first public actions in July 1968 when members kidnapped a government leader close to the president who backed a hard-line response to union strikes. Days later, they released him unharmed, making a point of protest and generosity. Marchesi notes that these symbolic measures "represented an effort to build an alternative power by way of 'armed propaganda.'"[67] In addition to multiple successful prison breaks which spotlighted the ineptitude of prison guards, the group also broke into military officers' homes and lectured them on changing careers. Tying up the officers and their families, the Tupamaros would be kind to the families and take only weapons and personal documents. The Tupamaros said these break-ins were intended to provide a supply of arms for their cause and undermine the morale of the force.[68] The Tupamaros also gained notoriety by robbing banks or other locations and then distributing the money to workers, such as when they gave lost wages back to the San Rafael Casino employees in 1969. The Tupamaros targeted big banks and establishments. At the same time, they promised to refrain from seizing the property of workers, small businessmen, and small producers.[69] Most of their initial public actions purposefully avoided bloodshed, a decision that garnered sympathy from the population, generated international attention, and stretched the imagination of what many considered "armed" struggle.[70] In Uruguay and around the world, their flashy actions aimed at embarrassing the Uruguayan military gained the group notoriety. The *New York Times* went so far as to call them "the best organized urban guerrillas in Latin America."[71]

Despite the Tupamaros' widespread popularity, some detractors expressed skepticism. Pro-Maoist and pro-Moscow critics among the Left in Uruguay contended that the group had little concrete philosophy for a utopian vision beyond armed action, which they considered problematic for a revolutionary movement.[72] The number of critics increased when the Tupamaros enacted a more violent version of armed struggle. They still claimed to use violence only at the "correct time against the correct target," such as in the name of self-defense or in cases where they needed to protect third parties.[73] Yet, under this philosophy from 1966 until 1971, the Tupamaros killed eleven police officers. Most famously, in 1970, the group kidnapped and eventually killed United States Agency for International Development (USAID) officer Dan Mitrione, whom they accused of teaching torture methods to the national police.[74] This move reversed earlier strategies of releasing prisoners, even those who were held for long periods of time.[75] At the time, one report noted a Gallup Poll that found that 20 percent of Uruguayans were against the execution of Mitrione, 20 percent were in favor, and 60 percent had no opinion.[76] Despite these equivocal numbers, the killing of Mitrione was a turning point in the widespread support for the Tupamaros and also triggered increasing backlash from the government. In this respect, the Tupamaros were subsequently blamed in many accounts for the governmental crackdown on the population and the move to military rule. While the military had begun to increase their repressive measures before the Tupamaros' killing of Mitrione, and continued well past the group's demise, in rhetoric the government framed the danger of the Tupamaros as justification for the state of emergency in the name of national security.[77] Many Uruguayans eventually believed this as well.

The Tupamaros' attention-grabbing acts, the force of international admiration, and their prominent presence in post-dictatorship politics have ensured that narratives of the Tupamaros have often dominated the Uruguayan historiography of the late 1960s and early 1970s. While their influence cannot be doubted, this focus tends to obscure the minor utopias, or as historian Jeffrey Gould explains, "imaginings of liberation usually on a smaller scale, without the grandiose pretensions or the almost unimaginable hubris and cruelties of the 'major' utopian projects" of the many different social actors, striving for a better future for Uruguay.[78] Many of these actors had divergent visions of how the country might respond to its political and economic predicament, which also shifted in response to the particularities of the 1960s moment. These ideals were also uniquely Uruguayan with their emphasis on social and economic rights that had been part of the Uruguayan ideal since the time of Batlle.

Unions; Convención Nacional de Trabajadores (CNT)

While labor unions have a storied history in Uruguay, their political relevance increased during the 1950s and 1960s in direct response to the deepening crisis.[79] By 1964, various unions started meeting to coordinate their actions. The following year, the trade union movement organized the 1965 People's Congress (*el Congreso del Pueblo*). Over seven hundred different social organizations attended, including workers, students, cooperativists, professionals, artists, doctors, neighborhood groups, housewives, and more.[80] These groups laid out an ambitious set of goals for how to respond to the national crisis which ranged from agrarian reform to workers' protections, and a minimum salary.[81] Perhaps most importantly, the meeting marked when labor and social movements became more political, identifying their aims as a response to Uruguay's deep and systematic crisis.[82] In 1966, the unions established the Convención Nacional de Trabajadores (National Convention of Workers) as a unified federation to represent all of the country's unions and increase their influence and lobbying power while pushing for concrete measures such as fair wages.[83] The CNT included groups such as electric power workers, teachers, bank workers, the press association, and the rubber workers. One of its first publicly disseminated documents asserted the CNT's goals as a fight for "bread, work, liberty, and progress"—particularly against increased government attacks.[84] Although its demands were vague at the time, the CNT ultimately focused its actions on collective workers' rights, which remained the centerpiece of its platform throughout the country's descent into dictatorship.

The root of the union-government confrontation stemmed from the increasingly draconian methods used to control unions through what the government termed "economic stabilization programs." With Uruguay in debt, the International Monetary Fund (IMF) became a major lender to the country, imposing strict conditions such as reducing state involvement in the economy and allowing greater openness to foreign investment and trade.[85] Budget cuts were imposed on many industries, often at the expense of workers. These burdens included limiting wage increases and laying off workers, even as inflation increased at astronomical rates. For example, inflation rose by 138 percent in 1967 alone, but wage increases were initially frozen by the government, and then when the freeze was lifted, wages increased by less than half the inflation rate.[86] These dire economic conditions challenged Uruguay's exceptionalist narrative, especially as the IMF's austerity policies offended the country's nationalist pride.

As the confrontation between the repressive government and a radicalizing Left grew, President Pacheco attempted to silence the CNT by invoking security measures to shut down its press and arresting labor leaders. In addition to battles against the government, the CNT also faced internal problems. It represented so many different unions from across the economic spectrum that infighting over its direction and tactics became debilitating.[87] Union members held divergent political sympathies, which included a strong Communist Party influence. There were fierce debates over how to balance promoting workers' particular rights against the general national crisis.[88] Despite these differences, documents emerged from CNT meetings that advocated for restoring a socially just Uruguay based in an economic rights discourse. From its founding in 1966 to 1973, when then-president Juan María Bordaberry outlawed the group, it consistently asserted the people's rights to a fair wage and living standard as part of the response to the cuts that the CNT believed were aiding the owners of many factories while hurting workers.

As the battle escalated between the CNT and the government, the CNT's demands expanded to respond to the repressive conditions.[89] The organization explained that the CNT did not only "coordinate the unions." Rather, as stated in their Declaration of Principles and Statutes, the CNT was a vehicle in workers' fight for social and economic justice. It advocated for improving material and cultural conditions, for national liberation and progress, and for creating a society without exploitation or exploiters.[90] However, one area the CNT did not fully address was women's rights. While women participated in the labor movement, women's rights were rarely a focus. As one female member, Mabel, recalled, "We never discussed women's issues in the union . . . the survival of the union movement was the main concern, not women."[91] And indeed, as Gestido and then Pacheco cracked down on the unions, the CNT increasingly focused on fighting against infringements on freedom of expression and cases of arbitrary arrests.

Advocacy for these principles continued to expand in scope and ferocity. In June 1971, the CNT called for a general strike to protest Pacheco's policies, centering their demands on a solution to the education crisis and reinstatement of workers who had been dismissed due to the Provisional Measures of Security for having what Pacheco deemed suspect beliefs.[92] Documents describing the demands behind these strikes reveal the unions' wide-ranging call for reform. For example, the CNT expanded on their political vision for an ideal society to include agrarian reform, public housing, and social security. They also increasingly advocated against cuts to education budgets and led protests to interrupt the functioning of schools in the late 1960s.[93] The 1971 official CNT platform ranged widely, starting specifically with a call for the right to protest against the government and the release of union leaders who had been arrested. The document also called for protection against foreign government intervention, protested IMF policies, and advocated for a change in the political functioning of government.[94] In *Marcha*, leaders of the CNT published demands, calling for unions to have free expression and the right to organize for fair wages.[95] Implicit in so many of these arguments was the invocation of historical rights that were now being curtailed. The CNT called for reform, went on strike, and protested for collective rights that it believed would improve society.[96]

While the CNT represented numerous unions, rarely did they center the problems of any specific industry, instead focusing on broader issues that workers faced across the country. At the root of these concerns was an argument for social and economic rights, once guaranteed by the Uruguayan government but now increasingly threatened amid economic and political crisis. These ideals united workers—and even students—as they faced escalating repression.

Student Movement; Federación de Estudiantes Universitarios del Uruguay (FEUU)

Unlike in other Latin American countries during this period, there was a high degree of coherence between the student movement, particularly the FEUU, and the CNT, which members claimed was part of "student-proletariat solidarity."[97] Together, they promoted the slogan "*Obreros y estudiantes; unidos y adelante!*" (Workers and students, forward united!).[98] This alliance provided for fruitful collaboration and a more forceful organizing effort, though the student movement had somewhat different objectives.[99]

From the FEUU's founding in 1929, the organization was a left-leaning force in Uruguay.[100] As an umbrella for student unions, the FEUU was organized by field of study, such as medicine, architecture, social sciences, or engineering. Between 1955 and 1975, the number of people receiving a university-level education increased by 117 percent, with the student population reaching around 22,000 during this time. During this surge in educational attainment, the university offered a place to debate and discuss various strategies and ideologies for political success during the growing political crisis.[101]

The FEUU's main focus during this period rested on attempts to gain university autonomy and establish a university government formed by faculty, alumni, and students. However, members also embraced what historian Megan Strom calls a "social mission" of engaging with wider societal issues.[102] For example, the FEUU adopted "a third way," rejecting many Cold War binaries and connecting to other global movements such as anti-Franco activism in Spain and Vietnam War protests. The FEUU hinged its identity on the idea that the university was a force for positive social change in the academic community and in society.[103] As the crisis in Uruguay deepened, the FEUU refocused on domestic issues that engaged these ideals.

For instance, in *Jornada*, the FEUU's paper, student leaders wrote articles protesting the increasingly repressive governmental measures and arguing for a way out of the crisis through a pathway of "social justice" for all.[104] Out of this discord, the FEUU articulated a platform based on three main principles aimed at combating the current political conditions and attracting a widespread following: a leftist political vision based on student discontent with the inability of the government and the two traditional parties to address the national crisis; strong nationalist sentiments, which pointed to capitalism and imperialism as contributing to the current economic problems; and university reforms such as autonomy for students to have a larger say in the curriculum and university governance.[105] Parliament had passed the Organic Law in 1958, which granted students "direct and significant" representation in the university's governing institutions. National unrest threatened this involvement as the government made reforms to the university budget without student input and moved to abolish autonomous governing councils to restructure government authority. While debates ensued on how to confront these measures, the movement leaned more toward a militant stance. Frequent clashes with the government further threatened the students' hard-won autonomy as Pacheco moved to effectively outlaw students' and teachers' strikes on the premise that all activities impeding the regular functioning of school had to be prohibited.

The FEUU's opposition to these actions rested on its long-standing belief in democratizing education and advancing a larger societal project of ending social injustice and economic exploitation.[106] In various columns in *Jornada*, the student movement explained that in response to the government's repression, they were fighting for solutions to problems such as hunger, for breaking relations with the "yanquis," for dignity, and for constructing a new society without "*latifundios*, misery, or traitors."[107] Even invoking explicit rights language at the time, the FEUU saw an independent university as playing a role in defending these values, which also included the "inalienable rights of the person and community."[108] The FEUU ultimately connected their advocacy to anti-imperialist movements and economic and social rights that extended beyond the educational realm. Missing in these broad claims, as was so often the case during this period of rights articulation, was any explicit mention of women's rights. As historian Vania Markarian notes with youth movements more generally, feminist issues were almost entirely overlooked and subordinated to larger societal goals and transformations.[109]

As the battles between students and the government intensified, students moved their protests from the papers into the streets.[110] The FEUU and students' involvement the political battles of the 1960s was unsurprising given the earlier history of student activism in Uruguay. The difference lay in the number of those who became involved, as well as the level of violence in the streets as clashes with the government became more common.[111] Líber Arce was the first student killed; he died of bullet wounds sustained by police shooting on the crowds during a large anti-government rally in 1968.[112] Following his death, massive protests and public displays of mourning took over the city. The government sought to control the public's outrage through arrests, torture, and outlawing public protest. These measures only further enraged the population and contributed to a cycle of escalation in the years leading up to 1973.[113]

By the latter part of the decade, the movement began to fracture and more radical student groups emerged, including the Frente Estudiantil Revolucionario (FER).[114] The FER rejected plans for gradual reform and instead supported a more combative stance against the government.[115] An article in *Marcha* further illuminated the diverging visions of what students at every educational level were striving toward. In interviews conducted around the secondary schools, students explained their hopes for the future. Some focused on economic equality, some stressed the importance of eliminating class lines, and others even focused on gender inequality. The students noted that their ideal societies differed, but they stood firm that they were all fighting for a "better ideal." The students also acknowledged that "sometimes there were different methods but that isn't to say they didn't have a good idea about where they wanted to go" as a society.[116] Ultimately, students promoted numerous ideas of social justice and minor utopian visions during these years.[117] While some students called for revolutionary change and even left the FER to join the Tupamaros, student groups fought inside and outside of the classroom for rights that ranged from social and economic to political and civil, especially when facing a crackdown by the government.[118]

In addition to the powerful student movement, professors at the oldest and only public university at the time, the Universidad de la República (UdelaR), also played a unique role in asserting rights. Leftist professors were the subject of scrutiny and intimidation. Dozens were arrested, detained, and tortured during this period.[119] In response, UdelaR's faculty governing body passed a resolution denouncing the regime's repressive acts and intimidation. Professors also created a commission with the aim of collecting information about university teachers who were detained and coordinated efforts to hire attorneys, address family concerns, and create a "solidarity fund and defense against fascism."[120] In this way, schools and universities acted as places of protest for students and professors to articulate a broad rights vision and organize against government repression.

Communist Party

Similar to the historic strength of the student movement, the Partido Comunista de Uruguay (Communist Party of Uruguay [PCU]) also emerged long before Cold War politics became pervasive. It held a unique and influential role in challenging the government's repression and contributing to a domestic discourse on rights.[121] The PCU had traditionally rejected violence as a means of political change, but the Party was a major force leading up to the 1973 coup, as members became a focus of the Pacheco and Bordaberry regimes' draconian policies.

At the start of the 1960s, the PCU was the largest group on the Left, with more than 40,000 votes cast for their candidates in the 1962 election.[122] During that decade, the PCU created a left-wing coalition, allying itself with middle-class sectors. By enlarging their base—including the specific targeting of women to mobilize as workers—the PCU believed Uruguay would be a step closer to fulfilling the "anti-imperialist agrarian" stage of an Uruguayan revolution.[123] Demonstrations targeted collective rights struggles against poverty, and for workers' rights, fair salaries, and justice. Despite the recruitment of more women, however, women's rights claims "lost ground and visibility" as the group pursued other goals.[124] The PCU focused on anti-militarism at this time. In many ways, the Tupamaros emerged out of Communist and Socialist Party reluctance to embrace a Cuba-like revolutionary mindset.[125]

As the decade wore on, the Communist Party struggled to articulate a platform amid the rapid political shifts. Historian Gerardo Leibner notes that the Party had trouble placing itself at the vanguard of the revolution when other groups such as the Tupamaros captured headlines.[126] After Che's death in Bolivia, and the setbacks and defeats of guerillas in neighboring countries, some activist groups in Uruguay became even more steadfast and revolutionary. The PCU, by contrast, moderated its position. Articles in *El Popular,* the communist newspaper, focused on creating alliances in defense of democracy, defending workers' rights amid an economic crisis, and ways to fight unjust government repression.[127]

The tactic was successful to some extent, and through the end of the decade the PCU recruited many new members, primarily disaffected workers who wanted to challenge the government but were unwilling to join revolutionary forces.[128] These increased numbers were not enough to secure real political power.[129] Attempting to overcome the deadlocked political scene, communists saw opportunity in the creation of a new political party of leftist group coalitions—the Frente Amplio. The formal coalition embraced the PCU's principles of anti-imperialism and anti-oligarchy, while joining forces with groups that the PCU had been working with in the preceding years to fight against the government's repressive actions.[130]

Creation of the Frente Amplio

The Communist Party was not alone in this shifting strategic decision. Many factions of the Uruguayan Left also hoped that a popular front party would offer electoral solutions to the country's problems. The Socialist Party and Christian Democratic Party joined together in 1971 along with the communists and half a dozen other small leftist groups. Importantly, major figures from the Colorado and Blanco parties also left the two historically prominent political parties to join this new coalition.[131] Notably, Zelmar Michelini and Alba Roballo were increasingly frustrated with the repression from their Colorado Party leadership and joined the new coalition. With impending elections in November of that year, these groups, inspired by the success of the Unidad Popular in Chile, officially founded the Frente Amplio on February 5, 1971.[132]

The Frente Amplio rejected violence as a method to resolve national problems.[133] It argued that the current government, which it considered unjust and unpopular, could be overcome through democratic organizing.[134] As Julio Castro, a teacher, labor leader, and one of the founders of the Frente Amplio, wrote in 1971, the leftist parties would unite around candidates who represented this ideal, who worked on a common program for change, and who could promote a strategy for how to achieve results.[135]

Frente Amplio's founding members recruited a viable presidential candidate who embodied these principles when it chose Líber Seregni. Seregni gained notoriety as an army commander who had been ordered by Pacheco to intervene militarily in a workers' strike in 1969. Refusing, he resigned in protest. With a great deal of moral authority, no previous party membership, and a history in the military that once believed in the subordination to civilian government, Seregni seemed like an ideal choice for the Frente in the 1971 elections. In his speeches, Seregni criticized the repressive government, emphasizing unity and dialogue.[136]

In addition to its selection of a presidential candidate, the Frente Amplio promoted an electoral platform called "The First 30 Government Measures," which laid out the group's ideas about social justice. These principles included, among other measures, agrarian reform, nationalizing private banks, invigorating state industry, and repealing the state's Security Measures.[137] Leaders such as Castro wrote about the party's platform in the press, explaining that the new political party would stand for nationalism, anti-imperialism, popular democracy, Latin Americanism, defense of people's rights and liberty, social peace, and widespread participation in the country's development.[138] Despite this broad vision, the Frente Amplio did not focus on women's rights or equality. Instead, it encouraged women's participation on the basis of traditional gender roles within the party's promotion of social rights such as public health clinics for children and mothers, medical assistance in rural areas, and guaranteed education.[139] Overall, while not explicitly invoking human rights, many of the core party tenets were imbued with collective social and economic rights claims that had been prominent in the country since the era of Batlle but had increasingly come under attack over the last decade.

The Frente Amplio emerged as citizens yearned for social change and many sought a path toward electoral reform. Even the Tupamaros promised to pause their battle against the government for the duration of the election and endorsed the Frente Amplio.[140] While frustration with the Tupamaros and revolutionary calls often take center stage in discussions about Uruguay's descent into dictatorship, the varied groups that formed the Frente Amplio articulated powerful messages of social justice. These visions of change emerged alongside specific claims for rights. As we shall see, they also reflected a growing awareness of the power of a rights discourse to appeal to universal claims when historically strong Uruguayan rights of citizenship were being undermined.

A Language of Rights

From the Frente Amplio to the student activists, Uruguay's political groups utilized a language of rights as they articulated their visions of social justice. In the 1960s, their political discourse rarely explicitly invoked the term "human rights." Still, some notable exceptions existed. For example, each year around the anniversary the UDHR's passage, many newspapers dedicated at least a small column to exploring either activities to celebrate the occasion or the meaning of the document. During the 1960s, these publications began including allusions to the government's increasing repression.[141] Similarly, writers invoked the UDHR when advocating for social justice issues. For example, Eduardo Galeano wrote in *Marcha* about the influence of the Marxist-Christian Colombian priest Camilo Torres, who was killed in a battle with the Colombian military patrol in 1966. In explaining Torres's impact on the current Christian Left in Latin America, Galeano invoked article 18 of the UDHR, claiming that every individual has a right to enjoy freedom of opinion and expression without being harassed for those beliefs.[142] Galeano's argument extended to the importance of securing freedom of expression and other civil and political rights at a time when these rights were increasingly insecure in his own country.

Newspapers, however, were not the only forums where leaders, intellectuals, and writers sporadically invoked the concept of human rights during these years. In one Parliamentary report, Alba Roballo, who would go on to be a founding member of the Frente Amplio, put forth a vote to investigate allegations of poor treatment in prisons, including torture. As a result of Roballo's advocacy, Parliament created the Special Investigatory Commission About Violations of Human Rights, Acts of Torture, and Detention Degrading Human Dignity in 1969. A year later, the committee submitted a report determining that, indeed, police employed systematic torture and horrific treatment to those being questioned as part of Pacheco's Security Measures.[143] Parliament also invoked human rights in response to the joint military-police force that killed eight unarmed members of the Communist Party in April 1972. Although the government justified the deaths as a legitimate response to Tupamaros' violence during a declared State of Emergency, Frente Amplio legislators criticized the systematic violation of human rights that the executive was refusing to investigate and condemn.[144] The Comité Nacional Femenino del Frente Izquierda (National Women's Committee of the Leftist Front) also denounced the government for "violating constitutional norms and human rights enshrined by the UN."[145] These reports and denunciations were important because they linked the government to violations against the citizenry, whose rights were being infringed upon not just because Pacheco and Bordaberry diverged from Batlle's legacy, but because everyone was entitled to universally recognized rights and guarantees. It was a minimalist vision, predicated on the right to be free from torture and arbitrary killings and divorced from some of the grander social justice platforms, but it was a preview of what would continue in the coming years. It also demonstrates the way violence against the populace began well before the official onset of the dictatorship. As the violations continued, political actors began to invoke human rights at a time when the term was not widely mobilized to advocate against governmental mistreatment.

The most comprehensive exploration of human rights in the pre-dictatorship period emerged from a conference hosted by UdelaR in September 1971 during a high point of confrontation between the electorate and the government. The organizers named the gathering the *Foro Internacional sobre la Vigencia de los Derechos Humanos en América Latina* (International Forum for the Exercise of Human Rights in Latin America). Lawyers, union members, and academics gathered to discuss the state of increased repression they faced in Uruguay and, more broadly, in the region.[146] The frustration with an increasingly repressive government, especially one that interfered in higher education and harassed and tortured professors and students, was palpable.[147]

The conference illustrates how various groups invoked human rights terminology in this pre-dictatorship period, using it to mean a range of ideas from protections against torture and imprisonment to a much broader social vision. Some speakers focused on the right to be free from dependency on imperialist and hegemonic powers that inflicted institutional violence on populations across Latin America.[148] Linked to this idea, others spoke about the right to revolution.[149] A variety of other participants concentrated on a range of negative rights, such as the right to be free from persecution, while others focused on positive rights such as the right to liberty and autonomy for university students and professors, and freedom of the press. In other discussions, conference attendees debated social and economic rights, focusing on decreasing literacy rates and poor nutrition as violations of human rights. In this way, the conference is notable for how the term human rights encompassed a broad array of collective rights, not just minimalist or individual rights.

Invoking the UDHR and harkening back to Uruguay's contributions to the foundation of an international human rights regime, speakers also explained how Latin American nations faced a myriad of problems that they had all pledged to fight against twenty-three years earlier when the UDHR was first passed.[150] Most participants spoke of these rights broadly and avoided direct invocation of the increasingly repressive government in the host country. However, despite this censorship and the danger of speaking directly about

Uruguay, one participant referred to the situation of human rights there, focusing on the arrests and torture by the Uruguayan military.[151]

The conference ultimately posed major questions about who had the power to enforce the human rights that were guaranteed in international treaties. This query was particularly poignant because of Uruguay's prominent role in the founding of these documents.[152] By pointing out that national governments—often deemed responsible for enforcing human rights—were also the ones responsible for violations, the conference exposed the frustration of millions of Latin Americans who lived under authoritarian governments. By invoking such a broad array of human rights, attendees also questioned what rights were guaranteed under the phrase "human rights." These questions ultimately endured during and after the dictatorship.

In the end, the conference's wide invocation of the term human rights proved to be the exception rather than the rule. Despite a few disparate uses of "human rights" prior to the dictatorship, the concept was not pervasively used. The fluidity with which human rights was invoked by various actors pointed to its presence in activists' vernacular, but it was not ubiquitous nor well defined. Few of those who utilized the phrase would have considered their advocacy for minor utopias or social justice part of a human rights movement. When it did arise in discussions, it was used to address a wide and sprawling set of issues, from torture to historically guaranteed social services. What many agreed on, though, was the profound crisis in the country and the government's failure to offer protections for almost any rights, which set the stage for a contentious 1971 election with profound consequences in the years to come.

A Stolen Election

The 1971 election remains one of the most controversial in Uruguayan history. It started when Pacheco, who was ineligible to run for a second consecutive term, nonetheless attempted to stand for reelection in 1971. To sidestep this legal prohibition, he proposed a constitutional amendment that would permit his reelection, which citizens voted on at the same time as the national election. He ran against the Colorado Party's desired candidate, Juan María Bordaberry, the Blanco Party's Wilson Ferreira Aldunate, and Líber Seregni from the newly formed Frente Amplio.

From abroad, the United States and Brazil sought to undermine the Frente Amplio's chances, as both countries feared a leftist victory similar to

Salvador Allende's in 1970 Chile.[153] Domestically, in addition to the increased polarization and violence, evidence points to the fact that Ferreira won the election, but the military snatched the victory away from him.

Early returns in Montevideo showed strong results for Bordaberry and the Colorados. Seregni and the Frente Amplio received 30 percent of the vote in the capital, but the new party had little support from the more rural areas of the nation, and that number fell continuously as results came in from the rest of the country. Ferreira and the Blancos saw the opposite occur. As votes from the interior streamed in throughout Election Day, the Colorados' early advantage narrowed. Projected returns eventually pointed to Ferreira as the winner. Then, when this information began to leak out and reached the radio waves, the vote count was mysteriously brought to a halt. At the end of tallying, the Colorado lead held, and Bordaberry was declared the official winner in an election that was widely seen as having been snatched from Ferreira.[154] Disillusionment and frustration with the electoral process was first seen in the end of the Tupamaros' truce just a few days after the results were announced.[155]

After his inauguration, Bordaberry addressed national security. He increased the military's budget at the expense of education and other social sectors, which were already suffering. The military also sought greater executive control and created a National Security Council, which was composed of members of the military who oversaw the presidency. Thus, although Bordaberry remained in office, his policies were overseen by a military intent on consolidating its power against the trumped-up threat of subversion and waging a war against the Tupamaros, communists, university protesters, and unions.[156]

The final consolidation of the military's power occurred on June 27, 1973. That morning, the Senate, still fighting against government repression, voted to investigate charges of torture by the military in the town of Paysandú.[157] Although no one knew it at the time, it was the body's final act for the next twelve years. After the vote, Bordaberry promulgated a measure closing Parliament and disbanding the elected governmental structures, which he declared necessary because of the national security threat the Tupamaros posed.[158] The act was a brazen move, not only because it was taken right after the Senate voted to investigate the military and signified that Bordaberry was abandoning Uruguay's strong democratic tradition. It was also bold because the threat posed by the Tupamaros had, by this point, been largely neutralized.[159] Almost a year earlier in September 1972, the military had arrested dozens of Tupamaros, including their leader, Raúl Sendic.[160] Sendic's capture was a huge victory for the Security Forces. Leaderless and with diminished public support after a series of missteps, the Tupamaros largely disbanded in defeat. Bordaberry, however, continued to invoke the Tupamaros as justification for his repressive measures. After closing Parliament, he prohibited criticism of his regime. Continuing Pacheco's censorship, the two Colorado leaders closed fifty-four different publications between 1967 and 1973. A climate of "absolute censorship" prevailed for the rest of the decade.[161]

A last breath of resistance arose from the FEUU and CNT with support of the Frente Amplio and the Blancos.[162] The FEUU issued a statement to fight the new dictatorship and "in defense of . . . the principles of justice, liberty, social wellbeing, human rights, and democracy."[163] The CNT responded to Bordaberry's decree by calling a general strike. For fifteen days, half a million workers and students occupied their places of work and study, paralyzing businesses and public services in Montevideo and interior parts of the country.[164] Bordaberry responded by forcibly removing workers from factories, arresting union leaders, and making the CNT illegal.[165] The strike ended when a purported deal was struck between the military and the unions to release some of the jailed leaders in exchange for ending the strike. Many of these union leaders fled into exile following their release. The military forcibly closed *Marcha* for three weeks following the coup. After it reopened, it published its response to the military's seizure of power by invoking an increasingly popular international language of human rights. It listed UDHR articles on its cover, including the rights to free speech, to be free from torture, and to organize.[166] After this final outcry, and foreshadowing the global human rights language to come, Bordaberry and the military consolidated their hold on the country and more brazenly waged a war against what it perceived as subversive elements. Within a year, they permanently closed *Marcha*.

Conclusion

What makes Uruguay's progression into this repressive state unique from some of its Latin American neighbors is the gradual way in which the government increased repressive measures and conceded power to the police and military. Unlike Chile's dramatic coup a few months later, which served in many ways to distract the international community from Uruguay's plight, Uruguay's military incrementally chipped away at the country's long-held rights guarantees and rule of law year after year until, by 1973, the military had destroyed any semblance of democratic balance in the nation. The closure of Congress on June 27, 1973 is often considered the official start of Uruguay's military dictatorship. Yet, Uruguayans had been living under a repressive government for years by the time Bordaberry dismissed the country's elected body. This slow process exposes the murky dichotomy between democracy and dictatorship, where violations began long before the military officially gained control.

During this progression, Uruguayans across the Left articulated various visions of rights. These invocations ranged from a defense of social democracy attuned to Uruguay's historical legacy, to a more radical assertion of equality focused on the politics of Third World revolution, to the search for a third way between oligarchical capitalism and communism. While these definitions varied, most failed to include women's rights within their purview, despite the strength of women's participation in politics and movements. In spite of this variety, many activist groups in the 1960s and the early 1970s reached for a shifting and fluid language of rights, that would grow more pronounced in the battle against the dictatorship. What differed between later concepts of rights and those articulated by the groups explained above is the collective rights nature of these earlier visions. In the face of crisis, many of these groups did not necessarily imagine a revolution for Uruguay like that in Cuba, nor did they focus only on individual rights. Instead, they articulated broad visions for social justice based on social and economic rights that were universally recognized and embedded in historic ideas of Uruguay's welfare state. This focus, however, changed during the dictatorship.

CHAPTER 2

Uruguay and the Rise of the Transnational
Human Rights Movement

On February 19, 1976, Amnesty International announced one of the largest international efforts it had ever waged, the purpose of which was "to focus public attention on the use of torture and other violations of human rights" in Uruguay.[1] Across the street from the UN headquarters in New York City, the organization held a "dramatic" press conference.[2] In front of journalists, activists, and even a few politicians, members of AI revealed the horrific, ongoing abuses in the small South American country. They called for people across the globe to write to Uruguayan government officials to demand the release of political prisoners and the cessation of the use of torture as a tool of repression.[3] Members of the group followed up the press conference by penning op-eds in papers around the world and organizing letter-writing campaigns to bring attention to conditions in Uruguay.[4]

Since its founding in 1961, AI had addressed individual cases of torture and political imprisonment from all over the world on an ad hoc basis. After learning about people who were incarcerated for their political views, the organization researched and released information about the person and the circumstances around their confinement. This strategy humanized the imprisoned person, generated public attention, and galvanized people to lobby government officials for immediate and unconditional release.[5] Working in local groups, volunteers sent hundreds of letters, postcards, and telegrams calling for the freedom of "prisoners of conscience." With this heightened scrutiny and public shaming, AI calculated that officials might yield, and indeed, this individual-based strategy proved remarkably successful.[6] A Ford Foundation report in 1975 even declared that "more than any single organization, governmental or nongovernmental, AI has been responsible for creating an international political climate of concern for political prisoners."[7] Yet, the press conference spotlighting conditions in Uruguay on a cold February morning in 1976 marked a considerable shift in the organization's strategy. Rather than focus on one individual prisoner of conscience, AI launched the first-ever campaign to spotlight the human rights situation in an entire country for the purpose of pressuring the government to improve its general practices. Why, though, was the small country of Uruguay the focus of this fundamental strategic shift for a transnational organization with global reach and international cache?

The answer is critical to tracing the relationship between Uruguay and the explosion of the international human rights movement in the 1970s. When the transnational human rights movement gained force in the 1970s, it focused on minimalist claims such as torture, disappearances, and political imprisonment.[8] While the UDHR in 1948 had offered a broad range of civil, political, social, and economic rights to aspire toward, the politics of the Cold War and the nature and extent of repression from Greece to Cambodia to the Southern Cone prompted a narrowing of how activists, exiles, and officials utilized the term around these more limited aims.[9]

Uruguay's own repression came into sharp focus at this perversely fortuitous moment. Torture, disappearances, and political imprisonment were three of the primary tools of repression that its military government utilized to maintain control. Indeed, at the time of the global human rights movement's maturation, Uruguay possessed the dubious distinction of having the highest percentage of political prisoners in the world, many of whom were also tortured.[10] Far from its vaunted title as the Switzerland of South America, Uruguay was now known across the globe as the "Torture Chamber of Latin America."[11] It was in this context that many Uruguayan exiles and activists moved away from the more contentious invocations of collective social and economic rights that had characterized their movements in the 1960s.[12] Instead, they constructed human rights in bounded and limited terms, focused on appealing to international groups to garner support from the widest possible constituency.[13] These calls were earnest; the discourse helped provide a globalizing call to rally against the very violations that they, family, and friends had suffered. The language of human rights, however, also served a political purpose, as a tool to appeal to foreign governments, transnational NGOs, and international funders.

Indeed, NGOs and funding organizations learned about the extent of the repression in Uruguay because Uruguayan exiles and activists began to frame the country's human rights problems as centering squarely on two of the same issues that these prominent international human rights groups were most concerned with addressing. The enormous number of exiles—approximately 10 percent of the entire population—that fled the nation's dictatorship had formed disparate solidarity groups that appealed to existing international concerns. Despite deep fissures in Uruguay's political culture and conceptions of human rights, the various visions and grandiose claims for revolutions that had divided Uruguayans during the 1960s were supplanted, at least temporarily, by minimalist calls for stopping a set of specific violations. While there was never any one movement or sustained alliance, various documents from solidarity groups, exile networks, major international organizations, and funding organizations during this period reveal a picture in which international actors focused on publicizing a specific set of rights that were remarkably consistent across organizations and continents. This consistency in defining the terms of abuse allowed exiles to drive attention to Uruguay.

As Amnesty International got increasingly involved in advocating on behalf of Uruguayan political prisoners, exiles helped push the organization to recognize the inadequacy of an individual-based approach to address the scope of abuses in the country. The conditions in Uruguay helped inspire AI's organizational shift and reoriented the very direction of human rights advocacy during this period beyond one individual at risk to broader country campaigns. As AI grew in stature and resources, it confronted the extent of abuses in Uruguay in a new way, which also served to shape the strategic direction of the organization by pushing against the bounds of their traditional organizing model and prompting new initiatives and ways of advocacy. Thus, although Uruguay is frequently left out of global analyses about the history of human rights in the 1970s, Uruguay was both a major contributor to and beneficiary of this international shift in human rights.

Yet, Uruguay's importance, impact, and visibility in the international arena had a paradoxical effect. By focusing on a minimal list of rights with deep international resonance to attract attention to Uruguay, exile groups neglected other violations taking place under the dictatorship and other victim groups. In the arena of transnational activism during the 1970s, the human rights crisis in the country was understood mainly as the violations of political imprisonment, torture, and disappearances. Social and economic rights dropped off the more visible agenda, and there was also very little activism around the treatment of minority groups such as Afro-Uruguayans; lesbian, gay, bisexual, transgender (LGBT) people; or Jews—all of whom were victims of particular and different types of persecution by the military regime.[14] While many reasons account for this silence—not least of which include resources, international connections, and prejudices within the movement—the primary reason activists ignored these violations was because they wanted to connect to international networks that already specifically advocated against torture and political imprisonment. The long-term, perhaps unintended effect of narrowly defining human rights influenced subsequent narratives about the dictatorship that ignore the treatment of these groups in Uruguay's history.

In this way, crafting a coherent narrative to appeal to international organizations also created an exclusionary human rights chronicle about the period. Ignoring a large group of victims, even if for valiant aims, had the effect of perpetuating the idea that only some violations and victims of the dictatorship were worthy of international attention.[15] This chapter explains how the coherence around specific rights at an international level drove strategic considerations for major transnational human rights organizations. It also recovers a narrative of human rights violations left out of most accounts of Uruguay's experience with dictatorship and human rights abuses in the 1970s.

Ultimately, this chapter offers an unromanticized account of Uruguay's contributions and limitations with respect to the rise of the international human rights movement. It first describes the nature of the dictatorship in Uruguay and explores the repression and human rights violations that Uruguayans suffered. The Southern Cone region experienced a wave of military regimes during the 1970s, although no two dictatorships were exactly alike.[16] This section contrasts Uruguay's experience with other repressive regimes in the Southern Cone, highlighting Uruguay's high rates of torture and political imprisonment. Second, it explains the emergence of exile networks and solidarity groups abroad that focused on a particular set of rights. While many exile communities had difficulty agreeing on how to challenge the dictatorship, groups did unite around a central human rights discourse, which specifically addressed torture, political imprisonment, and disappearance. The third section then explains the success of employing this strategy to appeal to the emergence of Uruguay as an area of concern for Amnesty International, the Washington Office on Latin America (WOLA), and the Ford Foundation, focusing on each group's efforts to address the dire situation in Uruguay. Finally, as opposed to narratives that leave out the dictatorship's impact on Afro-Uruguayans, homosexuals, and Jews, this chapter investigates violations that specifically targeted these groups to reveal the divergent experiences of abuse that occurred in Uruguay's dictatorship.

In explaining the growing international discourse on human rights around limited and specific issues, the chapter addresses how this minimalist discourse sought to overcome political cleavages that had evolved from the highly political but often divisive pre-dictatorship period. From the mid to late 1970s, these divides were, at least on the surface, subsumed to cohere around a limited but clear set of rights. This move did not mean that these groups' visions had changed; in fact, documents show just how political many of these groups still were. Even while appealing to international bodies such as the UN and Organization of American States (OAS), and international advocacy organizations such as WOLA and AI, groups of exiles scattered around the world did not work together on their campaigns. However, at a global level, they often privileged the potential impact of a focused human rights discourse. The irony here lies in the fact that while many of these groups focused their discourse on human rights to demonstrate solidarity around stopping political imprisonment and torture, fissures among these groups still existed below the surface. These differences in strategy and political ideals would resurface during the transition back to democratic rule in the 1980s.

Nature of Dictatorship

Throughout the 1960s crisis, Uruguayans questioned whether the country still upheld the values that had produced its vaunted title as the "Switzerland of South America." With Bordaberry's 1973 decree to close the legislative branch, the country now had its answer. The move completed the country's devolution into dictatorship. Accompanying the closure of the country's elected body was a surge in the reported number of people being arrested, tortured, and disappeared. Bordaberry also took actions to shut down various newspapers, even those only minimally critical of his inarguably violent regime. Censorship of the press was followed by outlawing political parties and "cleansing" the schools and universities of anyone who believed in what the military called "Marxist ideas" but in reality meant anyone on the left who pushed for state reform or challenged governmental power.[17] While the military had justified its takeover on the grounds of countering a subversive threat posed by the Tupamaros, once in power the military sought to create a "new Uruguay" by eliminating labor unions, leftist movements, and political opponents on the basis of an extreme ideology of Cold War anti-communism.[18]

The dictatorship started by decimating the organized labor movement—a key target of all military governments in the Southern Cone during this period.[19] Seeing unions as a leftist threat to their own rule, the military was determined to break the power of organized labor and restrict labor rights. In Uruguay, this process began when the government arrested labor leaders and outlawed the CNT, a coalition of unions. Some smaller unions were permitted to operate but had to register with the Labor Ministry. Registration, however, rarely translated into effective action—the repression made organizing impossible. Many of the tools that these smaller unions traditionally used to bargain with their employers, such as political strikes, became punishable crimes. By the end of 1973, reports surfaced that the military had "dismantled" the trade union movement.[20]

The new military government also targeted the country's education system. The government occupied the nation's only public university, which officially ended the previous hard-won guarantee of autonomy. Then it arrested the head of the university, along with more than 150 students and faculty members. Once the government had control over the university, it required everyone in, or applying for, teaching positions to sign a pledge declaring loyalty to the state and agreeing that they had not been part of "illicit" political organizations or unions such as the CNT or the FEUU.[21] Anyone considered disloyal was fired, including many left-leaning members of the faculty.[22] Government authorities then took over the positions. The stringent loyalty requirements expected from the university faculty extended to the secondary schools, and more than 2,000 teachers were also dismissed after administrative trials were hastily carried out in what was widely considered a harsh and arbitrary process.[23] The military also sought to control schools by approving curriculum and requiring uniforms for students, while teachers had to wear a tie and display patriotic symbols in classrooms.[24]

It was through these measures that the Uruguayan military, in the words of a leading human rights organization, established with "unprecedented sophistication . . . a hushed, progressive repression measured out in doses until it gained absolute control over the entire population."[25] Arrests began to extend well beyond teachers and labor leaders. In a country of only three million, the military imprisoned some 60,000 people for varying lengths of time. The result was the highest rate of political incarceration in the world—one in every fifty people. As one former political prisoner explained, "practically 100 percent of political prisoners experienced torture."[26] Hundreds more were disappeared in both Uruguay and neighboring countries. Operation Condor, a military campaign of repression coordinated between the South American governments to eliminate dissidents, began informally as early as 1968. It was officially affirmed in 1975 at a meeting in Santiago, Chile, when intelligence officials from Brazil, Chile, Argentina, Uruguay, Paraguay, and Bolivia met for a week to discuss plans to gather, exchange, and execute actions against perceived subversives across the region.[27] Uruguayans who had fled into exile in nearby nations, therefore, did not find refuge. Rather, they faced continued persecution, torture, and kidnapping.

The military even targeted the Church. The Church had criticized Bordaberry's arbitrary measures against the Tupamaros in 1972, and various religious groups spoke out against Bordaberry's seizure of power and mass arrests in 1973.[28] As a result, priests and religious women were arrested and interrogated as part of the general crackdown sweeping through the country.[29] The military even forbade religious processions meant to commemorate the annual feast of Corpus Christi, fearing they could turn into a form of political protest. In one of the more famous cases of religious persecution in Uruguay, a progressive bishop of the Catholic Church in Uruguay, Marcelo Mendiharat, was interrogated and expelled by the military in 1972. He did not return to the country until 1985 when the military had left power. Under these conditions, the Church increasingly understood the threat that the military posed, and its publicly critical attitude dissipated after a wave of arrests affected its leadership.[30]

Those who managed to avoid imprisonment still suffered under the dictatorship's repression. In Uruguay, half the population lived in Montevideo, and the military exercised a concentrated and precise method to sustain its power. One example was the categorization of the entire population into either an "A," "B," or "C" group. Military authorities assigned each and every Uruguayan citizen one of these three classifications. An "A" citizen was politically trustworthy and could be employed by the state, travel freely, and enjoy minimal restrictions. The "B" citizens were ideologically suspect and could be employed privately but not by the state. Their travel privileges were limited and they faced continual harassment by security services. Those categorized as "C," however, were not citizens. Rather, they were pariahs. Many people with a "C" categorization faced sustained imprisonment or torture.[31] The military stripped them of their right to hold public jobs and oftentimes even private employment. The military's reach extended even to small community elections. Nahum Bergstein recounted that he tried to run as a leader of the Ashkenazi Jewish community in 1975, but the military required approval of the ballot. When members of the military saw his name as a candidate, they banned him from running because he had a "C" classification.[32] As Uruguayan political scientist Carina Perelli wrote, the aim of the government was "total control . . . the whole country was transformed into a big prison."[33]

This state of terror was an explicit goal of the military. As political scientist Juan Rial explains, torture within the prisons had the specific goal of disseminating "fear among the general population . . . to manipulate the fear of marginal sectors of the population and to draft them as guardians of dissent."[34] The military became involved in matters as small as approving the election of the soccer team captain and taking over teacher aide positions so that it had a representative in every classroom across the educational spectrum.[35] Some Uruguayans described the scene in Montevideo as "hellish." Families were reduced to whispering to each other, even in their own homes. Everyone was assumed to be a spy and feared neighbors that might be watching their houses to report on suspicious activities.[36] Canadian politicians who visited the country in 1976 reported that they "were able to talk to very few people because of the totally controlled situation of military rule."[37]

Such repression had a great effect on human rights groups' capacities to operate in the country. The military rulers in Uruguay exerted "virtually total control over the HRNGO [human rights nongovernmental organization] sector."[38] Unlike in Chile and Argentina, where human rights groups found spaces to protest despite the heavily restricted and repressive environments, in Uruguay advocacy efforts during those initial years were nonexistent.[39] Individuals who many presumed would lead these movements were either in exile or in jail because the military was incredibly successful in clamping down on domestic organizing efforts. Those who attempted to resist saw their operations shut down and documentation destroyed.[40]

Under these harsh conditions, Uruguayans fled into exile at enormous rates. Between 300,000 and 400,000 people in a population of approximately three million in the entire country left during the dictatorship. With so many Uruguayans in exile and such deep repression at home, much of the organization against the dictatorship in the 1970s began to occur outside the borders of the country. Many transnational human rights organizations relied on exiles for information and firsthand evidence in the face of attempts at whitewashing by South American governments.[41] Uruguayan exiles recognized that there was no recourse to address the violent actions by the military domestically. Thus, many ended up employing a dual-track method of mass mobilization, wherein activists sought to shame the autocratic leaders into compliance with international norms, as well as lobbied foreign governments to put pressure on these states through bilateral relations and multilateral forums.[42] In practice, these actors also utilized personal connections and exile networks to get the word out about what was happening in their home states. For example, Robert Goldman, who had spent a Fulbright year from 1967 to 1968 in Uruguay and would go on to advocate for Uruguayan human rights for the next two decades, recalled receiving letters and calls from his friends or their contacts. These letters had to be smuggled out of the country, and they described people who had been arrested and tortured, imploring Goldman to help.[43] It was these types of measures that succeeded in getting information to transnational advocacy groups.

Before fleeing the country, many of these future exiles had stood in opposition to one another during the 1960s over what social justice could look like in Uruguay. Indeed, since the 1948 ratification of the UDHR, human rights around the globe had been subject to varied interpretations and fought over by both proponents and opponents alike. It was not until the 1970s that many began to witness a moment of coherence around what constituted violations for those concerned about Latin America. Uruguayan exiles still had diverse and individual motivations for getting involved in the emerging global human rights movement, but increasingly they did join the effort.[44] Even as their ideological differences continued, Uruguayans' urgency intersected with the work of a growing network of transnational groups with resources and connections, which helped to influence and define the contours of a minimalist language of political and civil rights that cohered around the most prominent violations of the military dictatorship.[45] Even while exiles' ideological battles still existed below the surface, this consensus took hold, inspiring a similar minimalist language of human rights among passionate activists around the globe.

Exiles Abroad

Uruguay was hardly the first nation, even in the Southern Cone, to garner the attention of the new transnational human rights movement. Coups across South America started as early as 1964 in Brazil, then in Uruguay and Chile in 1973 and finally in Argentina in 1976. The regional democratic collapse in many ways allowed the term human rights to become "a slogan of local response and international solidarity."[46] When addressing the situation in Uruguay, activists converged around the specific types of repression that many Uruguayans experienced during the dictatorship. Due to the repression at home and the large numbers of exiles worldwide, it was abroad that a growing voice protesting the abuses on the ground first emerged. Activists gave testimony, denouncing the military's repression and the most prominent problems facing Uruguayans back home.[47] These claims focused on the right to dignity of the person and argued against torture and political imprisonment, even at the expense of limiting their revolutionary language of the 1960s to a few specific human rights concerns.

Uruguayan exiles fled to a variety of places to find refuge, including neighboring Argentina.[48] Before its own military coup in 1976, Argentina was a natural first location for those fleeing Uruguayan repression because of its close proximity, relatively liberal environment in the early 1970s, and already sizeable Uruguayan population.[49] Like other leaders of the Frente Amplio, Zelmar Michelini condemned Uruguay's repression in newspapers and international forums from his new base in Buenos Aires, focusing on appealing for international help—oftentimes utilizing a human rights language.[50] Similarly, beginning in late 1973, two ex-deans of the Universidad de la República fled to Argentina and used an explicit human rights language to denounce torture and the military takeover of the university in Uruguay.[51] Mario Benedetti, a famous Uruguayan writer, wrote poems from exile in Argentina about the repressive conditions in his home country. Perhaps most well known is "Hombre Preso que Mira a Su Hijo" ("Imprisoned Man Watching His Son"), where Benedetti imagines a father writing to his son about his time in prison. He writes: "these sores welts and wounds / you can't / take your eyes off / all came from horrible beatings / boots kicking me in the face / too much pain for me to hide from you / too much torture not to leave a trace."[52] Benedetti already possessed an international reputation for his writing, and with his poems in Argentina he began to expose the horror of the dictatorship's methods of torture and imprisonment for the rest of the world to see. In April 1974, a meeting was held at the Headquarters of the Boxing Federation in Buenos Aires, where Uruguayans who had fled and those helping Uruguayans confront the dictatorship gathered together. The press reported over 7,000 in attendance, filling the venue with both people as well as "anger, pain, and hope" of forging a resistance from abroad.[53] For a brief time, Argentina provided a refuge for fleeing Uruguayan exiles to begin explicit human rights advocacy, even as their strategy about speaking out against the dictatorship varied from newspapers to poems to rallies in this initial period.

In 1976, the Argentine military initiated their own military coup. Shortly thereafter, two Uruguayan politicians who had found exile in the country, Michelini and former Speaker of the House of Deputies Héctor Gutiérrez Ruiz, were killed in Buenos Aires by agents of Operation Condor. While this was perhaps the most well-known such incident, many other Uruguayan activists were also targeted by the new Argentine junta.[54] With Argentina no longer a haven for Uruguayans fleeing from their country's military dictatorship, many fled instead to Mexico and Cuba, as well as Europe and the United States, where a growing international human rights movement had been developing an apparatus and language of protest.[55] In these new locales, exiles began to make valuable connections and draw attention to conditions in their home country, including with a few particularly prominent and growing organizations—AI and WOLA.

Advocacy Abroad: Amnesty International

For Uruguay, exiles proved most successful at bringing international attention to the plight in their nation with Amnesty International, which, as mentioned earlier, focused its first-ever country campaign on spotlighting human rights violations there in 1976. In fact, AI's involvement in Uruguay began several years prior to this campaign—even before the *autogolpe* (self-coup)— and reflects the organization's growing attention to the intertwined issues of political imprisonment and torture.[56]

AI's human rights approach historically centered on public exposure of abuse through active campaigns, documenting conditions and issuing press statements, interviews, and studies on the situation of political prisoners to produce a "clamorous drumbeat of public effort to arouse public interest and attract influential attention."[57] The organization focused on a limited number of prisoners of conscience who they could gather information about and for whom they could launch letter-writing campaigns to governments urging their release. As a *New Yorker* article blithely put it, the organization "made nagging an effective tactic in public affairs."[58] The narrow mandate was framed as above politics to give it credibility and broad appeal. This approach, coupled with some early successes and an increasing sense of moral authority, allowed AI to win a much higher level of popular support than almost any other organization at the time that was focused on human rights.

Yet, by the early 1970s, many leaders in AI began to realize that the extent of torture and abuses occurring around the world rendered an individual prisoner of conscience approach inadequate.[59] Partly informed by the organization's work in Greece and Brazil in the 1960s, AI expanded its operations to include denouncing torture.[60] David Hawk, AI-USA's executive director at the time, explained that AI members understood repression was widespread in many countries, but there was not always enough information and biographical data to launch individual campaigns for each person.[61] Therefore, AI began to look for ways to move beyond advocating solely for individual prisoners of conscience. It sought opportunities to address the larger problems of mass political imprisonment and what happened to people during imprisonment, namely torture and permanent disappearances.[62] A major turning point occurred when AI launched the worldwide Campaign for the Abolition of Torture (CAT) in December 1972.[63] The campaign had a multipronged strategy, with one major initiative focused on targeting the UN to take up these issues and declare torture an international crime.[64] AI recognized that the UN was both the "principal and the most effective instrument for promoting human rights throughout the world."[65] By focusing on the UN, the CAT believed it would make compliance with the Standard Minimum Rules for the Treatment of Prisoners compulsory under international law and provide an international authority for the punishment of offenders.[66]

AI found a receptive audience at the UN. In 1973, the UN passed a resolution expressing disapproval of torture and urging member states to forbid such practices. This was the first resolution in the history of the UN to exclusively address torture. Every subsequent year, the international body raised the issue, and torture even reached the main agenda of the General Assembly (GA) in 1974. The GA condemned the practice and commissioned forty-two reports on the state of torture around the world. In 1975, the Fifth UN Congress on the Prevention of Crime and Treatment of Offenders directly addressed torture and specifically drew attention to the situation in Latin America.[67] By the end of the year, the GA adopted the Declaration on Torture, which AI called the UN's "most important human rights document since the adoption of the Universal Declaration of Human Rights on December 10, 1948."[68] Amnesty International had achieved one of its major goals, and while CAT was a global effort targeting abuses in over sixty countries and involving coordination between the International Secretariat and national sections,

South America took on a particular urgency during this period of increasing concern over the issue of torture within the organization.[69]

As Amnesty International started to include denouncing torture among its core mandates, South American countries fell to authoritarian governments that regularly used torture. While AI's membership, prestige, and global reach grew in the early 1970s, the organization also began to invest its time and resources in the region for the first time in a sustained way. During this time, Uruguay became a particular focus of Amnesty International. As early as 1972, during the heightened repression but before the *autogolpe*, Uruguay emerged as a place of interest for the organization. AI cited it as a "Europe-anized country with a long tradition of liberal politics" where torture and arbitrary arrest had increased. AI was concerned about these conditions and believed it was a "country at the moment where we might have [the] most impact."[70] After the coup, AI's interest increased as the military regime's two most prominent means of control fell under AI's expanding mandate: political imprisonment and torture.[71] As such, Amnesty International, with the International Commission of Jurists, made an official visit to the country in 1974. The group met with political and judicial authorities and visited Libertad prison. What they found was worrying. As the trip report explained, Uruguay represented one of the "most extreme situations of human rights violations in terms of quality of political imprisonment and intensity of torture."[72] In the aftermath of the visit AI ramped up its press releases, urgent actions, and prisoners of conscience adoptions regarding Uruguay.[73]

How Uruguay went from a country where AI targeted actions to the subject of the organization's first international country campaign is multifaceted but important for understanding the iterative relationship between Uruguay's human rights issues and the growing operationalization of transnational human rights advocacy. Members recall that there were several imperatives compelling the decision. First, an organization-wide priority existed to focus more concertedly on repression in the Southern Cone. Andrew Blane, who served as a member of Amnesty International's International Executive Committee from 1974 to 1982, remembered that the focus on Uruguay was a product of this decision. Leaders believed it would be "most effective" to start work there by focusing on the smallest country.[74] In addition, while Chile received much international attention because of the dramatic coup, Uruguay flew under the radar by comparison.[75] AI's Latin America researcher, Edy Kaufman, said he had information on more than a dozen cases. Uruguayan exiles around the globe were particularly effective at making sure to get the information to him and other AI representatives so that Amnesty International could organize campaigns for friends and family members. Kaufman and his colleagues recognized the challenges of launching such a large number of individual cases and also strategically believed that a concerted campaign broadly about political imprisonment and torture in Uruguay could have an immense impact on the military government, as well as bring much-needed attention to a country that was largely being ignored.[76] Thus, between the horrific circumstances in Uruguay, the ability to draw substantial attention, and the hopes for a new type of advocacy process, AI decided to target Uruguay as its first-ever country-wide campaign.[77]

By the time AI made this decision in the mid-1970s, the organization had a global reach, with members in seventy-four countries. Leaders of the Uruguay campaign decided to launch their efforts in the AI-USA section on February 19, 1976, at the Church Center for the United Nations. The organization held a press conference highlighting the high rate of political prisoners, the systematic use of torture in political cases, and the death of dozens of people as a result of torture.[78] Members of the group, such as Jeri Laber, wrote powerful op-eds in the *New York Times* that publicized the government's abuses in horrific detail, ending with a plea to "show the offending government that the world was watching."[79] In the United States, the campaign information reached hundreds of colleges, while community groups across the country held vigils, public gatherings, and letter-writing meetings.[80] Even elected representatives such as Frank Leichter, a New York state senator, wrote to the Uruguayan embassy to "protest the torture and inhuman treatment in Uruguay."[81] Yet, the campaign was not just an AI-USA effort. Around the world, Amnesty International worked to collect signatures, petitioning the Uruguayan government to allow an independent observer to investigate allegations of torture and demand an end to human rights violations. Letters flooded into the Uruguayan government and local embassies from more than seventy countries. The campaign received widespread press coverage from Sri Lanka to Venezuela, Finland, and Morocco.[82]

With the world's attention turned to Uruguay, the campaign elicited a strong reaction from the military. The Uruguayan embassy first grew alarmed even before AI's launch because government officials "learn[ed] about a planned international campaign aimed at discrediting Uruguay." From their Washington embassy, foreign secretaries wrote memos about how best to respond to what they called AI's "accusations."[83] The military government decided on a preemptive, counteroffensive press conference. The day before AI gathered at the UN Church Center, Foreign Minister Juan Carlos Blanco organized his own media event to argue that Amnesty International "strives to harm Uruguay." He continued, stating that the government of Uruguay did "not recognize that . . . Amnesty International has either the competence or the moral authority to report on the internal affairs of Uruguay."[84] These efforts to counterattack the AI campaign continued in private. For example, General José Pérez Cáldez, the Uruguayan ambassador to the United States, attended a business leaders' meeting at the U.S. embassy in Montevideo in 1976 where he insinuated that Amnesty International was "directed by Communist sympathizers."[85] Uruguayan government-controlled media accused AI of "being a communist front."[86] Another paper in Uruguay attempted to discredit the organization by publishing a political cartoon depicting a devil with "Amnesty International" written across his chest who holds signs that say "slander" and "lies."[87]

All these efforts indicate that Uruguayan authorities considered Amnesty International's campaign to be a real threat. The government believed that there was a "coordinated campaign at the international level against [Uruguay] to paint a false picture of the national situation" and responded vigorously.[88] In addition to attempting to delegitimize Amnesty International, the military invited members of international organizations such as the Red Cross to a prison that temporarily hid any evidence of torture to "counter claims by organizations like Amnesty International that Uruguay is violating its citizens' human rights."[89] More ominously, the military searched accused subversives' apartments for AI materials, along with weapons, as the two most important potential pieces of incriminating evidence. In a testimony in 1985 before a Parliamentary Commission on the disappearance of Michelini and Gutiérrez Ruiz, José Luis Azarola Saint detailed his kidnapping and torture just one day before the two politicians' murder. In retelling the horrific ordeal, he explained that the military had not only searched his apartment for materials linking him to the international group, but also questioned whether he had been the one to tell AI about torture taking place in the Libertad prison, and whether he knew of others who had possibly told them.[90] While he was able to convince the military that he had no idea and was released about forty hours later, the incident illustrated the military's central preoccupation with the group. One CIA memo even mentioned that "some leaders of Amnesty International were mentioned as targets" as part of Operation Condor's mission to "liquidate" non-terrorists who were located abroad.[91]

The effects of AI's campaign are hard to measure. It was only one of many contemporaneous efforts by various international organizations such as

WOLA, the Committee in Defense of Political Prisoners in Uruguay (Comité de Defensa por los Prisoneros Políticos en el Uruguay), and the U.S. government, among others. All these groups' work intersected with domestic considerations during this period, mainly Bordaberry's removal and the military tightening its grip on power. AI, however, did believe that because of the campaign, torture in Uruguay "became a major international issue, particularly if compared with a situation of virtual ignorance about this problem" at the start of 1976.[92] A year later, AI contended that while no direct improvement in human rights could be detected, the government was beginning to address growing international criticism. AI reasoned its work had created "international awareness of Uruguay as one of the worst offenders against human rights."[93] Many years later, Hawk called the campaign an "enormous success," arguing that the Uruguayan government had gotten the message: "They understood that if they were going to torture political prisoners, that the world was going to find out about it and there would be consequences."[94]

Evidence from Uruguay seems to confirm this assessment. The practices did not immediately change. Instead, the government launched its own smear campaign against AI in the press. Then the Uruguayan government passed Institutional Act No. 5, which acknowledged human and individual rights—as long as they did not conflict with requirements for internal security.[95] The mere mention of a state's responsibility for human rights was a direct response to the international pressure, even though the military made clear that its definition of the concept differed from how international organizations portrayed human rights concerns.

More generally, the campaign illustrates some key points about Uruguay's impact on the transnational human rights movement. First, Uruguay became a focal point because of the possibility that AI's global membership and resources could be marshalled to have an effect in the country. Far from ignoring the abuses due to the small size of the country, Amnesty International selected Uruguay in part because of the nation's size—which the organization believed might make it more receptive to strong international pressure. Second, two key violations in Uruguay, torture and political imprisonment, were already on the international agenda of AI, and therefore it was a natural fit for the organization. Exiles were also critical in helping Amnesty International bring the plight of Uruguayans into the international spotlight. AI was able to organize a campaign because of the depth of information that came from exile groups in both Europe and the United States.[96] These groups connected with Amnesty International, provided accurate and extensive information about torture and arrests, and pressured AI to take up cases. Uruguayans focused their complaints on the issues already being investigated by these international organizations, which limited the scope of human rights issues, but did provide a rallying point for exiles and AI to work together to bring Uruguay's human rights situation to an international audience.

Advocacy Abroad: WOLA

AI was not the only organization working to bring the country's dilemma to international attention. WOLA also emerged as a strong player in the transnational human rights advocacy network of the 1970s.[97] Founders of the organization imagined WOLA as a space to elevate the voices of Latin Americans and allow them to "speak out and to have access to those making the policies that had a direct impact on their lives."[98] Joe Eldridge, a Methodist minister and ardent leftist, was one of the main organizers of WOLA. He helped bring together many ecumenical churches and other political activists to monitor and gather information about U.S. policy toward the region in order to influence policy makers. In addition, he sought to create a space where Latin Americans "could speak out in defense of human rights and social justice."[99] WOLA's staff conducted a host of connector activities such as contacting congressional offices and State Department officials, organizing and scheduling appointments for Latin American visitors and exiles, and often accompanying them to these meetings. The group served as a critical link between exiles, the public, and key policy makers, which both heightened WOLA's profile and also provided an invaluable resource for exiles.

WOLA emerged from a disparate group of leftist activists that were concerned about Latin America. Named the Latin America Strategy Committee, the group planned to meet on September 13, 1973, to discuss the deteriorating human rights conditions in Uruguay. Yet, the Chilean coup on September 11 put Uruguay temporarily on the back burner, and that meeting focused on the crisis in Chile instead. The urgency to address the Chilean coup created the impetus for WOLA, reshaping the mission and focus of the new organization for months to come.[100] It took until 1976 for WOLA to refocus the group's attention in earnest back to Uruguay, which occurred because of both Amnesty International's campaign and Juan Raúl Ferreira's efforts. Ferreira, the son of Wilson Ferreira, former senator and Blanco opposition leader, was one of the exiles who played a critical role in bringing Uruguay to the center of the group's activities. The military had briefly imprisoned him after the coup, and shortly thereafter Juan Raúl left Uruguay with his family and relocated to Buenos Aires. However, Argentine Security forces attempted to murder his father in 1976, the same day they kidnapped and killed Michelini and Gutiérrez Ruiz. Wilson Ferreira, however, narrowly evaded the same fate as his colleagues only because he was not there when the security forces arrived at his home. In the aftermath, the entire family fled Argentina, and eventually Juan Raúl found his way to the United States.[101]

Juan Raúl first connected with WOLA in late 1975 to raise awareness about the Uruguayan dictatorship and lobby Congress to cut off military aid to the country. While his father settled into exile in London, the main seat of Amnesty International, Juan Raúl remained in the United States, in part to have a permanent Uruguayan presence there to advocate on the country's behalf, and also, as he admitted, a bit to "try his own way" apart from his famous father.[102] WOLA welcomed him and gave him a job as an associate. He held this position from 1976 to 1980.[103] Ferreira considered WOLA "his work, his family, and his support" while in exile.[104] Ferreira also proved to be a critical link in bringing human rights issues such as torture and disappearances in Uruguay to the forefront of the small organization.

While Uruguay had fallen to the wayside as Chile took center stage during the early 1970s, Juan Raúl reinvigorated WOLA's attempt to lobby Congress, the UN, and the OAS about the situation in his home country. He also played a critical role in promoting a press strategy within the organization, writing frequent press releases and op-eds for the international news media based in Washington.[105] He helped provide new evidence to WOLA from friends who either called, sent telegrams, or smuggled information out of Uruguay—information that included new cases of torture, political imprisonment, or disappearances.[106] The deteriorating human rights situation in Uruguay went from being one of many issues discussed in the organization's newsletter, *Latin America Update*, to being a significant topic. In addition, WOLA began to release regular press statements concentrating solely on the country.[107] Following the success of AI's efforts to bring international attention to torture, political imprisonment, and disappearances in the country, WOLA focused on lobbying U.S. policy makers and the Inter-American Commission on Human Rights to pressure the Uruguayan government on the basis of a narrowly defined human rights vision. Juan Raúl was essential to this effort. As WOLA Deputy Director Jo Marie Griesgraber explained, he worked tirelessly during those years. He sometimes slept on the small couch in his office, and he furiously wrote press releases as soon as he received new information from friends and contacts who had made it beyond the closely monitored Uruguayan borders.[108] Embassy officials in Uruguay during the Carter administration also spoke of often working with WOLA, in particular as part of their NGO outreach strategy, "because of the role of Juan Raúl."[109]

While Juan Raúl's efforts were key in bringing Uruguay to the center of WOLA's agenda, WOLA also played a critical role in bringing visibility to Juan Raúl's work. It sent documents he helped draft to the State Department and key congressional offices, many of which made a direct impact on actors involved who read, noted, and took action on the memos.[110] In one memo, a State Department official even wrote explicitly that he wanted to be kept up to date on the Uruguay situation through WOLA.[111] WOLA also helped set up a meeting between Juan Raúl's father, Wilson, and U.S. Deputy Secretary of State Warren Christopher in 1977. The meeting took place at a time when the State Department was formulating a foreign policy toward Uruguay that centered on human rights for the first time.[112]

In these ways, Juan Raúl played the position of a key interlocutor between the repression on the ground in Uruguay and the lack of knowledge abroad about these events.[113] He advocated vigorously within WOLA and made sure that the emerging transnational human rights movement paid attention to Uruguay. While many advocacy organizations did not have a strong prior connection to the small Southern Cone nation, Juan Raúl focused his lobbying around issues of interest to these groups, mainly torture and political imprisonment. At the same time, WOLA provided important connections and visibility to help Juan Raúl reach policy makers in the United States, the OAS, and the UN.[114] What is striking in some ways, though, is the narrow focus of both Juan Raúl and WOLA. In WOLA's initial years of campaigning for the Uruguayan cause, its advocacy centered on a particular set of rights that were limited to political imprisonment, torture, and disappearances. Despite his firsthand experience of the unjust electoral politics or any number of other violations by the military regarding the press or freedom of expression, Juan Raúl pushed WOLA to campaign on issues of torture and political imprisonment. In turn, WOLA's narrow scope focused the attention of policy makers and government officials, complementing Amnesty International's more grassroots efforts. The combination of these two groups' efforts also set a limited but effective agenda for many other advocacy endeavors during the 1970s.

Advocacy Abroad: World Council of Churches

While WOLA described their organization as a "church-sponsored human rights organization," the World Council of Churches' (WCC) human rights advocacy was more explicitly religiously infused.[115] Their involvement in Uruguay during the early years of the dictatorship demonstrates the strength of ecumenical human rights activism, although the military conducted a smear campaign against them, similar to Amnesty International.

Indeed, the origins of ecumenical action in the Southern Cone began out of a politics of practicality during the dictatorship. While churches across Latin America had varied responses to military rule, ranging from outright support to fervent opposition, many member organizations of the WCC harbored victims who came to them for help after family members were beaten, arrested, or disappeared.[116] Based in Geneva, the WCC promoted a theory of Christian unity, specifically geared toward social justice and relieving suffering in the world for the love of Christ.[117] During the course of many Southern Cone dictatorships, this translated into action to protect victims of abuses, helping spur, as historian Patrick Kelly attests, "a linkage between Christianity and human rights."[118] The WCC's actions evolved from helping individuals who came to them for assistance to broader actions such as documenting information for the UN Commission on Human Rights' annual reports, speaking out against violations in order to put pressure on regimes, and mobilizing in solidarity with other groups around the world working to end abuses.[119] The WCC also made financial contributions to human rights activism, pooling donations from Western European social democratic governments to support the work of domestic groups such as Servicio Paz y Justicia (SERPAJ). From Argentina to Brazil, Paraguay, and Chile, the WCC's various activities played a critical role in supporting ecumenical opposition groups during the dictatorships.[120]

In Uruguay specifically, the WCC had strong connections with ecumenical churches dating back to the 1950s. Even before the official coup, the WCC spoke out in 1972 against human rights violations by the increasingly repressive government, sending a team to investigate allegations of abuse, writing and releasing reports on what they found, and sending public letters to Bordaberry to pressure him to restore human rights.[121] However, in response to this activism, the military dictatorship engaged in an orchestrated campaign against the WCC, painting them as communists and direct agents of the Soviets trying to infiltrate the country.[122] The military also shut down *Mensajero*

Valdense, the publication of an evangelical church in Uruguay that wrote about the WCC giving economic aid to churches in Uruguay, and imprisoned all of its staff members. Despite the church that published *Mensajero* not even being a WCC member, the decree against it specifically called out the WCC for promoting "armed subversion on national territory."[123] The military further targeted the WCC when Emilio Castro, an Uruguayan minister who had supported the Frente Amplio, took up an executive leadership position with the organization. After he traveled to Geneva for the job, the military refused to renew his passport and he remained unable to travel back to Uruguay for over a decade.[124] After these multiple upheavals, the WCC drew back from its direct involvement in Uruguay, playing a role mainly by documenting information and helping exiles or solidarity groups in Europe, and Geneva more specifically. Yet, based on its direct experience of repression, the WCC focused its activities on relieving suffering and publicizing the worst aspects of the dictatorship, similar to its more prominent counterparts Amnesty International and WOLA.

Advocacy Abroad: Additional Groups

While AI, WOLA, and WCC were certainly some of the largest organizations interested in taking action to stop human rights abuses in Uruguay during this period, various other organizations contributed to raising international awareness about the violations of torture and political imprisonment. Indeed, many other organizations and publications proliferated around the globe that aimed to raise the visibility of the human rights situation in Uruguay. For example, The Grupo de Información Sobre Uruguay (Information Group about Uruguay [GRISUR]) was founded in Geneva to gather and disseminate news from Uruguay to host countries and other exiles.[125] Further, the Secretariado Internacional de Juristas por la Amnistía en Uruguay (SIJAU) and the Committee in Defense of Political Prisoners in Uruguay were based in France, and the latter also had a New York presence.[126] Using firsthand information about the nation's horrific prison conditions, the Comité published a bulletin called *Uruguay Información*. The newsletter focused on raising awareness of the plight of political prisoners.[127] Other journals also proliferated in places such as Mexico City, Toronto, and Caracas, where groups publicized a broad range of concerns. The different publications spotlighted information that exiles received from friends and contacts still in Uruguay.[128] Meanwhile, labor leaders of the CNT who fled abroad also advocated on behalf of imprisoned comrades.[129] A solidarity group was organized in Israel called Comité Israelí de Solidaridad con los Presos Politicos en Uruguay (Israel Solidarity Committee with Political Prisoners in Uruguay), which tried to publicize information through both the Israeli embassy and foreign minister. In addition, the group staged acts of solidarity against the authoritarian regime.[130] Another group formed in 1971 in Madison, Wisconsin, called Community Action on Latin America (CALA). CALA focused broadly on publicizing the "nature and extent of U.S. involvement in the economy and politics of Latin America," but it also specifically raised visibility of human rights violations in Uruguay through its newsletters and events.[131] These smaller groups failed to unite as one major organization or movement due to geographic distance and political divisions, but their work collectively condemned torture, political imprisonment, and disappearances in the political arena. Although many at times had divergent causes and foci, their discursive unity and relative weight to these three prominent violations raised international awareness regarding Uruguay's human rights problems while also providing valuable information from their own experiences and contacts to some of the larger transnational groups such as Amnesty International and WOLA. Together, these networks of activists working on the Uruguayan cause contributed to a growing human rights consciousness around the world during the 1970s that overwhelmingly focused on a particular set of issues.

International Philanthropy

While transnational advocacy organizations were essential in raising awareness about Uruguay, another important but often overlooked force during the 1970s was the philanthropic community.[132] Foundations also drew attention to specific abuses such as torture and political imprisonment. Alarmed by human rights organizations' increasing reports of torture, the Ford Foundation emerged as an international force by funding and supporting their work.

The Ford Foundation had not always been quite so altruistic; when it was founded in 1936, it had a far less moral mission. In its conception, the foundation was created to protect Henry Ford's interest in the Ford Motor Company and prevent huge tax payments each year. While the Ford Foundation shifted to addressing "interests of the public welfare" in the 1950s, human rights issues in the Southern Cone did not arise until the 1970s, at which point Ford became what some scholars have called "an entrepreneur of ideas."[133]

The Ford Foundation began to focus on human rights on an ad hoc basis as early as 1973, after the Chilean coup.[134] Ford had a long-standing connection to the country, having extended grants to the country totaling $22.5 million between 1960 and 1970.[135] The organization also had its Latin American Southern Cone office in Chile's capital, Santiago. Pinochet's brutality appalled the Ford Foundation, as it countered Chile's strong democratic traditions and rule of law. In the first few years after Pinochet's takeover, the events in Chile compelled the Foundation to begin discussions about human rights as part of its broader conversation about the strategic allocation of resources.[136]

Yet, even as the Ford Foundation began to recognize that it could play a large role furthering human rights around the globe, it noted that "the area of human rights manifestly is ill-defined, contentious, delicate and relative." [137] As such, early on it focused on many of the same narrow set of rights as other international human rights organizations at the time, with internal reports noting that "whatever else we do we should concern ourselves with physical mistreatment, imprisonment on matters of conscience, and arbitrary arrest or deprivation."[138] A memo by program officer David Heaps and a follow-up *Draft Report on Human Rights* furthered those ideas.[139] In laying out how and why the Ford Foundation should commit itself to "the improvement of human rights," the report also paid particular attention to individual rights, asserting that "capricious and arbitrary abuse of individual rights no longer is an eccentric deviation from an accepted social norm. It has become an endemic characteristic of state power during the modern age."[140] Indeed, in subsequent pages, Heaps goes into detail about widespread problems of torture, political imprisonment, and killings or disappearances.

Despite Heaps stressing the moral imperative for Ford to fund human rights initiatives around these issues, it took time for a clear policy to form. In 1976, the Ford Foundation hosted a meeting that was devoted to discussing the Foundation's role regarding human rights in Latin America, which was seen as particularly important in light of the Argentine coup.[141] By 1978, the Foundation began more systematic investing in human rights. It aided scholars who were in danger as a result of the coups across the Southern Cone and funded several human rights organizations, particularly in Chile where Ford channeled the bulk of its initial support.[142]

Ford's relatively moderate support for human rights concerns in Uruguay also originated in 1978 when the Foundation commissioned a report regarding Uruguayan physicians whom the military had imprisoned and tortured.[143] Working with the New York Academy of Sciences, the American College of Physicians, the American Association for the Advancement of Science, and the National Academy of Sciences, the Ford Foundation convened a powerful group of professionals to pressure the Uruguayan government to allow an international visit to the prisons. In response, Uruguayan officials stonewalled such attempts by Foundation representatives. Not only were no visits allowed, but Uruguayan government officials responded to requests by dismissively stating that "any physician imprisoned in Uruguay was there for good reason and had been fairly treated."[144] Demonstrating a severe lack of engagement with the Foundation's concerns, Dr. Federico Garcia Capurro, a physician who served on the civilian advisory board to the military, described the prisons "as equivalent to a five-star hotel."[145]

The Ford Foundation's report admonished Uruguayan officials for blocking information. Unable to see the prisons firsthand, they also attempted to fill in the holes by turning to exiles for information. Both Uruguayan physicians and those not in the medical profession offered information from their family members and their own experiences. The Foundation's final report included testimonials of torture and political imprisonment. Once again, exiles provided the Ford Foundation with critical information that focused on two specific human rights violations—torture and political imprisonment.[146] In this way, it was not just activist organizations but also funding organizations that began to frame the human rights discussion around a limited and specific list of enumerated rights.

As the Foundation's experience with gathering information shows, the transnational human rights movement and exile connections were essential for bringing Uruguay's predicament to international attention. Not only did the government stonewall attempts by international organizations to gather information and denounce AI as a communist front, it also made domestic advocacy almost impossible through staggering repression. Government agencies and philanthropic organizations from the Global North became aware of just how difficult this advocacy was both through the process of Ford's report on physicians in Uruguay and through attempts to fund organizations in Uruguay in the late 1970s on human rights grounds.

In 1978, USAID offered a grant to the Washington-based Center for Law and Social Policy to provide assistance to lawyers and groups undertaking activities in defense of human rights in the Southern Cone that were focused on basic individual rights. Although the grant report touted success in reaching out to groups in Chile and Argentina, it painted a bleak picture of the ability to conduct human rights advocacy in Uruguay. While representatives were finally granted access to visit the country, the report noted almost no hope of even finding a group to work on human rights issues within the country. Accounts from meetings all drew the same conclusion—that "it would be very difficult to find lawyers willing to take a stand in support of fair procedures in the military justice system under which political prisoners are processed."[147] Uruguayans who chose to remain in the country believed that the military would act to "suppress any move made by lawyers to challenge the system and might arrest the lawyers concerned."[148] The Center even tried to arrange a group of respected lawyers whose credentials would appear impeccable to the military government. The organization hoped that an unimpeachable group of individuals might be able to raise issues with the government in cases where there was undeniable evidence of mistreatment. This idea was soon quashed as well.

The report concluded that, rather than pushing for marginal improvements in human rights, it would be better to work toward a restoration of civilian government. They believed any "frontal assault" on the military's human rights practices could be counterproductive in Uruguay.[149] An opportunity to push for an end to military rule began to appear possible in late 1980, which Chapter 4 of this book explores in more detail. Until then, however, human rights advocacy remained almost entirely within the realm of international efforts. These groups defined human rights through a minimal but coherent discourse addressing disappearances, torture, and political imprisonment that obscured fault lines and political divides in many of these exile communities, but the narrow framing also proved effective in bringing Uruguay to the attention of powerful and influential constituencies.

Transnational Human Rights Advocacy—and Its Limits

At a time of rising human rights concerns around the globe, the transnational human rights movement proved remarkably successful in bringing attention to Uruguay. In part, the rising interest in Uruguay's human rights violations was a product of a mutually constitutive process in which activists reacted to the increasing terror of the era and Uruguayans attempted to give voice to their trauma.[150] Uruguayans were not opportunists who merely rode the wave of international advocacy. Trauma theory argues that the experience of trauma is often beyond language.[151] This especially applied to torture, which characterized the majority of Uruguayans' suffering. One victim, Gabriel Mazzarovich, elaborated on this phenomenon. He was arrested at the age of sixteen after organizing clandestinely with other high school students and was tortured by the military for forty-two days. Talking about the experience years later, he noted that "the memory of torture . . . is a difficult memory to synthesize because language is a resource . . . words are inventions to which human beings give meaning, and torture is inhuman. There is no trace of humanity in it. It is very difficult to explain inhumanity with regular human resources."[152] As victims thus explain, putting their horrific experiences into words is extremely challenging. In Uruguay, those involved in human rights work were frequently advocating for either themselves or their loved ones who had been tortured. These people were directly affected and wanted to offer visibility to the horrors they had experienced. Their efforts were not aimed only at joining a powerful existing movement. Rather, in human rights, they found some language to describe their horrendous experiences and try to make others understand what had occurred. Human rights discourse was not merely a political object or tool to utilize for appealing to foreign governments and multilateral forums, but also a mobilizing language to give voice to an often indescribable experience.

This language helped create bridges, albeit temporary ones, across political divides. However, this rights vocabulary also centered on a minimal set of violations that came to characterize the dictatorship both at the time and in the historiography. The exiles' work brought Uruguay to international attention and influenced U.S. foreign policy, as the next chapter explores. Nevertheless, this language often ignored social and economic rights, in addition to obscuring other human rights violations that occurred during the dictatorship period—particularly against the country's most vulnerable populations.

Despite the country's liberal reputation, many scholars have concluded that even before the dictatorship, Uruguayans tended to accept myths of "racial democracy, homogeneity, and equality of opportunity."[153] This false construction of national identity rendered many issues and discrimination on the basis of race, gender, sexuality, and religion invisible, and continued to operate during the nation's experience with repression, even on the Left and for those involved in transnational human rights advocacy. Ultimately, these enduring myths impacted how activists portrayed human rights violations taking place and who drew international attention when it came to defining a set of violations. Silences about violations beyond individual rights point to human rights' narrow focus at a global level in this period, as well as taboos

within a larger context of Uruguayan history. However, unpacking and identifying how discrimination operated against these populations, as well as the
silencing within global advocacy networks, help reveal a deeper and more
complex narrative about Uruguay's experience under military rule. Considering violations based on race, religion, and sexual orientation during the
dictatorship speaks to structural and historic forms of discrimination within
the country that intensified and played out in diverse ways during the military's rule.

Afro-Uruguayans

Afro-Uruguayans suffered under this kind of silencing both historically
and during the dictatorship. The myth of Uruguay's racial homogeneity in
the early republic ignored indigenous groups as well as Afro-Uruguayans.
Starting in the colonial period, Montevideo was the port of entry for African
slaves for the entire Rio de la Plata region. While many slaves were shuttled
to Argentina, approximately 20,000 stayed in Uruguay. On the eve of independence in 1825, almost 25 percent of the country was estimated to be African or Afro-Uruguayan, and they influenced the country's cultural fabric in
a myriad of ways.[154] Slavery was abolished in 1842, and although the percentage of Afro-Uruguayans in the country decreased over time, they continued
to face pervasive discrimination and prejudice.[155]

Afro-Uruguayans lived at the physical and economic edges of society,
often ignored within the country's enduring mythology as a white nation.
Indeed, throughout the first half of the twentieth century, Uruguay promoted a process of *blanqueamiento* or whitening of its population—an image
that stressed its large population of immigrants from Western and Southern
Europe as proof of its modernity and racial progress.[156] Afro-descendants
were marginalized from the country's main institutions and did not obtain
educational benefits from the state, creating gross economic disparities and
rendering Afro-descendants invisible. As one textbook in the late 1800s
explicitly stated, "There are some blacks, children of those who were once
transported from Africa to serve as slaves, but only very few are left and they
will disappear rapidly."[157]

Despite this false perception of the makeup of the nation and the impact
it had on Black communities, José Batlle y Ordoñez's presidency in the early
twentieth century ushered in a national ethos of religious and racial tolerance.

This legacy, though, has often produced problems of discrimination and racism that are rendered invisible within the national consciousness.[158] By embracing a discourse that denied official racism in the twentieth century, the state ignored the specific problems and challenges that affected Afro-descendants.[159]

The military exacerbated these dynamics. During the dictatorship, the military regime denied that any racial problems existed within the nation because, as Bordaberry tried to justify, nonwhite people were nonexistent in Uruguay. Bordaberry ignored the nation's history of slavery entirely and stated that "all of [Uruguay's] inhabitants are descended from the first Spanish colonists, later joined by large numbers of European immigrants from different countries."[160] The military government allowed a historic black organization, the Asociación Cultural y Social del Uruguay (Cultural and Social Association of Uruguay [ACSU]), to remain open throughout the dictatorship despite shutting down many other civil society groups, but this was done mainly to boost the military's own image.[161] The ACSU was traditionally conservative, did not challenge the military, and posed little threat to the government.[162] Bordaberry cited its continued operation as evidence of the nation's acceptance of its Afro-Uruguayan population. Yet, despite these claims of tolerance, the regime displayed its true feelings toward Afro-descendants in a variety of discriminatory practices.

On the one hand, Afro-Uruguayans endured the same treatment as the rest of the population, which included torture and political imprisonment as the military's main modes of repression.[163] Yet, Afro-Uruguayans also suffered additional violations that were outside the official discourse of human rights that was developing internationally and focused on political repression while eliding violations of economic and social rights. For example, most Afro-Uruguayans had lived in *conventillos*, a type of planned housing tenement building in the Montevideo neighborhoods of Barrio Sur and Palermo. These tenements were racially diverse and integrated but stood out for their strong Afro-Uruguayan presence and the cultural importance that Black communities place in the housing structures. As scholar Vannina Sztainbok notes, many Afro-Uruguayans remember them as "sites of family solidarity, hardship, and very humble beginnings . . . cultural heritage sites" that featured frequent *candombe* and were places of Afro-community and culture.[164]

Yet during the dictatorship, the military passed laws supporting neoliberal policies, including massive gentrification projects in the central part of the city as a way to attract foreign investment and private capital.[165] The military targeted traditionally Afro-Uruguayan neighborhoods because they had, over time, become prime real estate. Prices for land in these areas increased, and many stood to benefit from the construction of new homes in the neighborhood which would enhance the city and promote Montevideo as an international banking center. Rent in these buildings had also been controlled since 1947 and thus remained artificially low.[166] This dynamic produced a situation where landlords decided not to invest or maintain these buildings, leaving decaying housing structures. The Afro-Uruguayans who occupied these buildings had strong cultural connections to the area and oftentimes could not afford to leave.

Endorsed by the military government, the city passed laws in 1978 that allowed landlords to evict tenants from buildings that were in a "state of emergency," which the government defined as being "covered with filth and moral degradation."[167] Newspaper articles in the heavily censored press explained that one famous structure, Medio Mundo, needed to be destroyed for its "failure of progress" and because it was a "danger to the occupants."[168] This racialized discourse, based on long-held prejudices, allowed these areas to be targeted for eviction as part of the military's broader neoliberal economic plan and "civilizing mission."

As a result, the government destroyed—literally bulldozed—the conventillos, and their residents were displaced. These evictions often occurred through brutal force.[169] As activist and politician Romero Jorge Rodríguez notes, more than 1,200 people were evicted during this project, the majority of them Afro-Uruguayans.[170] Beatriz Santos Arrascaeta, a writer and activist, explained that the experience of eviction felt connected to her ancestors' similarly dehumanizing removals from the continent of Africa.[171]

The government did not offer tenants adequate housing or other compensation. These communities and historical centers of Afro-Uruguayan life were gone, their residents dispersed to far-flung neighborhoods scattered on the margins of the city. This removal created a sense of double exile from both their African heritage and their Uruguayan birthright.[172] These new "homes" lacked many basic services. In one case, residents were brought to former city stables, a group of sheds in Barrio Sur. Afro-Uruguayans were told to make their homes "out of cardboard and other found materials."[173] In another case, they were taken to an abandoned factory that some scholars have described as having concentration camp-like conditions.[174] These actions served not only to erase blackness from the city center, but to further target an already struggling population. The government's decision to move Afro-Uruguayans served as another kind of disappearance during the dictatorship—a way to make the population vanish from literal sight in the center of the city and move it further away from national consciousness.[175]

The military also forbade candombe from the city center. Candombe music originated with African slaves, but it had become mainstream in Uruguayan culture by the time of the dictatorship. However, the military attempted to move the carnival celebrations out of the center of the city, claiming that the poor housing conditions were linked with the "vibrations of the drums of candombe groups."[176] Since the music was still deeply associated with Afro-Uruguayan populations, it ultimately proved to be a thinly veiled way to justify evictions that in fact held deep racial implications.[177] In addition, the military blamed the paltry living conditions in conventillos on the lifestyle of the inhabitants, passing judgment on the different cultural norms of the Afro-Uruguayan population.

These policies reveal the contradictions between the regime's claims of racial blindness and the reality of its policies. Even on the identification cards that the military handed out to monitor the population, the regime recognized racial difference in a way that stood out in Uruguayan history. Despite no question about race on the country's census since 1854, *cédulas* (ID cards) during the dictatorship included people's date of birth, place of birth, and skin color.[178] The inclusion of race indicates that the dictatorship took notice of race in a way that belies its purported tolerance.

The military also displayed other forms of racism toward Black populations in the global sphere. For example, an Uruguayan official at the OAS made the argument that the Organization "is degrading itself to accept into their ranks Jamaica, Trinidad and Tobago, and Grenada because they are former British colonies with mixed populations of negros, chinese, Malays, Hindus, and other ethnic elements from Africa and Asia. This means that the unity has been broken and that the OAS has ceased to be an organization of Spanish-Portuguese origin of Western culture, with a majority of Catholics, and with a large indigenous population, and an important contribution from the white race."[179]

Further, at a time when countries around the world were enacting boycotts and sanctions as well as cutting diplomatic relations with South Africa in attempts to pressure the government to end the apartheid regime, Uruguay opened an embassy in Pretoria in 1975.[180] Later the same year, Uruguay received an official trade mission from the country, and then separately hosted

Prime Minister John Vorster.[181] These actions resulted in Uruguay being censured by the UN Special Committee Against Apartheid.[182] In contrast to the global anti-apartheid movement, Uruguay found itself making strides to strengthen relations with South Africa, which gave international credibility and legitimacy to the racist regime.[183] In these cases, the military's words and actions belied claims of acceptance and tolerance of African and Afro-descendent populations.

Despite the different nature of the abuses and particular discrimination toward Afro-descendants in Uruguay, these violations were never brought to the attention of international human rights groups.[184] Part of this inaction was due to a lack of representation abroad. Whereas many persecuted members of the CNT and the FEUU fled into foreign exile, Afro-Uruguayan groups were displaced domestically. Many Afro-Uruguayans did not have the financial or social capital to flee abroad to centers of the transnational human rights movement. Their lack of international presence meant that the human rights movement focused on constructing narrow definitions of human rights during this period, which included political imprisonment and torture, not the violent displacement of Afro-Uruguayans. The narrow articulation of human rights to appeal to international funding groups and U.S. lobbying meant that displacement was outside the framework of recognized human rights violations in the period.

Jews

In addition to the military government making false claims of racial tolerance, Uruguay also celebrated an illusion of religious tolerance that was not always present in practice. Dating back to Batlle's separation of church and state in the early twentieth century, the state had prohibited religious instruction in schools.[185] This contrasted sharply with other Latin American countries, particularly Argentina and Chile, where Catholicism's strength remained inextricably linked with politics, including under military regimes. When asked about antisemitism under their military regime, Uruguayans consistently responded that despite the horrors of its governance, the military was not hostile toward Jews. They replied by asking how a secular society could be antisemitic. These claims, however, are undermined by other forms of discrimination and the targeting of Jews during the dictatorship. As early as the 1960s, a series of groups on the extreme right carried out attacks on left-wing social activists and Jews, elements that by the 1970s were integrated into the mainstream security apparatus of the dictatorship.[186]

The military was in part inspired by the Nazis in designing how to carry out its control over society. In an interview with the magazine *Posdata* in 1996, General Alberto Ballestrino admitted that the military took ideas about its own rule from the regimes of General Franco (of Spain) and other leaders in Europe such as Mussolini and Hitler. He confessed that they considered themselves nationalists, not Nazis, but found great inspiration in the Nazi model.[187] Human rights groups did not hesitate to also make these connections during the dictatorship. Far from the glib comparisons that are sometimes used to liken any authoritarian impulse to Hitler or Nazism, a four-page spread in one exile newsletter in the 1970s outlined the links between the philosophies and methods of the two regimes.[188] The military itself even articulated that its regime was responding to a Jewish-Masonic-Batllista-Bolshevik-Tupamaro threat.[189]

While the armed forces linked a Jewish threat to part of a broader leftist conspiracy, the military regime never directly laid out an antisemitic strategy in the way that the Nazis targeted the extermination of all Jews. Scholar Marguerite Feitlowitz explains that in Argentina, "there was no official anti-Jewish policy at the highest levels of the regime. The generals were too careful of their image vis-à-vis Washington for that."[190] Uruguay followed a similar rulebook. Although not explicitly targeted, the Uruguayan dictatorship often assumed that being Jewish meant being associated with communists due to their Eastern European descent.[191] Many Uruguayans were arrested on suspicion of being associated with communist beliefs; their heritage was considered sufficient justification. In jail, various men recounted being called "*ruso*" (Russian) during their torture sessions because of their Jewish descent, even though they had been born in Uruguay.[192] What research uncovers is that even though there were no directives of institutional antisemitism within the military, Jews did often suffer because of their origins. Jews were perceived as subversives and often experienced unusually cruel treatment as political prisoners.[193] For example, Jewish *detenidos* (detainees) recounted that in jail they were punished specifically for their Jewish origins and heard repeated antisemitic remarks from the prison guards.[194] Oftentimes Jewish prisoners received harsher punishments, such as double or triple torture sessions, or torture that was described as being conducted with "particular severity."[195] Even for those who were never political prisoners, Jews with Polish or Jewish-sounding last names were harassed in the streets. After the military would see their names on their documents, they could become targeted on a regular basis.[196] Due to the fact that even one's last name could make the military suspect him or her of being a subversive, some Jews registered under pseudonyms or changed their last names to avoid the heightened scrutiny.[197]

Reports also surfaced of increased antisemitism across the country. For example, the Nazi Youth organization was revived in Uruguay and held meetings in the Pocitos neighborhood of Montevideo. The group explained that they adhered to Hitler's ideas and sought to "eliminate Jews and Communists," which further demonstrated the inherent links among some Uruguayans between those two groups.[198] Exile newsletters reported on increased antisemitism, such as Jewish cemeteries painted with swastika graffiti in Canelones and flyers distributed in Jewish neighborhoods in Montevideo by the "Comité Antijudío" (Anti-Jew Committee) that declared "the Jew and the communists . . . the two worst enemies of the state" and called for a "Jewish boycott."[199] Jews also reported receiving death threats and hearing groups of people in the street chanting praise of Hitler. A synagogue in Montevideo was destroyed in a bomb explosion on Yom Kippur in 1978.[200] The Anti-Defamation League raised concerns about these issues, writing to the Uruguayan embassy about reports of these incidents and of Nazi graffiti and the sale of antisemitic books around the country.[201]

Despite this activity, the main Jewish institutions were often left alone by the state.[202] Afraid of another Holocaust or further "othering" by the regime, Jewish organizations such as the Comité Central Israelita del Uruguay remained largely silent about the crimes of the dictatorship during this period. Similarly, besides occasionally mentioning antisemitic actions, *Semenario Hebreo*, a weekly newspaper for the Uruguayan Zionist Youth Federation, also was careful not to criticize the military regime.[203] Since these groups were not under attack by the regime, many leaders did not speak out. They chose not to make waves lest they come under suspicion themselves and endanger the entire community.[204] The institutional silence meant that no larger effort was mobilized on an international scale to speak out against these abuses, in contrast to the effort made on behalf of Soviet Jewry during this period. Thus, besides occasional denunciations by U.S.-based Jewish groups, neither international human rights groups during the dictatorship, nor scholars in the historiography, have focused on the particular abuse that Jews endured under the military's rule.

"Homosexuales"

The Uruguayan military targeted the LGBT community during the nation's dictatorship, but this discrimination also dated back further than the 1973 coup. Long before the military took over in the country, Uruguay's psychiatric community classified homosexuality as a sickness and published various articles about the endocrinological problems of the "disease" in its premier psychological journal.[205] The medical community in Uruguay attributed homosexuality to a combination of biological problems and environmental influences, which led to the proliferation of "treatments" to cure homosexual "inclinations," including electroshock therapy.[206] Pathologized from the perspective of medicine and psychology, gay life in Uruguay was also targeted by the police for a large part of the twentieth century under directives "to clean the capital of sexual depravity."[207] Fear of arrest and public shaming drove gay life underground even in the pre-dictatorship period.

The military dictatorship, however, discriminated against gay populations in various ways that shifted and intensified after 1973. First, the military imposed a ban on "homosexuals" serving in the armed forces, stating that "open sexual deviation" precluded anyone from enrolling in a military academy.[208] During the dictatorship, there were several publicized cases of officers being discharged with dishonor for "homosexual practices." The dictatorship also institutionalized a homophobic agenda by instituting a school curriculum that taught that homosexuality was a representation of deviation and a loss of morality.[209] This was all part of the military's larger doctrine of national security that sought to preserve the nation and reestablish its moral base, which included the idea of heteronormative, patriarchal families and did not tolerate "sexual deviance." The military saw homosexuality as a form of subversion.[210]

Testimonies have also begun to surface about the ways in which homosexuality was particularly targeted and punished among the general population during the dictatorship.[211] First, anyone who openly identified as gay was immediately classified by the military as category "C," meaning that the person lost many employment opportunities and was subject to surveillance and harassment.[212] The military purportedly kept a list of people they considered homosexuals so that these individuals could be carefully watched.[213] Any bars or public spaces known to tolerate homosexual activity were frequently raided, a practice that became common during the dictatorship.[214] Police would surround bars and arrest anyone inside. In one raid in 1981,

120 men were brought down to the police station, with the military separating them by presumed sexual roles—active or passive. Those who were considered "active" were released first because the military "didn't believe 'active' men were 'real' homosexuals."[215]

If gay men and women were arrested and incarcerated as political prisoners, their circumstances usually further deteriorated. They often received particularly harsh treatment in the prisons. The military wanted to "keep the incidence of homosexuality within the jail low" and demonstrate control over the prison population. In one report from a prisoner in 1980, Eugenio Bentaberry noted that the military started by singling out "the three or four individuals that tried to advertise . . . and spread their numbers"—referring to gay people in the prisons—punishing them harshly to show its intolerance for these activities.[216] This punishment included torture and solitary confinement. In fact, when the British diplomat John Sharland was allowed to visit the Libertad prison in 1977, military officials explained that the longest and maximum sentences for solitary were for "reserved for homosexuals."[217] Despite these attempts to control sexual behavior, oral histories indicate that relations among prisoners of the same sex were at times a means of survival during the brutal imprisonment, even if normative negative perceptions of homosexuality discouraged an open discourse about this occurrence.[218] If these prisoners were caught, the consequences were harsh. One *ex-preso politico* (ex-political prisoner) recalled a guard raping her and explaining that the act was "ridding her of her homosexuality." Similar to how Jews received particularly harsh treatment once they were in the prison system, gay people during the dictatorship also reported being subjected to harsher treatment in the jails.[219]

While the dictatorship openly discriminated against what it considered sexual deviance, many leftist groups also did not provide an open environment for homosexuality. Particularly among the Tupamaros, homosexuality was considered counterrevolutionary and bourgeois. Sexuality belonged to the revolution and any deviations from heterosexual lifestyles could prohibit one from being allowed to join the movement. Homosexuality was associated with "passivity" and therefore deemed undesirable among militants.[220] Further, in the early 1970s after the Tupamaros successfully conducted two prison breaks, the Tupamaros complained not only about aggressive treatment by guards, poor nutrition, and poor medical care, but also about exposure to homosexual practices.[221] Indeed, most sectors of Uruguayan society marginalized LGBT issues during the 1970s and the 1980s. As historian Lindsey Churchill notes, "homosexuality, like nonwhiteness, seemed to be invisible to Uruguayan society."[222] Both human rights actors at the time, and scholars since, ignored these abuses to advocate for a narrower set of violations.

Conclusion

As the international human rights movement flourished in the 1970s, Uruguay became a major catalyst for and contributor to the growing activism of the era. While Uruguayan political parties and exiles never formed a cohesive solidarity movement against the dictatorship abroad, a discourse about the violations of torture and political imprisonment linked these groups and added to a rising awareness and international activism against the abuses of the military regime. At times, this proved immensely effective in garnering attention from international NGOs, the OAS, and the UN and, as the next chapter will show, in influencing U.S. foreign policy. The military also bristled against the international condemnation and spent an enormous amount of energy coming up with plans to denounce, stonewall, and counter the effects of these groups. Thus, human rights, and the convergence perhaps not of political exiles but of a discourse, became utilized for political aims—often to great effect.

Far from just being a tool, though, this discourse of human rights was immensely important to Uruguayans who had been tortured or who had family members who were tortured or who disappeared. At the national level, the language had deep moral and political resonance. Split into various visions of social justice throughout the 1960s and early 1970s, advocacy against harsh treatment by the military was one area that these groups could agree to organize around. The ability to get this critical information to international groups was part of the reason Amnesty International took up Uruguay as its first country campaign against torture in 1976. While debate still raged internally and various groups continued to publish their own leaflets articulating their political platforms, stopping torture and political imprisonment became a common cause for the large exile population to converge around.

The rise of human rights internationally presented an opportunity for Uruguayans to advocate on these grounds and successfully garner attention, and thousands of pages have been published on the larger human rights movement in Uruguay. However, there is still very little research that spotlights the treatment of Afro-Uruguayans, Jews, or gay people during this period. The abuses or targeting that these groups suffered were not only ignored during the period, but have been largely ignored in the historiography as well, creating a particular narrative about what human rights victims experienced and what they looked like. These stories about race, religion, and sexuality challenge who and what qualified as subjects of human rights violations.

Part of this absence in the 1970s was due to activists connecting to a prevalent discourse that the international rights movement was already utilizing. Torture had become a major international issue before Uruguayans attempted to advocate against the dictatorship. However, another reason involves a larger strand in Uruguay's history. Homogeneity was always a part of Uruguay's founding myth.[223] Both in its strong historical Eurocentric construction and in the implications of its descriptive phrase, "the Switzerland of South America," Uruguay has relied on an identification with Europe to obscure the heterogeneity in its culture and set itself apart from other countries in the region. Writer Alicia Midgal aptly explains that Uruguay constructed a national myth that was a "sum of exceptionalities . . . so literate, so cultured, so European, so Indianless."[224] The implications of this exceptionalist narrative influenced both the discourse of human rights and the construction of the dictatorship's history as well. The exclusion of these violations from the dictatorship period was thus consistent with a certain preexisting national mythology. The dictatorship's policies amplified the prejudices these groups faced both before and after the period from 1973 to 1985, and later chapters will explore how this manifested in a renewed civil society movement in the late 1980s.

This chapter has sought to recover some of these groups' histories during the period of the 1970s. The years 1973 to 1980 in Uruguay were characterized by crushing repression, which sent enormous numbers of exiles abroad. These individuals helped put Uruguay on the international human rights agenda, albeit around specific violations of torture and political imprisonment. Uruguay thus became an important contributor to and beneficiary of the emerging transnational human rights movements of the period through relentless advocacy and a narrowly defined focus. The effects of the discursive unity are undeniable, but also created silences around a broader array of violations. These silences expose the limits of an emerging human rights language. When listened to carefully, they are quite expressive in exposing some of Uruguay's historic and structural forms of discrimination.[225] The international human rights discourse of Uruguayans that *was* utilized during this period did not have an indelible effect just on transnational activists, who were openly receptive to help from exiles, but also on a seemingly more impermeable institution—U.S. foreign policy.

CHAPTER 3

Human Rights in U.S.-Uruguayan
Bilateral Relations

In a memo from Director of Policy Planning Anthony Lake to Secretary of State Cyrus Vance, Lake noted that in Uruguay, "our bilateral interests are so modest that our prime interest is human rights."[1] Indeed, during four years in office, the Carter administration focused its policies regarding the country around a human rights strategy by cutting aid to the Uruguayan military, publicly and privately condemning abuses in the nation, and supporting opposition groups. Despite Carter's difficulty in implementing a human rights policy around the globe, examining his policies with Uruguay offers a window into one of his administration's most vigorous human rights efforts. This consistent human rights pressure was possible because the country represented a best-case scenario—Carter had little to lose diplomatically in relations with the small Southern Cone nation, and therefore his administration, and the local embassy officials he handpicked for their human rights commitment, could afford to be more insistent in their human rights stance. In this way, Carter's policies toward Uruguay reveal the internal logic and instruments his administration employed without the tradeoffs and limits that are evident in his human rights policies toward many other regions and countries around the world.

Carter, however, did not lead the worldwide human rights battle against the Uruguayan military; he was perhaps the last to join the fight.[2] Despite the rapid ascension of transnational human rights activism in the 1970s, U.S. presidents lacked the same enthusiastic embrace. In fact, they were often at best reluctant and at worst dismissive of integrating human rights into policy decisions. Yet, in the early to mid-1970s, Congress dragged the executive branch into the human rights "explosion."[3] The legislative body's move constituted a reaction to the growing transnational human rights movement and the abuses of the imperial presidency.

Carter's reversal of executive intransigence toward human rights, however, encountered significant challenges as he tried to define how to translate high moral rhetoric into actual policy directives. In many contexts, Carter's earnest approach proved to be broadly defined and expansively envisioned, but unevenly enforced in different contexts around the globe.[4] Yet, while early administration debates about a broader social and economic rights agenda reveal a robust understanding of rights, in South America, and particularly Uruguay, policy focused on a narrow set of rights, mainly political imprisonment, disappearances, and torture. It was a strategy that followed in the footsteps of the transnational human rights movement and congressional efforts over the previous five years to address the dictatorship's violence in the name of Cold War concerns. Thus, Uruguay influenced the Carter administration's strategic human rights calculations by employing a minimal and confined set of objectives and adding pressure to transnational momentum by withdrawing the United States' symbolic and material support for the authoritarian regime.

This chapter traces the emergence of a U.S. human rights policy toward Uruguay that started even before Carter took office. It begins by revealing Richard Nixon and Henry Kissinger's willingness to ignore human rights abuses in the country in favor of Cold War concerns. It then shows how transnational human rights activists and Uruguayan exiles raised U.S. congresspeople's awareness about ongoing events in the nation in the early to mid-1970s, and the tensions that resulted between the Nixon and Ford administrations and congressional action. Carter's shift in policy is thus framed as a response to this external pressure, illustrating how Uruguay and other high-profile Latin American countries informed his broader policy goals and ultimately allowed him to implement one of his most robust human rights policies. Although U.S. foreign policy makers reluctantly and inconsistently incorporated human rights over the "long 1970s," the process of developing and deploying these policies offers crucial insight into the U.S. government's approach to debates about the expanding international discourse, and which rights ultimately became politically possible to implement.[5] Indeed, examining U.S. foreign policy with Uruguay illustrates how initially resistant and then ultimately reactive U.S. presidents were to one of the most pressing issues of the day.[6]

Beyond demonstrating U.S. reticence in implementing human rights policies, analyzing U.S. policy toward Uruguay in the 1970s contributes to scholarship on human rights in two other significant ways. First, it illustrates the importance of small states in understanding the varied implementation of Carter's policy around the globe.[7] Recently, scholars have recognized the limits of analyzing the "great powers" and paid more attention to how actors from and events in smaller nations influence international history.[8] Certainly, the dictatorship and role of Uruguayan exiles in garnering Carter's attention around a specific set of rights speaks to this trend. Second, this chapter spotlights the critical role of ambassadors and embassy officials in influencing how U.S. policy played out on the ground, especially in smaller states that were not a daily focus of the administration.[9]

Ultimately, due to Uruguay's strong democratic history and the fervent advocacy of Congress and human rights organizations, the Carter administration believed a focused human rights policy around pressuring for the cessation of a limited set of violations—mainly torture and political imprisonment at the hands of the state—could have a significant impact. This belief, combined with consistent policies and establishing a strong human rights team on the ground, led to Uruguay becoming one of the key frontiers to advance Carter's human rights policy—to decidedly mixed results.

Nixon, Rockefeller, and Uruguay's Democratic Breakdown

When scholars discuss Nixon's foreign policy, they frequently speak of Nixon and Kissinger in the same breath, focusing—rightfully so—on their mutual interest in fighting communism as an overriding strategy. Indeed, first as National Security Advisor and then as Secretary of State, Kissinger had an outsized influence on Nixon's international outlook.[10] Yet, in Latin America, Nixon's policies were initially shaped in part by Nelson Rockefeller, who Nixon asked to travel to the region to prepare an extensive report on inter-American relations. Despite the heated 1968 Republican primary between the two men, Nixon called on Rockefeller due to his extensive background in Latin American affairs. Rockefeller had served as Franklin Delano Roosevelt's Coordinator of Inter-American Affairs, and some policy makers considered him a friend of the region.[11] In fact, Galo Plaza, the secretary-general for the OAS, advised Nixon that the best thing he could do to develop a successful policy in Latin America during his first term in office would be to send Nelson Rockefeller to the region.[12] Nixon did just that.

Yet, not everyone in the region viewed Rockefeller in terms as positive as Plaza's. For many, Rockefeller's name was "handy political shorthand . . . for imperialism and repression" throughout the region.[13] In some places, U.S.-based companies controlled 85 percent of sources of raw materials, and Rockefeller's family owned or held major stakes in many of these. Illustrating this perspective, some of the first few countries Rockefeller visited were Colombia and Ecuador where he was met with riots, which caused Chile and Venezuela to cancel their invitations to Rockefeller entirely.[14]

When faced with a visit by Nixon's envoy, Uruguayans also took to the streets to protest Rockefeller. Many leftists had viewed the United States with suspicion since the 1950s. Eisenhower's policies toward Latin America were motivated by the idea of protecting the continent from a communist threat. His administration called communism "a hidden enemy that would subvert a society from within" and sent public safety advisers to the region.[15] For over a decade, these U.S. advisers traveled to Uruguay "to improve the capacity of the nation's police to put down the insurgents."[16] This capacity building included providing resources and training for the Uruguayan police and military to conduct harsh interrogation methods. Although Rockefeller was not one of these officers, many Uruguayans connected Rockefeller to these advisors and further saw him as an "agent of Yankee imperialism."[17] In anticipation of his arrival, protesters stoned and firebombed U.S. businesses, hit the U.S. military mission with a Molotov cocktail, and broke the windows of official U.S. automobiles.[18] The leftist weekly *Marcha* headlined an entire issue in the lead-up to Rockefeller's visit "Rockefeller, Go Home," complete with cartoons and articles denouncing the tour. Then, the day before Rockefeller arrived, the Tupamaros destroyed the General Motors display room on the grounds that the company had sold one hundred police cars to the Uruguayan government for the "repression of Uruguayan students."[19] Costs of the damages reached over a million dollars.[20] Fundamentally, the protests against Rockefeller's visit were part of a growing popular frustration with U.S. policies that privileged embracing the government's anti-communist posture and funding and training police and military in the increasingly repressive measures the Uruguayan state employed against its own people.

Opposition to Rockefeller's visit extended from the streets to the halls of Parliament and press rooms where senators and writers alike leveraged the upheaval to pressure President Jorge Pacheco Areco to cancel the diplomatic meeting. Senators Héctor Gutiérrez Ruiz, Julio Sanguinetti, Jorge Larrañaga, and Antonio Hernández proposed a resolution that would require Pacheco to rescind Rockefeller's invitation while writers excoriated the "unlimited arrogance" that would allow an "undesirable and unwanted visit" to proceed.[21] However, Pacheco was firm in his desire to proceed with the diplomatic mission and imposed a "limited state of siege."[22] He also switched the meeting location from the densely populated capital city of Montevideo to the beach town of Punta del Este in midwinter. Pacheco hoped that hosting Rockefeller there in Punta's off-season would isolate Rockefeller from possible violence and protests.[23]

Ultimately, the venue change accomplished its objective as Pacheco's intuition proved correct. The Left protested in Montevideo during the visit. Groups of students barricaded themselves inside university and high school buildings, while the Tupamaros took over a radio station to broadcast an anti-Rockefeller message. The police silenced this broadcast by cutting off electricity to part of the capital city.[24] In moving the meeting location, the government shielded Rockefeller from the upheaval and limited his interactions to meetings with ministers and high-ranking officials to discuss the future of U.S.-Uruguayan relations.

Despite the controversy preceding his arrival, most governmental reports considered the trip a success. In his recommendations to Nixon, Rockefeller explored the possibility of the United States providing Uruguay with agricultural assistance, military training, and investment opportunities. Rockefeller even described the trip as a "turning point" for the Presidential fact-finding mission. He explained that in Uruguay a pattern emerged over issues the entire region faced, which provided the points of view, information, and counsel that the president wanted to hear to formulate U.S. foreign policy toward Latin America.[25]

Yet, while Rockefeller's post-trip report focused on a vast array of topics, he did not make a single reference to the social upheaval or human rights situation in Uruguay.[26] The silence is noteworthy. As the turmoil surrounding his trip illustrates, Rockefeller arrived amid substantial unrest and repression. The social discord, while unique to Uruguay's own sociopolitical circumstances, also reflected the widespread unrest around the region and the world. However, Rockefeller neglected to address any of these issues or the government's handling of the situation.

Instead, Rockefeller's report on Uruguay, and Latin America more broadly, reflected the U.S. Cold War perspective of the region. It acknowledged the emergence of Latin American military regimes but did not challenge their violent tactics. In fact, just the opposite occurred; Rockefeller urged Nixon to learn to tolerate governments that used repression rather than isolate them, even recommending further military assistance to Uruguay.[27] His staffers tried on multiple occasions to include language that would point to the abuses inflicted by these regimes and to argue for a return to democracy and political freedoms. However, Rockefeller removed the language.[28] In congressional testimony delivered just months after he issued the report, Rockefeller explained that "military juntas were becoming forces for social change and were in many cases the only alternative to 'anarchy and chaos.'"[29] While Kissinger and Nixon ignored much of Rockefeller's advice about topics such as debt refinancing, they endorsed Rockefeller's Cold War framework. Indeed, Nixon's approach to formulating policy toward Latin America demonstrated the application of the Nixon Doctrine, wherein the United States would build up the military capacity of allies by providing economic and military aid and training to contain communism. This strategy prevented the United States from putting boots on the ground as it had with Vietnam, but allowed antidemocratic regimes to impose order and stability regardless of the brutal measures they employed against their own citizens to do so.[30]

The principle of "anti-communism at any cost" proved particularly salient in Uruguay in the coming years.[31] During the 1971 election, Nixon sought to prevent what the State Department described as a "takeover" by the Frente Amplio. While the party presented a platform of peaceful, legal, and democratic ways to reform the government, the Nixon administration painted the Frente as a threat to "Uruguay's traditional institutions" that sought only "radical solutions" to Uruguay's problems.[32] Nixon was particularly concerned with Uruguay because he wanted to prevent "another Chile." In 1970, Salvador Allende had been elected to the Chilean presidency as a socialist candidate on the strength of a leftist coalition. Nixon feared a similar outcome in Uruguay. Documents now support the claim that the Nixon administration knew about and was possibly complicit in rigging the election in Uruguay.[33] The United States pursued overt and covert actions to counter the Frente campaign's efforts. Further, Nixon supported Brazil's and Argentina's attempts to intervene in the Uruguayan election.[34]

As a result of foreign and domestic meddling, Bordaberry, the most conservative candidate, became president. Within two years, he closed Parliament and handed over power to the military.[35] The Nixon administration, predictably, failed to condemn the suspension of democracy. Despite the U.S.

government's role in supporting these actions, it sought to deflect this perception. The embassy explained that its silence on Parliament's closure was based on trying not to give "any indications or grounds for suspicion that we are in any way intervening in developments." Instead, it determined Bordaberry's actions represented Uruguayans' efforts to "find Uruguayan solutions to Uruguayan problems."[36]

While trying to stave off any appearances of being involved in the *auto-golpe*, the Nixon administration subsequently backed Bordaberry in a variety of ways. For example, it provided military aid and grants to Uruguay. It also carried out public relations activities such as visits from high-ranking SOUTHCOM officers and conducting U.S.-South American Allied exercises. When the Peace Corps had to withdraw all operations from Uruguay in 1973 due to budget constraints, the Nixon administration went out of its way to make sure Bordaberry's government knew it was only a fiscal decision and not based on "recent events" in the country.[37] Nixon's ambassador to Uruguay, Ernest Siracusa, ultimately expressed a "widespread sense of optimism" based on the hope that Bordaberry's government "will be effective in solving some of the long-standing economic problems in the country."[38] Despite a growing human rights conscience in Congress, Nixon's support of the new military regime reflected his use of national security as the main interpretive framework for determining policy, particularly in the Southern Cone.

This position was predicated on Nixon's belief that the military was well placed to restore stability in Uruguay. More broadly, Nixon's reaction to the elections demonstrates the anti-communist orientation that had characterized U.S. foreign policy since the 1940s and grew more dominant after the 1959 Cuban Revolution. Nixon continued a Cold War tradition of the United States supporting Latin American militaries to protect what he perceived as U.S. anti-communist and national security interests in the region.[39] Indeed, between 1970 and 1973, the administration dedicated 9.5 percent of its Latin American military aid budget to Uruguay. In 1970, that meant Uruguay received the second-highest military assistance in the entire hemisphere.[40] This money was primarily used to train Uruguayan police forces in repressing potential revolutionary threats, especially the Tupamaros. For a country with a population of fewer than three million people, this financial commitment reflected Nixon's policy emphasis on fighting communism in the region by strengthening the militaries of Latin American countries. By supporting right-wing candidates and offering strategic aid, Nixon pushed a strong Cold War agenda in U.S. relations with Uruguay.

Ford and Kissinger vs. Congress

By the time Nixon resigned from office in 1974, U.S. policy toward Uruguay and Latin America had begun to shift. Nixon's replacement, Gerald Ford, faced increased pressure to confront abusive military dictatorships from the human rights movement and Congress. However, during his administration, public criticism of repressive regimes was rare, and private diplomacy was at best sporadic. Kissinger, who stayed on as Secretary of State, also defied new congressional legislation which mandated reporting on violations and reducing aid to governments that abused their citizens' human rights.[41] Because of this intransigence, Congress implemented what historian Barbara Keys calls a "reactive, punitive, and unilateral approach" to human rights, which sought to circumvent the presidency to pressure foreign governments to respect the human rights of their citizens.[42]

This congressional assertiveness stemmed from the growing influence of a group called "the new internationalists" who advocated for economic cooperation, cultural exchange, human rights, support for democracy, and a less interventionist foreign policy. Individuals such as Donald Fraser (D-Minnesota) and Tom Harkin (D-Iowa) emerged as dominant voices in the late 1960s, expressing the belief that U.S. foreign policy needed to be "grounded in the same kind of social values that their party had promoted in the domestic realm with civil rights and other aspects of the Great Society."[43] Congress grew bolder as abuses proliferated during the Vietnam War and Watergate. Human rights issues crossed political divides during this period. Indeed, Congress worked with increasingly vocal human rights groups to pass legislation such as Section 502B of the Foreign Assistance Act, create the Bureau of Human Rights and Humanitarian Affairs, and institute the Harkin Amendment prohibiting economic assistance to any country that commits gross human rights abuses.[44] Kissinger resisted these measures, repeatedly focusing foreign policy decisions on the primacy of the national security doctrine to fight terrorism and largely ignoring human rights concerns.[45]

This resistance emboldened Congress to be more persistent in pursuing international human rights issues and challenging executive power in foreign affairs. The primary tactics Congress deployed to influence foreign affairs included controlling spending measures, using individual efforts to publicize issues, and creating subcommittees to investigate countries.[46] These strategies were especially important in U.S. relations with Uruguay.

For example, Edward Koch (D-New York), a member of the House Appropriations Subcommittee on Foreign Operations, spearheaded cutting off aid to Uruguay on human rights grounds.[47] Koch's interest in human rights stemmed from his work in support of Soviet dissidents. One of Koch's staffers, Charles Flynn, looked for other human rights issues for him to address. While Chile occupied many liberal congresspeople's attentions, Koch was a strident anti-communist, and he was uneasy about staking his human rights policy on objecting to Allende's overthrow. Meanwhile, Uruguay appeared on Flynn's radar because of Amnesty International's February 1976 country campaign. AI possessed a stellar reputation for being objective toward both communist and anti-communist regimes, which increased Flynn's belief that Koch would be interested in working to discontinue aid to the regime.[48] Indeed, Koch began to work on raising the issue in Congress soon thereafter.

Koch's commitment to working to stop U.S. aid to the military regime increased after connecting with WOLA. When Koch published a statement on Uruguay in the *Congressional Record*, WOLA's executive director, Joe Eldridge, contacted Flynn to work together. Eldridge also introduced Koch to Wilson Ferreira, a moderate politician from the country's centrist Blanco Party. According to Flynn, Koch had "incredible chemistry" with Ferreira.[49] Amnesty International's campaign and WOLA's efforts compelled Koch to use the information and discourse from these human rights groups to direct the House's attention to the human rights abuses in Uruguay.[50] Throughout 1976, Koch publicized information from these reports, worked with human rights groups to question the efficacy of sending aid to Uruguay's security forces, and lobbied Congress to end such aid.[51]

Fraser, the head of the House Subcommittee on International Organizations, also played a large role in the congressional campaign against human rights violations in Uruguay. Fraser first entered Congress in 1963 and was an outspoken opponent of the Vietnam War. By the late 1960s, he also began working to move the United States away from supporting repressive anti-communist governments on the basis of Cold War alliances. One of his main levers for doing so in his position came from holding subcommittee hearings addressing international human rights, of which he held seventeen between 1973 and 1976. Historian Sarah Snyder notes that these hearings, the subcommittee's subsequent reports, and the legislation that resulted from these discussions "marked a key turning point in the rise of human rights as a priority in U.S. foreign policy."[52] In the summer of 1976, Fraser held a hearing specifically to address the human rights situation in Uruguay.

Fraser's interest in the human rights situation there originated several years prior, when his constituents wrote letters to him about abuses. For example, one group sent him a report about torture in the nation, while another, the Authors' League of America, Inc., wrote requesting help in advocating for the release of authors imprisoned in Uruguay.[53] Meanwhile, Fraser also began to hear from Uruguayan exiles seeking to garner international attention for Uruguay's plight. This group included Wilson Ferreira, his son Juan Raúl Ferreira, and Senator Zelmar Michelini. These men worked closely with AI and WOLA, which helped connect them to Fraser and advocated on their behalf. As WOLA's director Eldridge recalled, he would go to talk with Fraser and his aide, John Salzberg, to explain the need to hold a hearing on a specific nation.[54] WOLA singled out Uruguay in September 1975 as Latin America's most brutal dictatorship.[55] Government officials noted the report as "an example of Uruguay's high profile on the human rights issue."[56] Together, constituents, human rights activists, and Uruguayan exiles convinced Fraser that the U.S. government needed to reevaluate its policies toward Uruguay in light of the extensive political imprisonment and torture taking place there.

Fraser took various actions in response to this advocacy. He set up meetings with constituents, worked to create international networks of people interested in human rights, and tried to gather more information about Uruguay. On the latter, Fraser contacted Niall MacDermot, the Secretary General of the International Commission of Jurists, who was planning a trip to survey and report on human rights abuses in the Southern Cone. In his letter to MacDermot, Fraser requested a report on Uruguay and raised the possibility of the Inter-American subcommittee holding a hearing on the topic. The hearing came to fruition two years later.[57]

At 2 P.M. on June 17, 1976, in the Rayburn House Office Building, the House of Representatives Subcommittee on International Organizations convened to explore the issue of human rights in Uruguay. Considering new evidence of abuses by the Uruguayan government, the committee stated its purpose of reviewing section 502B of the 1974 Foreign Assistance Act, which specified no military assistance be provided to oppressive regimes.[58] In this way, the hearing was a means to reconsider U.S. funding to anti-communist dictatorships in the name of its Cold War objectives. As historian Vanessa Walker argues, cutting off military aid was aimed at signaling "moral condemnation and materially affect[ing] the ability of foreign governments to perpetrate abuse against their own citizens."[59] With that objective, one of the most powerful governments in the world turned its attention to the human rights situation in Uruguay.

Notably, Zelmar Michelini was absent from the hearing. He had been slated to testify along with Wilson Ferreira but, as explained in Chapter 2, he was assassinated as part of Operation Condor while in exile in neighboring Buenos Aires on May 20, 1976.[60] Ferreira had narrowly escaped the same fate and now relayed this information to open the testimony.[61] His presence drew widespread attention in the United States, where there was "standing room only" during his two hours of testimony.[62] Next to him was an empty seat purposefully reserved for Michelini, who had not survived.[63] With that powerful display of the very real dangers facing Uruguayans across the Southern Cone, Ferreira explained the political situation in Uruguay and recounted the terror he had experienced. He shared that thousands of Uruguayan citizens were detained without legitimate justification, accused of "attempting to undermine the morale of the armed forces."[64] In fact, Ferreira relayed, Uruguay possessed the highest per capita number of political prisoners in the world, with most subjected to some form of torture. His testimony described some of these violations in detail and illuminated how the government's violations extended beyond physical abuses to breaches of political and civil rights, such as the dissolution of Congress, censorship, prohibition of freedom of association, and monitoring of private communications.

Ferreira next requested an end to "U.S. intervention" in support of the military government. Ferreira argued that the United States "openly and publicly . . . sustained those sectors responsible for the most diabolic forms of repression imaginable" and contributed to the "artificial stabilization of tyranny."[65] He ended his testimony with an impassioned plea for Uruguay to be "left alone" and for the United States to stop the "material and technical aid" to the military regime.[66] His testimony highlighted the juxtaposition between Congress's growing concern for human rights and the executive branch's support for repressive military regimes. It further revealed the influence of Uruguayan exiles on U.S. policy debates.

Hearings continued a month later when political scientist Martin Weinstein and AI's Edy Kaufman testified. Weinstein outlined the relationship between the United States and Uruguay. He argued that by increasing aid to the Uruguayan armed forces and maintaining a close, supportive relationship with the dictatorship, the United States had strengthened the military's hold on society. Weinstein called these policies "morally bankrupt and politically unwise."[67] Meanwhile, Kaufman outlined AI's efforts to document human rights abuses in Uruguay.[68] He urged the United States to suspend all military aid to the country. Kaufman's testimony was particularly poignant. AI had a stellar reputation for impartial documentation and influenced congressional debate on Uruguay. The discussion shifted from whether the United States. should single out the nation as a gross violator of human rights to what the response should be toward an Uruguayan government that was widely seen as repressive. Congressional representatives increasingly utilized AI's widely circulated reports that focused on the issues of political imprisonment and torture, demonstrating the influence of NGOs on the policy-making process.[69]

The hearings on Uruguay ultimately had two main implications. First, despite the fact that the State Department responded to the hearings by defending U.S. policies toward Uruguay, Koch's resolution to cut military aid to Uruguay on human rights grounds passed into law in September 1976.[70] This measure sent a message to Uruguay that U.S. policy had shifted from ardent support to at least partial condemnation from Congress. Second, the Uruguayan government was forced to respond as it closely followed the public campaigns in the United States. Starting in January 1976, the Ministry of Foreign Affairs issued an internal memo to track how U.S. news outlets and Congress portrayed Uruguay.[71] Accordingly, the Ministry collected voluminous amounts of information, particularly the congressional hearings and all mentions of Uruguay in the *Congressional Record*.[72] Ministry employees blamed the negative attention on a worldwide Marxist-communist conspiracy and called Amnesty International an organization of communists.[73] In meetings with Pinochet and Bolivia's repressive Hugo Banzer, Bordaberry further revealed his fears of the U.S. proceedings, stressing concern over "intervention in [Uruguayan] internal affairs, subversion, seditious movements, and campaigns to discredit their image."[74] To marginalize the impact of the hearings, Uruguay even initiated its own public relations campaign in the United States to challenge the negative perceptions of the country.[75]

Within Uruguay, these hearings also had major repercussions. Newspapers published the testimony verbatim, even though the press was heavily censored.[76] Around Montevideo, citizens rushed to purchase papers and clustered in small groups around the capital to read about the violations their government had committed. The military misjudged the impact of the testimony. As an isolated institution, it believed that the hearings were evidence of slanderous claims perpetrated against the country internationally. The government went on to release a long list of figures it claimed were active in the international leftist conspiracy to defame Uruguay. Presumably, the Uruguayan government believed the list proved how important the military was in fighting against a subversive threat. However, the act of publishing the testimony ultimately exposed the gap between the military and its citizens. To many Uruguayans, the list revealed that there was growing international support against the military's abuses.[77]

The United States' termination of aid after the hearings and Kissinger's continued support for the government also illustrated the chasm between the U.S. Congress and administration policy over human rights, which weakened the possible impact of aid cuts. Despite Congress's focus on human rights measures, Kissinger and Ford's State Department ultimately sent a different message to leaders in Uruguay by attempting to stall congressional measures. In fact, the State Department viewed Congress as an impediment to its foreign policy initiatives. In a meeting with Uruguay's foreign minister, Kissinger argued that, for the United States, the "biggest problem in this country is the role of the legislature."[78] As one 1974 State Department briefing paper explained, the administration believed that military regimes in South America "favored U.S. interests," and efforts to support them were "seriously hampered by hostile Congressional attitudes."[79]

Political scientist Kathryn Sikkink notes that, during Ford's administration, State Department personnel appeared to be "uninformed about the human rights situation in Uruguay."[80] However, documents suggest that they were not so much unaware as intransigent. Ambassador Siracusa maintained close ties to the dictatorship and was often an "apologist" for the Uruguayan regime at the "expense of human rights."[81] In Uruguay, he was known as the "public relations agent for the dictatorship."[82] Siracusa explained that Uruguay and other Southern Cone nations believed that "communist manipulation and infiltration . . . are really responsible for the mounting attacks against them on human rights issues." Meanwhile, Siracusa noted his belief that these countries "face[d] a regional, coordinated therrorist [sic] threat is fact, not fiction" and even encouraged a coordinated regional response that ultimately cohered as Operation Condor.[83]

As early as 1975, Kissinger also had the State Department Congressional Relations representative respond to Fraser's request for action with justifications for the Uruguayan government's actions against "subversives." In addition, he stated that the State Department "believe[s] the number of arrests has been greatly diminished."[84] The letter explained that Uruguay's traditional democratic institutions were just undergoing a restructuring as a temporary measure to fight against the communist "menace." In January 1976, Siracusa reiterated this viewpoint, acknowledging that the military committed human rights abuses, but they were isolated to a "small minority of people" who were

members of "terrorist or subversive organizations."[85] In essence, he understood the measures to be justified since they were part of operations focused
on national security.[86] Overall, Ford's government at every level of policy
formation disregarded growing evidence of human rights abuses in favor of
supporting these governments' anti-communist policies.

The State Department's reaction to the Koch Amendment proved to be
the most revealing measure of Ford's human rights policy—or lack thereof.
Acting Assistant Secretary for Inter-American Affairs Hewson Ryan had publicly endorsed Uruguay's "success in restoring order and safety for ordinary
citizens after years of terrorist assaults."[87] Ryan also followed up privately to
Koch, revealing his agitation with the congressman. Ryan explained that he
did "not share the same conclusions about the human rights situation" and
instead cited a communist threat as justification for the military's actions. He
argued, "it is in our national interest to maintain good relations with Uruguay . . . Uruguay has been consistently friendly toward the United States," by
allying with the United States on key international issues in the OAS and the
UN. Ryan also explained that Uruguay's human rights had improved since
the fight against the Tupamaros had abated. He wrote to Koch that he was
"sorry that you have sponsored an amendment."[88]

Then, in a meeting with Uruguay's foreign minister, Juan Carlos Blanco,
Siracusa tried to reaffirm his commitment to blocking pro-human rights
measures in Congress and maintaining a strong relationship with the military. Blanco noted his country's "extremely negative" reaction to the Koch
Amendment, a stance that was supported by newspapers across the country
deploring U.S. "interference in Uruguay's affairs."[89] Siracusa acknowledged
that "the question of human rights" had become the "fulcrum of relations"
between the two countries, but added that the State Department had opposed
the Koch Amendment. Siracusa attempted to assuage Blanco's concerns and
downplay the government's evidence of abuses. Siracusa explained that any
cuts to U.S. funding had to be tied to a *consistent* pattern of gross violations of
human rights. Siracusa argued that proving a consistent pattern was a "difficult
one" and had "not yet been defined." He noted that he "personally accept[ed]
the GOU's [government of Uruguay] statement that it did not advocate or
condone torture" but only that "instances" of torture and political confinement had occurred in the past.[90] Through these types of legal and linguistic
gymnastics, the State Department worked against congressional attempts
to integrate human rights into the foreign policy calculus. Ultimately, these
moves succeeded in sending a weak message to the Uruguayan government

about how much its northern neighbor cared about human rights violations in Uruguay.

At a basic level, Kissinger's State Department never embraced a human rights agenda.[91] To the extent that he evolved at all on human rights issues, Kissinger encapsulated his and Ford's approach in a speech to the Synagogue Council on October 19, 1976, at the height of the Carter-Ford campaign season, when Carter was pushing the issue as a defining component of his electoral platform. Here, Kissinger acquiesced that while the administration "must bend every effort to enhance respect for human rights ... a public crusade is frequently not the most effective." Kissinger opposed attempts to deal with sensitive international human rights issues through legislation and stated that quiet diplomacy was a better method. Since human rights issues were complex, he claimed, only diplomats could address both the inherent contradictions between universal claims and conflicts with power, and balance moral aims with finite resources and competing goals.[92] When forced to confront the human rights revolution, Kissinger claimed that human rights could be an element of foreign policy only if morality was understood to be a measure of national power. These beliefs ultimately structured the Ford administration's approach to addressing abuses in Uruguay throughout his two and a half years in office.[93]

Carter's Policy Shifts

Jimmy Carter's election in November 1976 placed human rights concerns at the highest levels of U.S. foreign policy. The focus had served as a touchstone for Carter's presidential platform and offered a fundamental change from the Nixon-Ford-Kissinger foreign policy approach.[94] Carter hoped he could convince the country to move past the legacy of the Vietnam War and the American "struggle for the soul of the country" that had followed.[95] Carter believed human rights could appeal to individuals of all political stripes and reunite a nation that had been torn apart by political discord and government scandals.[96] His human rights policy was also part of his larger aim to refocus American foreign policy beyond the bipolarity of the Cold War. In a commencement speech at the University of Notre Dame, Carter contended that the United States' "inordinate fear of communism" had led the country to bad policy decisions.[97] Carter saw human rights as a way to organize a new, comprehensive, and long-term strategy that would reflect stronger North-South ties.[98]

The Southern Cone specifically informed how Carter would incorporate human rights into his foreign policy in critical ways. The region was replete with military dictatorships committing massive violations, and even before he entered office activists and members of Congress were confronting the executive branch over how to reverse previous interventionism and complicity in citizen repression. Thus, from debates about how to weigh human rights concerns against other administrative priorities to the tools for how to most effectively withdraw material and symbolic support for these right-wing dictatorships, the region played a role in influencing Carter's strategic thinking and priorities on human rights as a whole. Uruguay was specifically important to this process because of the way activists presented the administration with a very narrow set of rights to focus on. Therefore, in a country without many competing national interests, Uruguay allowed the administration to test a best-case scenario for implementing human rights policies and think through how to translate these broader ideas into practice.

Latin America's importance to the administration's human rights policy became immediately evident through both private and public actions. First, it was the only region of the world that received a comprehensive policy review.[99] In the directive, the administration asked for all departments to consider options for U.S. foreign policy to "reflect a higher and more effective level of concern for fundamental human rights" in the region.[100] Additionally, right after Carter's inauguration, officials frequently gave speeches about how to change the United States' relationship with Latin America, which often included a rights priority.[101] For example, in April 1977 Carter spoke before the OAS, detailing his administration's realignment toward human rights and respect for the sovereignty of "each Latin American and Caribbean nation."[102] A month later, in May 1977, Rosalyn Carter went to Latin America on a goodwill mission to talk about "strengthen[ing] ... ties with our friends to the south."[103] She conspicuously did not visit the region's worst human rights offenders, and in the countries that were included on her trip, a consistent theme in her discussions was the way human rights affected "the overall shape of US policy."[104] President Carter also sought to reorient relations with Latin America in one of his first major policy initiatives—negotiating a new Panama Canal Treaty.[105] As Secretary of State Vance explained, these measures sought to "forge a new and more constructive relationship with the nations of the Western hemisphere and the Third World."[106] Historian Adam Clymer reaffirms that position, explaining that the negotiations were part of Carter's policy of conveying "respect for human rights, small nations, and moral principle."[107]

Despite these early efforts, the administration was initially and purposefully "vague and general" about its human rights policy.[108] Carter waited for direction from his administration on how to bring the high ideal of promoting human rights into the difficult terrain of foreign policy implementation. During this period, the administration began working on how to define what a human rights approach would look like and where these strategies could be most effective. In the administration's Policy Review Memorandum-28 (PRM) and in speeches by Vance, Carter's administration started by articulating a classification system for human rights. The first category included the idea that human rights were to be free from governmental violations of the integrity of the individual. This was particularly important in cases concerning freedom from torture, freedom from inhumane treatment or punishment, and freedom from being denied fair public trials—issues that related closely to Southern Cone nations such as Uruguay. His administration also articulated other categories, including human rights as defined by basic human needs, such as food, shelter, and health care. Finally, the third major category related to civil and political rights, such as the freedom of thought, religion, assembly, and speech.[109] This classification system enabled the administration to define a broad array of human rights, although there was vigorous debate over how to prioritize these different categories and how to reconcile competing objectives. For example, officials expressed concern over utilizing aid primarily as a punitive measure against gross and consistent violations versus how cutting off nonmilitary aid and loans conflicted with potential social and economic rights initiatives such as food security.[110] Ultimately, the administration had to determine how to apply these broader principles on a case-by-case bilateral basis.

Early policy drafts point toward Carter starting to implement his human rights policy by concentrating on a "limited number of 'worst' cases" early in his tenure. Indeed, when the administration narrowly focused on that first category of rights, Uruguay quickly became a prime candidate.[111] Uruguay's prominence was bolstered by the work of NGOs and Congress in the years prior to Carter taking office. As Chapter 2 explained, in 1976 Amnesty International had identified Uruguay as a particularly egregious place where human rights abuses were taking place, which led to it being the organization's first targeted country campaign. This attention was replicated in Congress, particularly through Koch's work to cut off aid to the country, also in 1976. At one point, Koch even contended that Uruguay was of no real strategic importance to the United States, which meant that it could be a natural place to "make the point with other Latin American countries that we were no longer going to sit back and support repression."[112] This justification held weight with Carter when he was deciding where to focus his efforts as well. As John Youle, the Political Officer in the Montevideo office from 1977 to 1981, explained, Uruguay was "smaller and less complex than Argentina. It was much more malleable, and the Uruguayan military was the weakest in South America at the time."[113] Despite tensions and conflicts that emerged in defining Carter's broader human rights policy objectives, such as between security and economic interests, the Carter administration viewed Uruguay as a place where they had the potential to have an "easy win."[114] The administration could focus on human rights concerns in the country without many other strategic calculations taking precedence. Thus, Carter's categorization of Uruguay as one of the worst violators of human rights allowed his administration to center a human rights–based strategy in bilateral relations.[115] As such, the study of Carter's foreign policy toward Uruguay offers an opportunity to test different tools for implementing human rights policies. It also makes it a particularly interesting case for examining how smaller states did not elide administration prioritization, but rather served as a place to try out broader initiatives and ideas.

One way this was done was within the State Department, where the Uruguay embassy team was handpicked to be a model in these human rights efforts. Youle explained that the embassy under Nixon and Ford had been viewed as outspokenly supportive of the military, with continual pushes to provide them arms and spare parts. Under Vance's State Department, the administration implemented an entirely new team at the top that was strongly supportive of Carter's human rights initiatives.[116] This new team included Lawrence Pezzullo as ambassador, who made human rights "the central issue" in diplomatic relations.[117] For example, after the Senate confirmed him, one of the first things Pezzullo did was go to Koch, the author behind the 1976 amendment to cut off aid to Uruguay on human rights grounds, to explain that there would be a change at the embassy to focus on a human rights perspective.[118] Indeed, by the midpoint of the administration, Carter's Assistant Secretary of State for Human Rights and Humanitarian Affairs, Patricia M. Derian, acknowledged that "the U.S. Embassy in Montevideo is by far 'the most active in human rights issues.'"[119] Appointing local human rights–oriented bureaucrats to implement day-to-day policy was an important initiative in the Carter administration's prioritization of human rights considerations in individual countries.

In addition to selecting particular State Department personnel, the Carter administration incorporated many of the tools Congress had employed in the early 1970s into the executive branch. Rather than serving as a point of contention between the legislature and presidency, these instruments were utilized by Carter to promote human rights, especially toward Uruguay. For example, the State Department's *Country Reports on Human Rights Practices* came to play a key role in the administration. While Kissinger had been "willing to engage in quite blatant evasion of the law" to avoid their implementation, Carter and Vance declassified and publicized these reports, using them to inform policy decisions.[120] These actions meant that Carter no longer followed a long line of presidents who claimed ignorance about abuses in other countries. Documentation of the abuses educated the administration and the public regarding human rights violations abroad.[121] The reports about Uruguay were critical of the military regime, detailing the incarceration of long-term political detainees, disappearances, and torture.[122] Human rights groups had first laid out these abuses in their reports, and the State Department now publicized these violations as well.

The reports also informed decisions on aid. In one of Carter's first interdepartmental meetings on February 3, 1977, the administration began working to eliminate foreign military sales (FMS) to Uruguay.[123] While previous administrations linked continued aid with national interest, Carter, following the logic of activists and congressional actors, rejected this view with respect to Uruguay and dismissed the assumption that security assistance to repressive regimes furthered Cold War aims. Instead, the Carter administration adopted the view that, particularly in the Southern Cone, U.S. support for such regimes had damaged its global leadership and made the United States complicit in human rights abuses. Thus, on February 24, 1977, Vance addressed a Senate subcommittee and explained that the administration was reducing foreign aid to Uruguay, Argentina, and Ethiopia due to their human rights violations. This meant Koch did not need to focus on passing another amendment forcing the administration to cut off aid during a budget approval process; it would be supported and employed by the administration.[124] Carter followed through on this policy despite protests from a variety of groups. The Uruguayan government protested that they were being unfairly targeted, while U.S. businesses with economic interests in the region complained about potential financial repercussions. In addition, some senators such as Jesse Helms believed that cutting aid to countries such as Argentina and Uruguay was a "mistake" because they had strong anti-communist policies.[125] Carter's determination on this issue, despite these voices of dissent, symbolized a shift in the executive branch's support for human rights in foreign policy in relation to Uruguay and constituted a break from Nixon and Ford's intransigent opposition to communism no matter the human rights costs.

Carter's initial human rights stance had two divergent effects in Uruguay—one at the grassroots level and one at the governmental level. First, his policy gave hope to some Uruguayans who viewed his election as the triumph of peaceful democratic change and an inspired human rights policy.[126] Although the military government's censorship prohibited the celebration of Carter's Uruguay policy, Enrique Tarigo, who later became an opposition leader, extolled Carter's policy toward the Soviet dissident Andrei Sakharov. In praising this human rights stance, Tarigo wrote about the possibility for forces of democracy to triumph. Although he was ostensibly speaking about the moral discrepancy between the Ford and Carter presidencies with respect to Soviet dissidents (Ford had refused to meet with dissident Aleksandr Solzhenitsyn in 1975 for fear of damaging the White House's détente policy), it was clear that Tarigo was using the democratic shift in the United States to discuss the possibility that the forces of democracy could promote human rights in Uruguay.[127] In addition, although they were not yet an organized group, mothers of the disappeared wrote letters to the State Department and the U.S. Embassy in Uruguay appealing for U.S. help in finding their missing children. In their pleas, they acknowledged Carter's changed human rights policies and cited the "special concern of his government with the defense of human rights."[128]

Second, and conversely, the Uruguayan government reacted with confusion and then outrage to Carter's morality platform. One of the administration's early memos on relations with Uruguay noted that Aparicio Méndez claimed not to understand the Carter administration's seeming reversal of U.S. policy. Méndez was bewildered that Carter was attacking Uruguay's human rights practices, when only years before the United States had encouraged his government "to suppress all forms of subversion."[129] By the latter part of the year, this confusion turned to outright obstruction. As Carter wrote in his diary, his first meeting with Méndez, in September 1977, went poorly. All Latin American heads of state had been invited to Washington, DC, for the signing of the Panama Canal treaty. The press, liberals, and exile groups criticized Carter for inviting Méndez and other "repressive heads of state" to the White House, which they viewed as a fundamental hypocrisy considering his purported human rights policy.[130]

In their private meeting, however, Carter pushed his human rights agenda. As reported in his diaries, when Carter brought up the issue, Méndez was "highly defensive." Méndez denied that there were any political prisoners in Uruguay, despite the fact that the U.S. government had credible information that Uruguay held somewhere between 2,000 and 5,000 prisoners at the time of the meeting. Méndez also rejected the possibility of the UN Human Rights Council monitoring the country. Carter noted that Méndez was evasive, more so than any other Latin American head of state.[131] Carter continued to pursue the issue after the meeting, encouraging the Uruguayan president to improve the country's domestic situation since "allegations of human rights violations now make it most difficult to sustain past relations [between the countries]."[132] While the quiet diplomatic approach proved confusing to activists concerned about his commitment to human rights, Carter's administration saw the private meetings as a "unique opportunity" to promote his human rights policy.[133]

The Uruguayan government reacted indignantly to other external pressure as well. In September 1977, Congress hosted a conference on U.S.-Latin American policy and human rights, which brought together members of Congress along with representatives from the National Security Council and State Department, and activists from the human rights community.[134] The conference sought to analyze current U.S. policy and discuss alternatives for the future, including the material and symbolic withdrawal of U.S. support for regimes committing massive human rights abuses. In response, Uruguayan ambassador to the United States José Pérez Caldas wrote a scathing letter to Senator George McGovern (D-South Dakota), one of the conference organizers. Pérez Caldas rejected the conference's criticism of Uruguay's human rights violations as "absolutely false" and "based on wrong information about the political reality of the Southern Cone."[135] After years of mixed signals, the Uruguayan government initially responded to diplomatic pressure during the Carter years the same way it had reacted to Congress in the early 1970s—with ardent denials and counteraccusations.

Méndez, along with other Latin American leaders whom Carter criticized, also complained that the U.S. government's policies of cutting aid unfairly pressured them, while ignoring the domestic threats they faced. Both Jorge Videla in Argentina and Augusto Pinochet in Chile charged the United States with meddling in their domestic affairs and violating their sovereignty by pushing a human rights agenda.[136] All three leaders also accused the United States of hypocrisy, pointing to the United States' continued aid to South Korea despite its poor human rights record, and frequently accused the United States of moral imperialism.[137] In the end, the Uruguayan government vehemently protested the Carter administration's cutting of aid and argued that the United States was "punishing" them since the United States had few economic or security interests there.[138] Demonstrating the limitations of Carter's ability to influence human rights internationally through cutting aid, Uruguay preempted the cuts by rejecting the aid first. By spurning the aid on its own terms, Uruguay sought to limit U.S. influence.[139]

As Carter's first year in office ended, Uruguay and other South American authoritarian regimes appeared somewhat impervious to the new frontier of human rights diplomacy. The Bureau of Intelligence and Research noted that human rights progress in Uruguay was blocked by the government's "unwillingness or inability to take effective measures to resolve its serious human rights problem."[140] A report to the UN on the period of August 1977 to January 1978 similarly confirmed that "the Uruguayan government has not stopped its violations of human rights, but has in fact increased them."[141]

Despite the initial intransigence, there was sustained pressure from human rights groups for Carter to continue pressing the Uruguayan government to change its practices. The administration received a steady stream of letters from Uruguayans and transnational human rights groups requesting help locating imprisoned or disappeared friends and relatives.[142] Furthermore, WOLA, working with Juan Raúl Ferreira, stayed in frequent contact with government officials about the continued abuses taking place. One example in particular illustrates this continual pressure from WOLA, as well as the debates within the government over how best to achieve human rights progress. In mid-1978, Derian praised the "emerging trend toward improvement in the human rights situation of Uruguay," including sharp reductions in reports of new arrests and mistreatment of detainees.[143] Yet, while the Carter administration saw praise as necessary to try to encourage further reform, it was met with vehement criticism from activist circles who saw the military as trying to manipulate the United States over, at best, cosmetic changes.[144] Indeed, WOLA criticized the Carter administration's "uncritical" approval of "token gestures made by dictatorial regimes in an effort to gain favor without really altering policy."[145] In response to this incident, WOLA also wrote to Carter administration officials with extensive documentation of increases in the number of political prisoners and use of torture, in contrast to the Uruguayan government's own reported improvements.[146] While demonstrative of the difficult choices the Carter administration faced over how best to carry out its human rights policy, the human rights community's lobbying produced a consistent stream of information and pressure on the administration to follow up on its rhetorical commitment to human rights.

At least partially in response to this petitioning, the Carter administration continued to implement human rights policies in relations with Uruguay into his second year in office. Embassy officials led the way, launching a human rights walk-in program, during which the embassy could discuss the plight of political prisoners or the disappeared with the population.[147] One memo with a large and devastating collection of stories from the program explained that the initiative had created a "tragi-comic effect" wherein the United States was almost saying "step right up with your tales of human rights violations!"[148] Ambassador Pezzullo also pushed for the Uruguayan military to release lists of political prisoners who were currently detained or already released, urged judicial processing of detainees, encouraged independent human rights observations, and emphasized that "an improvement in U.S.-Uruguay relations will be conditioned upon visible and marked improvements in its human rights performance."[149] Embassy officials further made public statements criticizing the military, which citizens later reported gave them hope that the United States was ready to "stand up" and make sure changes occurred.[150] Groups such as the National Academy of Sciences found that the embassy's policies had its desired effect; it became well known in Uruguay that human rights advocacy was an official element of U.S. foreign policy.[151] As lines of citizens grew outside the U.S. embassy, the Uruguayan government could not ignore that the United States was promoting a human rights consciousness and a right to protest conditions on the ground.[152]

The United States also kept up its public campaign against the human rights abuses in various multilateral forums. In January 1978, the United States voted against a request from Uruguay to host the OAS General Assembly meeting due to its poor human rights record. After lobbying hard to host the meeting, Uruguay considered the rejection both a "humiliation" and a "defeat" for the military.[153] Then, in February, the United States strongly criticized the Uruguayan government during the meeting of the UN Commission on Human Rights in Geneva.[154]

Some limited progress occurred in 1978 when the Uruguayan government allowed the American Bar Association (ABA) to send two investigators to examine the human rights situation in the country. Previous attempts to dispatch human rights delegations had been rejected. However, by April of that year, international pressure had made the denial of such requests costly, and the military allowed a five-day visit. The ABA subsequently issued a report urging the Uruguayan government to reform its human rights practices. Recommendations included improving treatment of political detainees, transferring the jurisdiction for subversive crimes from military to civilian courts, and increasing lawyers' independence. Rather than refute the report, Uruguayan officials responded by declaring the state's intent to publish the ABA's recommendations. This small concession was indicative of the Uruguayan government's increasing sensitivity to its image abroad in the face of unwavering pressure. The *New York Times* noted that "nobody sees a likelihood of any major change soon, but the signs of military concern over the international effects of their policy include the release of some prisoners and the better treatment of others."[155] All of these limited steps were in many cases cosmetic and narrow in scope. However, permitting a team of observers to come, accepting a report, and making some limited improvements indicated a desire to diminish U.S. focus on repressive practices, even though the regime was uninterested in major changes.

Surprisingly, even some Uruguayan officials responded positively to the Carter administration's policies. For example, in March 1978, Uruguay's UN ambassador Carlos Giambruno approached U.S. representatives from the Human Rights and Humanitarian Affairs Bureau at a cocktail party to express his belief that Carter's human rights policy "benefits the moderates [in Uruguayan government] . . . despite occasionally pressing too hard."[156] This conversation demonstrated the various ways members of the Uruguayan government reacted to the Carter administration's policies, indicating a growing divide between hard-liners and moderates. By the midpoint of his term in office, Carter and the State Department opined that improvements had begun to occur in Uruguay. The spotlight on human rights abuses had made complete denial of such abuses impossible for the first time since the military government had come into power.[157]

The Carter administration continued to press human rights concerns in the latter half of his term.[158] First, the State Department focused on addressing the continued abuses committed by the military government. For example, Roberta Cohen, the Deputy Assistant Secretary in the State Department's Bureau on Human Rights and Humanitarian Affairs, met with a U.S. medical team traveling to Uruguay to investigate the status of imprisoned doctors. She discussed international standards on torture and medical ethics, provided the team with documents relating to these standards, and offered recommendations that it could make to the Uruguayan government. These recommendations included establishing a medical association in Uruguay, publishing the UN Convention on Torture in the country, and allowing foreigners to investigate abuses. These actions focused on ways to immediately decrease the rates of torture and political imprisonment through various channels.[159]

In addition, Carter continued to reject military aid requests to Uruguay on the grounds that torture was still occurring and almost 1,500 political prisoners remained in jail.[160] Although some members of Congress accused the Carter administration of being "overly rigid" in bringing human rights considerations into economic assistance decisions, Carter believed that withholding these loans could have a significant impact.[161] It is important to emphasize that Uruguay was an outlier in this administration strategy. In responding to over four hundred loan requests during Carter's administration, the United States voted against only nine requests on human rights grounds, of which Uruguay was one. Furthermore, of hundreds of USAID projects with economic aid, only seventeen were denied on human rights grounds during his administration. Once again, Uruguay was included in this latter group. Despite the selective and limited scope of implementation, the U.S. ambassador to Uruguay indicated that U.S. hard-line policy might have begun to make a dent in the military government's impervious exterior.[162]

Even in private meetings, Carter continued to place an emphasis on improving human rights in Uruguay. In January 1980, Carter met with the neoconservative group Coalition for a Democratic Majority (CDM) to mend fences ahead of his reelection campaign. Over breakfast, Carter attempted to use human rights as an area for common ground. Thinking the blatant abuses in Uruguay could be a nonconfrontational rallying point, he asked the group for help in dealing with human rights issues in the country. The group, however, reacted with outrage, and the CDM urged Carter to focus his human rights policy on the Soviet Union. While demonstrating the growing divide between Carter and neoconservatives who defected to the Republicans in 1980, Carter's focus on Uruguay is further proof of his attention to the country throughout his administration.[163]

His administration also utilized 502B reports to publicize Uruguay's human rights violations. The 1979 report noted some improvements, such as four hundred political prisoners being released. However, it focused on the remaining 1,500 prisoners, which resulted in a "high per capita ratio of political detainees to the general population."[164] The report also noted that there had been "few reforms in the area of civil and political rights" and that "intimidation of detainees through psychological abuse during interrogation continued."[165] The Uruguayan government objected to these critiques, calling the report a "'clear interference' in its domestic affairs and an 'uncalled for insult' [sic] ... which 'calls for categorical rejection and formal protest.'"[166] Until the end of Carter's four years in office, the military attempted to dispute attacks on its human rights record, even as these abuses continued to occur. The Carter administration, however, remained consistent in its critiques by largely following international human rights groups and focusing on issues of political imprisonment, torture, and disappearances. Due to a relative lack of conflicting interests in Uruguay, examining Carter's policies toward the country offers a window into one of his administration's most vigorous human rights efforts that extended from the local embassy all the way to the president. Ultimately, despite this coordinated policy, it had varying degrees of effect on the regime's practices.

Conclusion

Despite a narrow focus on a particular set of human rights concerns, even Carter's exceptionally strong human rights policy toward Uruguay suffered from several categorical problems he encountered in implementing human rights into a broader foreign policy framework. As Derian noted in an internal memo to the administration in 1979, public understanding of the term "human rights" was "thin ... behind the vague phrase 'human rights policy.'"[167] Indeed, in various countries around the globe, Carter struggled with exactly how to define his human rights policy and how to implement the various tenets of the policy as they related to other strategic considerations.

Carter's global human rights policies had two main weaknesses. First, while internal administrative debates discussed the various tradeoffs of different categories of human rights, Carter did not publicly offer specific insight into how to address the challenges of a broad notion of human rights. Second, he failed to publicly acknowledge the limited power of foreign governments to change human rights practices in other sovereign states. By according the broad notion of "human rights" such a prominent place in his administration, Carter raised expectations without clearly defining the limitations of human rights and the reach of his policy. This vagueness, combined with his inability to articulate the limited capacity of U.S. influence, hampered his policy and the public's perception of his effectiveness.

In contrast to these overall policies, U.S. relations with Uruguay were striking in their specificity as a policy centered on an explicit set of individual human rights. By divorcing the circumstances that produced these violations from the actual horrific acts, the U.S. government utilized the coherent discourse and documentation of transnational human rights movements to identify a "consistent pattern of gross abuses" in very narrow categories.[168] Therefore, Uruguay readily met the criteria for a "gross violator of human rights" and received targeted pressure, particularly from a strong human rights–focused team at the U.S. embassy in Uruguay.[169] Indeed, as policy makers made challenging day-to-day decisions about the implementation of human rights policies, they struggled over which categorization to prioritize. In Uruguay, the administration's principal preoccupation focused on the narrowly defined rights of freedom from torture and political imprisonment. As a result, it was not the policy makers who granted legitimacy to the human rights movement's claims, but the other way around. Years of activism surrounding Uruguay's human rights abuses generated a discourse and paved the way for embassy officials on the ground to implement a targeted policy toward Uruguay.

The Carter administration used several diplomatic tools to address human rights in Uruguay, including cutting aid, denying loans, meeting with leaders, encouraging political opposition, supporting a human rights–focused embassy staff, and working with NGOs.[170] In Uruguay, the narrow definition of human rights, along with focused diplomatic pressure, were consistent during the Carter administration. As one memo on U.S. human rights policy during his term noted, while no military regimes fell in the Southern Cone, "some political systems are becoming somewhat freer . . . a trend seems to have begun which could gather momentum and which already is improving the plight of individuals . . . and individuals are what the human rights policy is primarily about."[171] The Carter administration's focus on these actions in Uruguay, especially in the absence of conflicting strategic priorities, helped the administration develop policy tools and influence Carter's thinking on human rights implementation that could be applied to other countries around the globe. Years later, Julio María Sanguinetti, who became the first Uruguayan president after the transition back to democratic rule, praised Carter. He believed that "in those years of dictatorship, those of us in the opposition had to struggle practically in the dark. One of the few significant sources of support we had was the policy of the U.S. government, which was constantly looking for human rights violations."[172]

Despite Sanguinetti's effusiveness, Carter had, at best, a limited impact in changing the regime's practices. First, as Senator Harkin noted, U.S. foreign aid to Uruguay had been minimal in the 1970s before Carter took office. Therefore, "the denial of nominal amounts of aid [was] not likely to be felt economically."[173] The strategy rested on rhetorical disapproval. Second, the democratic transition in Uruguay did not occur until almost five years after Carter had been voted out of office. As one memo on Carter's impact in Latin America noted, "net incremental changes [in human rights practices] are difficult to identify and impossible to quantify. No government is likely to admit that it is pursuing a more civilized and humane policy towards its own citizens because of outside advice or pressure."[174]

Indeed, it is impossible to know if Carter had a substantial impact on the Uruguayan military or whether changes during those four years were the result of any combination of factors, including transnational advocacy and domestic politics. While external pressure can be a powerful element influencing local dynamics, social scientists have effectively demonstrated that it cannot be the only factor and that norm shifts often take a long time. Carter's failure to explain these limitations was part of his perception problem.[175] He never clarified that instituting a human rights policy was part of his administration's desire to encourage the long-term improvement of human rights and that he could not stop every human rights violation around the globe. While this point was perhaps obvious to Carter, by not laying out a limited vision for his human rights policy he left himself vulnerable to being blamed for any international violation of human rights as a problem of his foreign policy.

Despite these shortcomings, Carter's specific human rights discourse about violations and consistent policies in Uruguay placed some pressure on the regime and emboldened soft-liners in the military.[176] For example, in the latter part of his presidency, Carter sent spare parts for a small squadron of eight A-37 warplanes to the elite air force. The Uruguayan air force had been the most constitutionalist institution in the nation, and thus the most in favor of returning the country to democracy. After years of denying any military aid to Uruguay, this limited measure exploited divisions within the military, helped to influence internal negotiations, and gave more credibility to soft-liners.[177] The Carter administration's policies thus impacted political and military opposition groups. As one WOLA report noted, the Carter administration "encouraged the democratic opposition ... [and] restored the United States to a position of prestige ... who for years, regarded their neighbor to the north as the hidden power behind every dictatorship on the continent."[178] In this way, Carter's policies offered a fundamental change from previous administrations' support for repressive regimes in Latin America in the name of Cold War objectives. It might even have had the greatest impact in Uruguay by providing support to opposition groups, as opposed to having a direct impact on the military regime's calculations about its use of torture and political imprisonment.[179]

By 1980, seven years into the government's military rule and long after the military had soundly defeated its leftist opposition, a wide variety of factors compelled the government to seek to reestablish its legitimacy. The pressure from Carter and the transnational human rights groups, along with domestic opposition groups and soft-liners in the military, pushed the Uruguayan government to adopt a *cronograma* (timetable) to return to a limited notion of democratic rule in the nation. This process involved initiating a plebiscite on a military-drafted constitution. The Uruguayan government thought this move would appease internal detractors and international critics. In fact, it became a critical juncture in the human rights struggle in Uruguay, which transpired just as Carter was leaving office. However, as the next chapter explains, the gambit backfired.

CHAPTER 4

Plebiscite and Politics

The dictatorship of Uruguay calls a plebiscite and loses.
The people forced into silence seemed dumb, but when
it opens its mouth, it says no. The silence of these years
has been so deafening that the military mistook it for
resignation. They never expected such a response. They
asked only for the sake of asking, like a chef who orders his
chickens to say with what sauce they prefer to be eaten.
                                                —Eduardo Galeano, 1988

On November 30, 1980, just a few weeks after U.S. voters sent Jimmy Carter
home to Georgia in favor of Ronald Reagan, Uruguayans headed to the polls
for a very different type of vote. The military held a plebiscite, attempting
to legitimize their rule with a "yes" or "no" vote on a constitutional expansion of their power. In spite of the country's strong democratic history, it was
the first vote in nine years. During this time, the country had been ruled
by a brutal military regime, its citizens subjected to constant monitoring
and harassment, while thousands across the country had been arrested and
tortured. The military had justified its rule, and these repressive actions, by
pointing to its need to counter the armed Left and ensure the nation's survival. This argument had always been, in large part, based on a false premise, and by 1980 even those justifications had disappeared. The Tupamaros
had long been defeated and no other threat was imminent. Yet, the military
maintained a violent and apparently firm grip on power. The regime found
itself under increasing pressure from multiple actors about their brutal tactics, which included criticism from foreign governments, intergovernmen-
tal organizations, exiles, and a transnational human rights movement.[1] The

lack of any armed leftist challenge, combined with increasing criticism from abroad, ultimately compelled the military's decision to draw up a charter that would actually give the armed forces a permanent and more sizeable control of power in the country.[2] It then submitted the document to the country for approval, which it believed would grant the regime a veneer of democratic sanction as a way to respond to both domestic and international pressures.

While holding a popular vote under military rule might at first glance appear surprising, this practice of staging elections to confer legitimacy on a regime had deep roots in the region.[3] Just two months prior, for instance, Chile's own strongman, Augusto Pinochet, organized a similar electoral gambit with great success. Under growing international scrutiny, he held a referendum on his rule and won a landslide victory, with over two-thirds of Chileans casting their ballot in his favor. Despite using repression and voter intimidation to secure the results, he claimed that the vote affirmed the regime's legitimacy.[4]

The Uruguayan military's plebiscite followed this example and sought to establish a constitutional façade that would legitimate its continued role in Uruguayan society. While giving the opposition a few limited opportunities to speak against the proposed constitution, the military used the force of its power to promote its cause—it took over the airwaves, blasted TV commercials across programming, and used the heavily censored newspapers to frame the vote as for or against chaos and insecurity. Between the persistent pressure and the generally assumed faith in the adage that "dictators don't lose plebiscites," the military entered Election Day confident about the outcome.

When media outlets finally announced the results, though, this belief proved misplaced. No such victory emerged. Uruguayan voters rejected the constitutional reform by a margin of 57 to 43 percent. Efraín Olivera, who worked for the "no" vote and later went on to found one of the country's first human rights groups, encapsulated the feelings of many Uruguayans when he said that the outcome "seemed like a miracle."[5]

This chapter explores the conditions and effects in Uruguay surrounding this remarkable plebiscite. In historical accounts, this plebiscite is primarily viewed as a critical juncture that cracked open a door to the long transitional phase and return to democratic rule, but analysis usually ends there.[6] While the result was an extraordinary moment, in some ways it was just that—a moment. It took four more years of harsh military rule before meaningful elections for new representatives occurred. However, the importance of the plebiscite in human rights terms is broader than just marking a shift; it demonstrates the impact of this burgeoning global cause in interesting but perhaps counterintuitive ways. While observers and activists from abroad regularly invoked human rights when discussing the plebiscite, the domestic opposition to the military's project rarely relied on a human rights language. Instead, during the campaign, the military more regularly tried to justify their project by redefining human rights in ways that focused on the shield of state sovereignty and sought to refute the global movement's critiques.

In this way, the plebiscite demonstrates the political and ideological nature of the emerging global human rights language that could be bent, interpreted, and deployed by divergent and, at times, competing groups that ranged from international NGOs to state actors and opposition organizers. For example, an international movement that started in the 1970s linked transnational organizations such as Amnesty International and WOLA, as well as various foreign governments and multilateral institutions. These actors invoked a narrow concept of human rights that focused on the pervasive repression of Uruguay's military rule—the right to be free from disappearances, torture, and political imprisonment. During the campaign for the plebiscite, they cited these violations as a reason to oppose the military's exercise. In policy memos, press statements, and newspaper op-eds, they argued that the consti-tution would institutionalize the military's repressive apparatus that allowed these abuses to occur. Domestic advocates did not make this same argument. After seven years of fear and silence, the plebiscite did provide a small open-ing domestically for Uruguayans to speak out against the military's project, but they rarely did so in explicit human rights terms due to regular repression and arrests. Instead, domestic activists argued in terms of restoring historic models of Uruguayan democracy that removed the military from power. When direct critiques of the military's violations occurred during the lead-up to the vote, they mostly came from abroad.

Representatives of the military government, however, not only blasted these international groups but also utilized a very different definition of human rights in framing their constitutional project to serve their own interests. The military disputed transnational movements' and foreign gov-ernments' invocation of human rights. It argued that the military, indeed, defended and upheld human rights but that they were fighting an imminent domestic threat that legitimized their practices. In essence, they, like many other Latin American military governments at the time, argued that they sup-ported and adhered to the idea of human rights but it was not absolute. The military explained that claims by international organizations, human rights groups, and foreign governments were lies, and calls to change practices were a violation of Uruguay's sovereignty. In this way, the military disputed the very meaning of human rights that had burst onto the international scene in the 1970s and challenged these prevailing notions of state sovereignty, largely in response to the violations of Southern Cone military governments.[7] Instead, the military desperately tried to cling to an increasingly archaic notion of human rights as a concept that resided within states to determine and balance with its self-defined security needs. It challenged the transnational discourse by employing human rights as an internal question, not one subject to international standards and pressures. The military hearkened back to an older notion that no longer held in the changed international environment. Thus, the defeat of the plebiscite in Uruguay was also the defeat of the military's anachronistic invocation of a state's sovereignty to commit massive human rights abuses within their own borders, demonstrating the success of the 1970s activism and paving the way for the emergence of a domestic human rights movement in the years that followed.

Lead-Up to the Plebiscite

While the human rights stakes linked to the plebiscite came to light most starkly in the immediate period around the constitutional campaigns, the idea of a plebiscite can be traced back to several years before Uruguayans went to the polls, when the military first set the wheels in motion to conduct the electoral exercise. During the 1973 coup, the military justified its takeover in national security terms. It defended its actions to dissolve Parliament and institute repressive measures as the only way to protect the country against dangerous threats within society—primarily referring to the Tupamaros as symbols of a wider communist peril threatening the nation. Though in reality the military had crushed the Tupamaros prior to the coup, they served as an effective justification for the military's brutal rule. By the late 1970s, however, it was clear that the guerrilla group was no longer a viable threat, and the military had a harder time explaining their tactics and the necessity of the military being in power in terms of pressing national security concerns.[8] As the previous chapters have shown, this internal pressure was exacerbated by increasing international scrutiny, particularly in the form of a transnational human rights movement and U.S. foreign policy pressure. Consequently, the military sought legitimacy through institutional reform, with the goal of creating a more comprehensive legal framework for its continued rule.[9]

The process began in 1976 when Juan María Bordaberry, the civilian figurehead of the military regime, suggested a new governmental structure that, among other measures, eliminated traditional political parties. The military rejected his plan, in part because the proposal reduced the military's role in government while strengthening the civilian leader. The military, perhaps unsurprisingly, subsequently dismissed Bordaberry. Alberto Demicheli served an interim three-month term before the military empowered Aparicio Méndez as the de facto president of the nation. Méndez was a seventy-two-year-old former law professor who had been active in Blanco Party politics prior to the military regime. In the aftermath of the 1973 coup, however, he endorsed the military government, and the military rewarded this support by handing him the position in late 1976.

His swearing-in ceremony provided a visual representation of the subservient role the military required him to play as an acting civilian head of the military regime. A short, bulky man with thick-rimmed glasses, a bushy gray mustache, and a balding head of hair, he wore a subtle gray suit and projected a nonthreatening appearance. This marked a stark contrast to the large military presence that day, all of whom had dark, full heads of hair, were tall, and dressed in strapping dark-brown uniforms. A panel of three stern-looking commanders stood behind the meek-looking Méndez as he signed to take over the ceremonial post.[10] The moment encapsulated Méndez's docile position, which was exactly what the military wanted after its power struggle with Bordaberry. Indeed, Méndez proved willing to carry out the wishes of the armed forces; his first act in office was to issue a decree that further restricted the political rights of former political party leaders.

After years of de facto military control of the government, Méndez was the right civilian leader to usher in a new institutional model that officially and legally placed the state under the jurisdiction of a military group called Consejo de Seguridad (Security Council [COSENA]), which focused on national security measures. Importantly, it defined "national security" loosely, as the defense of "the national patrimony in all its forms, and defense of the process of development toward national objectives against internal or external aggression or interference." Under COSENA, national security even encompassed the control of economic and educational policies to defend the nation against potential threats.[11] This meant that the military had a sweeping mandate for carrying out whatever measures it thought would be necessary to "protect the nation."

The proposed alterations to the constitution placed these changes within a more permanent and legal framework that only cosmetically, but not functionally, would shift the military's role in politics. For example, the new constitution gave the COSENA veto power over all the actions of future Uruguayan governments.[12] Moreover, while a weak legislature and judicial body would be appointed with military approval, the military would also have the discretion to remove any member of either body without giving a reason. Most politicians who had formerly held office as Blanco or Colorado political party officials were proscribed from participating in politics. Those from the leftist political coalition faced an even harsher fate. Anyone who had been a member of the Frente Amplio, ranging from Christian Democrats to communists, was permanently barred from holding office or even working in the civil service sector. The new constitution also prohibited public-sector strikes. Equally egregious was the military's proposed form of an "election" of public figures, which it slated for 1981. The election allowed the Blancos and Colorados to agree on only a single candidate to put forward, with the military's approval. That is, it would be a military-approved candidate, and no leftist party candidates would be allowed to contend, or even have a say in who would occupy the slot. Thus, despite the proposed "changes," the military would maintain complete control over the government's functioning and even increase its role in certain areas.[13] It was this document that the military submitted to the population for approval as a way to legitimate an expansion of their rule and appease international outcry.

The Campaigns Around the Plebiscite

When the campaigning around the plebiscite began, observers from around the world were not optimistic about the opposition's chances to triumph over the military. The *Los Angeles Times* called the vote a "political charade," and the *New York Times* accused the military of using the plebiscite as a stunt to rubber-stamp its repressive policies.[14] In London, newspapers pessimistically interpreted the constitutional referendum as a way for the military "to stay in firm control for at least the next two decades."[15]

The referendum in Chile two months prior had served to reaffirm the difficulty of a fair, democratic vote under a repressive military regime. On September 11, 1980, Chilean voters had cast their ballots on expanding and institutionalizing Pinochet's rule. Pinochet framed the referendum on a new constitution in his country as a vote for order and tranquility. Meanwhile, he warned that any vote against the constitution indicated a desire to return the country to disorder and insecurity.[16] As mentioned at the beginning of this chapter, Pinochet won easily, with 67 percent of the vote. He claimed that the results affirmed the regime's legitimacy. Pinochet sharply controlled the vote, requiring the population to cast a ballot, supervising voting tables and the vote count, and framing the debate over the constitution as being for or against peace. Activists working for the "no" vote were also arrested and, at times, beaten and tortured. This violence further silenced the opposition. As a result, the "election" became a one-sided ratification process.[17]

In neighboring Uruguay, his triumph served to reassure military officers that, with a similarly firm grip on power, they too would have success in the upcoming plebiscite. Both regimes found themselves caught between trying to carry out their repressive military projects and trying to bolster their domestic and international legitimacy against increasing criticism. These electoral exercises were seen as a way to overcome this tension, and the Uruguayan military sought the same success.

Upon releasing the text of the new constitution, the military set the terms of the campaign by using its resources to invoke fear about returning to the chaos of the late 1960s and early 1970s. The military controlled most of the airwaves and printed press, launching a massive public campaign in support of the "yes" vote. The military utilized the *Dirección Nacional de Relaciones Públicas* (National Directorate of Public Relations [DINARP]), which the military founded in 1975 to produce propaganda and censor the remaining papers within the country. In 1980, the military deployed DINARP to promote the constitutional changes. The military spent approximately $30 million and used every available medium to ardently promote the plebiscite as a choice between the evils of communism and the protection of the homeland.[18] Governmental representatives argued that the constitution was a way to "adjust to the new realities of life in which we live."[19] They painted a possible rejection of the constitutional reform as being equivalent to communist subversion and defined their mission as needing to continue countering this threat. A "yes" vote would secure Uruguayan safety and allow the military to provide services to the community.[20] One military commander, Raúl J. Bendahan, explained his view in terms that mirrored many of the campaign ads, in which "terrorists, Marxists, and other people who do not love the country are those who are inclined to vote no in the plebiscite."[21] Thus, he implied that only voters who were members of those despised categories would reject the constitution.

These political messages bombarded radio listeners and TV watchers with jingles every fifteen minutes. Newspapers provided visual representations of the military's intended contrast. For example, some ads in favor of the new constitution depicted adorable babies with happy parents, invoking an emotional tug at the military's ability to secure a happy future for one's family. Other ads were even more heavy-handed. They juxtaposed pictures of smoke, bombs, and violence to smiling friends walking carefree in the streets, implying that a "no" vote would guarantee a return to chaos while a "yes" could ensure happiness and safety.[22] Most of the censored newspapers and TV stations also openly endorsed the plebiscite, with the few holdouts remaining neutral.[23]

The military combined its emotional campaign with attempts to couch the proposed constitutional changes in a discourse of democracy, albeit a definition more closely associated with century-old ideas about democracy as limited and not broadly participatory.[24] For example, Méndez described the constitutional changes as a "purer, cleaner form of democracy . . . purged of the vices and defects."[25] Minister of National Defense Walter Ravenna described the project similarly as an attempt by the leaders of the country to "work in the spirit of democratization."[26] An editorial in the heavily censored *El País* also echoed the governmental argument for democratic achievement, explaining that the plebiscite aimed to "restore the country to democratic normalcy" while still maintaining "peace and security."[27] Uruguay's strong democratic traditions compelled the military to explain its project in these terms of democratic reform. In each case, the military defined democracy in terms that remained unrecognizable to Uruguayans as any form of modern democracy. In the end, the military attempted to shift normative understandings of democracy during the dictatorship closer to a restricted model.

This appropriation of a democratic discourse was also evident in the military's attempts to co-opt the language of human rights from transnational groups by claiming that rights derived from states' protection. In these arguments, the military centered the importance of sovereignty as an organizing principle in international relations. It argued that states had an absolute right to dictate what happened within their own borders, which included defining and protecting citizens' rights. While at one point these arguments might have held more weight, this notion of absolute sovereignty had shifted considerably in the 1960s. In the following decade, activists and increasingly some diplomats began to challenge this idea and argue that repression was subject to international condemnation and no longer the sole purview of a state's own jurisdiction.[28] By utilizing the UDHR, and rights treaties and documents from the UN and OAS, activists argued that certain essential rights superseded state primacy. In essence, state actors could no longer claim the principle of nonintervention in the face of massive violations.[29] Yet, the Uruguayan military fought vociferously against this international normative shift. Claiming its sovereign right, the regime, like so many of its Southern Cone counterparts in this era, argued that the meaning and definition of human rights were found within states and did not interfere with the purported project of national security.[30]

Indeed, the military began using a rights discourse as early as 1974 for its own purposes. Just a year after the coup, the military's Council of States approved the formation of the Commission for the Respect of Individual Rights.[31] While the Commission did little but pay lip service to the idea that the military respected and supported a narrow idea of rights, the military eventually took more formal measures. For example, a few years later, the military promulgated Institutional Acts to legitimate its power. Institutional Act No. 5 specifically addressed human rights, qualifying that human rights ultimately had to be "regulated in accordance with internal security."[32] In effect, the military declared its belief that human rights, as defined by international groups in their condemnation of the regime, were not absolute. Instead, the Act confirmed a commitment to the concept only when it did not conflict with the military's stated mission of fighting perceived subversives. Therefore, the military rejected accusations of human rights violations by promoting a neutered definition of the term.[33] It located the protection of rights within the state apparatus that was subject to the principle of nonintervention.

This perspective was reaffirmed in 1977 when, in response to a request to help a school in San Francisco with a model OAS simulation on human rights, the Uruguayan Foreign Ministry went through multiple levels of approval to write back articulating the country's perspective on the topic. The letter declared that Uruguay "has always been known as a defender of human rights . . . working to make the idea succeed." It went on to say that the international campaign denouncing the regime on human rights terms failed to understand the subversive elements the regime was fighting, a fight they linked with other nations of "the free world." Instead, the letter explained that Uruguay's government maintained "a clear principle against the politicization of the issue of human rights," having the "moral constraint of their own conscience and the unbearable sense of responsibility" to strike a balance between battling to uphold national security as well as the individual rights and liberties of its citizens.[34]

This letter to a school group in northern California was revealing. It painted Uruguay as the victim of an international smear campaign and failed to recognize the contradiction between its measures against perceived sub-versives and a vague notion of human rights that could be defined by the regime and limited in a way that it did not interfere with the military's anti-communist project and national security measures. Rather, it saw foreign governments and advocacy groups' use of human rights discourse as a viola-tion of state sovereignty and a politicization of the concept.

A year later, Uruguayan representatives to the actual OAS used the same justification. In rejecting a request from the OAS to visit Uruguay and investi-gate allegations of human rights violations, the Uruguayan official José María Araneo wrote that Uruguay "has confirmed and does confirm its traditional dedication to and efforts aimed at defending human rights." He asserted Uru-guay's right to national sovereignty and noted a "discrepancy" between the Inter-American Commission of Human Rights and Uruguayan authorities on the topic.[35] Less explicitly than in the letter to the school group, Uruguay was reaffirming its limited view of human rights when it conflicted with Uru-guay's stated need to battle what they declared as security threats. Fundamen-tally, the military ignored the way that transnational groups had transformed the idea of human rights in the international sphere as piercing the cloak of state sovereignty and attempted to reassert its own view of the term to serve its ideological project.

This articulation of human rights by the regime was also evident during the plebiscite campaign. At a domestic level, the military argued during debates that the constitution would allow the country to "continue being democratic, representative . . . and protect human rights . . . similar to what we have had previously that also repairs the problems we had before."[36] Internationally, at the height of the campaign, Uruguay's Minister of Foreign Relations, Adolfo Folle Martínez, also gave the opening plenary speech at the General Assem-bly of the UN. In his remarks, he reiterated the regime's previous take on human rights. He accused other states of using them as "an instrument for political struggle among States or groups with different social and economic philosophies," reaffirmed Uruguay's historic commitment to the cause of human rights, and explained that the breaches of human rights came only when defending the nation against "insidious and criminal subversive move-ments."[37] In this way, the regime did not shy away from human rights, but rather argued that the concept was defined by the state and limited when it conflicted with its ideas of national security.[38] Therefore, institutionalizing its power through the constitutional changes was a way to ensure a broader protection of Uruguay's historic rights. While claims against the regime were predicated on the massive human rights violations the military committed between 1973 and 1980, the military attempted to appropriate the language of human rights for its own purposes. They claimed to uphold a different definition of the concept that privileged the idea of individual rights and the preeminence of state sovereignty over the fundamental ways the concept had changed over the previous decade when massive violations were, indeed, subject to international scrutiny and pressure.

Wielding its economic and physical control of the country, the military ultimately ran a multifaceted campaign to support its constitutional project. At first, it was difficult for the opposition to counter these messages and speak out against the plebiscite. After seven years of harsh rule, the population already lived in a state of fear. Many of the former politicians who attempted to protest the government monopoly were prohibited from accessing radio or television, or writing in papers to debate the merits of the constitution.[39] Further, many were detained in the months leading up to the vote to further discourage voting against the military.[40] The previous decade had enforced a silence among Uruguayans. Once-vibrant cafes along the country's main thoroughfare, the Avenida 18 de Julio, transformed from a destination for passionate political discussion to silent spaces in which even neighbors were afraid to acknowledge one another, each believing that the other might be an informant. In the years of the descent into dictatorship, the Left had fractured into sectors over varying visions of political reform. By 1980, there were no longer distinct groups debating different futures, but rather individuals who were generally afraid to work in alliances.

With the domestic environment so constrained, it was around the world that a chorus of voices first emerged to support a "no" vote. Exile groups and international human rights organizations led the charge. While many exile groups were pessimistic that the vote would be fair, they still saw the plebiscite as the first opening that the military had provided since taking power. Some even explicitly opposed the vote in human rights terms. For years, opposition parties in exile had been fairly disjointed. These groups were deeply divided over the future direction of the country and proved unable to come up with a cohesive plan to oppose the military and mount a joint challenge from abroad.[41] However, these exile groups, joined by international organizations and foreign governments, found the plebiscite to be a focal point around which to rally. They called for a return to democracy and discussed the imperative of this vote by focusing on the human rights violations committed by the Uruguayan military.

One important group of exiles that demonstrated this view was the Grupo de Convergencia Democrática en Uruguay (Union for a Democratic Convergence [CDU]). Founded by a cross-party coalition immediately before the plebiscite was announced in April 1980, it revealed a growing inclination to find common ground among exiles from multiple political persuasions. The group strengthened efforts to counter the plebiscite. In its first press statement issued from New York City, the group blasted the repressive military apparatus in Uruguay for continuing to carry out disappearances, imprisonment, and torture.[42] Vowing to work across party lines, the CDU committed to joint efforts.[43] As the WOLA noted in a press release, the group "underscore[d] the antidemocratic character of the Uruguayan regime."[44]

In May 1980, an alliance of political party leaders in the CDU gathered in Mexico to meet for the first time. They selected the month of May for their first meeting to commemorate the murders of Héctor Gutiérrez Ruiz and Zelmar Michelini four years earlier. Led by Juan Raúl Ferreira, Wilson Ferreira's son, and joined by members of the Blancos and the Frente Amplio as well as independents, the group pledged that it would fight to reestablish democracy in Uruguay on a nonpartisan basis.[45] The location of the group's first meeting was also important. During the dictatorship, Mexico served as a refuge for fleeing Uruguayan exiles. By 1980, there were more than 1,000 Uruguayan exiles in Mexico, many of whom had been assisted by a sympathetic Mexican ambassador in Uruguay.[46] The country's celebration of its "revolutionary tradition" and open immigration policies allowed Mexico to offer asylum to thousands of refugees fleeing from various other South American dictatorships.[47] From the safety of Mexico, the CDU realized that although each individual had different political, ideological, and philosophical ideas for Uruguay, they could all agree that the root of their opposition stemmed from the defense of their vision of democracy against the military's self-described democratic trappings, and from their desire for an end to human rights violations.[48] Working together, the CDU became the most outspoken and well-defined voice of the country's political opposition.[49]

As the date of the referendum drew closer, the CDU began to grow more ardent in their calls for a "no" vote on the plebiscite as a repudiation of the military regime. The group connected with government officials and civil society groups across Europe, Latin America, and the United States, arguing that nothing less could be accepted than the full legalization of political parties and party leaders, complete restoration of civil liberties, and an open and free election.[50] Ferreira spoke out against the plebiscite, explaining that the "only way to make sure there is no torture or political prisoners is to return the government to popular rule."[51] In addition to its call for a vote against the military's new constitution, the CDU argued for a host of other human rights reforms, such as liberty for political prisoners, a return of exiles, and guarantees of free speech and expression.[52] The CDU also managed to downplay the ideological differences between the various parties. Instead, it tended to emphasize the goals of restoring "democratic freedoms and a political regime that will fully respect internationally recognized human rights."[53] Therefore, while the group was dedicated to advocating for a return to democracy in Uruguay, its discourse about the plebiscite emphasized and highlighted these human rights issues.

This discourse linked the CDU's advocacy efforts with international human rights groups that had been gaining prestige and influence throughout the 1970s and which many of the CDU organizers had been part of. Organizations such as AI and WOLA also spoke out to encourage a "no" vote, which invoked a coherent and narrow human rights discourse. For example, AI expressed its concern "that the proposed constitution would legitimize practices which have encouraged human rights violations in recent years."[54] Therefore, AI centered its efforts on garnering grassroots support and led an urgent action campaign in November 1980 to focus international attention on the upcoming plebiscite. This strategy included a letter-writing effort to Uruguayan authorities urging them to release prisoners and open public debate for campaigning in the lead-up to the plebiscite.[55] Amnesty International also organized a formal protest against the exercise and circulated a twenty-page analysis of the proposed constitution to AI members and Patricia Derian. The organization called the new Uruguayan constitution an instrument to forward the "institutionalization of repression."[56]

Similarly, WOLA focused considerable attention on the upcoming plebiscite. Its strategy focused on lobbying governments and multilateral organizations. For instance, the organization's president, Joseph Eldridge, joined a group of government officials from around Latin America to form the *Comisión por la democracia y derechos humanos en Uruguay* (Commission for Democracy and Human Rights in Uruguay). The group organized directly in response to the military's plebiscite by working to reject the constitution. The group explained its opposition on the basis of stopping torture and freeing political prisoners.[57] It lobbied the OAS, raised public awareness, and met with members of the U.S. Congress to discuss the situation in Uruguay. It was the first time that so many important Latin American political leaders came together to voluntarily discuss and take action on a human rights situation in a neighboring country.[58] Its efforts were joined by declarations of support from the governments in Sweden, Holland, Spain, France, and the United States, who all sought to focus attention on rejecting the constitution in the name of democracy and human rights.[59]

The United States had a particularly interesting position in this regard. Most international groups called the plebiscite a farce. President Carter, however, after hammering Uruguay's military government's human rights record for much of his presidency, believed the plebiscite was a positive sign. Therefore, Carter was more muted in his public criticism of the government in the months leading up to the vote. Memos from the State Department note that the administration was aware of the "extreme sensitivity" of the Uruguayan military prior to the constitutional plebiscite and took a public stance to encourage the military to follow through on the exercise.[60] For example, Carter noted the "substantial improvements" in the Uruguayan human rights situation and endorsed the plebiscite vote as "an encouraging effort to restore normality" to the country.[61] Carter was criticized for praising the regime's human rights improvements as exile groups lobbied the Carter administration to take a hard public stance against the "farce of pretended democratic intentions . . . in open and grotesque imitation of the Chilean dictatorship."[62] Instead, Carter opted for a behind-the-scenes approach to avoid potential accusations of interference in the electoral results. Privately, the Carter administration warned the military that the vote would be viewed as credible internationally only if the military allowed freedom of the press and did not ban opponents' political participation.[63]

Multilateral organizations also put pressure on the military's project. A week before the election, the OAS put forward a statement condemning the constitutional proposal. The statement was drafted by the Commission for Democracy and Human Rights, and sixteen different countries across Latin America signed it, a move that incurred the wrath of Uruguay's representative to the OAS.[64] The OAS's annual report also argued that the constitution "contains serious contradictions of the standards contained in the American Declaration of the Rights and Duties of Man," and further doubted the open environment in which voters were being allowed to evaluate their choices.[65] The OAS thus used explicit human rights terms to criticize the military government during the campaign.

In the lead-up to the vote, the UN also nudged Uruguay to improve its human rights compliance.[66] Although not without controversy, the United

Nations Commission on Human Rights voted in early 1980 to keep Uruguay under review for continuing violations as well.[67] The European Parliament also put forth a statement that the referendum "would not guarantee democratic rights" and condemned the vote that offered "the Uruguayan people no real choice and which seeks to institutionalize the dictatorship."[68] Together, these organizations added pressure to the regime's attempts at legitimacy and often focused on the explicit human rights violations the government had committed throughout the 1970s.

Whether as a result of this mix of encouragement and pressure, or more broadly the need to make the plebiscite seem legitimate, the Uruguayan military government did ultimately allow debate about the constitution—to a limited extent. In the final weeks of the campaign, the government permitted a regulated expression of contrary opinions.

With the slight political opening, Enrique Tarigo surfaced as a domestic force behind the "no" vote in those final weeks. Tarigo projected a commanding presence; he was a larger man with full eyebrows that strikingly framed his big, searing eyes. He most often slicked back his graying hair and never seemed to have a strand out of place. It shone even in black-and-white photos.[69] Born in Montevideo in 1927, Tarigo started his career as a lawyer, teaching at the country's only public university, La Universidad de la República, until 1973 when the military took over. During the early years of the dictatorship, he worked as a somewhat obscure columnist for *El Día*, one of the few Uruguayan newspapers still allowed to publish. In the late 1970s, when the military announced the possibility for a *cronograma* or political reform process, Tarigo emerged as an outspoken critic of the process. His editors feared reprisal and pushed Tarigo to leave the paper. However, when the government opened up the debate on the constitution in the lead-up to the plebiscite, Tarigo resumed his campaign against the military's claims of democratic reform. After an incredibly difficult approval process, he founded his own weekly paper, *Opinar*.[70] Covering "no" rallies and promising to provide an independent perspective, the paper's circulation soared in the final weeks before the plebiscite.[71] Tarigo also offered a voice for the opposition in the public debates with the military about the efficacy of the new constitution. He was an emerging, prominent, and incredibly important opposition figure, but he expressed his opposition in both his writing and his speeches without an explicit invocation of the regime's human rights abuses.

A monthly magazine, *La Plaza*, surfaced outside of Montevideo in Canelones during this time. This publication also criticized the plebiscite, though perhaps more subtly at first. Felisberto Carámbula and his two sons founded the periodical in 1979. Carámbula was a Batllista adherent who had held positions in the government prior to the dictatorship, but had lost his right to participate in politics during the military's rule.[72] The periodical had the original aim of "playing an educational role in our city [Las Piedras]."[73] In the period leading up the plebiscite, the magazine challenged the military's propaganda for a "yes" vote. For example, some articles addressed the broad idea of the importance of political parties in a democracy, which the current constitution would have not empowered.[74] *La Plaza* also published pictures of two windows, one closed with "si" in it and one open with "no" in it, referring to the paper's stance toward the plebiscite.[75] Many of the writers also worked tirelessly going door to door to campaign against the plebiscite and used the publication as a place to discuss broad ideas of freedom, democracy, and how to achieve these ideals under the dictatorship. Both *Opinar* and *La Plaza* were closely monitored and periodically shut down during this period. As a result, human rights language was not explicitly used in the articles; doing so would have almost certainly meant further reprisals. However, the periodicals provided important alternative spaces in which to discuss challenges to the military dictatorship during a period when censorship still dominated. They gave an organized voice to the domestic opposition for the first time in seven years.

In addition to written criticism, on November 14, 1980, the military granted the drafters of the constitution and its opponents the opportunity to debate its merits on national television for over two hours.[76] On an episode of *En Profundidad* (In Depth) on channel 4, Néstor Bolentini, a retired Army colonel who was also the former Minister of the Interior, and Enrique Viana Reyes, a member of the Consejo de Estado for the military, faced off against Tarigo and Eduardo Pons Echeverry, the former Minister of Education and member of the Blanco political party. In this venue, the four debaters and two moderators sat around a small round table. All the men were dressed in suits and ties and smoked throughout the discussion, which caused thick plumes of smoke to fill the set, at times obscuring the close-up views of the debaters. But it was riveting television for the Uruguayan electorate. For two hours, the men debated the merits of the constitutional reform in an intense but largely calm demeanor.[77] Members of the military reiterated claims that the reform was intended to secure the country against subversives and the "tragedy and chaos" prior to their rule. They also relied on the idea of protecting Uruguayan rights and invoked a vague commitment of the regime to human rights, a term they used three times during the debate. The military's invocation of the concept referred to a limited definition. Human rights, according to the military, were within the state's jurisdiction to enforce, and were not subject to international meddling. The state defined human rights in a way that did not conflict with national security.

However, Pons and particularly Tarigo took advantage of this limited airtime opportunity to provide a counterargument, even without utilizing an explicit human rights language. Tarigo explained that the constitution was in line with those of authoritarian states, not allowing any rights or guarantees to the people. Even without directly needling the military by bringing up international criticism and definitions of the human rights abuses going on, he was able to dispute the military's definition by talking broadly about the military's takeover of everyday life. In addition, turning the argument by the military about subversives on its head, Tarigo accused the proposed document of being more similar to those of communist states than those of the free world, since it lacked any "reasonable guarantees for all."[78] Uruguayans across the nation watched the government being criticized openly after no one had dared to speak out against the military for years. As one former leader of the Socialist Party who had been jailed several times, Eduardo Fernández, recalled, the debate made many "realize that we were not the only ones who were against the military."[79] It marked a critical juncture in the political campaign.[80]

The military also granted the opposition a platform by approving exactly three rallies against the constitutional changes. Despite the military's heavy monitoring of the rallies and their requirement that they be held in rented auditoriums and not in the streets, these rallies were widely attended.[81] Surreptitiously, some opposition members campaigned by word of mouth and even distributed small "no" pamphlets around the city.[82] These activists worked to circulate tape-recorded speeches and messages of support from exiled Blanco leader Wilson Ferreira, which were smuggled into the country. Members of the Brigada Líber Arce de la Juventud Comunista (UJC) went in the middle of the night to hang a poster with "NO" in huge red letters on the Hospital de Clínicas, a building located on one of the busy avenues in Montevideo.[83] Lacking the same powerful mouthpiece as the military government, the opposition relied on these furtive activities and the few permitted spaces to hear alternative sources of information. Much of the information that did filter in explained the differences between the military and the opposition as predicated on a democratic vision.[84] This work continued unabated even as the military arrested various "no" activists.[85] The Uruguay Catholic Church, a

traditionally weak institution in the country relative to its regional counterparts, also called for "open channels of participation" as an essential part of
the plebiscite being seen as legitimate. The Church was also more forceful in
issuing a public declaration that criticized the constitution's repressive tenets.[86]
Thus, even in spite of the enormous resources and power that the military
wielded, a small but important opposition began to emerge domestically as
a result of the referendum. This opposition became enormously important in
the years that followed. Yet, fearful of reprisals, they did not utilize a discourse
of human rights; it was the military who more often attempted to invoke a
framework of rights that relied on states' own definition of the term as a means
to counter international criticism and promote its constitutional project.

Even in spite of these small opportunities to contest the military's claims,
most people around the world were skeptical about the open nature of the
referendum, suspecting that the plebiscite was a political scam. A *New York
Times* article the week before the vote noted that "Uruguayans are under pressure to approve a document about which they know very little . . . there is little
doubt that on Dec. 1 the Government will announce overwhelming support
for the constitution."[87] Much of the exiled opposition similarly believed that
the complete repression Uruguayans had been living under had sufficiently
scared the population into voting for the constitution. On the remote chance
that was not the case, they predicted that the government would manipulate
the results.[88] To put it mildly, expectations were not very high.

The Results

Going into Election Day, international skepticism about the fairness of the
vote was replicated in Uruguay. Most voters believed that "the results were
a foregone conclusion . . . everyone assumed that everyone would be voting with the military."[89] Early polls supported this idea and had the military
leading by more than 2 to 1, although polltakers said that almost half of the
individuals they approached had refused to respond. This silence illustrates
the extent to which Uruguayans feared the government.[90] A week before the
election, however, at least one poll indicated that the gap had closed, but it
was never published. The pollsters did not dare to publish the results, unsure
about how the government might respond.

Under these conditions, Uruguayans nervously headed to the polls on
November 30, 1980, to cast their first vote in nine years. While the voting

tables were not monitored, this was largely because the military did not believe the "no" vote could win.[91] An estimated 12,000 people returned from abroad, mainly from neighboring Argentina, to participate in the electoral exercise.[92] Of the 1,944,941 Uruguayans permitted to vote, 1,689,424 submitted a ballot, which equals 86.9 percent of those with a valid registration.

What came next shocked many Uruguayans and the world. When the vote tally was announced, Uruguayans had rejected the new military-drafted constitution by a margin of 57 to 43 percent of the popular vote. Despite all the predictions of failure, despite seven years of oppressive military rule, despite all the military's censorship and propaganda, the Uruguayan people voted against the new charter. The citizens' voices had prevailed.

How the military would react to this triumph was still unknown. It sent an ominous sign to the population by banning all political activity and press commentary for three days while the military "reconsidered" the political liberalization program.[93] Continuing under the censorship that had governed the press for the past seven years, the major papers failed to ascribe any significant meaning to the vote. Instead, they merely reported the tallies without any political analysis of what the results might mean for the military. After weeks of printing articles in support of a "yes" vote, papers spent two days covering the president's cautious remarks praising the "calm and participatory" nature of the elections.[94]

Nevertheless, to many Uruguayans who had suffered for years under the regime, the outcome was incredible. Wilson Ferreira's wife recalled learning about the results from exile in Brazil: "When we heard the first news reports from *El Espectador,* we were all silent, each one of us thought we had heard wrong. There was a tremendous silence, and then someone began to cry and the rest of us began to yell and applaud 'Como el Uruguay no hay!' How amazing that we can celebrate a victory after so many years of suffering and shame! Then, we all sang the national anthem and honored the courage of the Uruguayan people."[95]

Susana Ferreira's reaction captured what the rejection of the military meant to many Uruguayans, both at home and in exile, after living so long under a repressive dictatorship. For them, the results helped citizens "regain their dignity and hope . . . [after] seven years of humiliation."[96] The vote had clearly expressed the disapproval that many felt toward the dictatorship, and it was, as *Opinar* noted, "an unforgettable day."[97]

The "no" vote allowed Uruguayans to hope and celebrate possibilities for the return of rule of law, political activism, and a resurgent human rights culture that could end the torture and political imprisonment that had been the focus of so much global attention. One article in Tarigo's *Opinar* extolled the restoration of his version of democratic principles that he believed had prevailed after the long winter of repression. It captured the renewed excitement by exclaiming, "What a wonderful blessed country is Uruguay! What wonderful people in this blessed Uruguay in which all of us were born by chance but if we had the possibility, surely we would have chosen it!"[98]

Others around the country were a bit more wary, unsure of what the vote would mean in concrete terms. Marcos Carámbula, Felisberto's son and one of the founders of *La Plaza*, remembers that Uruguayans did not celebrate in the streets, but rather the next day they displayed their happiness with smiles and flashes of the V-sign, waiting for indications of how the military would respond.[99] Their caution reflected a wariness that had built up after years of fear and repression.

On the other hand, from abroad, the accolades flowed in. WOLA's director, Joseph Eldridge, whose organization had been persistently working against the dictatorship, declared that "in a most remarkable test of political will, the Uruguayan people have sharply reproached the military and unequivocally repudiated their plan for permanently participating in government." He called the military the "bearer of one of the worst human rights records in the hemisphere" and heralded the victory as bringing "renewed hope" to all of Latin America.[100]

U.S. senator Edward Kennedy followed suit, explaining that he had long been an opponent of the military government in Uruguay. Indeed, Kennedy had lobbied to end U.S. support of Latin American military dictatorships throughout the 1970s.[101] In Uruguay, he had worked with Juan Raúl Ferreira to publicize the government's abuses and signed petitions against the imprisonment of political figures such as the Frente Amplio's Líber Seregni.[102] After the vote, Kennedy noted that he "was heartened by the recent popular rejection of a new constitution which would prolong military rule virtually indefinitely in that nation . . . the plebiscite is one more reminder of the historic importance of the struggle for democracy and liberty throughout Latin America."[103] In Congress, his celebration was joined by other members who had worked on human rights–focused initiatives, such as Representative Elizabeth Holtzman (D-NY).[104]

Press in the United States and abroad also lauded the vote. The U.S. media called on Carter to "nourish" the results and stated that the vote "vindicates the Administration's periodic pleas for human rights in Uruguay."[105] After years of criticism of Carter's human rights policy, the now lame-duck president finally received some praise. In Mexico, journalists called the results a "triumph of democracy by the people."[106] Overall, there was a mix of excitement and caution while everyone waited to see how the military would respond to the vote.

The Aftermath

Both domestically and abroad, the vote was immediately interpreted as a historical novelty and an "unexpected opening."[107] Nevertheless, the question remained as to whether the military would cling to power and attempt to reinterpret the election returns, or whether they would accept the defeat. This uncertainty introduced a cautious side to the widespread excitement, particularly within Uruguay.

A few days after the results were announced, the military's response finally became clear: it would try to manage the results and maintain power. The civilian figurehead of the government, Aparicio Méndez, tried to twist the meaning of the "no" vote and rejected the idea that it indicated a political setback for the government. Instead, he explained that the results were actually a "defeat for the people."[108] The leader of the military junta, General Luis Quierolo, reinvoked the national security justification and said that "all emergency periods, like the ones we have suffered to date, cannot suffer a brusque change . . . the transition from this process to the next of complete normalization should be slow."[109]

The military leaders began to suggest that the vast majority of those who voted "no" did so because they were content with the current governance structure and did not want a change. According to this logic, the "no" vote was not a rejection of the military, but rather represented the fact that the people "preferred the current situation."[110] Clearly, this interpretation differed from the pre-electoral assertions that only Marxists, terrorists, or unpatriotic citizens would vote "no." However, the explanation served to justify the military's continued power in the face of the defeated charter.

Indeed, the government tried to manage the terms of a possible transition. Less than a year later, a thirty-five-member Council of the State was installed, and a new president, Gregorio Álvarez Armelino, took office without a vote. The Council of the State also took on expanded responsibilities, which included the ability to call constitutional assemblies, plebiscites, and general elections. This Council of State was not an elected body. Rather, it supported Álvarez and acted as an arm of his military rule, as opposed to a check on the balance of power. The immediate defeat of the proposed constitution led to a new wave of arrests, and human rights violations in the form of torture, political imprisonment, and disappearances also continued to occur.[111] The results had weakened the military, but it was not a foregone conclusion that they would leave power.

Conclusion

Despite the military's intransigence after the plebiscite, the same level of repression that the military employed before the plebiscite proved impossible to maintain. Thus began a long negotiation process over the transition back to democratic rule. The vote galvanized a population that had previously been too fearful to work overtly against the dictatorship. For years, many Uruguayans had been afraid to talk to each other about the horrors of the dictatorship, let alone to organize against it. No one knew who might inform on them, which could result in torture, incarceration, and possibly worse. However, armed with the plebiscite results, Uruguayans now saw that others also were willing to stand up to the dictatorship and fight to return the country to a broader notion of democracy that excluded these human rights violations. As one editorial in *Opinar* explained, at the end of 1980 and the beginning of 1981, there was a "climate of expectation in Uruguay, and of hope. Of hope for a new national direction."[112]

Indeed, as this chapter has demonstrated, the plebiscite provided the first crack in the dictatorship's tight control on society. Yet, it also showed how domestic and international actors employed varied uses of human rights. The paradox during the plebiscite campaign is that the military government's representatives were the ones to invoke the language of human rights, not the opposition, who feared a direct link to the international discourse might provoke retaliation from the military. The opposition's success, therefore, was not only defeating the constitutional project, but also countering the military's invocation of human rights that transnational groups had been fighting against over the previous decade. Despite the military's hopes to bend and reinterpret the term to support their repression, it failed.

Thus, the plebiscite provides an important origin point for the domestic opposition in explicit human rights terms. Whereas the 1970s had been an important decade for the mobilization of transnational groups and international advocacy, the vote became a defining moment for human rights domestically. Despite the lack of human rights language during the campaign by the opposition, the constitution's defeat at the polls shifted the landscape considerably. The 1980s would witness the emergence of a domestic movement, despite the difficulties opponents of the dictatorship would encounter during the long transitional process back to democratic rule.

CHAPTER 5

———

Human Rights Emergence
and Military Retrenchment

April 1984 marked three and a half years since the Uruguayan electorate had voted "no" on the military's proposed constitution for an expansion of its power. Military rule remained and, despite ongoing negotiations, a transition back to democracy was anything but assured. Opposition leaders and members of the military still could not agree on terms for a transfer of power. While newspapers and human rights groups formed in the aftermath of the November 1980 plebiscite, they did not operate in a completely open and free environment. They were periodically shut down and their leaders imprisoned at the military's whim.[1] Perhaps most emblematic of the stalled progress was Vladimir Roslik's death during a torture session on April 15, 1984, in San Javier, a small town in the western part of the country bordering Argentina.

Roslik had been well known in his small and close-knit community as one of the town's few doctors. San Javier was founded in 1913 by 750 dissidents who had fled Czarist Russia in search of religious freedom. By the 1950s, San Javier had a community center, the *Centro Cultural Máximo Gorki de San Javier*, as well as culinary and linguistic influences from the town's early founders.[2] While these cultural connections linked the Soviet Union and San Javier, most residents were two or three generations removed from those immigrants and had assimilated to their new South American home. Nevertheless, the town's history resulted in increased scrutiny by the military, including frequent and widespread detentions, home searches, and intimidation.[3] Roslik was among those targeted. A former member of the Communist Party, he received his degree from the Soviet Union during the 1960s, an affiliation that automatically placed him on the military's radar as a potential subversive.[4] In 1980, the same year as the plebiscite, the military raided the town's Gorki Center and arrested about a dozen residents, including Roslik. The military questioned and tortured the detainees, and Roslik remained in jail for fifteen months. Even after his release, the military monitored him closely.

On April 15, 1984, at approximately 4 A.M., the military appeared at his house again. Dragging him out of his bed, members of the armed forces blindfolded Roslik and took him in for questioning with six other people from the area. Roslik's wife, María Cristina Zabalkin, never saw him alive again. The next day, the military informed her that Roslik had died of cardiac arrest in detention. Roslik was forty-two years old and the father of a four-month-old child.[5]

María was told to collect the body. Doubtful that her otherwise healthy husband had suffered from a heart attack, she secretly had another autopsy done, which determined that he was killed by injuries sustained during torture.[6] She later learned from the other men who had been brought in for questioning that the military had accused the group of having arms hidden around town. The military believed the men had smuggled weapons into the country, possibly from the Soviet Union. The men had been questioned and tortured for hours, even though none of them had any knowledge of weapons in the area. Far from an aberration, Roslik's death served as another example of the continued use of state violence by the military to maintain control over the Uruguayan population.

The murder of another citizen, even as the military was supposedly negotiating their exit from power, demonstrated the intransigence of the regime and how uncertain it was at the time that the military would ultimately leave power. Political scientist Martin Weinstein suggests, "If Uruguay's descent into dictatorship was slow and occurred in stages, much the same may be said of the return to constitutional government."[7] Close to four years after the people's plebiscite victory, the military continued to use violence against opposition groups and perceived leftist subversives. Indeed, the 1980 vote was only the first step in what was ultimately a five-year battle for democratization. Roslik's death highlights just how prolonged, arduous, and contingent the process really was.

Despite these continuities, domestic activists' response to his death also exemplified the ways that the country had changed since the plebiscite. Earlier deaths and disappearances had been the focus of international activism, but within the country they were swept under the rug by the military and ignored by a tightly censored press. In contrast, Roslik's murder ignited open and vociferous outrage and condemnation in Uruguay. Journalists from various publications that had emerged after the plebiscite reported widely on Roslik's death. In addition, domestic human rights groups had formed in the years since the plebiscite. They also worked to spotlight his murder as a reason to push for a transition.[8] The people of San Javier even filed a racial discrimination suit with the Uruguayan Supreme Court, asking the judicial body to investigate the military's treatment of the town's citizens. While the courts eventually dropped the suit, even its filing demonstrated how far Uruguayans had come in standing up to continued military rule in the push for democratization and how much human rights activism had become part of the domestic landscape.[9]

This chapter charts the mutually constitutive relationship between local and international forces that led to the reemergence and development of Uruguay's civil society after the plebiscite, and ultimately allowed for the possibility of groups to protest against the military. At the domestic level, it examines the multiple actors that became prominent opposition forces during the years of transition. After seven years of repression, the plebiscite opened up space for many important newspapers and weeklies to form, the first explicit human rights groups to organize, and the unions and student groups to reconstitute themselves under new names after having been outlawed during the height of the dictatorship. All three of these sectors began to utilize a human rights language as a tool to challenge the military regime. While explicit references to human rights by the opposition had been largely absent during debates over the plebiscite, human rights language emerged during the transition as a mechanism to push for substantive social change, although exactly how the various actors defined human rights differed, sometimes significantly.[10]

While tracing the emergence of a domestic human rights discourse, this chapter also spotlights the international influences on this activism. At one level, international groups such as AI and WOLA continued their work from the 1970s, joined by the newly formed Americas Watch. They exposed the military's continued violations to an international audience and lobbied the U.S. government to try to implement a human rights component in bilateral relations. As international human rights groups matured and gained even more traction in the Global North during the 1980s, they still worked on issues related to Uruguay. However, to consider the international human rights regime to be the only or even dominant influence in Uruguay overlooks the enormous effect that regional advocacy groups played in inspiring Uruguay's civil society. Human rights groups in neighboring Chile, Brazil, and, most importantly, Argentina also provided a vital source of support and encouragement to domestic activists. Facing similarly repressive governments, Uruguay's neighbors differed in that the regimes permitted some domestic human rights groups to operate in those countries, even during the dictatorship's harshest years. With respect to Uruguay's own reemerging civil society movement, its regional counterparts provided essential support and examples of effective advocacy against similarly intransigent governments. As a result, this chapter recenters the influence of regional human rights groups. Uruguayans drew support from international groups such as Amnesty International, but used groups in neighboring Argentina such as SERPAJ and Centro de Estudios Legales y Sociales (Center for Legal and Social Studies [CELS]) as important models for the emergence of domestic groups.

As such, this chapter stitches together the domestic, regional, and international human rights dynamics during Uruguay's push for a transition from 1981 to 1984. The country's return to democratic rule was far from a linear trajectory or a predetermined outcome. The military's retrenchment imposed severe limitations on the birth of a domestic human rights movement. Using further arrests, censorship, and intimidation tactics, the military attempted to manage the negotiations to assert control over the terms of leaving office and maintain some power, especially as it received renewed U.S. support when the Reagan administration entered office in early 1981 and embraced military regimes as part of its Cold War refocusing. Ultimately, the excitement following the plebiscite proved essential to launching a domestic human rights movement, but the continued repression and lengthy negotiations exposed the fissures over the definition of human rights, including on issues such as justice and the prominence of social and economic rights—divisions that would emerge even more fully in the late 1980s.

An Emboldened Press

Newspapers provided one of the first avenues for public discussion of human rights in the aftermath of the plebiscite. Since 1973, when the military shut down most of Uruguay's papers, there had been a dearth of independent news. However, the "no" vote in the plebiscite opened the space to permit a greater degree of freedom of expression than had been allowed in the previous seven years. *Opinar* and *La Plaza,* which emerged in the months before the vote, continued to operate. They were joined by other important outlets as well, such as *Jaque*, *Aquí*, and dozens of others. While the mere existence of these new papers signaled an important change in the post-plebiscite period, the papers also became important spaces for a new human rights discourse. At first indirectly and then increasingly directly, they challenged the military dictatorship's policies and practices, even as the military regularly intervened to shut them down and attempt to silence criticism.

Opinar, the weekly newspaper founded during the plebiscite campaign by Enrique Tarigo, grew as an important opposition voice to the dictatorship. In many articles, the newspaper questioned the regime's authority, a daring move by Uruguayan press standards after years of censorship. In the first issue after the plebiscite, for example, the writers stressed that they would continue to fight for the freedom of expression.[11] In subsequent issues, reporters highlighted Uruguay's historical commitment to liberty and called for restoring political rights.[12] Despite challenging the dictatorship's rule in this way, the newspaper did not broach the topic of torture or political imprisonment.[13] Throughout its first year of publication, the only article that invoked the specific term "human rights" in relation to Uruguay was centered on covering the launch of the first domestic human rights organization, SERPAJ, and the Argentine Nobel Peace Prize winner Adolfo Pérez Esquivel's visit to Uruguay. The article merely provided a summary of Esquivel's message, because the newspaper feared the potential reprisals of a larger discussion.[14] After all the closures and arrests of journalists in the previous seven years, this fear was well founded. Despite this restraint, a *New York Times* article covering Tarigo's efforts made the notable observation that he kept a copy of the UDHR in his office on the wall behind his desk.[15] While this detail indicated a belief in the broader idea of human rights, the paper itself was cautious about its invocation in this initial period.

La Plaza also continued to publish after the plebiscite and spent more energy focused on covering human rights issues in neighboring Argentina as a lens to explore Uruguay's own plight without directly evoking the military's wrath. The magazine was similarly tepid in its approach to criticizing the government. Writers frequently focused on cultural issues, such as the return of Uruguayan art and movies.[16] Nevertheless, they also went a step further than *Opinar* and explored controversial topics about issues affecting life under the dictatorship. For instance, the paper discussed a possible path toward democratization, which included lifting the restrictions on political parties.[17] Other articles mentioned Argentina's struggle with human rights through its discussion of the Argentine branch of SERPAJ. Through this lens,

the periodical discussed Esquivel's efforts in defense of Uruguayans who had
disappeared in Argentina, albeit without discussing the Uruguayan government's own complicity.[18] Thus, the magazine was careful not to overtly criticize the military government and to only indirectly address issues of human
rights through reporting on neighboring Latin American nations. This tactic
allowed the writers to discuss, for example, torture and disappearances, since
all Uruguayans knew that Argentina's issues closely resembled their own. Yet,
the periodical was restrained about the extent to which it directly challenged
the Uruguayan government's conduct.

As negotiations with the military continued in fits and starts, more publications appeared, including ones that increasingly and more overtly challenged the dictatorship. For example, the Christian Democratic Party, one of
the coalition parties of the leftist Frente Amplio, founded *Aqui* in 1983. In its
first issue, writers explained the paper's purpose as assuming a "promise and
responsibility" to contribute to the democratization process already underway
and to assist in the search for solutions with truthful and independent reporting. The article boldly explained the history of "individual rights" and its hope
of transforming fear into liberty through the open discussion of ideas.[19] While
focused on freedom of the press, similar to the earlier weeklies, it also spotlighted conversations in Argentina about the disappeared.[20] *Aqui* was different
from the other papers that had first appeared in 1980 and 1981 when Argentina was still struggling with human rights violations under a dictatorship. By
1983, Argentina was in the midst of transitioning to a democratic government
and discussing accountability for the crimes of the dictatorship. Therefore,
without talking directly about issues of human rights violations in Uruguay,
Aqui continually highlighted conversations of truth and justice regarding the
military's disappearances in Argentina. These articles included examining the
actions of the Madres de uruguayos detenidos-desaparecidos en Argentina
(Mothers of Uruguayans detained and disappeared in Argentina).[21] Spotlighting Argentina allowed the press to expose Uruguayans to possibilities of
accountability without directly discussing Uruguay's own plight.

Jaque followed *Aqui*'s creation in the later transitional period to "contribute to the effort to create a free and democratic press."[22] Manuel Flores Silva
founded the weekly after working at *Opinar* for two years. Flores came from
a political dynasty in Uruguay. He was the son of former Colorado representative Manuel Flores Mora, but his political lineage dated back to the nineteenth century and former Colorado president Venancio Flores (1865–1868).
A tall, young man with a flowing head of brown hair and a well-groomed but

bushy beard, he had the political acumen to recognize the importance of the press in these critical years, particularly for his generation who came of age during the fear and silence of the dictatorship.[23] The first issue set the parameters of these objectives:

> Jaque is not just another weekly that tries to provide an additional layer of commentary. It comes, on the contrary, to fill a gap with a new model and a different message. Because we feel we are natural representatives of a different generation, a generation that was integrated into national life in the darkest moment in the history of the country's freedoms. We come from a generation that does not hold resentment but also that does not have the luxury of unrecognized innocence. Our generation arrives without our eyes closed to the reality of politics. A generation which grew up in the eclipse of the rights of speech and assembly. And one that learned to read looking beyond an immediate message between the lines. A generation reclaiming their place and voice. Because there are many things to say.[24]

The newspaper discussed various topics in its first few weeks, including the reappearance of a union movement and press freedoms.[25] The paper also addressed human rights. For example, in the December 9, 1983, issue, the magazine included a full-page spread on the disappeared throughout Latin America, with statistics on Uruguay.[26] A week later, in the December 16 issue, an article commemorated International Human Rights Day and asserted the need to return the concept of human rights to the hands of the people. Previously, the article argued, treaties had been signed and enforced by generals and leaders of countries. Now, it was time for human rights to be entrusted to the people who understood the pain that accompanies violations and abuse.[27] It was a powerful call to adopt a domestic approach to the universal conception of human rights protection that rejected the idea that rights could be defined solely by heads of state. While in the past human rights had sometimes been understood as moral imperialism or solely within the domain of a state's jurisdictional definition, Jaque readily embraced human rights as part of a vision for a better future for the country that regarded certain rights as penetrating the sovereign veil. This shift exemplified the evolution of a domestic human rights discourse to articulate the people's struggle against the dictatorship and considered broader international rights standards that transnational human rights groups had been promoting over the last decade.

Between the plebiscite in November 1980 and the elections four years later, over a dozen papers ultimately emerged. Many of them struggled with how to advocate openly for democracy and human rights in the face of periodic crackdowns and closures by the military as it attempted to maintain control over the transitional process.[28] Nevertheless, the mere existence of these publications after years of censorship reveals how the press offered a space for citizens to voice tentative and diverse opinions about human rights. While the press was far from being open and free, there was an important change. Before the dictatorship began in 1973, papers rarely discussed human rights directly. In the early 1980s, a flurry of articles surfaced to demonstrate how the emergence of a human rights discourse had become relevant in the prolonged battle to push the government toward a transition to a more democratic society. While these papers rarely challenged the Uruguayan dictatorship directly, the discussion of a broad array of rights marked an increasing use of human rights language at the national level. The newly formed domestic human rights groups, however, proved bolder in confronting the military's continued abuses.

The Formation of Human Rights Groups

During the first seven years of military rule, no human rights groups existed openly in Uruguay.[29] By contrast, human rights groups formed and protested against military rule in both Chile and Argentina even during each country's dictatorship's initial years.[30] However, the severity of Uruguay's repression precluded the possibility.[31] Thus, in addition to other forms of popular protest following the plebiscite, civil society's reemergence encapsulated a burgeoning domestic human rights movement that often looked to its regional counterparts for how to organize.[32] As scholars argue, defending human rights became one of the first expressions of civil disobedience in Uruguayan society. After such a long time under repressive rule, it was the first type of public protest considered lawful—to a limited extent.[33] During this critical period, Uruguay relied heavily on its neighbors for inspiration and models.[34] The groups that emerged in Uruguay combined a deep historical commitment to Uruguay's own social justice history with with an eye toward regional strategies for how to protest against military rule.

One group that emerged in Uruguay after years of operating abroad was known as the Madres y Familiares de Uruguayos Detenidos Desaparecidos, which merged several groups that had been operating abroad in the years prior.[35] As early as 1976, Uruguayan women began traveling to Argentina in search of their loved ones who had disappeared there after the neighboring country experienced its own military takeover.[36] In documents relating to the organization's history, its founders explain that they met each other during the desperate search for their sons, brothers, and spouses, oftentimes abroad where they joined the Madres de la Plaza de Mayo.[37] In Argentina, the government initially dismissed these women who began to organize in search of their loved ones as "*locas*" (madwomen), rather than viewing them as a legitimate threat and putting an end to their demonstrations immediately. Scholar Jean Franco explains that the military believed nobody would take a group of "old, tired, and obviously crazy women" seriously.[38] The Madres de la Plaza de Mayo began marching in April 1977 in Argentina, within a year of the country's military takeover.

Because Argentina allowed for limited protests, and because many Uruguayans had been disappeared in Argentina, Uruguayan women joined their suffering Argentine *compañeras* on the streets.[39] These women eventually started their own formal group under the name Grupo de Madres de Uruguayos Desaparecidos en Argentina (Group of Uruguayan Mothers of the Disappeared in Argentina), which was modeled on the Argentine group. Together they presented petitions of habeas corpus, submitted complaints to governments in Uruguay and Argentina, and connected with international organizations such as the UN, the Red Cross, and Amnesty International to publicize their plight.[40] During those initial years, complaints from Argentina were completely ignored within Uruguay where the repression continued through torture, jail, and in some cases disappearances. No domestic news outlets covered these women's pleas since the press was so heavily censored.[41] When Aparicio Méndez announced the plebiscite in 1980, the group sent him a note urging for a fair vote and for information regarding the disappeared. The government denied the group's claims in all cases and refused to answer any of its letters.[42]

After the plebiscite, however, the mothers gained some traction domestically for the first time. Some women used their experience from Argentina to work within the limited spaces for activism within Uruguay. Others who had never gone abroad had met on buses that took them to the prisons to visit family members who were political prisoners, and began to participate in political activity outside of the domestic sphere for the first time. These women began to organize solidarity networks and collections for relatives of prisoners, since often the removal of the head of household for extended prison sentences

meant that families struggled to make ends meet. The group grew as it incorporated grandmothers into the movement, and then eventually men as well.[43]
Human rights, as one madre, María Magdalena "Quica" Salvia, explained,
began as a women's movement but grew as a space for those who sought a
solution to the state-sponsored violations.[44] The women also expanded their
aims through the early part of the decade. While groups continued to work in
Brazil and Argentina to connect its message to its regional counterparts, they
also took a more directly political approach by engaging with members of the
newly reconstituted political parties in Uruguay. In addition, the reemerging
domestic press reported on the women's work for the first time, including publishing a list of disappeared Uruguayans.[45] In 1982, the women officially created
a group within Uruguay, Asociación de Familiares de Uruguayos Desaparecidos (AFUDE). This group consolidated with other Madres y Familiares sections from abroad the following year under the name Madres y Familiares de
Uruguayos Detenidos Desaparecidos (Familiares).[46] Among other events that
took place that first year in Uruguay, the group participated in a "*Semana del
Detenido y Desaparecido*" (Week for the Detained and Disappeared) in May to
protest the growing number of disappearances across the region.[47]

     In this work both before and after the plebiscite, the women maintained two
very specific goals: the search for children and spouses who had disappeared
and the release of loved ones who were being held in prison. Women seeking
information about their sons and daughters banded together at a time when
political parties and political action did not exist. In those years, few institutions had the capacity to mediate between the state and individuals. The loss of
their children, however, transcended many mothers' fear of death and moved
women from the domestic realm into a direct confrontation with the state.[48]
In juxtaposition to the all-male military regime, women dominated Familiares
and exploited the traditional view that mothers were just "vessels of reproduction." These women transformed the traditional role of motherhood from
being a private calling into a more broadly ethical mission. Crossing traditional
national and class boundaries, the group provided an alternative public sphere
of protest.[49] This new role was particularly notable in Uruguay. A report by the
Ford Foundation explained that while there was not a strong, preexisting structure within the country for women to advocate for their rights against the state,
this situation changed during the dictatorship as the repression increasingly
put women in a precarious position.[50] In turn, they were motivated to become
more involved in public life to advocate for rights.[51] Thus, women surfaced as a
strong societal force in this period.

Familiares also expanded its vision in 1983. Emboldened by forming partnerships with other groups, it spearheaded the creation of a movement to defend human rights more broadly. Starting in 1983, human rights committees began to form in trade unions and student organizations. With the strong influence and support from Argentina's group in Familiares' founding, the group followed Argentina's discursive change as well.[52] Its calls shifted from merely discovering what happened to loved ones to using the phrase "truth and justice," which was being sought with some success in Argentina immediately following the country's transition back to democracy. It now seemed possible to advocate for accountability in Uruguay as well.[53] Even before the last prisoners were released, Familiares began to explain its desire for truth and justice. The group said that if Uruguay was going to try to build a strong democratic foundation, it was necessary to know what happened to the young lives that were lost. The group began to print calls asking both "when?" referring to justice, but also "how and why?" One memo in particular went on to explain that this process was necessary to ensure that those who were gone would not be forgotten and advocated that those who were responsible be brought to justice.[54] Thus, Familiares was one of the most visible groups to challenge the dictatorship on human rights grounds after moving and consolidating its work from abroad to within Uruguay after the plebiscite.

Like Familiares, SERPAJ had strong connections to Argentina as both a model and a source of early support.[55] A branch of SERPAJ was founded in Argentina in 1974 and an Uruguayan section opened after the plebiscite, demonstrating the impact of global ecumenical human rights work, and more specifically the direct impact of Argentina's group. As noted in Chapter 2, ecumenical groups such as the WCC played a critical role across the Southern Cone in response to the military dictatorships by focusing on relieving the suffering of the most vulnerable populations and advocating against repressive regimes. Yet, the Uruguayan military conducted a fervent smear campaign against the WCC, effectively causing the group to withdraw from its direct involvement in Uruguay by 1975, even as it continued to support the work of Uruguayan exiles and human rights groups proliferating around the globe throughout the 1970s. In the early 1980s, the WCC supported the renewed domestic fight against the dictatorship by endorsing the establishment of SERPAJ Uruguay; yet, they mainly played a role from afar. Due to the military's earlier attack on the WCC, they did not want to potentially undermine the group's work by inviting false claims that its efforts were just the result of foreign entities trying to spread communist ideas.[56]

Therefore, endowed with the ethos of the global ecumenical movement and the symbolic support from the WCC, it was the direct influence from neighboring Argentina that ultimately had the biggest impact on SERPAJ. Luis Pérez Aguirre led the founding of SERPAJ's country branch and worked closely with his Argentine counterparts. Born in 1941, Pérez Aguirre was a Jesuit priest who came from a prestigious, wealthy family. When he was young, he eschewed his privilege, wanting to dedicate his life to addressing, through religious work, the suffering that he saw around him. He was ordained in Uruguay in 1970 and began working with university students and sex workers just prior to the official military coup. By the latter part of the decade, he wanted to advocate more directly against the military government's abuses. Pérez Aguirre, known affectionately by his friends as Perico, helped found and wrote for *La Plaza* as one venue to address what was occurring in the country.[57] For the publication, he covered the work of Adolfo Pérez Esquivel in SERPAJ Argentina, which is how they got to know each other initially. SERPAJ Argentina had also been involved in Uruguay's human rights plight since it began receiving appeals in 1979 for help with cases of Uruguayans who disappeared in Argentina.[58] After the Argentine organization won the Nobel Peace Prize in 1980, Esquivel and Pérez Aguirre began discussing how to form an Uruguayan branch of the organization.[59]

Esquivel offered external support to found SERPAJ in Uruguay in 1981, even though the situation in the country was still very dangerous at the time. Francisco "Pancho" Bustamante, one of the earliest members of the organization, recalled that many people thought "we were completely crazy" for opposing the military outright.[60] Yet the group's founders persevered with the support of Esquivel, who had the added prestige of being a Nobel Peace Prize winner and offered a model for how Uruguay could operate in a repressive environment. Indeed, Pérez Aguirre noted in October 1981 that the government was "watching us closely" as the group worked to establish a presence.[61]

Due to continued repression in Uruguay, SERPAJ was careful in how it articulated its mission. SERPAJ promoted a broad vision of human rights, not directly challenging the military at first. For example, the week SERPAJ launched, Pérez Aguirre wrote a long article about disability rights as human rights in *La Plaza*.[62] Furthermore, the periodical published a letter from Esquivel describing SERPAJ's mission within an ecumenical frame as helping those who were poor and most in need.[63] Another article in the same edition went on to explain SERPAJ in more detail, touching upon the mission of the organization, which sought to affirm respect for human rights, to search for the promotion of these values, and to defend against human rights violations.[64] As a result, SERPAJ emerged on the scene in a very different way than Familiares, which focused on disappearances and political imprisonment of family members. SERPAJ attempted cautiously to promote the idea of broad human rights values that did not just focus on the military's violations but also included social and economic rights that fit within a broader ecumenical tradition. Members who worked at SERPAJ during those initial months noted that the military's continued repression impeded their organizing even at this early stage when the group advocated for a general moral platform.[65]

However, SERPAJ eventually took cautious steps to address the Uruguayan human rights situation in relation to the dictatorship. For example, while it was very careful to define human rights broadly as defending the right to life, the right to health, socioeconomic rights, and political-cultural rights, SERPAJ also articulated the right to be free from torture and political imprisonment.[66] To counter claims of subversion, SERPAJ also defined its mission very specifically as a service, not as a movement with any political leaning.[67] This careful positioning carried over into SERPAJ's first public actions, which involved organizing a day of support for the families of Uruguayans who were disappeared in Argentina, and noticeably not in Uruguay. This led to other churches organizing days of support for peace in El Salvador, against war in the Malvinas, and against murder "with hunger or bullets."[68] These initial actions were not directly aimed at challenging the dictatorship, but rather sought to position the group as a broader peace movement. In this respect, SERPAJ became a symbol of a reviving civil society sector and a place for individuals to begin to gather and discuss broad human rights ideals. It tested what the military dictatorship would allow in the post-plebiscite period while simultaneously trying not to directly incur the wrath of the dictatorship.

By 1982, though, Pérez Aguirre began to speak and write more publicly about Uruguay's own human rights problems, arguing that justice could help form a true peace.[69] In 1983, Pérez Aguirre explained in an interview that SERPAJ had different foci within the organization: one on political prisoners, one to support the families of the disappeared, and another on union issues.[70] SERPAJ took the lead in denouncing the torture of university students, and soon thereafter Pérez Aguirre led a fast to protest the torture of political prisoners. In another example of the link between SERPAJ Argentina and SERPAJ Uruguay, Pérez Esquivel led a similar fast in May 1983 in Buenos Aires.[71] The contexts were very different, however. Argentina was already transitioning back to democratic rule, where no such clear end was in sight in Uruguay. Therefore, as the leader of the protest action, SERPAJ Uruguay was put squarely in the national spotlight as standing up to the government.[72] In this way, the organization began to narrow its focus from a broader list of social and economic rights to advocating for the resumption of a specific set of rights based on countering the repression of the dictatorship. This shift revealed two important components of the human rights embrace in Uruguayan civil society. First, it indicated the emergence of a human rights discourse under a broad interpretation of political, civil, social, and economic rights—even in its early invocations, it was never segregated. However, it importantly also showed how groups increasingly focused during this period on utilizing the discourse as a tool to challenge the dictatorship and push for a transition.

Another important group to emerge during this period was the Instituto de Estudios Legales y Sociales (Institute for Legal and Social Studies [IEL-SUR]), which its founders modeled on a similar Argentine organization, CELS. Although officially founded in 1984, it had begun its work a few years earlier as a small group of progressive lawyers who were frustrated by the unwillingness of the Uruguayan *Colegio de Abogados* to work for the legal defense of human rights abuse victims.[73] Many members were young and, armed with law degrees, sought to help the country's many political prisoners.[74]

CELS in Buenos Aires had emerged in 1979 to foster and protect human rights. CELS focused on investigating the disappeared, providing legal help to those families, and documenting the terrorism of the state. One Ford Foundation officer, Margaret Crahan, praised CELS for "doing the most important human rights legal work" that is also "highly effective."[75] CELS even provided a home for Uruguayan exiles, such as Octavio Carsen, who worked on Uruguayan issues from the Buenos Aires office and remained close to many of the lawyers who founded IELSUR.[76] IELSUR attempted to follow CELS's lead by clarifying the fate of the disappeared in Uruguay. The group also engaged in a more diverse range of activities that reflected the particularities of Uruguay's dictatorship. For instance, it focused on advocating to release the remaining prisoners, repealing the nation's repressive laws, and winning amnesty for political prisoners and exiles.[77]

In its early years, IELSUR also worked abroad to discover what had happened to the many Uruguayan nationals who had disappeared in other Southern Cone countries during the dictatorship, particularly in Paraguay, Chile, Argentina, and Brazil.[78] The group's legal claims expanded dramatically after the country transitioned to democratic rule, but during those first years, it worked with SERPAJ and Familiares to advocate for a set of rights that the dictatorship had denied the population.[79] Like the other civil society groups that emerged in the initial years, the organization was born out of a human rights ideal that focused on promoting the human rights of current or former political prisoners, a set of rights that required robust advocacy efforts in the transitional phase.[80]

Each organization played a different and critical role during this period, emerging and growing at various points before the formal transition occurred, while also focusing on different aspects of human rights. Still, these three civil society groups shared some fundamental similarities in the initial years after the plebiscite. First, they were all profoundly influenced by other regional human rights groups. While Argentina, Brazil, and Chile had all suffered under similarly repressive dictatorships, these three countries also had a substantial domestic human rights presence prior to Uruguay's November 1980 plebiscite. Therefore, after the space opened for a domestic rebirth of civil society in Uruguay, these countries provided the most important models and, at times, organizational support to Uruguay's own burgeoning human rights movement. Scholars are now beginning to study this dissemination effect, drawing strong connections in the flow of ideas and inspiration to mobilize national movements.[81] In Uruguay, this influence clearly occurred at a regional level. Thus, the most important connections and influences were not with transnational groups in the Global North, whom some Uruguayans, particularly on the Left, at times viewed with suspicion. Rather, other regional actors, with whom Uruguayans had direct contact during years in exile or in the search for loved ones, had a stronger human rights impact and provided a model for Uruguayans.

Second, while all three groups at times employed different tenets of human rights in explaining their work and mission, all three groups made general and unrestricted amnesty for political exiles and political prisoners a goal in their early years of operation. For example, in one of Familiares' early meetings, the group explained that its objectives were to obtain truth and justice with respect to the disappeared, to punish those responsible for the disappearances, and to ensure that those still in prison received general and unrestricted amnesty.[82] Similarly, Pérez Aguirre, writing in *La Plaza* as the leader of SERPAJ, reiterated the idea that amnesty was necessary as part of the country's transition to reconciliation and peace.[83] Pérez Aguirre also led SERPAJ to sign a public letter in 1982 asking President Álvarez for amnesty for political prisoners.[84] SERPAJ consistently included amnesty for those still in jail as an important component of its primary goals, citing its "hope that amnesty would serve as a base for reconciliation for all."[85] IELSUR also wrote position papers advocating for amnesty, describing how it could be promulgated and carried out.[86]

Thus, amnesty for political prisoners was a critical aspect of civil society demands during the emergence of local human rights groups. After Uruguay garnered the dubious distinction of being the country with the highest rate of political prisoners in the world during the 1970s, the goal of obtaining prisoners' freedom proved to be a unifying factor among these opposition actors. The issue of amnesty would resurface after the transition, however, invoked by the military in an entirely different context with respect to human rights.[87] In these initial years, though, it remained a key point of contention and a rallying call for domestic human rights groups in their fight against the dictatorship, even as their other prime objectives and invocations of human rights differed.

Reconstituting Unions and the Student Movement

Alongside these new domestic human rights groups, labor unions and the student movement regained a public presence after the plebiscite. Both had been proscribed during most of the military dictatorship, and their reemergence demonstrated the various ways that civil society began to challenge and pressure the dictatorship in the post-plebiscite period. The labor movement resurfaced under the new name of Plenario Intersindical de Trabajadores (PIT), while the military allowed a new student movement to form as the Asociación de Estudiantes de la Enseñanza Pública (ASCEEP). While these groups sought to pressure for an end to the dictatorship, their ideas about what rights to put at the forefront of their mobilizing efforts differed. In many ways, union workers and students focused on reviving historical claims to social and economic rights that had long been part of the Uruguayan public sphere prior to the dictatorship.

Unions began to organize again after the plebiscite when the military passed a 1981 law that granted private-sector unions the chance to operate so long as they received governmental approval. Initially, approval was purposely difficult to obtain, and only a few did. In addition, the military passed a series of other restrictions, which included prohibiting anyone who had held a union post prior to 1973 from assuming a leadership position. In spite of these challenges, workers began publishing a magazine to articulate the importance of reviving the workers' movement as early as 1981.[88] Then, when unions resumed organizing in the streets, they ultimately did little to follow the military's strict rules. In the first protest since the early years of the dictatorship, the unions organized a May Day demonstration in 1983 to push toward democratization. Under the banner of "peace and freedom," over 100,000 demonstrators took to the streets, representing forty-eight reorganized unions.[89] The unions called for an end to the military's aggression and injustice, after which union leaders declared the event to be an historic success.[90] The protesters helped to reestablish unions as a political force within civil society. Subsequent demonstrations occurred in September of the same year around the slogan that would be their motto for the rest of the dictatorship: "Freedom, jobs, higher wages, and amnesty."[91]

The slogan ultimately captured a broad vision of the PIT's main goals. When the PIT advocated for "freedom," it was vaguely defined but widely understood as freedom to organize, to participate in union activities, and to challenge the dictatorship.[92] Through these ideas, the unions revived many of their pre-dictatorship demands such as higher wages and more jobs. They also now included a unique anti-dictatorship bent incorporating a call for amnesty for imprisoned comrades who had been targeted by the regime. However, when the PIT talked about rights it was generally in reference to the right to strike, the right to make a living wage, or the right not to be summarily dismissed from their jobs.[93] Only occasionally did the PIT actually use the term human rights explicitly, and when it did it was in reference to reviving and reestablishing the rights that the unions had advocated for throughout the twentieth century.[94]

Another important civil society group to resurface during this period was the student movement: ASCEEP. This group replaced the old FEUU, which had been banned during the dictatorship. Because the university had been an active site for organizing during the 1960s and early 1970s, the military government took control of the university during its rule, purging professors and administrators, putting its own people in their place, and then rewriting the curriculum and budget to root out any perceived subversive influences. ASCEEP announced its founding in April 1982 to unite students as a challenge to the "individualism and silence of dictatorship." In addition, ASCEEP sought to reverse the "the lack of autonomy" that characterized the university over the previous decade.[95]

The new student movement differed from other groups that were reorganizing out of the wreckage of repression. Political parties and most other unions saw participants from the period before the dictatorship return to prominent positions , even if it was behind the scenes due to the military's official prohibition. The student movement, however, was comprised of entirely new individuals, a younger generation who had grown up largely under the cloud of dictatorship. The group joined other movements organizing events to pressure the dictatorship's policies of repression, and amplified similar concerns.[96] For example, in materials published and distributed around the university, ASCEEP explained its goals in its initial years as a long list, including the fall of dictatorship, general and unrestricted amnesty, liberty for all political prisoners, information on the disappeared, free return of exiles, justice for all those that committed crimes against humanity, dismantling of repressive apparatus, reinstatement of all those who had been dismissed for political reasons from the university, trial of civilians in civilian courts (not military ones), open elections, and freedom of the press. Reinvigorating the worker-student alliance from the 1960s, the group also pushed for unionization, health services, and social security programs. Economically, it sought to remove Uruguay from World Bank economic pressures, to allow for civil society to participate in decisions with respect to the national economy, and to redistribute the wasteful security and defense budgets to health and education. In 1984, ASCEEP even organized a "Human Rights Week" where they hosted a widely attended conference on topics as diverse as union rights, social and psychological repercussions of exile, and the detained and disappeared throughout Latin America. This range of topics demonstrates the diverse ways ASCEEP invoked human rights terminology.[97]

Yet, ASCEEP focused primarily on solutions to problems specifically related to the university.[98] As one prominent member of the movement explained, "First clandestinely and then through legal spaces that we had reconquered, we questioned the intervention [of the military in the university system] and little by little we opened up more spaces for participation."[99] ASCEEP dedicated much of its energy to education reform, advocating against private universities, opening a school of fine arts, and reclaiming the autonomy of the university.[100] One of the most prominent events ASCEEP staged in this period occurred in September 1983. The group organized a weeklong conference to commemorate the statute that had granted the university independence twenty-five years earlier, highlighting the contrast to the current military control. The conference ended in a march, which was estimated to have 60,000 protesters. The strength of actions such as this demonstrated the resurgence of the student movement after having been thoroughly targeted during the early years of the dictatorship, a movement that did at times utilize human rights language to encompass a wide range of issues affecting the entire country, even if most of their organizing centered on issues specific to the university community.

The revival of both the unions and the student movements revealed a burgeoning civil society during the initial years after the plebiscite. The military government faced increasing pressure as human rights groups worked alongside unions and the student movement to push for a transition back to democratic rule. What is clear though is the discrepancy in these groups' understanding of human rights. At a basic level, the student movement, unions, and human rights groups were all working for a transition. However, whereas the human rights groups focused on eliminating political imprisonment, torture, and disappearances, the unions and student movement had much broader concerns that were equal in weight to, or exceeded, the oftentimes more narrow emphasis of the human rights groups. They were generally much more concerned with resurrecting the struggles of their pre-dictatorship counterparts, and only occasionally at this point described their prime motivations in explicit human rights terms. Although the goal of a transition transcended these discrepancies in the initial years, below the surface, fundamentally different ideas existed about what constituted human rights. What banded these groups together in the early 1980s was a common enemy: the enduring repression of the dictatorship even in light of renewed activism.

The Military Pushes Back

Even as civil society emerged from a variety of sectors to challenge the government, continued repression often stymied substantial progress.[101] Gabriel Mazzarovich recalls that the plebiscite's results "unleashed [the military's] fury." At the time of the plebiscite, he was sixteen and a high school student, active in the clandestine student movement. He recalled that in the year after the plebiscite, more than 4,000 people were arrested and tortured, including himself and other high school students, many as young as fourteen. While he was "only" in jail for forty-two days because of his young age, he noted that the arrests and torture were used as a warning to the rest of the population of "what could happen to you if you got involved."[102]

Indeed, the military employed its typical modes of repression to attempt and reassert control over any political concessions it offered. For example, the military relegalized political parties and called for internal party primaries in

November 1982. This measure aimed to elect leaders who were allies of the
military and could negotiate a restricted democracy similar to what they had
proposed in the 1980 constitution. Former top Blanco and Colorado leaders
were prohibited from running for internal leadership positions, and the leftist
Frente Amplio Party remained illegal. Many Frente Amplio adherents either
submitted blank ballots (7 percent) or voted for anti-regime candidates within
the traditional parties.[103] Even with all these restrictions, anti-military candidates running on both the Blanco and Colorado Party tickets won by overwhelming numbers, approximately 77 percent of the vote.[104] As the results
came in, hundreds of people streamed out onto the main street of Avenida
18 de Julio to celebrate.[105] Scholar Charles Gillespie explains that "the clear
message of the primaries was an even greater rejection of the regime than in
the plebiscite held two years previously."[106] Instead of prompting a quicker
transition, however, this second defeat only served to further reinforce the
military's recalcitrance. The military continued to use force to maintain control of the negotiations in any potential moves toward civilian rule.

In addition to the mass arrests and torture in the immediate aftermath
of the plebiscite, the military also reasserted its authority through sporadic
but sustained efforts to censor the press. This began as early as April 1981,
when the military closed *Opinar* for four weeks after the paper published two
articles calling for elections and criticizing the armed forces.[107] Shutdowns
increased as the media grew more strident in challenging the military. In the
months that followed, the military temporarily forced a dozen newspapers
and magazines, including *Jaque*, to halt publication. The military closed others such as *La Plaza* permanently. At first, the military had only provisionally
closed the periodical after Pérez Aguirre published an article on the human
rights implications behind the murder of Oscar Romero in El Salvador.[108]
Even the comparative discussion of human rights was seen as threatening to
the military. When *La Plaza* made a direct critique of the military by calling
for amnesty of political prisoners in Uruguay, it received a final notice to close
its doors.[109] Other papers were shut down for mentioning banned politicians,
criticizing government policies, or asking questions about the nation's disappeared.[110] The military required that they approve weeklies before they were
sent to press, and a number of issues were rejected outright.[111] The government also closed Radio CX30, an independent station that had adopted an
increasingly defiant stance regarding the military after the 1980 plebiscite.[112]
The closure prompted the station director, Germán Araujo, to embark on a
hunger strike protesting the closure, during which he occupied the station.[113]

All these repressive actions received international condemnation when the Committee to Protect Journalists (CPJ) appealed to UNESCO to protest the closures of a slew of other papers such as *Cinco Días, Tribuna Amplia, Somos Idea,* and *Convicción.* In the complaint, the CPJ explained that the dictatorship still enforced decrees forbidding "(1) news reports or media commentary about political activities, (2) attacks on the morale of the armed forces, (3) news coverage of politically banned persons, (4) reports on strikes, rallies, and trade union activities, and (5) any direct or indirect criticism of the government."[114] As late as June 1984, the military was still closing newspapers, while journalists endured threats, had their homes shot at, and were even arrested and tortured.[115]

The military also targeted the emerging human rights organizations. After its founding, SERPAJ had grown increasingly bold in calling attention to the military's continued human rights abuses. Members supported efforts to appeal for amnesty for political prisoners, denounced the torture of twenty-five detained young people, and went on a hunger strike to draw attention to the human rights abuses.[116] For these actions, the group found itself under strict government surveillance. First, the Minister of Culture forbade publication of SERPAJ's information bulletin about human rights in 1982.[117] Then, in April 1983, *El País,* the national newspaper that was largely controlled by the military, published an article accusing SERPAJ of being a "very suspicious organization with deceitful aims."[118] Despite SERPAJ's attempts to counter the claims, shortly thereafter the military closed down SERPAJ's office, outlawed any actions, and confiscated much of its materials. It destroyed most of the organization's files, and they were never recovered. From this point forward, SERPAJ was forced to operate clandestinely until after the transition.[119]

The head of SERPAJ, Father Luis Pérez Aguirre, had also personally faced the "wrath of the dictatorship" since the organization's founding. He was arrested, questioned, and imprisoned multiple times for his work.[120] Before being shut down, SERPAJ struggled with external funding for this reason. They feared being arrested and tortured for accepting international money, which the military viewed as part of an international leftist conspiracy seeking to undermine its regime. In contrast to Chile, where money funneled in through the Church, which acted as a moral shield, SERPAJ's founders did not want to risk their safety by accepting international assistance during those initial years.[121] Human rights groups were particularly vulnerable to the military's abuses. As political scientist Alexandra Barahona de Brito notes, although the regime in Uruguay lost the plebiscite in 1980, it was truly a surprise to all involved, which meant that opposition parties never developed an interparty practice of human rights defense in cooperation with the nascent human rights organizations.[122] As such, each group acted alone to protect themselves from the armed forces.

The reconstituted student movement and labor unions were also subjected to the military's harassment.[123] Soon after the May Day protest, in June 1983, the military detained and tortured several dozen protesting university students.[124] Furthermore, in July of that year, the military cracked down on the PIT, preventing the organization from holding an airport rally to welcome home representatives from an International Labour Organization meeting. In September, the government banned a press conference by the group. Two months later in November, the police broke up a protest and arrested five hundred people.[125] This crackdown continued into 1984. After a twenty-four-hour strike in January to protest a 28 percent increase in prices and the continued repression, the military declared the PIT illegal and banned all media coverage of their protest.[126] In all these measures, the military clamped down on these groups' increasing challenge to its rule and sought to assert its control.

The military also rearrested members of the PCU. Juan Acuna, a former member of the PCU, was held in prison for his membership in the Party from 1977 to 1980. Although the military released him in 1980, they rearrested him in March 1983 with his wife and mother-in-law. Acuna serves as just one example of many who were victimized as part of a general crackdown on the Left during the increasing activism of this period.[127] As a leader of the Communist Party in Uruguay, Rodney Arismendi, noted, despite President Gregorio Álvarez's public avowals that the military was open to starting a conversation about Uruguay's future, "a dialogue was not possible ... while the military was threatening the people and practicing repression."[128]

The contradiction of the political aperture with continued repression was captured in a letter by Ema Julia Massera, the daughter of mathematician José Luis Massera. Due to his affiliation with the Communist Party, the military had him arrested and imprisoned in 1975. His renowned academic work garnered international attention for his plight, and in 1982 his daughter wrote to a professor who was gathering global support for her petition to the Uruguayan government to release her father. In the letters, she described the domestic situation, explaining that while some openings had emerged, "more censorship appears ... with violent repression of various opposition groups, closing of newspapers, etc. and attacks within prisons."[129] Even as human rights groups formed, trade unions and a student movement reappeared, and the press increasingly challenged the official military narrative, the violence did not cease. The military's repressive apparatus was largely still in place. As such, the reemergence of a domestic civil society was met with force as the military sought to maintain control of the negotiations about the possibility of leaving office.

The Paradox of International Attention

While domestic groups fought for human rights amid continual crackdowns by the military in the early 1980s, international pressure operated in two contradictory ways. On the one hand, established transnational organizations headquartered in the Global North such as AI and WOLA continued to advocate for the military to change its practices. They were joined by a new organization, Americas Watch, that also kept Uruguay's plight on the international radar. These groups served an important role in continuing to spotlight issues of disappearances, torture, and political imprisonment in the country, and offered a vital connection for people such as Ema Julia Massera to appeal to when repression persisted. In addition, these actions sought to put pressure on the military to continue its transition to civilian rule. On the other hand, Reagan's assumption of the presidency saw a reversal of many of Carter's human rights–focused policies. In this way, an important force that had urged the military to improve its human rights record dissipated, empowering the military to make only small and symbolic gestures toward human rights improvements to satisfy its most vociferous critics, while it continued to stifle domestic dissent and negotiate its exit from power on the best terms possible with the renewed support of the U.S. government.

From a transnational human rights group perspective, AI and WOLA demonstrated a high degree of continuity in their advocacy before and after the plebiscite. For example, Amnesty International, which played a fundamental role in the 1970s in raising awareness about Uruguay's plight to international audiences, continued to spotlight abuses by the military government and push for transition. The organization issued urgent actions, adopted prisoners of conscience, waged letter writing campaigns, sent a delegation to the country to investigate human rights practices, and submitted materials to the UN documenting Uruguay's "consistent pattern of gross human rights violations."[130] WOLA also publicized continual abuses such as military-mandated newspaper closures and crackdowns on writers, editors, and activists.[131] With these efforts, AI and WOLA continued to raise global awareness about the military's ongoing human rights violations, focusing on disappearances, political imprisonment, and torture.

These two groups' advocacy was also joined by a new international human rights organization: Americas Watch. Although scholars studying Americas Watch tend to focus on its advocacy against U.S. intervention in Central America, its work on Uruguay demonstrates how the group also became an important player in raising awareness of human rights abuses by dictatorships of the Southern Cone. Aryeh Neier helped found Americas Watch as a spin-off of Helsinki Watch. Helsinki Watch was a U.S.-based group created in 1978 to monitor Soviet repression and the rights guaranteed in the 1975 Helsinki Accords through writing reports and issuing statements about human rights abuses.[132] Founded a few years later in 1981, Americas Watch emerged as a response to concerns about the Reagan administration's actions in Central America and the co-opting of human rights for Cold War purposes. Americas Watch sought to focus its efforts explicitly on holding the U.S. government responsible for the same abuses Helsinki Watch was denouncing in the Soviet Union.[133] Together, they formed the Watch Committees, operating out of the same office with the same leadership, finances, staff, and philosophy.[134]

With its focus on Reagan, Americas Watch opened a Washington, DC, office in 1982 under the direction of Argentine exile and former political prisoner Juan Méndez.[135] Indeed, Americas Watch's hiring of Méndez demonstrates the group's commitment to advocating against Southern Cone dictatorships, which it did by sending missions to the region and conducting its own research, testifying at congressional hearings, and alerting the press to violations. Neier also recruited Robert Goldman as one of Americas Watch's founding members, for both his expertise on international humanitarian law and his deep experience working on human rights issues in Uruguay. Before his work with Americas Watch, he had been hired by the Inter-American Commission on Human Rights, SIJAU, and WOLA to write reports and speak out against the abuses by the military.[136] He brought this expertise to Americas Watch and helped it develop expertise within the Southern Cone, including Uruguay.

Americas Watch devoted most of its initial work on Uruguay to raising awareness about the continued mistreatment of political prisoners. For the first few years after the plebiscite, Patricia "Polly" Pittman was Americas Watch's representative in the region. She first came to Argentina in 1982 on a Ford Foundation internship at CELS.[137] There, she shared an office with two Uruguayan exiles who were working to oppose the dictatorship. However, due to the repression in Uruguay, they were unable to travel back to the country, so she went frequently on their behalf, smuggling out information about the human rights violations taking place.[138] This role led to more extensive work for several Uruguayan and international organizations, including Americas Watch, that lasted throughout the decade. According to Americas Watch's own reports, Pittman played a "leading role in helping human rights activists" in Uruguay.[139] Pittman helped develop the organization's portfolio on Uruguay, and in 1984 Americas Watch sent its first mission to the country to report on the continued violations by the military government.[140] Although it was the youngest of these international groups, Americas Watch played an important role in publicizing the abuses still occurring and in keeping up pressure on the regime. Amnesty International, WOLA, and Americas Watch often worked with each other, went on joint fact-finding missions, and amplified each other's efforts.[141] Yet, each had its own concerted focus and methods, serving to keep Uruguay on the international radar. Thus, international human rights groups continued and even increased their efforts on behalf of human rights in Uruguay.

Adding to the international clamor was the Ford Foundation's interest in providing financial support to Uruguayan groups challenging the dictatorship. The Ford Foundation's work on Uruguay began in 1978 when it commissioned a report on the high rate of physician imprisonment.[142] However, it took four years to even complete this report because, as described in Chapter 2, the Uruguayan military stonewalled the Foundation's attempts to investigate conditions on the ground. Early efforts to fund human rights work in Uruguay were met with fear from lawyers and activists and failed to get off the ground in the 1970s. Following the plebiscite, however, Ford attempted again to make connections with domestic groups.

As the plebiscite occurred in Uruguay in November 1980, human rights became one of the Foundation's six major programmatic themes.[143] The first grant issued in Uruguay that was directly related to human rights was for the Grupo de Estudios sobre la Condición de la Mujer en Uruguay (Study Group on the Situation of Women in Uruguay [GRECMU]). GRECMU was a group of social scientists that investigated women's participation in the labor force, and Ford supported their research on how women were impacted by the military's repression by, for example, having to become the family's primary breadwinner when husbands or brothers were imprisoned or blacklisted from employment opportunities. Thus, Ford's first grant in Uruguay provided funding to study these effects of the dictatorship, rather than funding to directly challenge the military.[144] In 1984, the Ford Foundation's human rights program began to explore how to support Uruguayan groups engaged in the investigation and documentation of human rights abuses.[145] The grant was not awarded until 1985, after elections were held, and Ford ended up having more of an impact in Uruguay's post-transition period. Yet, the origins of its involvement and support of domestic human rights work began in the early 1980s, when its work, along with that of other international NGOs, played a role in keeping Uruguay's plight on the international radar as a means to keep pressure on the regime.

In contrast to these human rights groups, which continued to spotlight ongoing abuses in Uruguay, Reagan embraced the dictatorship.[146] Upon taking office, the Reagan administration eschewed Carter's foreign policy objectives and refocused U.S. strategic goals within a binary anti-communist framework, particularly in the first years of his administration.[147] Through these efforts, Reagan promoted a limited perspective on what constituted human rights within a narrow civil and political lens and focused criticism of abuses toward communist regimes. These priority shifts reshaped relations between the United States and Uruguay, as Reagan viewed the military's actions as part of the cost of fighting the Cold War against potential subversives. As such, his administration reinstated military aid, ceased public criticism of Uruguay's human rights abuses, and cheered small and symbolic improvements, even when continued repression on the ground contradicted the U.S.'s public praise.

At a broader administration level, Reagan reflected these changes in some of his choices for key cabinet positions. First, Reagan nominated Jeanne Kirkpatrick as the U.S. ambassador to the UN. Kirkpatrick gained notoriety for her 1979 article in *Commentary*, which criticized Carter's human rights policy toward South American nations. It argued that anti-communist governments, even if authoritarian, should be embraced while pushing for gradual liberalization, rather than focusing on direct criticism, economic pressure, and shaming.[148] This appealed to Reagan's Cold War objectives, and once she was confirmed, he dispatched Kirkpatrick, along with "roving" ambassador Vernon Walter, to South America.[149] On the trip, Reagan's emissaries relayed the administration's anti-communist objectives, overlooking the very human rights violations that Carter had tried to pressure these governments to improve. Similarly, Reagan nominated Ernest Lefever to replace Patricia Derian as the Assistant Secretary of State for Human Rights and Humanitarian Affairs. Despite being named to the position most responsible for bringing a human rights perspective to the administration, Lefever was on record as vocally opposed to "giving human rights a central place" in foreign policy considerations.[150] While Derian had been a forceful advocate behind Carter's human rights policies, particularly in Latin America, Lefever openly derided human rights as a diplomatic tool.[151] WOLA's Joe Eldridge explained that the human rights community "had held Pat Derian in very high regard, we kind of revered her. To try to replace her with Ernest Lefever was an insult, an abomination."[152] Eldridge's reaction epitomized the feelings of many congressional Democrats and human rights advocates, and after intense mobilization by both groups, the panel voted 13-4 to recommend that the Senate reject his nomination. Lefever withdrew his name from consideration soon after.[153] Elliott Abrams was eventually confirmed for the position, although he too adopted the Kirkpatrick view of human rights, illustrating how Reagan reoriented his human rights policy to primarily use it as a tool against the Soviet Union and leftist regimes, while embracing anti-communist authoritarians.[154]

Uruguayans' reactions to Reagan's electoral victory reflected this shift in human rights policy—the military celebrated Carter's defeat while the burgeoning domestic human rights movement despaired.[155] In the weeks following the election, the Uruguayan government tried to determine exactly how these changes would impact bilateral relations. In carefully catalogued clippings from U.S. newspapers, the Foreign Ministry highlighted statements from various U.S. officials, such as Secretary of State Alexander Haig, who asserted that in the Reagan policy calculus, "international terrorism will take the place of human rights."[156] They also marked up statements from U.S. representative Clement Zablocki, who explained that "there would be a revision of foreign policy based on the interest of national security." This change from a focus on human rights, he explained, included a review of U.S. "sale[s] of military equipment to Latin America . . . including perhaps the sale to some places that they didn't currently sell."[157] Thus, as Reagan laid out his desire to strengthen relations between the United States and South American anti-communist military regimes, the government kept a close, hopeful watch on any indication that its stance toward Uruguay would change.

The first positive sign for the military came soon after Reagan's inauguration, when the government received word that Reagan was reevaluating the Carter administration's foreign aid standards. Indeed, one of Reagan's first foreign meetings upon taking office was with Argentine military president-designee Roberto Eduardo Viola. At the meeting in March 1981, Reagan indicated that the United States would like to resume assistance, a move that flashed a clear signal across the Rio de la Plata of similar aid renewals.[158] As this news reached Uruguayan shores, Rear Admiral Hugo Márquez responded to this possibility of receiving military aid by telling reporters that he was "very satisfied with the presence of Ronald Reagan in the U.S. government. He is a man with the right idea about things."[159]

Uruguay saw tangible changes by the summer of 1981, when Reagan reversed Carter's policy of blocking loan requests from Chile, Argentina, Paraguay, and Uruguay in development banks.[160] This shift released a $40 million loan to Uruguay for a project to improve its telecommunications services. The Reagan administration also green-lighted a third-country transfer of arms from South Korea to Uruguay.[161] Much to the delight of the Uruguayan embassy in the U.S., which sent a flurry of excited memos about the shift back to Montevideo, the Reagan administration cited its improvement in human rights since the plebiscite and added that the United States no longer viewed punitive aid measures as an effective means to influence governments.[162] In doing so, the Reagan administration cheered superficial and small human rights improvements, prioritizing warming relations between the United States and Southern Cone countries, which Reagan saw as the "true bastions of anti-communism in Latin America."[163] Focused on "preventing another Cuba," the Reagan administration centered what it viewed as its primary national security objective of countering Soviet expansionism in its foreign policy. Particularly at this early stage of the administration, it was more important for allies to be anti-communist than to uphold human rights standards.

Reagan's changes did not go uncontested by the human rights community in the United States. Forty-nine members of Congress sent a letter to Treasury Secretary Donald Regan protesting these decisions and citing continued reports from Uruguay that the same violations were still occurring.[164] Democratic representative Samuel Gejdenson also tried to pass a House bill prohibiting the sale of weapons to the country, similar to what Koch did in 1976.[165] Despite public hearings and testimony by U.S. activists and Uruguayan exiles in the House Committee on Foreign Relations, there were not enough votes in Congress to block the sale. Reagan's reversal of Carter's human rights policy extended from the administration to the legislative branch, enabling Reagan to effectively shift U.S. foreign policy priorities to a more Cold War–centered framework.[166]

While the Uruguayan military applauded these changes, the opposition found these policy shifts unsettling as it fought to gain momentum after the plebiscite. When Juan Raúl Ferreira testified before the Senate Committee on Foreign Relations in September 1981, he criticized these changes, explaining that the administration's "rush to applaud" superficial improvements "undermined the context in which they were made and did not focus on whether any real steps were to be taken to improve the human rights record of the regime."[167] As Ferreira went on to explain, the Reagan administration's actions "have strengthened the position of the dictatorship in our country, and the position of hardliners within the regime, precisely at a time when the pressure of the democratic forces in Uruguay and the initiative of the democratic sectors of the Armed forces were making a political opening realistically possible."[168] A SERPAJ spokesperson also decried Reagan's policy, relaying that under Carter, the U.S. Embassy was a place where "there were people we could go to, people that would receive us and listen to our problems. But that doesn't happen anymore."[169] WOLA further acknowledged Reagan's impact on its advocacy strategy. Instead of lobbying the executive branch to put pressure on Uruguay's military regime, the organization began to focus on Congress and the media, since the Reagan administration was not receptive to the organization's efforts.[170] Finally, the recently resurgent Uruguayan press decried this new U.S. foreign policy, publishing articles with the blazing headline "Go Home Kirkpatrick!" when the UN ambassador was in Montevideo in August 1981.[171] Although the press was at times unable to directly criticize the Uruguayan government, it was within its new freedoms to excoriate the United States' resurgent focus on battling communism in Latin America.

These rebukes appear to have had no effect on the Reagan administration. Just a few weeks later, on September 24, 1981, Haig met with Uruguay's Foreign Minister, Estanislao Valdés Otero, and confirmed friendly relations with the Uruguayan military in a meeting that was "noteworthy for the high degree of candor and goodwill evident on both sides." Reaffirming all of Ferreira's criticisms, Haig lauded Uruguay for "insisting upon a return to the democratic process, thereby serving as a model of encouragement for the rest of Latin America." In return, the Uruguayan government sought assurances that the United States would no longer criticize its human rights record and even requested that the administration control the State Department and discourage unfriendly acts by Congress and the U.S. press.[172]

Valdés's wish was at least partially granted in the next round of State Department 502B country reports. Instead of using the annual reports on the state of human rights in Uruguay to spotlight abuses as Carter had done, Reagan's State Department praised the way that the military's timetable for transition "has been adhered to, and the Government has often publicly renewed its commitment to it." The report emphasized these cosmetic moves, even in the face of political actors being prohibited from participating in elections and the continual collapse of talks between the military and the civil society.[173] As Neier explains, the reports became skewed so that they assessed the practices of left-wing governments far more harshly than those of governments that portrayed themselves as anti-communist allies of the United States.[174] While human rights groups criticized these whitewashed reports, the Reagan administration continued to applaud the military government's improvements.[175] These flattering assessments demonstrate the low bar the Reagan administration set for praising Uruguayan human rights improvements as a way to recenter its bilateral relationship with the country on fighting the Cold War. They were not a thorough analysis of the various types of violations that were occurring in Uruguay.

In what proved to be circular logic, the Reagan administration used its biased assessment to justify further increases in aid. In 1982, Reagan resumed direct military aid to the Uruguayan military. A year later, in 1983, Reagan requested $50,000 in direct military training funds for the Uruguayan government, which was set to increase to $60,000 a year later.[176] These new funding initiatives demonstrate how Reagan reframed Uruguay's stunted negotiations about a possible return to democracy as human rights successes, even as groups such as Americas Watch mobilized to try and block these measures, citing over 1,000 political prisoners and the military's continued abuses.[177]

There was ultimately a disconnect between how the U.S. government spoke publicly of Uruguay's transition as being orderly and on schedule with substantial human rights improvements, and the tenuous and fraught advances playing out on the ground.[178] As one international NGO pointed out, there were "distortions and contradictory assessments" of the state of human rights.[179] Another group called Reagan's policy "shockingly uninformed about severe encroachments on the basic rights of Uruguayans; much less do they [Reagan officials] seem interested in supporting efforts to bring them to an end."[180] This disconnect was perhaps no better exemplified then in mid-1984, when the Uruguayan government arrested and imprisoned two of the most prominent opposition actors who had spent much of the dictatorship in exile, Wilson Ferreira and his son, Juan Raúl Ferreira. The Reagan administration failed to reproach the government for this blatant act of political repression, a silence that the *New York Times* called "stunning." Instead, Reagan's team just said that Wilson's return represented a "complicating factor" in the elections.[181]

As historian Hal Brands explains, Reagan's policy toward Latin America more broadly was a shift from Carter's human rights focus to, by the end of

Reagan's first term in office, the promotion of democracy, with "a rather simplistic view of what constituted democracy."[182] In other words, he considered that countries had reached a basic threshold of democracy if they elected a government (or, in the case of Uruguay, were moving toward elections). This proved true even if the country's practices were undemocratic, or even if the elections were not completely fair and open, as long as the regimes were anti-communist.[183] As the Reagan administration asserted in 1983, "Our interest remains constant: to encourage Uruguay's return to democracy as the best means of ensuring the country's longer-term political stability, and to support the government's commitment to an open economy as the most effective means for economic recovery and sound growth."[184] Reagan viewed democracy and economic liberalization as fundamentally intertwined, and therefore encouraged political reform as part of a push toward neoliberalism. However, the broader human rights emphasis of the Carter administration was gone. Therefore, even while international human rights groups persisted in their efforts to draw attention to abuses, the U.S. government's changed position gave the Uruguayan military some international legitimacy and cover to continue its repression during the extended negotiation process.[185]

Negotiations Stalled

As the years dragged on, there were further setbacks in negotiations over a possible return to civilian rule. In May 1983, talks at the Parque Hotel collapsed amid disagreements over national security and further retrenchment by the military. Two months later, in July, the Blanco and Colorado parties submitted a list of conditions for the talks to continue, which included allowing more political involvement, opening the press, and trade union freedoms. Meanwhile, the military's demands had hardly shifted from the 1980 plebiscite. Its proposals included keeping the National Security Council, allowing the president to declare a state of subversion, holding suspects for fifteen days without trial, and incorporating military judges into the judiciary.[186] Unable to bridge the gap amid continued arrests of politicians, the parties felt obliged to withdraw in protest. The hope for progress dissolved yet again.[187]

By the end of 1983, few advances had been made. For almost a year after the Parque Hotel talks failed, attempts to return to a formal negotiation process were thwarted by an unwillingness on both sides to agree on the terms of discussion. This difficulty was evident in some of the more prominent and contradictory cases of political imprisonment. For example, Líber Seregni, the leader of the Frente Amplio who had been in jail for nine years of the military dictatorship, was released in March 1984.[188] While this seemed like a positive development, the military proscribed him from running for office or voting for two years. Then, as mentioned earlier, the military arrested former Blanco leader Wilson Ferreira soon after his return to Uruguay. In June 1984, the former leader of the Blanco Party returned to his home country with his son following eleven years of exile. Awaiting his ferry from Buenos Aires was a large group of about four hundred supporters and journalists. Upon stepping onto the Uruguayan shores, he and his son were immediately imprisoned. The elder Ferreira was charged with aiding the Tupamaros and inviting foreign intervention by criticizing the military, while his son was arrested on accusations of insulting the military and attempting to undermine the government.[189] For most of the dictatorship, any public references to his name or references in newspaper articles had been prohibited. In addition, the military proscribed him from participating in politics. This latest arrest was the final straw. Ferreira's imprisonment stymied attempts at negotiation. Members of his party pulled out of the negotiations until the military would release him from prison.[190] The push and pull of these advancements and setbacks continued throughout this period.

Meanwhile, the Uruguayan economy faltered. Right before the primaries in 1982, the peso collapsed in value.[191] From 1982 to 1983, the gross domestic product (GDP) fell by 14 percent, and inflation exceeded 50 percent in 1983, which led to high unemployment and a sharp decline in incomes.[192] The military had boasted about its strong economic policies for years, and this unraveling caused even previous supporters to begin to lose faith in the military and its economic project, compounding mounting frustration from opposition actors.

The stalled talks ultimately produced paradoxical results. On the one hand, civil society actors grew more emboldened as the intransigence of the military became evident. On Independence Day, August 25, 1983, Uruguayans in Montevideo staged a *caceroleo*, a coordinated banging of pots and pans across the city to protest the continued military rule. As negotiating delays dragged on, the protest movement grew. In late November of the same year, over 300,000 citizens converged at the Obelisco monument to call for the military to abrogate power and return the country to democracy.[193] Located at the intersection of the main streets of Avenida 18 de Julio and Artigas Boulevard, the obelisk was a carefully chosen symbolic location for the rally, as it commemorated the one hundredth anniversary of the country's constitution. Read by one of Uruguay's most well-known actors and writers, Alberto Candeau, a proclamation was presented by the people declaring their right to exercise suffrage and reinstitute democracy in Uruguay.[194] Among those gathered were Familiares, which took to the streets for the first time.[195] Protests continued in January 1984 with a coordinated general strike that paralyzed the capital. Another strike in June preceded the restart of talks, this time at the Naval Club.

While civil society increasingly challenged the military directly, the further repression and failed negotiations tempered expectations and revealed the limits of the transition. For example, after the January 1984 strike, the military outlawed the PIT and forbade the press to publish any information about strikes and workers' occupation.[196] Roslik was killed in San Javier a few months later, and by May 1984 there were still at least eight hundred political prisoners.[197] These new rules and decrees as late as 1984 sent a powerful signal to the population about the difficult process of negotiating with the military. Publicly, the military appeared intent on retaining some semblance of power. Behind the scenes, an internal power struggle emerged between those who believed that losing the plebiscite meant continuing the redemocratization process and those who thought democracy should be taken off the table completely.[198] Nevertheless, politicians were determined to find a solution and made more and more compromises to try to enact a pragmatic transition. Fundamentally, the transition centered on the negotiations with the political elite rather than those involved in the social mobilization.[199] In fact, the Blancos and Colorados had very little contact with human rights organizations between 1980 and 1984. Only the Frente Amplio maintained consistent communication. However, the military sidelined the Frente Amplio for much of the negotiation process because of their leftist beliefs.[200] As a result, the explicit issue of human rights was largely absent from the negotiations.

The final round of negotiations began in June 1984, and even then talks were constantly on the verge of collapsing. Some politicians almost abandoned the discussion over disagreements about whether civilians would still be allowed to be held without charges. Military justice similarly created stumbling blocks. Disagreements erupted over whether violent acts committed by the military "within their exercise of duty" would be handled by civilian or military courts. These conflicts illustrated the extent to which the negotiations struggled with the most basic questions of the military's future role in a democratic environment. By the end of negotiations, opposition politicians had reduced their major issue to "how to persuade the military (which still had complete control of the country) to hand over power to democratically elected civilians."[201] Meanwhile, the military leaders hoped to figure out "how to extricate themselves from rule without damaging their institution or risking human-rights trials."[202] In late August, both sides finally announced that elections would be held in November 1984 to pave the way for a democratic government to take over in March 1985. A compromise had been reached.

In the month that followed the talks, the military repealed many of its institutional acts that created and sustained its repressive apparatus. Meanwhile, arrangements for elections accelerated.[203] What is still largely debated was whether there was an agreement about impunity for the military, or at the very least a tacit recognition of the military's institutional autonomy.[204] There is evidence suggesting that while such a pact might have been implicit in the success of such difficult negotiations, participants most likely sidestepped any explicit discussion of trials since negotiations had stalled so many times over controversial issues. Scholars acknowledge that one of the reasons the Naval Club talks even occurred was the ambiguity of some of the thornier issues, a lesson that all sides had learned after the collapse of the talks at the Parque Hotel. Any insistence on the total resolution of all these disputes would have resulted in another round of failed negotiations, which is partially why no formal document ever emerged.[205]

When a democratic government did finally take office in March 1985, the nature of these negotiations had deep implications. The very long and difficult process to agree on the conditions of democratic rule discouraged contentious topics, such as human rights.[206] In addition, it exposed the tenuous alliance between the political elite and civil society. The political elite focused on negotiation and agreed to a more limited vision of a reconstituted democratic country. Therefore, hopes for promoting human rights considerations were considerably dampened. As editor and future politician Manuel Flores Silva would later state, "It is not whether the subject of human rights were considered or not at the Naval Club. There is a consensus that the topic was not addressed but sidestepped."[207] In contrast to Argentina where much of the negotiations process and the elections discourse focused on human rights violations, very few political conversations in Uruguay grappled with these issues as part of the negotiation process. Instead, opposition actors pushed a much smaller list of human rights concerns, focusing primarily on amnesty for political prisoners, the return of exiles, and job restoration for the thousands of individuals who had been fired for political reasons. In the end, the decision to sidestep the topic of possible trials during negotiations left the issue of accountability to be fought over by future politicians and civil society actors, creating new fault lines and an even wider gap between those who had suffered losses during the dictatorship and many who would go on to hold political power. And, as the subsequent chapters explain, politicians ultimately had long memories with respect to how easily discussions over human rights and accountability could produce backlash from the military.

Conclusion

It had taken four years from the date of the plebiscite to reach an agreement on the transitional terms amid continued repression and suffering. Fundamentally, 1981 to 1984 encompassed a profound and challenging period in Uruguay. While the emergence of a domestic human rights movement reflected the resilience of the population and connections with both international and regional groups, the long negotiations and retrenchment by the military exposed the gaps in what human rights in a new democracy would focus on, and the extent to which activists and politicians might diverge on their priorities. All sides also had to grapple with the implications of a new U.S. administration, demonstrating further divergences in how actors were defining, and redefining, human rights. At a broader level, the long process of negotiation revealed the blurry boundaries between dictatorship and democracy that had also characterized Uruguay's slow descent into military rule. Scholar Charles Gillespie described this process in the early 1980s as a "tortuous path to democratic transition."[208] Indeed, while it is easy to look back and assume the transition was inevitable after the plebiscite, in reality it had been fraught with twists and turns over an incredibly long period. The effects of this arduous process were felt immediately but became even more evident in the initial years after a civilian government was finally restored.

CHAPTER 6

From Elections to the Ley de Caducidad

Uruguay's election was far from perfect. In November 1984, the military permitted Uruguayans to vote for new representatives for the first time in thirteen years, but many restrictions remained in place. Blanco leader Wilson Ferreira languished in prison and the military prohibited him from appearing on the ballot. Líber Seregni, the founder and spiritual head of the leftist Frente Amplio, had been out of jail for eight months, but the military still barred him from participating in the election. Only the center-right Colorado Party had its top candidate, Julio María Sanguinetti, lead the ticket without the military imposing any obstacles. These proscriptions on who could run compounded the difficult conditions in which the voting took place. When polls opened, four long and arduous years had passed since Uruguayans rejected the military's repressive charter. Despite the excitement following the success of the "no" vote in 1980, further crackdowns and stalled negotiations had tempered citizens' expectations about the possibilities of a new democracy as month after month went by with continued military rule.

A breakthrough in negotiations had finally occurred in August 1984 with the Naval Club Pact, which paved the path for elections in November of that year. By the time Election Day arrived, the atmosphere in Uruguay reflected little of this difficult history. Reporters chronicled the week leading up to the vote, during which buses, ferries, and planes from neighboring countries filled with eager expatriates returning to cast their ballots. Many of the passengers had been living in exile and came streaming back across the border to participate in the momentous election.[1]

As the polls opened on the morning of November 25, the excitement was palpable. Smiling citizens flooded the streets on their way to cast their ballots, while restaurants filled with jubilant gatherers indulging in celebratory sausages and juicy steaks. People drove their cars through the streets honking enthusiastically, waving Uruguayan flags from the roofs and windows.[2] For a brief moment in time, the election results mattered less than the physical act of casting ballots after such a long wait. A poll worker for the Frente Amplio remarked with a smile, "This is what we have been waiting for."[3]

Two days later, the country turned its attention to the results. The electoral commission declared Sanguinetti the winner. Almost 90 percent of eligible voters had cast their ballot with just over 40 percent in favor of the moderate Colorado Party. The Blancos, traditionally the other strong party in the country, earned approximately 34 percent of the vote. Meanwhile, the Frente Amplio also saw a strong showing in the capital city and garnered just over 20 percent of the national vote—far behind the other two parties, but more than the military had projected after proscribing so many of their candidates. While it was another three months until Sanguinetti or a new legislature assumed power, the military government's departure was officially underway.

What remained uncertain was what the restored democracy would look like. Ever since the 1980 plebiscite, citizens had battled to reconstruct civil society through the reemergence of a vibrant student movement, unions, and new human rights groups. However, the difficult transitional years had revealed divisions between these sectors, particularly over their different conceptions of human rights. During the lead-up to the elections, different factions increasingly began to look beyond minimalist visions of being free from torture, political imprisonment, and disappearances. In many cases, they started to advocate for a more expansive vision of human rights based on a socioeconomic rights platform. For example, unions turned much of their attention to the right to fair wages, while the student movement focused on recovering an autonomous education system. Based on their own concerns and advocacy aims, these groups often diverged along interest lines as other important projects of reconstituting democracy took center stage.

These divisions became even more evident after Sanguinetti's inauguration. Both the legislature and civil society groups advocated for a much broader rights vision that oftentimes recalled earlier social justice visions from the 1960s. The difference in the post-dictatorship period was that these groups now began at times to articulate these claims within a human rights discourse that had grown in prominence throughout the 1970s. In this way, there was a paradoxical cost of human rights success. The powerful international language bolstered a varied and robust rights agenda but also lessened the impact and focus on accountability for the military's crimes. This became a major issue as the new government grappled with whether to address the military's past human rights abuses. The debate over accountability became an even more pressing concern as Uruguay watched neighboring Argentina struggle with the consequences of bringing the generals of its military regime to trial for crimes during its dictatorship.

This chapter explores these domestic dynamics and the changing uses of a human rights discourse between the electoral campaigns starting in August 1984 until December 22, 1986, when Parliament passed an amnesty law for the military's crimes. Fundamentally, it examines claims within the literature on this period, which tends to trace the amnesty law directly to the Naval Club Pact in August 1984, when political parties and the military agreed to hold elections. Many accounts of this period draw a direct link between the two events, arguing that part of the deal to hold elections involved the promise not to prosecute members of the military for human rights abuses.[4] Yet, examining this twenty-two-month interlude reveals that amnesty was not a foregone conclusion. Justice for human rights abuses committed during the dictatorship was hotly debated at various societal levels after the election. Reading legislative minutes, newspapers, and the archives of human rights groups exposes that it initially appeared likely that there would be some societal reckoning with and accountability for these past violations. Among other moves, Parliament passed various measures to begin investigations into the crimes of the dictatorship, and human rights groups began to file cases within the court system—actions that existing scholarship often overlooks.

However, as Sanguinetti's presidency continued and cases began to reach the courts, Sanguinetti started working more closely with the military and received increasing pressure to stop these moves toward accountability. As such, a sense of anxiety about the hard-won pact for elections spread throughout society, reigniting fears of a possible return to dictatorship and invoking the difficult negotiations for transition. The hope that justice for the military's human rights violations could actually occur diminished, especially as amnesty proposals began to flood the legislature. On the one hand, the legislative move toward amnesty reunited a civil society that had fractured along interest lines. Together, they advocated to continue measures for justice. On the other hand, it also exposed the fragility of the new democracy and human rights culture within the halls of power that split along clear party lines at this critical moment.

Surveying the period between the November 1984 elections and the passage of the amnesty law reveals three key insights. First, the new government attempted to enact accountability measures in the first months of its rule. These initial proposals challenge historiographical narratives that brush over these important initiatives, revealing the way the commitment to accountability measures for human rights violations evolved after the elections. Second, the debates over justice in this period expose the precarity of Uruguay's promised democratic transition and the fluidity of competing rights concerns. In addition to confronting the abuses of the dictatorship, activists began to organize and fight for a broader idea of social and economic rights. This discourse recaptured many of the tenets of the 1960s social justice visions that had been subsumed during the direct battles against the military. Finally, this chapter explores the complex reintegration of the political parties as human rights allies in flux. Many of the fiercest critics of the dictatorship on human rights grounds were much less concerned about justice for these abuses once they assumed elected posts and began working with the military to maintain a tenuous balance of power. Examining the Parliamentary debates about the amnesty law raises questions about the changing human rights priorities, not only among leftist activists, but also among various political actors in the complex interplay between justice and access to power, particularly during the key transitional period between the election and the passage of the amnesty law.

The Election

Campaigns for the November elections began as soon as the military announced the date at the conclusion of the Naval Club talks, albeit under continued military censorship and further threats of candidate proscription.[5] After the collapse of the Argentine regime amid the failed Malvinas (Falkland) invasion and economic emergency, the presidential campaign there openly discussed human rights issues. A year before Uruguay's election, Raúl Alfonsín's candidacy hinged on "a triple promise" of human, social, and political rights that included a vow to investigate human rights abuses, while his opponent, Peronist candidate Ítalo Luder, guaranteed to uphold the military's self-amnesty.[6] No such debate occurred in Uruguay.[7] While the Blanco and Frente Amplio candidates expressed tepid support for accountability, they did not "consistently or determinedly champion it" as part of their electoral platform.[8] It had taken four years for the military to agree to finally transition to civilian rule, and candidates stayed focused on making sure the elections wouldn't be called off. Therefore, under the military's careful watch, politicians in Uruguay

limited the terms of debate in the lead-up to the election, and no accountability promises emerged in the official campaigns.

Instead, the election took place amid what some scholars have called a
"unanimous rejection of the regime's economic policies."[9] Economic issues
dominated the campaign and debates in the press about the future of the
country. Inflation in 1984 reached 66 percent while unemployment in Montevideo lingered at about 13 percent. Meanwhile, real wages were half the
level they were when the military first came to power in 1973.[10] These concerns animated discussions about the election, whereas there was an absence
of debate about the crimes committed during the dictatorship. For example,
many young writers defined their vision for a new democracy in economic
terms. Instead of framing ideas for the future in terms of being free from
torture or political imprisonment, they disparaged the military for their poor
policies that put so many Uruguayans in a precarious economic condition.
Editorials called for a transition that would ensure that the military would be
outside of the governing structure. Juan Carlos Doyenart was one of many
writers who began to imagine a country where workers were "the main ben-
eficiaries" of a new social order, "achieving substantial improvements in the
level of wages, employment opportunities and freedom of union activities . . .
all which gives them the real capacity to negotiate and participate in the definition of economic policies."[11] These concerns were motivated by the poor
economic conditions of the early 1980s that helped drive the military from
power, but they also contributed to defining the terms of a future democracy.

Other election issues focused on the myriad of other concerns the nation
faced in light of the military's transition. These included how to reconstitute a
vibrant and independent university system, the reinstatement of social security benefits, and the guarantee of workers' rights. Candidates and the press
agreed that these issues needed to be addressed.[12] In the months leading up
to the election, candidates wrote articles about these concerns, and the press
covered their responses to a variety of economic and social topics that animated the electoral debate. However, in all the media coverage devoted to the
impending vote, rarely did candidates or the press address how the nation
would deal with the military's crimes. To the extent that a rights language was
invoked, it was mostly in reaction to social and economic rights rather than
the military's violations.

The one exception to discussing human rights issues resided with the
Concertación Nacional Programática (CONAPRO), a forum for dialogue
between political party representatives, social organizations, unions, and

employers in the country.[13] Starting in September 1984, they worked to secure a consensus on transitional issues ranging from the reincorporation of returning exiles to housing and health policies, educational concerns, and human rights topics.[14] Their goals centered not only on the military's institutional transition back to the barracks, but also on a project of reconstructing the country and recovering a civil society that had been devastated during the twelve years of the dictatorship from an economic, social, cultural, and moral perspective. Within CONAPRO, the subject of human rights earned some consideration in the sense that the group worked on specific aspects of how to recover guarantees of human rights in a democratic society and how to confront the possibility of moving forward with trials regarding crimes against humanity.[15] The group even debated how to empower the judiciary to be able to carry out these investigations. While at best vague, these efforts demonstrate that discussions about accountability for human rights violations were not completely absent during the electoral period.[16] Belying the idea that the Naval Club Pact a few months earlier had shut the door completely, CONAPRO offers evidence that the idea was discussed in the lead-up to elections.[17]

However, human rights discussions, both from the press and from CONAPRO, focused less on accountability and more on securing an agreement to release all political prisoners who were still incarcerated.[18] With violations still occurring daily as the elections neared, debate regarding human rights centered on officially ending torture as a governmental policy and on the release of the hundreds of people still in prison—two of the main human rights issues that had dominated discussions since the 1970s.[19] Accountability for members of the military, while discussed, was not the emphasis.

Therefore, while CONAPRO provides evidence that all three political parties were discussing human rights accountability at least in vague terms, the election debates eventually split along traditional party lines as jockeying for power took center stage. The temporary unity against the dictatorship dissipated as the groups battled over who would be elected to lead the country in its new democratic period. The CDU, which had been such an important force in uniting the political parties during the 1980 plebiscite, dissolved in the final stages of negotiations in 1984. In part, the rupture revealed diverging platforms over what took precedence in establishing a new democracy, and also a growing realization of party interests in the upcoming elections.

Even candidates on the Left, those most sympathetic to accountability claims, did not focus on this issue during the campaign. Frente candidates concentrated on dismantling the apparatus of the repressive dictatorship and ensuring that amnesty for their fellow compatriots was part of the transition process.[20] While some prominent Frente Amplistas had been released from jail in the months leading up to the elections, hundreds remained imprisoned and thus provided a focal point for campaigns.[21] Other prominent members of the party concentrated on unifying the Frente Amplio coalition around modest objectives and not upsetting the tenuous agreement to hold elections. Indeed, beyond ensuring the military returned to the barracks and political prisoners received general and unrestricted amnesty, the Frente platform promoted the right to health and fair wages, increasing pensions for workers, recovering independent education, and promoting agrarian reform.[22] These were broad leftist objectives around socioeconomic rights that didn't center justice as part of their platform. When mentioned at all, for example by the *sublema* Democracia Avanzado, it was included as a small point in a large eight-page program in a vague reference to autonomy for the judicial branch to oversee national reconciliation and protect human rights—not a specific call to justice for members of the military.[23] Others, such as the Christian Democrats, studiously avoided the discussion of justice, stressing instead the importance of reparative measures to "avoid latent misgivings and mutual resentment that would affect future coexistence."[24] If anything, the Christian Democrats appeared to be arguing against the idea of justice for human rights abuses altogether, instead focusing on the reestablishment of democratic governance, amnesty for political prisoners, and the return of exiles.

Raúl Sendic encapsulates this moderating impulse in the elections. Sendic, the leftist leader and former Tupamaro head, had been in jail from September 1972 to March 1984.[25] During the election, he encouraged former Tupamaros to engage in political activity, despite concerns about the large number of leftists being proscribed from the ballot. Once the leader and founder of the guerrilla movement that had organized for the violent overthrow of the government rather than participate further in a broken political system, his advocacy for getting involved in the electoral process contributed to the process of pacification and democratization. Sendic's shift reflected a widespread feeling that the overriding national aim was to bring the regime to an end rather than push a controversial political agenda.[26] It was a platform that rested on an expansive vision of socioeconomic human rights—which more closely mirrored activists' collective rights vision from the pre-dictatorship period and which some civil society groups had begun to argue for once again.

One exception to this impulse was the Izquierda Democrática Independiente (IDI), another *sublema* of the Frente Amplio. Overall, this group fit into the general trend of focusing its efforts on legitimate political avenues and how to revive a viable Left. Many of its members in the party had been among those most affected by the military's oppressive rule, and candidates explained their new policy as predicated on "the construction of a just society based on nationalism and progressivism." They articulated this platform by advocating policies of agrarian reform, nationalization of the banks, restoration of labor party rights, and domestic energy development.[27] However, they also discussed human rights in terms of justice. In one campaign document, the IDI explained that they would fight for "parliament to investigate all violations of human rights committed by the military and also economic crimes. Not for vengeance but for JUSTICE."[28] Despite this focus, the IDI never gained much traction. Only one of their members was elected to the Chamber of Deputies in 1984, Nelson Lorenzo Rovira, and he served only one term.[29] Thus, the IDI offers a view of the ideas of a small subsection of the electorate, but does not represent the most widespread electoral emphasis.

In other political parties, another aspect of moderating the call for justice in the military's crimes was the absorption of some of the most outspoken opposition activists of the military into formal political channels. Political scientist Charles Gillespie explains that the most significant renovators in the Colorado Party were Enrique Tarigo, who helped form *Libertad y Cambio*, and Manuel Flores Silva, who led the Corriente Batllista Independiente (CBI), a party with a younger, more progressive following.[30] These men had been two of the most ardent protestors against the dictatorship, founding two critical newspapers during the early 1980s that called for respecting human rights.[31] During the plebiscite and pre-transition period, they used informal political channels to protest and challenge the military regime. Throughout the campaign, however, the introduction of elections and the reemergence of political parties allowed for formal political participation. As a result, their calls for change became less radical within this constrained and censored environment as they sought to gain political office.[32]

Their party was also led by Sanguinetti, who staked his election on moderation and negotiation. Sanguinetti stood out physically for his bushy eyebrows, a trait that had made him instantly recognizable since his emergence on the political scene two decades prior at the age of twenty-six. Before the dictatorship, Sanguinetti had served in various government positions, but during the military's rule, he mainly worked as a journalist. By the early

1980s, he had reentered politics by proving willing to compromise and work with the military during the negotiations after the constitutional plebiscite.[33] Members of the Colorado Party elected him Secretary General in the 1982 internal party elections, and by the time of the general elections in 1984, Sanguinetti was forty-eight years old. His defining eyebrows were graying and his hairline receding, but his moderating impulse made his candidacy palatable to both the military and the broader public. He even had the support of the United States, as the Reagan administration flew him there in early 1984 for top-level meetings with various U.S. officials, demonstrating its clear preference for the Colorado candidate.[34] In campaign materials, Sanguinetti called for "peace, tolerance and change," and focused his policy proposals around economic issues and governmental transparency.[35] The two former agitators assumed Sanguinetti and the Colorados' more moderate position in the final stages of the election.[36]

What all these various voices demonstrate is that, from August to November 1984, the campaigning period witnessed a general moderating impulse, particularly with respect to human rights issues. Worried that the military might crack down again, or perhaps even call off the elections, candidates and social actors from across the political spectrum did not focus on the possibility for justice. Instead, they emphasized the less ambitious goal of ensuring that the elections were carried out. Human rights rhetoric, to the extent that there was any, largely centered around freeing the remaining political prisoners rather than other accountability measures. This abatement in terms of justice for human rights concerns, however, did not mean that leftist candidates had abandoned their advocacy for a more democratic society. Instead, editorials, campaign materials, and organizational minutes illustrate that many Uruguayans began to slowly move toward advocating for recovering a broad array of collective rights that included claims for a strong labor union, fair living wages, and vibrant autonomous universities, rather than focus on the individual rights claims that had been prominent as a protest mechanism during the height of the dictatorship.

The final tallies of the election in late 1984 reflected much of this moderation, as well as the strength of party loyalty within the country. Even with all the turmoil from over a decade of dictatorship, no party received more than a 5 percent difference in the vote from the last elections that had been held in 1971.[37] The primary difference came from those leaving the Blancos and voting for the Frente Amplio, which many attributed to the main Blanco candidate, Wilson Ferreira, being in jail for the elections. When the votes were all counted, the Colorados received 40.2 percent; the Blancos 34.2 percent; and the Frente Amplio 20.8 percent.[38] These results reaffirmed traditional party politics that had largely broken down prior to the coup. It suggested that the voters sought stability and reassurance within traditional party structures over the more radical but less predictable alternatives. With these results, Sanguinetti became the first democratically elected president of the country since 1971.[39]

The Return to Democratic Rule and
Moves Toward Accountability

On March 1, 1985, Sanguinetti, along with his vice president, Enrique Tarigo, were sworn in amid great fanfare. The president rode in an open vehicle from Parliament to the Government House in Independence Plaza, while cheering crowds lined the streets to celebrate their new leader. Foreign dignitaries from around the globe, including the U.S. Secretary of State, George Shultz, also marked the momentous occasion by attending the inauguration.[40] Most human rights groups had a more cautious approach to the day; they waited anxiously to see whether Sanguinetti would live up to the promise of releasing the remaining political prisoners. As one of the main human rights groups, las Madres y Familiares de Uruguayos Desaparecidos Detenidos expressed their hopes that the return to democracy would be interwoven with the remaining prisoners' release, as well as truth and justice.[41] They did not have to wait long. Just days later, one of Sanguinetti's first actions as president was a proposal to release the remaining 340 political prisoners who were still in jail. The move garnered praise from across the political spectrum and from international groups such as Amnesty International, which had been invested in the Uruguayan cause for almost a decade.[42]

Some accounts view the election as the end of the transition—and indeed, it marked the official shift from military rule to elected representation. While some papers declared an end to the dictatorship on the day of the elections back in November, other papers, such as the *Washington Post,* saw the inauguration of Sanguinetti four months later as the official arrival of democracy.[43] Indeed, in March 1985, the president and Parliament assumed control over military issues such as promotions, budgets, and missions, while establishing civilian authority over the Ministry of Defense. Although the military was again legally subordinated to an elected government, questions remained regarding exactly how much influence the military would continue to have over the newly elected government and if there would be accountability for the crimes committed during the dictatorship.

On some level, the idea of military action to stop accountability efforts was a dark threat that hung over the new administration's triumphant inauguration. For example, on the eve of Sanguinetti taking office, Lieutenant General Hugo Medina warned that "if we are obliged (by the courts), we will have no choice but to carry out another coup d'etat," explicitly stating Uruguayans' greatest fears and stirring a political firestorm.[44] These statements and the moderate nature of the elections with respect to addressing human rights has led some scholars to trace a direct line between the agreements made in the 1984 Naval Club Pact and the amnesty law's passage twenty-two months later.[45] Still, the amnesty was not a foregone conclusion. The excitement of a democratic transition brought hope to many citizens. In fact, as part of the transition, all military-appointed judges on the Supreme Court were dismissed and replaced by professionally trained ones, which many believed would offer judicial independence to the body.[46] Indeed, the initial months of Sanguinetti's presidency showed some promise in terms of moving toward a human rights definition that included truth and justice for the military's abuses.

Sanguinetti's first actions in office reflected two main priorities: the economy and human rights. First, he began to adopt neoliberal policies to address the economic crisis. In an attempt to ameliorate the fiscal crisis, Sanguinetti made an IMF agreement and implemented fiscal adjustments such as drastic reductions in public expenditures, trade liberalization measures, and limitations on wage increases, and he moved toward privatization of the economy.[47] These moves upset many on the Left because the initiatives conflicted with attempts to reconstitute the union movement and focus on social and economic rights. However, human rights accountability for past abuses was also very much a part of these initial government conversations. On a visit to Venezuela after the election but before his inauguration, Sanguinetti declared that the military should be judged in civilian courts for any crimes committed during the dictatorship.[48] Then, it was a mere two weeks into his tenure that he signed the Ley de Pacificación Nacional (Law of National Pacification). Sanguinetti had immediately proposed releasing the final political prisoners upon taking office, and now he made good on the plan. While Parliament had begun debating and proposing amnesty terms for the remaining political prisoners as early as February (Parliament took their seats before the presidential inauguration), a compromise bill passed on March 8, 1985, and less than a week later, on

March 14, 1985, the last political prisoners were released. Although prisoners accused of violent crimes involving bloodshed were not given amnesty, their sentences were reduced and prisoner conditions improved.[49] The rest were finally free. Assets that had been seized by the military were also returned to those who received amnesty. As part of the law, public employees fired by the dictatorship for political reasons were rehired, and the law supported the reinsertion of exiles and ex-prisoners into society.[50] Article 5 also explicitly stated that the military was not included in the law's amnesty.[51]

The extent to which the Law of National Pacification addressed the conditions of those who had been most adversely affected by the dictatorship has at times been lauded as a model for political transition. For Uruguay in 1985, it proved essential in moving toward strengthening the democratic government, through both the release and reinstitution of prisoners as well as attention to exiles and those who had been fired for political reasons. It was an important first step toward committing the government to justice initiatives and showed these possibilities early on. The battles undergirding Article 5, however, were just beginning.

During Sanguinetti's second month in office, he affirmed his intention to try members of the military. He gave a speech in which he declared that "the civil justice system would judge the members of the military that had violated human rights."[52] Parliament also assumed a large role in beginning to open national discussions on accountability. While much of the pressure came from the Frente Amplio, these measures demonstrate the ways that the government did, at the very least, discuss the legacy of abuses at an official level. For example, Frente Amplio representative Eduardo Jaurena looked across the border at Argentina's truth commission and Nunca Más report and, without directly accusing Uruguay, questioned the coordination and role Uruguay played in the atrocities across the Río de la Plata. He encouraged Uruguay to confront its own chapter of violence.[53] Frente Amplio Representative Yamandú Sica Blanco invoked Vladimir Roslik's memory, the last death of the Uruguayan dictatorship, to call for justice "and those responsible for [his] death to be found."[54] Soon after, Parliament established two commissions that were tasked with investigating the deaths of Héctor Gutiérrez Ruiz, Zelmar Michelini, and the other disappeared.[55] The commissions cost less than Argentina's truth-seeking efforts but still indicated a governmental initiative toward grappling with the human rights abuses that had occurred during the dictatorship. Las Familiares later called this the high point of hope for accountability in the new democracy.[56]

Indeed, human rights groups used the positive signs stemming from the government as an opening for other actions. Following the establishment of the investigatory commissions, many Uruguayans filed petitions in court in the hope that trials would move forward.[57] Twenty lawyers began gathering information on human rights violations, particularly regarding disappearances, and announced they would file lawsuits against people who they found had committed abuses.[58] In Parliament, one representative suggested building memorials for those "that shed their blood for the tree of liberty, democracy, and justice."[59] As these claims and proposals poured in to address accountability for human rights through a broad array of initiatives, many Uruguayans were hopeful about the country's democratic direction. Between the opening of investigatory commissions, and proposals for memorials, trials, and restitution for former political prisoners, the first few months of Uruguay's return to democracy showed a great deal of potential for a multipronged approach to seeking justice for the crimes of the dictatorship. In the proposals put forth, the government resolutely linked ideas of human rights, justice, and accountability to consolidating democracy.

Civil Society and the Push for Justice

The reemergence of civil society strengthened this optimism. In addition to the aforementioned measures, a legislative decree reopened SERPAJ in early 1985. The organization had been operating clandestinely or in international forums since 1983 when the military had closed its office.[60] As Parliament began to discuss and pass measures to address various abuses, SERPAJ's president, Luis Pérez Aguirre, forcefully argued in favor of the country taking substantial steps that would address past violations. Writing in the leftist paper *Brecha,* he advocated for the legislature to deal with the human rights abuses of torture, political imprisonment, and disappearances. He also addressed the kidnapping and disappearances of pregnant women and their children, whose whereabouts were unknown but whom many believed were possibly alive and residing within the country. He said that "we do not want a democracy based on forgetting without memory. We do not want a peace based on impunity of terrorism without justice."[61] In this way, Pérez Aguirre laid out SERPAJ's idea that accountability for the military's human rights abuses was a necessary component of the country's transition back to democratic rule.

In July 1986, SERPAJ also launched a campaign for human rights, which specifically addressed the issue of justice for crimes committed during the dictatorship.[62] The organization called the campaign "justice for peace" because, it argued, those who violate human rights are a threat to peace.[63] Calling on other human rights groups to join them, SERPAJ wrote a letter to fellow organizations and political partners, such as the Frente Amplio, to urge these groups to promote the idea of human rights and justice. The main slogan was: "Uruguayans want to live without fear and impunity of those who violated human rights, it is a threat to our peace. Justice for peace (*Justicia para la paz*)."[64] In addition, in a press release, SERPAJ explained that the campaign was part of a larger societal need to "clarify all of the allegations of human rights violations during the previous regime and [for] those responsible for the crimes [to] be judged and sentenced." This, SERPAJ declared, was a necessary part of national reconciliation.[65] Pérez Aguirre argued that the country should actively pursue trials, focusing that call around a human rights imperative.[66]

Las Familiares joined SERPAJ in its calls for justice. In many ways, justice had been a key component of its movement since 1984, when the organization adopted the slogan *"aministia, verdad, y justicia"* (amnesty, truth, and justice).[67] For Familiares, accountability and finding out what happened to family members were key parts of its mission. After the renewal of democratic rule, the group remained committed to pursuing justice as an important part of stabilizing democracy. In May 1985, the group organized a week for the detained and disappeared in which it addressed Parliament's creation of a commission to investigate disappearances during the dictatorship. As part of the efforts, Familiares marched to Avenida 18 de Julio. In speeches at the march, group leaders praised the commission as a good first step, but also explained that they "demanded the broadest powers" for the committee so that it "can effectively fulfill its mission and cite those responsible, civilian or military." They sought to "lift the veil of secrecy" that had been "clouded in the name of national security."[68] In August, the group participated in the World Day Against Forced Disappearance by protesting in the Plaza Libertad to keep attention on the issue.[69] During all of these actions, the group explained that it could not fully enjoy democracy because it still did not know what or why violence had been visited upon loved ones. For them, democracy could not be complete without grappling with the human rights violations of the dictatorship. They saw some possible first steps from the Sanguinetti government and sought to push the issue of accountability further.

IELSUR, which had emerged during the early 1980s, also grew in importance and size over the course of the transition, particularly as it received additional international funding from the Ford Foundation.[70] Working with other human rights groups in the country, IELSUR advocated for financial settlements for former political detainees. These efforts included those whose jobs had been taken away by the military government. IELSUR also joined the group of lawyers who initiated dozens of cases on behalf of the tortured and disappeared, despite the legal limbo that dominated this period regarding jurisdiction over these crimes.[71] It brought charges against former members of the military regime and uncovered evidence of a clandestine cemetery for those who had been killed in detention. Furthermore, IELSUR helped reform the state's mental institutions and improve conditions, since so many of them were populated by former tortured detainees.[72] The group also worked on initiating civil suits for those who had lost homes, belongings, or jobs as a result of being classified as a "C" by the military. In addition, while most political prisoners were granted amnesty, those who were accused of intentional homicides were not; however, much of the evidence used in those cases was obtained through torture, which IELSUR now challenged in the court system.[73] Through legal efforts, IELSUR led the charge for accountability in the form of both prosecutions and reparations.

Some in the press eventually followed these groups' calls for justice as well. The most prominent paper from the Left in the 1960s and early 1970s, *Marcha*, had been shut down during the dictatorship in the early 1970s, but reopened under a new name, *Brecha*, in October 1985. In the very first issue, editors placed the issue of accountability front and center, asking on the cover, "*Justicia, para cuándo?*" (Justice, When?)[74] The paper followed the cover with a story about the lack of information about the disappearance of journalist Julio Castro. The weekly noted that it would continue to publish confirmed information about disappearances since "respect for human rights and the application of justice are as essential as the air we breathe for the existence of a civilized society."[75] Human rights groups, as well as the reemergence of a leftist press, made it clear that there was a desire for accountability among certain sectors of the population, and they followed government indications that some justice might be possible by organizing around these ideas as a core part of their mission in the new democracy.

Civil Society Actors and a Human Rights Vision

Governmental and civil society actions aimed at addressing justice for past human rights abuses in the initial months of democratic rule indicate some political will to focus efforts on accountability for narrow human rights aims. Yet, many of these civil society groups were not singularly focused on these concerns. A much broader vision of rights took firm hold during this period. Indeed, many of these human rights groups' greatest allies focused their energy on other essential challenges of the period, demonstrating the resurgence in activism around the rights and issues that had been fundamental to these groups in the pre-dictatorship period.

Unions, for example, argued for a broad view on rights. As one leader of the newly reconstituted labor union, Juan Ángel Toledo, explained, many workers saw human rights as pertaining to "problems of the situation of the disappeared, the judgment and punishment of those responsible for assassinations and torturing."[76] However, other union workers, which had historically had a lot of power in Uruguay, struggled to regain their place in the new democratic environment and began to make rights-based arguments.[77] In the electoral period, they challenged business leaders who pushed to maintain a "legally decentralized labor market" as well as restrictions on union activities such as strikes and occupation-based bargaining.[78] After Sanguinetti's inauguration, they shifted their focus to regaining negotiating power. No longer illegal, the PIT reconstituted as the PIT-CNT, combining their new name with the name of the union that had been outlawed during the dictatorship. This move was meant to reflect the institution's history and values of the pre-dictatorship era. To a certain degree, the unions proved successful in fulfilling their objectives. The PIT-CNT regained the right to strike, reinstituted the wage board, legalized voluntary union affiliation, and permitted freedom of action for collective activity.[79] However, the unions also struggled against the costs of the dictatorship's economic policy failures and Sanguinetti's neoliberal economic program. For example, in mid-1985, union leaders organized campaigns to improve workers' rights to health, social security such as pensions, and education.[80] They even threatened to strike and shut down the city's essential services because of the way the dire economic conditions in the country affected so many citizens.[81] Unions proved strongly critical of Sanguinetti's IMF agreements and called on the government to place a moratorium on external debt payments—to no avail.[82] As the year progressed and

economic improvement proved slower than expected, unions fought vociferously with the government over issues such as a national minimum salary
amid a struggling economy.[83]

Increasingly worried about the sluggish economy and technological
changes that replaced many workers, unions proposed programs for training workers for the new labor market.[84] The variety of issues these unions
faced captured much of their time and attention as they struggled to adjust to
the new economic environment. After the 1985 Congreso del PIT-CNT, the
organization reported that members were almost unanimous on two things:
questioning Sanguinetti's economic policies and the need to demand trials
and punishment for those responsible for human rights violations.[85] Despite
these declared principles, workers' rights took up the majority of the conversation and organizing of the congress, and members sought ways to address
the historical concern of collective socioeconomic rights and began to rein-
vest their energies in a broad idea of rights.[86] This shift illustrates a growing divide between the unions and human rights groups. Labor unions now
focused on workers' rights as their main concern.[87] Meanwhile, groups such
as IELSUR and SERPAJ were committing their energy to realizing the idea
of accountability measures, and the coalition's energies dispersed into these
distinct projects.

Similar to the country's unions, Uruguay's public education system had
been among the most advanced in Latin America throughout the twentieth
century. However, the dictatorship nearly destroyed it. The military reduced
funding for education from 21 percent to only 13.5 percent of the national
budget. Fearing that the university was a refuge for subversives, the military
withheld funds for research, carried out armed attacks against student groups
in the university, and then formally took control over university affairs in
1973. This last intervention included setting the educational agenda to
exclude any teaching of "equality" as a dogma of dangerous liberal and Marxist thought. The military also fired between 70 and 90 percent of the university teaching staff for disloyalty. They imprisoned hundreds of professors
amid accusations that they were subversives.[88] In the period following the
return to democratic rule, the student movement also struggled with balanc-
ing human rights accountability for the military's crimes and how to expand
the definition of the concept in the educational sector.

Many medical students focused on accountability, since military doctors
had helped the dictatorship conduct torture by overseeing and monitoring the
military's torture sessions to the point of extreme pain without causing death.

Doctors also performed autopsies during the dictatorship to certify that deaths occurred from natural causes rather than by torture. They willingly falsified these notices. In the aftermath of the dictatorship, the medical school grappled with its own justice issues and the responsibility of doctors to maintain the Hippocratic Oath and help humanity despite this sullied history. Therefore, the medical student group maintained its commitment to justice by promising to "not cease our struggle until achieving the trial and imprisonment of the guilty that participated in the harassment, torture, omission of assistance, falsification of death certificates or other crimes against humanity."[89] In October 1985, the group extended this argument more broadly to the state of accountability within the country when the official newsletter of the medical school students explained that many people believed that the issue of human rights was receding in democratic rule. It claimed that the larger civil society movement was no longer mobilized around accountability issues. The group made an impassioned argument to ask for truth and justice, to locate the disappeared, and to hold those responsible for crimes against humanity.[90] Along with SERPAJ and Familiares, this was one of the first examples of a broader population grappling with the question of accountability.

Despite these accountability arguments, the larger student movement was comprised of a new generation of leaders that also focused on other concerns. For the newly reconstituted student movement, ASCEEP, a return to democracy also meant the possibility to organize around ridding the schools of military oversight. Students and professors alike launched a campaign to "rebuild the university" and focused on issues including salary, health insurance, research support, and sabbaticals.[91] After a decade of the military gutting the university of both its finances and workers, this proved to be a difficult job, made harder by Sanguinetti's strict economic policies. In October 1985, the university's union accused Sanguinetti as being no different from the dictatorship in his policies toward the university. Later in the same month, it occupied the university to protest the administration's failure to address its concerns.[92] Students continued to support accountability issues for the military, especially since many students had been gravely affected by the violence. However, students fundamentally questioned what human rights organizing looked like in the post-dictatorship period. Now that amnesty for political prisoners had been achieved, was human rights a quest for justice for these abuses or broader ideas about a fair salaries and university access and autonomy?[93] Indeed, most of ASCEEP's organizing efforts centered around the pressing issue of how to rebuild the university.

In this way, the activities of both unions and the student movement reflected a variety of concerns in dealing with post-authoritarian Uruguay. Many of these issues could be traced back to its rights visions of the 1960s. The fight for collective rights—for fair living wages and an education—had been a critical part of 1960s activism in the years prior to the dictatorship. Now, in the post-authoritarian environment, the radical nature of calls for revolution to achieve rights was absent, but the desire for collective rights reemerged in new social movements. These initial ideas about societal change were sought through more formal venues of protest. While the language and venue for change were toned down, these groups were still ambitious in their ability to imagine a new political environment endowed with rights—rights that extended beyond truth and justice.

A Shift from Accountability

Within the government, attention was diverted from its initial rhetoric for justice measures. The all-male Parliament began to focus on economic concerns and social issues such as improving the schools, financial reform, hospital improvement, and even abortion.[94] As the year progressed, both the president and Parliament moved away from some of the original measures for even limited truth and justice. First, in August 1985, military courts challenged the civilian jurisdiction over the trials that were being processed. The military claimed that cases involving military personnel should be handled under the Supreme Military Tribunal and not in civilian courts. Some members of government backed this claim as well, with the confusion ultimately paralyzing the movement of the cases brought before the courts.[95]

Then in November, the investigatory commission reports came back with their results. The Investigative Commission on the Situation of Disappeared People and Its Causes and the Investigative Commission on the Kidnapping and Assassination of National Representatives Zelmar Michelini and Héctor Gutiérrez Ruiz had very narrowly defined missions. The first sought to establish the fate of the disappeared, while the latter explored the most notorious killings of two Uruguayan politicians in Argentina. While showing some commitment to exploring the abuses during the dictatorship, these mandates were extremely limited. Therefore, they did not investigate the military's repressive tactics such as torture, which were more common than actual disappearances in Uruguay. In addition, the commissions were relatively weak and could not compel information or testimony from the military. In the end, the commissions offered some information on the disappeared, but it was minimal at best.[96] They also were unable to find proof of institutional decision-making about disappearances as a military tactic. The findings caused major rifts both between and within the political parties, resulting in the commissions' findings never being widely distributed, covered, or even officially announced to the public.[97]

Human rights groups such as Familiares and Amnesty International criticized the commission for producing almost no new information.[98] They argued that, among other faults, the commission did not have the power to compel official information or even to interview members of the military, particularly about the whereabouts of children or grandchildren who had been disappeared and might still be alive. Sanguinetti opposed attempts to investigate past abuses more broadly and sought to investigate only "dramatic episodes" of the disappeared rather than engaging in a more thorough undertaking.[99] Many Uruguayans began to view the commissions as a political exercise rather than a serious initiative for human rights.[100] After seven months, the commission reported on only 164 disappearances without establishing the systematic abuses of the security forces or the influence of Operation Condor—a coordinated campaign of political repression and terror by the dictatorships of the Southern Cone aimed at eradicating alleged socialist and communist influence and ideas.[101] Instead, the reports affirmed information that the disappeared were dead but did not even offer specific evidence in each case.[102]

Despite the shortcomings of the process, many activists still believed that trials would proceed.[103] In the months following the investigations' findings, criminal complaints continued to flood the judiciary. However, judges who agreed to hear the claims faced threats, and the military courts continued to assert that they should have jurisdiction over the cases. IELSUR noted that the investigation by the commission prompted a backlash by some in the military and government who argued that the search for justice could destabilize democracy.[104]

Events in neighboring Argentina exacerbated these delays. Argentina's transition was substantively different than Uruguay's, particularly with respect to Argentina's military defeat in the Falklands in 1982 and the collapse of public support. This, coupled with a crippling economic crisis, forced out the Argentine military in defeat, which contrasted sharply with Uruguay's long-negotiated transition. Argentina's transition also occurred approximately two years before Uruguay. Both chronologically and because Uruguay had always been a keen observer of Argentine politics, the leaders in Uruguay were undoubtedly influenced by Argentina's transitional process.[105] In the first two years of Alfonsín's democratic presidency, he began to address the crimes of the dictatorship with a truth commission that was much more extensive and had more authority than the investigatory commissions in Uruguay. Limited prosecutions followed as well, starting with nine high-level military commanders who were tried on 709 charges including murder, unlawful deprivation of liberty, torture, and robbery. After convictions of some of the defendants in December 1985, over 3,000 cases were filed in Argentine courts by victims and their families.

By the time Uruguay dealt with its own history of abuse, however, Argentina's forward momentum in its justice initiatives had stalled as the country began to confront a backlash and insubordination from the military. Fears of a military coup began to grow amid unrest from the military, and by late 1986 the Argentine government began to consider ways to reduce the cases moving through the courts.[106]

This resistance reverberated across the Rio de la Plata as procedural delays and rumblings by the military slowed the progress of trials. Public opinion polls demonstrate the extent to which Uruguayans feared military involvement in the newly democratic environment. In one survey, for example, only 10 percent of Uruguayans believed that the military did not maintain any power. Forty-four percent of the population believed they maintained power over questions of salaries, trials for crimes of the dictatorship, and the ability to continually surveil people and political groups. Fifty-one percent of respondents also said that they did not believe that the military would be required to testify at trials if they were allowed to proceed.[107] The president and Parliament also felt the effects of the coup attempt rumors.

Under these circumstances, Amnesty International visited Uruguay in early 1986 and registered concerns about the current state of investigations into past human rights abuses, which the organization argued hurt the prospect of protecting human rights in the future. In a meeting between the group and Sanguinetti, the president explained that he did not have the power to improve investigatory commissions or trials, since the measures were initiated by Parliament which lacked the legal power to compel testimony. While Sanguinetti said the issue was not under his jurisdiction, AI made the argument that more leadership should come from the executive to condemn torture so it could not be used as an excuse in extraordinary measures. The group also pushed for him to support accountability with trials; yet, the meeting appears to have had little impact on the president. At a fundamental level, though, AI's criticism marked a continued interest in Uruguay's human rights situation by the international community, which had largely celebrated Sanguinetti's election. Now, it continued to spotlight the importance of human rights accountability.[108] The paradox of the continued pressure was that although the international community maintained some interest in Uruguay's quest for justice, domestically only a few human rights groups sustained their focus on that issue while a broader array of human rights concerns competed for unions' and student movements' attention and efforts.

Amnesty Law Debates

By mid-1986, Parliament began to debate amnesty bills that would provide varying degrees of coverage to members of the military. Uruguayan civil society's focus on other concerns, along with pressure from the military, all contributed to this shift. Sanguinetti offered the first proposal, an illustration of his move away from his initial position of, at the very least, passively supporting justice. It was in this moment that Sanguinetti began to articulate the idea that the military did not need to be tried and that it was normal to provide amnesty for the military. He argued that any jurisdiction over investigations should be left to military justice, even though military courts rejected requests to investigate crimes.[109]

In August 1986, Sanguinetti introduced an amnesty bill that supported these ideas. Attesting to the power of the military's pressure to obtain amnesty, his proposal encompassed a broad, sweeping time frame that covered crimes related to "fighting subversives" from January 1962 to March 1985. However, many Uruguayans opposed this bill, and over 10,000 people gathered to demand it be rejected.[110] Parliament did just that—defeating the bill in September on the basis that it was too broad.[111] Then the Blancos introduced a bill that offered amnesty to the military except for those who had engaged in the gravest human rights abuses, such as rape, murder, and disappearances— as long as the complaints were filed before September 1986. This proposal attempted to allow certain cases already in the system to continue while at the same time precluding thousands of others, many of which focused on claims of torture. The armed forces objected loudly to this bill, and the measure was defeated in October 1986.[112]

As these proposals continued to fail under pressure by various factions, the Supreme Court handed its own blow to the military. Under repeated appeal to determine the jurisdiction of the petitions, it ruled that the cases would move forward in the civilian system and not a military one. By the time the decision came down, there were over seven hundred cases of past abuses under judicial investigation, and the first military commanders were ordered to appear in court on December 23, 1986. General Medina declared his opposition to any members of the military appearing before civilian judges, which set up a showdown between the military and the government—and also imposed a deadline for Parliament to try to come up a solution. Legislators scrambled to draft a proposal that they could pass.[113]

At a basic level, the debates that transpired during the month of December reflected a broader societal engagement in the issue of truth and justice for the crimes of the dictatorship in the new democratic era. With so many challenges facing the democratic fabric of society, citizens asked where accountability fit into the hierarchy and what took precedence, particularly amid the uproar among the armed forces. While politicians had differed in their answers to these questions during the first twenty months of democratic rule, in December 1986 strong fault lines emerged among Parliamentarians that indicated an important shift in the new democratic period. As opposed to the broad commitment to some form of accountability that prevailed during the initial transition, both the Colorados and Blancos now exhibited a willingness to forgo trials. The Frente Amplio, however, continued to push for truth and justice. What resulted was a hastily passed amnesty law with a majority of votes being cast in favor of impunity. Still, the Parliamentary debates during this frantic period reveal a nuanced struggle within Parliament over what human rights actually meant in the new democratic rule, and how they would be defined in this period. While deliberations occurred under the fear of a military coup and an impending deadline for the military to appear in court, the reconstruction of these debates uncovers the various meanings of democracy and human rights to different groups during this tumultuous time.

When a new amnesty law was proposed to cover the years of 1973 to 1985, the three dominant parties discussed what was at stake in markedly different ways.[114] First, the Colorados strongly opposed trials and favored the amnesty law. They had been the party closest to the military who worked hand in hand with them on the transitional process. Voting almost unanimously for the bill in both the Senate and Chamber of Representatives, many elected Colorado officials stressed the future of a firm stable democracy over "drowning in the problems of the past."[115] As Flores Silva stated years later, his party believed that the dilemma in 1986 was "either we turn the page or apply transitional justice and the theme of peace would go to hell . . . as hard as it was, peace was more important than justice in that moment because without peace, there would be even more injustice."[116] These leaders did not ignore the fact that the military committed human rights violations. However, they pointed out that extraordinary times necessitated these measures. Just as Parliament had granted amnesty to political prisoners for the sake of reconciliation, Colorados argued that it should be extended to the military.[117] Colorados viewed amnesty as a reconciliation tool to pacify former political prisoners *and* the military. The meaning of democracy encompassed compromises and turning the page on the difficult history rather than pushing for justice when both sides had committed crimes. Despite the vast gap in scale and design of abuses, the Colorados propagated the "two demons" theory that gave equal weight to crimes on both sides of the conflict. Instead of focusing on justice issues, these legislators looked for the best way to secure new democratic freedoms such as the rights to freedom of speech, freedom of the press, and freedom from arbitrary imprisonment. They saw an agreement with the military over amnesty as a way to secure these elemental components of democracy, and the leaders proved willing to compromise on accountability to achieve them.

The Blanco Party was likewise supportive of the bill, but much less enthusiastically. Members argued that the amnesty law was a necessary evil to have democracy continue, avoid a military coup, and be able to secure broader human rights in a democratic future. Many members of the party, including Guillermo García Costa, explained that impunity was the only way to preserve the new and fragile democracy.[118] Even though Wilson Ferreira had not been allowed to stand for election and was therefore not a member of the Senate, his spiritual leadership of the party also played an important role when he made various public statements against pursuing justice.[119] The Blancos' reluctance to vote for the bill was also encapsulated in their argument that a form of amnesty had been promised in the Naval Club Pact. The Blancos had protested those negotiations over Ferreira's imprisonment and thus had not been present at the talks. By claiming that an agreement had been made in the Naval Club Pact, they exempted themselves from blame for the bill and claimed that they were just going along with a promise that others had made. In this way, the Blancos did not argue that the human rights abuses or claims for justice should be ignored as a matter of principle, merely that this stance was necessary in the current situation to avoid a return to military rule, which would create even more abuses.

The Frente Amplio, however, refused to accept this justification and argued for the triumph of human rights and accountability. Pointing to the CONAPRO agreement to pursue justice and the explicit exclusion of the military in the Law of National Pacification, members of the Frente Amplio advocated firmly against protecting the military.[120] They declined to vote for impunity of massive human rights violations, which would "justify what is unjustifiable."[121] Advocating for the primacy of human rights and rule of law as necessary elements to secure a democratic future, their claims ultimately fell on the deaf ears of their fellow Parliamentarians.[122]

In some respects, the fracturing consensus among political parties accelerated the move away from accountability. Political scientist Alexandra Barahona de Brito argues that the unity of political parties committed to truth and justice is an important predictor in determining the success of accountability efforts. In Uruguay, the divide among parties promoted further fragmentation, and "discouraged parties of principles, and reduced internal programmatic consistency."[123] This division made coherence on fighting against the amnesty laws even more difficult.

Beyond exposing the cracks among the political parties, the Parliamentary debates also revealed the widening gap between the population and lawmakers. Many prominent politicians had been among the fiercest critics of the military during the dictatorship, but now that they held positions of power, they changed their views. Vice President Enrique Tarigo surfaced as one of the most blatant examples of a shifting human rights ally. As editor of *Opinar,* he had led the popular movement against the military beginning in 1980. Senator José Germán Araújo, the former head of the independent radio station who also now entered politics, had worked closely with Tarigo to push for a transition to democratic rule. He believed his former ally was betraying the cause. He pointed out that when Tarigo was a newspaper editor, he had called for justice to be an integral part of the new democracy. Araújo stood on the floor of the Senate and quoted Tarigo's own words: "while some countries want to turn the page and begin anew . . . those who were responsible [for crimes committed during the dictatorship] should be sanctioned by the law."[124] By December 1986, though, Tarigo and many of his former compatriots who had fought against the dictatorship were arguing for the passage of an amnesty law.[125] The newly reconstituted student movement also noted this perceived betrayal, arguing that a majority of the public wanted to try military leaders, but Sanguinetti, and particularly Tarigo who had been a leader in the fight against the military government, now advocated "for complicity and amnesty."[126]

Wilson Ferreira provides another example. He still held considerable sway in his party, and his public support for the law felt like a betrayal to many who had seen him as one of the most important opponents of the military regime during its twelve years in power.[127] Some accused him of taking the stance in order to make his candidacy for president palatable to the military in 1989.[128] As WOLA Executive Director Joe Eldridge recalled, he was "afraid to provoke the military . . . so surrendered his human rights credentials."[129] Struggling to maintain a tenuous balance between governing, future elections, and angering the military, Tarigo and Ferreira are just two examples of how former advocates against the military emerged as their protectors against trials. These two politicians proved to be unreliable allies for the human rights movement as their roles shifted from protestors of the military to positions of power.

In the end, months of Parliamentary debates resulted in a hurried three days of legislative activity to pass Law 15.848, known as the *Ley de Caducidad de la Pretensión Punitiva del Estado* (Law on the Expiration of the Punitive Claims of the States). Pressure mounted as a constitutional crisis appeared imminent; the military declared that they would not appear in court to face proceedings.[130] Debates on a possible agreement continued all through the night before the supposed showdown, and the arguments were fierce—one fistfight even erupted during the proceedings. At the end of the debates, Parliament finished voting just one hour before a federal court was supposed to open a hearing for an army colonel accused of kidnapping a journalist in 1976. [131] The law avoided a confrontation between the military and the judiciary, with the Ley de Caducidad entering into force on December 22, 1986.[132] In the final text, the law gave immunity to the members of the armed forces and police (but not civilians) who had committed crimes for political motives between June 1973 and March 1985. The only cases that were excluded were ones where illicit profit was made as a result of violations.[133] Sanguinetti explained that, in the end, the vote on the law was about "choosing between war and peace."[134]

The law engendered the passions of many in civil society who saw the amnesty as the Colorado and Blanco representatives conceding to the predominance of the military in the new civilian government. One activist, Omar Mazzeo, later called it the "saddest day in the country's parliamentary history."[135]

Even Wilson's son, Juan Raúl Ferreira, explained that he and his father had felt the law was necessary to save democracy, but he had not wanted to vote for it. He recalled leaving Parliament with his father that night crying.[136] Many others were not just sad; they reacted with outrage. Senator Araújo did not care why Blanco leaders, such as Wilson Ferreira, Alberto Zumarán, and Elías Porras, had supported the law. He called them traitors and enemies for compromising their principles and supporting the law.[137] Protestors also congregated around the city to oppose the law's passage. Some participated in *caceroleos* and went to rally at the house of military leaders who were accused of human rights violations.[138] Other protesters directed their anger toward Ferreira and assembled outside his home, shouting slogans against the law long into the night.[139] The biggest crowd gathered outside the Palacio Legislativo, where some protesters scuffled with the police and legislatures while others expressed their anger by destroying the windows of cars parked around the building.[140] The military arrived on the scene as well, arresting nineteen protesters for "serious acts of disturbance."[141] A few days later, Araújo was expelled from the Senate, accused of inciting the violence that transpired. The media contributed to the fevered environment. After largely failing to cover the legislative debate in Parliament, they reported on Araújo's expulsion and the violence that followed the passage of the law more than the actual debate over it.[142]

The physical unrest that accompanied the law's passage foreshadowed the battles that would be fought in the public sphere, in the legal system, and at the ballot box in the coming years. It also reunited civil society actors who had diverged in purpose since the return to democratic rule over the hard work of how to reconstitute democracy and what human rights would mean in the post-dictatorship era. The amnesty prompted a return, albeit temporarily, among many of these groups to accountability over the earlier, more individually focused rights that had been the focus of protests against the dictatorship, and that now under democratic rule required a renewed form of organization and fight.

Conclusion

The twenty-two months between Sanguinetti taking the oath of office and the passage of the amnesty law proved to be a critical time in Uruguay. Reexamining this period reveals the complexities involved in negotiating the terrain of a "pacted" transition and new democratic governance. In addition, it demonstrates the ways that human rights evolved both within civil society and governmentally, including the fissures that had developed between these groups.

Historian Steve Stern explains that "pacted" transitions are often limiting because both sides come to an agreement based on a "necessary fiction" of what the transition will be like. In this situation, construction of a fiction is the only way that an agreement can be reached. However, problems arise because no one actually trusts this necessary fiction to hold. Therefore, the years following these pacts often include a "struggle to redraw the lines of effective power."[143] Uruguay witnessed this phenomenon amid other countervailing societal forces, which partly explains the evolving attitudes toward justice during these initial months.

An additionally important shift was the ways Uruguayans utilized a discourse of human rights more expansively. As the country's transition proceeded through 1985 and into 1986, civil society addressed human rights issues that expanded beyond justice for crimes committed during the dictatorship to address issues related to economic struggles, social concerns, and educational efforts as fundamental human rights to be protected. The evolving definition of what constituted human rights recovered ideas of the pre-dictatorship era, and collective rights reemerged as critical societal issues. While no longer within a revolutionary framework, these actors began to reimagine dreams that had been lost during the height of the repression. Although this inclusion expanded the discourse of human rights to these other spheres, it also diverted attention and efforts from human rights issues specifically regarding justice for members of the military.

What also shifted during those twenty-two months was the argument linking full recuperation of democracy to justice for human rights. At first, activists tied democracy to rule of law, which meant punishing the officers for human rights abuses.[144] The separation between consolidating democracy and human rights began in 1986 as confrontations with the military emerged. The debates over delinking these two concepts started over three rushed days in Parliament in December 1986, but they would captivate the nation for the remainder of the decade.

CHAPTER 7

The Fights for Human Rights
and Accountability

Less than twenty-four hours after Parliament passed the amnesty law, two separate groups announced their intention to challenge its implementation. First was the MLN-T, the former guerilla group that now regrouped as a political force and called for repealing the law through a referendum.[1] The second group was led by three women who called a press conference. On December 23, 1986, the widows of two murdered politicians, Elisa Dellepiane and Matilde Rodríguez, and the mother of a *desaparecido*, María Ester Gatti, stood at the Asociación Cristiana de Jóvenes (Christian Youth Association) and declared their intention to challenge the Ley de Caducidad with a national referendum.[2] They announced the creation of the Comisión Nacional Pro-Referendum (National Pro-Referendum Commission [CNPR]), a group that would eventually take the lead to place the law before a popular vote and give Uruguayans a chance to overturn it.

Since 1934, Uruguay's constitution had allowed for these types of direct democratic procedures.[3] Citizens could hold a referendum on a law if 25 percent of the electorate requested it. They had one year from the date of the law's passage to collect the requisite signatures, after which an electoral court would verify the names and then set a future date for the referendum. Although it was a lengthy and daunting process, the organizers of the commission felt that it was their only option to fight the impunity that the amnesty law imposed on Uruguayans. Thus, the CNPR launched what would be an almost three-year battle to overturn the Ley de Caducidad, one beleaguered by lawsuits, political attempts to undermine the work of the CNPR, and an onerous and slow verification process. Despite making it through all the hurdles to even conduct a referendum, their efforts were ultimately unsuccessful. When the vote was finally held in April 1989, the population voted to keep the amnesty law in place with a 55.95 percent majority.[4]

Scholars have often portrayed the referendum's outcome as a human rights failure. In many ways, it was just that. The impunity that took hold after the vote prevented human rights accountability and devastated many of the activists who sought justice for the various violations. Yet, a close examination of the changing human rights landscape during the battles to overturn the amnesty law challenges this interpretation in two primary ways.

First, during much of the campaign the CNPR retreated from couching their activities in a human rights imperative. At first glance, it might appear counterintuitive that the organizers of a referendum to overturn the protection of human rights abusers concentrated a public campaign on an argument that largely avoided addressing such violations. Yet, in attempts to appeal to the widest majority of potential voters, the CNPR focused its campaign strategy on appealing to the population by arguing that the referendum would restore people's voices in democracy, rather than making the more controversial argument that it was necessary to obtain justice for past human rights abuses. In this way, the campaign concentrated on the importance of democratic engagement by casting a vote over a human rights argument. Exploring the difficulties of the campaign process and strategies suggests multiple causes for the referendum's failure beyond just a narrative of fear about another coup.[5]

Second, while human rights receded as the primary justification for the CNPR, it exploded in other sectors to encompass a broad array of social and economic rights. In this way, the referendum laid bare the paradox of the increasing ubiquity of a human rights discourse: as human rights language came to encompass an expanded set of rights claims within the reconstituted democracy, concerns for justice for the military's violations lost some of their domestic force as priority values. During the nearly three years it took for the government to allow the population to vote on the amnesty law, political rights and accountability lost some of their organizing force. Instead, activists were at times more focused on other pressing needs, which ranged from reviving social justice battles in the social and economic rights spheres to launching new human rights movements that centered on women's rights, LGBT rights, and Afro-Uruguayan rights. As such, human rights became, as historian Jennifer Adair has explained in exploring a comparative Argentine context, a "multivalent political language" used by a broad array of social actors.[6]

A critical component of this story includes looking at various effects of the ebb and flow of international involvement during this period. Attention from NGOs and philanthropic foundations varied considerably during the referendum battle as other pressing human rights violations around the world took precedence, particularly in Central America. The international human rights movement, which had been so critical in the years of the dictatorship, had a much reduced, or at times even negative, role in events during the referendum battle. In addition, U.S. foreign policy continued to withdraw support for explicit human rights aims.[7] The Reagan administration had hardly been a defender of human rights in Uruguay throughout its first term in office, and during the referendum battle the administration focused on how bilateral or regional concerns could be furthered by the continuation of democratic rule without any major upheavals that might result from the possibility of the referendum's success. As such, just as this chapter charts the domestic changes in human rights, it also takes account of the effects of international and transnational groups during this critical time to understand the changes in human rights activism in the late 1980s.

The chapter proceeds chronologically to examine the diverse invocations and impacts of human rights from 1987 to 1989. Despite the failure of the objective of overturning the law, examining the various human rights dynamics pushes us toward a rethinking of how a human rights discourse in Uruguay underwent a fundamental transformation during the 1980s transition back to democratic rule. While activists had utilized human rights as a mechanism to challenge state oppression during the dictatorship, the term came to be invoked as a tool for substantive social change in a variety of spheres in the years immediately following the return of a civilian government. Further, this chapter reconsiders the implications of this narrative with emerging ideas about transitional justice. At some level, the triumph of the amnesty law and the lack of other accountability mechanisms that followed demonstrated the shortcomings of the justice movement during the 1980s transitional decade. As a result, Uruguay is often left out of early histories of transitional justice.[8] Yet, exploring the tension and debates about justice and human rights during the referendum campaign reveals some of the tradeoffs in how citizens prioritize accountability and social and economic rights that still exist in the field today. As such, this chapter recenters Uruguay as an important country to explore the origins of transitional justice debates and the enduring battles for accountability that far outlasted the referendum's defeat.

Collecting Signatures

When Dellepiane, Rodríguez, and Gatti announced the creation of the CNPR, they launched a powerful challenge to the legislature's amnesty law. The women sought to channel the outcry and unrest on the streets that accompanied the law's passage toward productive means. Despite the fact that politicians and civil society actors had focused attention over the past several years on a multitude of challenges facing the fragile democracy, many groups now joined together and issued official statements expressing their opposition to the law.[9] Líber Seregni encapsulated this renewed solidarity when, speaking for the Frente Amplio, he explained that "our people have reliably demonstrated that they want truth and justice and no pact with the military. That our people want peace, yearn for peace, they know certainly there is no peace without justice."[10] The outpouring of concern from the press, politicians, and civil society groups signaled a renewed attention to the issue of amnesty.

These statements translated into action in the form of a march just days after the law's passage in December 1986, affirming that there was widespread support for the referendum. More than 50,000 demonstrators filled the main street of Montevideo, Avenida 18 de Julio, from the University to the *Obelisco*. Organized by the major labor union, the PIT-CNT, and led by members of the Madres y Familiares de Uruguayos Desaparecidos Detenidos, they declared that the march was an act to reclaim "Uruguayan dignity" after the past few tumultuous days.[11]

Many of the marchers later formed grassroots committees to organize to overturn the law. Less than forty days after the CNPR declared their intention to collect signatures for a referendum, two hundred neighborhood committees appeared in the capital and continued to grow over the year. Initially, at least one committee was also established in each of the other eighteen interior departments in the country, and eventually there were over eighty in the interior.[12] Overall, the total number of committees in the nation ultimately reached between 350 and 400.[13]

The enthusiasm for recourse against the law produced groups that were largely "self-organizing networks and pluralist forces of civil society, dissociated from traditional parties, although supported by individual politicians."[14] While the leftist political party, the Frente Amplio, and human rights groups such as SERPAJ helped encourage people to join the efforts, the groups were all independent.[15] Yet, they came together under the central CNPR agenda, which had promised to transcend political party banners. One of the initial petitions submitted to the government demonstrated this unity among the groups by having representatives of the labor union, major human rights groups, political party representatives, and even the famous author Mario Benedetti sign a single letter expressing opposition to the law.

In analyzing this loose alliance, two important insights emerge that directly influenced the CNPR's initial strategy to focus on democracy over a human rights discourse. First, the diversity of this large movement produced tensions, particularly among members who were also involved in the Frente Amplio. This political party, representing a coalition of leftist political groups, experienced internal party struggles during this period that manifested in debates over how to conduct the campaign strategy. For example, arguments arose in the group when the Communist Party criticized the lack of orthodoxy among other Left groups and blasted the CNPR for accepting international money to conduct the campaign.[16] With internal struggles surfacing early on, the CNPR realized the importance of advancing a cohesive approach in order to attract the greatest number of Uruguayans to sign the petition for a referendum and reduce internal tension. This issue was at the forefront of debates over how to organize a public campaign and helped impact the decision to focus around the less controversial argument that the referendum would restore people's voices in democracy. What was absent, though, was an appeal to the population based on the importance of pursuing justice for past human rights abuses.

Second, the CNPR's gender dynamic reveals the expanding role of women in the social sphere, a process that had begun during the dictatorship and continued in the democratic environment.[17] This stood in contrast to the halls of political power. For example, only men had participated in the Parliamentary debates about the law. No women had even been elected in the 1984 vote. The Chamber of Deputies was composed of ninety-nine men and the Senate of thirty. The CNPR, however, represented a very different dynamic. It was formally constituted by a group of three women who were publicly known figures already linked to the painful violation of human rights. Although men eventually did enter the upper ranks, its leadership was still largely comprised of women. Throughout Latin America, scholars argue that women drew on their role as activist mothers to enter the public sphere and form the backbone of the human rights movement during this period.[18] Rodríguez remembers this phenomenon in Uruguay, recalling that the CNPR was "full of women." While she had never considered herself to be a feminist, she noted that challenging the military's impunity was her first "contact with feminist militancy . . . and it was phenomenal."[19] This aspect had a profound societal effect. Women's leadership at the top of the CNPR played an important role in inspiring other women who might not have traditionally gotten involved in politics to become involved in the campaign and lead neighborhood groups. They organized solidarity networks in their communities, at home, and even in churches.[20] Members of neighborhood committees recalled women distributing leaflets about the referendum while running errands in the market.[21] Women also canvassed the vast territories in the interior parts of the country and attended local labor group assemblies, church meetings, and political gatherings to collect signatures and organize other members.[22] In this way, women who had not traditionally seen themselves as political actors found a point of entry into the political sphere.

Women serving on the committees recalled organizing in an atmosphere "removed from the ideological rhetoric" and "not thinking about political returns."[23] Instead, many of these women entered the public sphere as a form of gendered solidarity, attempting to find common principles and return to "values, the value that all were equal before the law and the values that had been lost during the dictatorship."[24] They approached the referendum battles with "sympathy, warmth, and simplicity," to counter the tremendous fear the country had experienced throughout the dictatorship.[25] Rodríguez explained that the campaign was not presented as a radical challenge to the social order. Rather, it allowed for the inclusion of women who did not rely on affiliation with a specific political party. Their status as "concerned women" made their participation a nonthreatening entry into the public turmoil that had thus far characterized the amnesty debates.[26] As a result, some of these women also sought to focus the campaign on a noncontroversial argument about restoring rule of law to remove the issue from the contentious politics of human rights and accountability that had produced physical violence after the all-male Parliament passed the Ley de Caducidad.

There was another motivation that influenced the CNPR's initial strategy, and that was responding to government arguments in support of the law. In particular, the government claimed that the Ley de Caducidad was essential to save democracy. During the Parliament's debates on the law, Blanco leaders had stressed that amnesty was the only way to prevent a breakdown in the fragile democracy. For example, one of the party's leaders in the Senate, Gonzalo Aguirre, explained that Uruguay was "facing a serious institutional crisis" and argued that only an amnesty for the military would "guarantee peace, tranquility, and fundamentally, making institutions safe from any impending risk."[27] After the law was passed, Wilson Ferreira wrote an editorial in *La Democracia* rationalizing that the path to democracy had been incredibly long and difficult. He stressed that the law was the only way to prevent an imminent institutional crisis.[28]

The Colorado Party made similar claims. President Sanguinetti asserted that the amnesty was "not only about liberty, but also security and tranquility."[29] He stressed equivalency of granting amnesty to political prisoners in March 1985 with the new law, declaring that the country needed to "judge all or judge no one to honor the future. The country should adopt a political solution to leave the past definitively behind and consolidate national institutions."[30] Thus, the law's proponents justified their support by pointing to the need for peace to safeguard a fragile democracy, and by asserting the necessity of turning the page on the past era.

The CNPR's campaign strategy reflected a direct response to both these claims and many of the women leaders' desire to create a common purpose removed from political ideology. Documents from some of the initial CNPR meetings illustrate that group members debated the best way to counter the government's arguments. They ultimately decided to explicitly emphasize democracy over a direct human rights appeal.[31] The official call for a referendum, for example, asserted that the amnesty law was an "affront to the people's democratic sentiments" that were rooted in the "recognized principles of universal law and the most pure national traditions of Artigas."[32] The referendum process, the press release went on to explain, was essential to counter the threat to the newly reconstituted democracy after "so much effort and sacrifice to overcome more than a decade of dictatorship."[33] These broad values of democratic affirmation made a specific call to all political parties and sectors of society to sign the petition and have their voices heard. This strategy is reflected in the campaign slogan the CNPR ultimately chose: "I sign for the people to decide."[34] While members of the CNPR considered using language that invoked truth and justice, the heterogeneity of the actors compelled the leaders to choose a less controversial slogan that appealed to a democratic consciousness following the long military dictatorship and the importance of ensuring the return of citizens' voices in politics.[35]

This initial strategy proved effective as the campaign got off to a rather amazing start. The CNPR organized a big kickoff around the country on February 22, 1987.[36] In the first three weeks, committees around the country collected 160,000 signatures, averaging a staggering 7,619 names each day. On Sunday, March 15, the CNPR held a national event to collect signatures and set up over three hundred tables, mostly in Montevideo but with some other locations in the interior as well. Between 8,000 and 9,000 people collected signatures, going door to door and zone to zone.[37] Meanwhile, referendum proponents painted signs and murals around the city with the campaign's slogan, "*Yo firmo, para que el pueblo decida.*" Bands played in front of similar posters to attract large crowds and generate excitement about the campaign.[38] The day was a huge success and the CNPR collected almost 100,000 additional signatures—which brought the total to just under 50 percent of the number needed.[39] While no other event brought in that quantity of votes, independent groups continued to organize debates, show films with discussions afterward, and bring citizens out in the neighborhood to sign the petition.[40] During this time, the Commission enjoyed enthusiastic global support. Amnesty International launched a letter-writing campaign to protest the law.[41] The PEN American Center and Americas Watch both wrote and circulated letters to President Sanguinetti, expressing concern and condemnation over the amnesty law.[42] Meanwhile, activists in Argentina launched a campaign to collect signatures of Uruguayans living in the neighboring country.[43]

The remarkable pace of these efforts proved unsustainable as the colder months set in. Door-to-door campaigning and getting to less-populated areas became more difficult as the seasons changed. During this slower period, the campaign planned for the next stage of its efforts. In this moment, they decided to appeal to possible signers by expanding their message beyond just "let the people decide." The CNPR drew up a series of new slogans to roll out. Just as was true in its first phrase, the new strategy also barely touched on justice for human rights issues. The new CNPR slogans similarly centered on democratic appeals, using language such as "I sign because I have confidence in democracy" and "I sign because I have confidence in the future" as a direct repudiation of the government's campaign of fear, and "I sign because I have confidence in Uruguayans" as another appeal to the democratic impulse in "letting the people decide."[44]

It was not the case that appealing to human rights just did not occur to the group. Indeed, one proposed radio jingle touched on human rights. It asserted that "for Uruguayans, judging who violated human rights of the past only has one meaning, to look with calm toward the future; I sign because I have confidence in the future."[45] Yet even in this context, human rights served the larger purpose of appealing to a broad audience by countering the government's claims that a referendum would cause upheaval in the country.

In contrast to the general CNPR message, there were other independent groups that, from the beginning, spoke about the crimes of the dictatorship as part of the reason why they supported the CNPR's efforts. For example, the Comisión Nacional de Liberados Políticos (National Commission of Liberated Politicians) used opportunities such as the anniversary of the final release of political prisoners to support the referendum. It stressed the continuing financial and psychological difficulties many Uruguayans faced as a result of imprisonment and torture. The group declared support for the CNPR by arguing that "democracy cannot be consolidated by ignoring the crimes of the dictatorship."[46] The Tupamaros also described the referendum in human rights terms. The MLN-T issued a statement which described the referendum as a "historical battle." They went on to explain, "For the first time ever in the Southern Cone and perhaps all of the Americas, the issue of human rights violations and its punishment, of facing the military problem under a controlled democracy, and how to define what kind of democracy we want will be determined by a popular decision."[47] Many of the Tupamaros had been imprisoned for the entire length of the dictatorship and were more invested in linking the referendum with accountability. For these two groups, the referendum was not about being allowed to participate in politics, but rather about justice for the suffering so many experienced. These groups proved the exception to the CNPR's general silence.

Interestingly, some of the opposition to the campaign focused more on a human rights argument than the CNPR. Throughout 1987, members of the Colorado and Blanco parties waged a campaign against the referendum attempt. They never formed a formal commission as the supporters of the referendum did, but they still managed to argue publicly to uphold the amnesty.[48] Specifically, Vice President Tarigo and Senator Eduardo Paz Aguirre spoke out, citing other countries' successful use of amnesties to secure a peaceful transition. They even used the language of the human rights movement to make an argument declaring that "peace is the guarantee of human rights."[49] They stated that a successful referendum and trials could be a return to the "confrontations of the past," which played on the population's fear of another military coup and invoked the dictatorship's human rights violations, but by arguing that the amnesty law was the only way to prevent more.[50]

This argument was particularly poignant in light of events in neighboring Argentina. During *Semana Santa* (the week before Easter) in April 1987, a group of military officers mounted a dramatic protest against the impending trials in the country. The day before Major Ernesto Barreiro was supposed to appear in court for his human rights trial, the military overtook the Campo de Mayo Infantry School and converged on the city dressed in combat uniforms as if preparing for battle. The military demanded that the trials come to an end and that members of the armed forces be granted amnesty. President Alfonsín brokered a peace deal that included placing the leader of the rebellion, Aldo Rico, under house arrest. However, Alfonsín also passed the *Obedencia Debida* (Due Obedience) law that offered impunity for those below the rank of colonel from responsibility for any actions taken during the Dirty War.[51] Although the result was ultimately a peaceful conclusion, it exposed the fragility of Argentina's new democracy. Politicians in Uruguay who opposed the referendum used the incident as evidence of the possible ramifications that could come from pursuing trials.[52]

Anti-referendum voices in Uruguay also depicted the amnesty law as a preemptive peace between the new government and the military that would actually guarantee a *more* expansive vision of social and economic human rights.[53] Colorado and Blanco party members argued that trials might prompt another coup, while guaranteeing peace with the amnesty law actually had the possibility of advancing other types of rights in a stable, democratic context. While not explicit, this stance worked against the idea that human rights stemmed from truth, justice, and accountability. Here the opposition hit on a key debate in this emerging transitional justice movement—which path had the best chance of preventing future violations: justice or peace? Were these goals mutually exclusive? In this way, the referendum's opposition positioned themselves as defenders of human rights by articulating an alternative theory of how to obtain such rights.[54]

Despite these claims from referendum critics, the CNPR proved successful in achieving its most immediate goal—collecting well over the required number of signatures to put the amnesty law before a referendum. On December 17, 1987, at around 3 P.M., members of the CNPR went to the Banco República in the Old City in Montevideo, where the signatures had been kept in a vault.[55] In an armored vehicle, 634,702 signatures were transported to the Electoral Court.[56] A line of CNPR members walked behind the truck to personally present the signatures.[57] After depositing the petitions, Rodríguez's widow spoke to a crowd assembled outside the building and stressed that the collected signatures allowed the people to decide. She reaffirmed the group's democratic discourse and declared that a vote by the people would "provide national dignity." [58] A CNPR press statement echoed her discourse, stating that reaching the required number of signatures was a "testament to [the people's] faith in democracy." It argued that they could celebrate in the knowledge that Uruguayans would now have "the power to decide what future we want."[59] Optimistic after collecting so many signatures, the campaign that had centered on exalting democracy celebrated its victory in a discourse that mirrored the winning strategy.

The Response and Verification Process

Sanguinetti's government had actively supported the amnesty law, but it had no organized campaign against the collection of signatures—just periodic statements by party members.[60] However, immediately after the CNPR presented the signatures needed to hold the referendum, the government went on the offensive. Sanguinetti dispatched Vice President Tarigo to counter claims of success, stating that the number of signatures the CNPR obtained was still only a minority of the population, implying that most people wanted the amnesty to stay in place. Trying to turn the narrative on its head, he argued that almost 75 percent of the population did not sign because they were actively against a referendum.[61]

Despite these claims, the mood was largely celebratory in the capital as organizers gathered to revel in the streets of Montevideo. Assuming that the electoral commission would soon announce a date for the referendum, the CNPR began to work on the next stage of the process—convincing the population to vote to overturn the amnesty law. With this goal in mind, the Commission expanded its discourse beyond a democratic appeal and toward a broader grappling with the issues of justice. In fact, the day it submitted the signatures, the CNPR produced a set of posters announcing "now we vote for justice." For the first time, the CNPR centered the importance of the referendum based on justice for the human rights abuses that were committed during the dictatorship.

The Electoral Court soon stopped this new strategy dead in its tracks. Original estimates predicted that it would take the Court between four and six months to count the signatures. However, immediately after receiving the petition, the Electoral Court implemented new, complicated measures to verify the signatures.[62] Now every signature had to be reviewed and certified at least twice, and then checked against the original signer's registration papers. Depending on when a given person had registered, this meant going back to try to find original papers in government warehouses that were up to over half a century old and often lost in a sea of decaying papers. Journalist Lawrence Weschler called this process the "equivalent of a filibuster."[63]

Thus, in the midst of this already onerous process, the Court disqualified thousands of signatures on seemingly dubious grounds for arguably partisan reasons. For example, signatures in Uruguay required a voter ID number on the form, which is called the *credencial cívica número*, and often shortened to CC. However, even if the numbers were correct, signatures were disqualified if the person wrote the letters "CC" in the box in front of the letters. Signatures were thrown out if a U looked too much like a V in a signature, or vice versa. If a person made a mistake in their signature and crossed out anything or attempted to write over a letter in darker pen, the signature was disqualified. If anyone wrote both their old and new ID numbers to make sure that they had the right one with a particular registry, they were also disqualified.[64] Perhaps the greatest affront occurred when Senator Carlos Julio Pereyra and General Líber Seregni had their signatures disqualified, despite being two of the most outspoken leaders supporting the referendum.[65] One was discarded in what was later found to be a transcription error and the other because the S in his last name looked too different from his original registry of over forty years before.[66] By implementing these practices, the Court engaged in blatant partisanship that aligned with the government's position and against the efforts of the CNPR. These measures only served to further discourage the population about the efficacy of the process and detract from the CNPR's message.

This arduous months-long verification process was coupled with the Uruguayan government's renewed fear tactics. The government warned that a referendum threatening to overturn the amnesty law would actually endanger democracy by upsetting the military. Sanguinetti led a multifaceted campaign, particularly fierce in the country's interior, with statements to the press and ads on TV and in the newspapers threatening that chaos would return if the amnesty law was overturned.[67] In January 1988, the government's claims were bolstered just as the Electoral Court battle was beginning. In neighboring Argentina, Colonel Rico escaped from the house arrest that had been imposed after his first attempted uprising and launched another mutiny effort.[68] Although his second coup attempt ultimately failed as well, the Colorado Party touted the attempted uprising as evidence that moving forward with trials could produce a similar, and perhaps victorious, move by the Uruguayan military. Newspapers in Uruguay debated this possible scenario at length across the country.[69]

The Uruguayan military's arrest of Naval Captain Bernardo Gastón Silberman and Lieutenant Sergio Retamoso only exacerbated these fears. Their arrests transpired after it was discovered that both men had signed the petition in support of the referendum. The military claimed that officers were not allowed to participate in political activity. Historically, referendum petitions had always qualified as mandatory voting, an exception to the general political activity ban for the military under Uruguayan law.[70] Nevertheless, both men spent weeks in jail, attracting international outcry and urgent action calls from Amnesty International.[71] Although they were eventually both released, the move sent a powerful signal to the country that the military was not completely subordinate to civilian rule.[72] It also signaled to signees that should they support overturning the amnesty law, they could expect repercussions at the hands of the military.

Despite the CNPR's initial intentions to broaden its messages, during this time it paused the objective of moving toward discussion of accountability for human rights, since even the possibility of holding a referendum was in doubt. The CNPR returned to its original slogan, which changed only slightly from "I sign for the people to decide" to "I signed for the people to decide." (*Yo firmé para que el pueblo decida*). Taking a more defensive posture, the CNPR spent an enormous amount of energy attempting to counter the misinformation originating from the Electoral Court and fighting against the disqualification of signatures. For example, the CNPR issued a press release as early as January 1988 denouncing signature disqualifications. It argued for the will of the people to prevail since Uruguay was once again a democratic nation and deserved to have the voice of the people heard. The issue of justice that had surfaced so briefly as part of the CNPR's strategy in the immediate aftermath of turning in signatures to the Electoral Court vanished yet again.[73]

As the battle over the signatures dragged on, the CNPR continued to focus its efforts on fighting the disqualifications. First, it launched a massive public information campaign about civil rights, which centered on denouncing the dubious reasons for the Court disqualifying signatures and urging the Court to allow people's signatures to count.[74] The CNPR also used key anniversaries from the dictatorship to garner attention. For example, on May 20, the anniversary of the deaths of Michelini and Gutiérrez Ruiz, the CNPR held a press conference to memorialize the leaders and made a statement that the referendum was "inexorable" and needed to move forward.[75] They held a public protest in August that attracted an estimated 50,000 people to push for the Electoral Court to allow the referendum to move forward.[76] When these efforts had no effect, the CNPR tried to overturn the amnesty law by challenging the very constitutionality of amnesty in the courts. However, the Supreme Court upheld the constitutionality of amnesties with a close 3-2 vote. This left the flawed referendum process as the CNPR's only avenue to stop the impunity of the military. However, masses of signatures were still being disqualified daily and the campaign grew more exasperated, explaining that the Court was working against the will of the people. It also argued that for the good of the country, the referendum needed to be held without further delay. The CNPR believed the people's very confidence in the democratic institutions was at stake.[77] Even Cynthia Brown of Americas Watch, who visited the country in 1988, realized the terms of debate were not around the human rights violations.[78] She wrote, "I came away from Uruguay believing that the issue [of the referendum] has gone beyond the amnesty itself and has become in addition a matter of protecting the rights to free expression and to disinterested legal processes."[79] Brown's observations proved spot on. Throughout the verification year, public discussion centered on protecting the democratic process. As the months wore on and frustration grew, the issue of justice for human rights stayed in the background.

Waning International Support as the Battle Continues

Brown's trip for Americas Watch in 1988 was part of intermittent efforts by international groups to shine a spotlight on the country's referendum battle. As WOLA's Joe Eldridge explained, "after the elections the focus was on Central America, we took our foot off the pedal with regards to Uruguay."[80] These transnational organizations had been a critical source of support during the previous years by providing funding, attention, and continued global pressure on human rights. Yet many were now beginning to focus attention and their limited resources elsewhere.[81] Their efforts on Uruguay over the course of the long referendum campaign ebbed and flowed considerably, despite attempts on behalf of the CNPR to keep them engaged.

Indeed, the CNPR aspired to earn international support on the referendum campaign. They even created a subgroup specifically aimed at this objective, which was headed by Luis Pérez Aguirre. These efforts had three purposes: to obtain monetary support, to put outside pressure on the government to follow through with the referendum, and to get exiles still living abroad to sign the petition. To do this, the CNPR regularly sent updates about the referendum process to international organizations such as WOLA and Americas Watch, as they had been critical partners in spotlighting human rights abuses during the dictatorship. These letters asked for financial support to defeat the law in order to print materials, to fund trips throughout the country to spread their message, and most importantly "to counter the enormous propaganda by the government."[82] They extolled "our international friends that have united with the Uruguayan people in demanding that human rights be respected" and asked them to "maintain an alert lookout with respect to the unfolding events in Uruguay."[83] Local affiliate and support groups also popped up in places such as New York, New Jersey, and Toronto.[84] Comprised of local activists and Uruguayans living abroad, these groups sought to implore international "institutions and individuals concerned with the protection and advancement of human rights worldwide to support [the CNPR's] efforts in every way possible."[85] Additionally, these groups set up stations for Uruguayans in the area to sign the petition.[86]

The CNPR's work connecting with international audiences is revealing at two levels. First, while the CNPR often elided or toned down its human rights message domestically in favor of an argument for democratic discourse, it had the opposite strategy abroad. Realizing that human rights language was fundamentally galvanizing for these transnational groups, the CNPR's messages asking for support abroad focused centrally on justice for human rights violations as the reason that they should support the referendum. These efforts were part of a longer tradition of employing a global language of human rights to appeal to international audiences for support.[87] Additionally, this work reflected the CNPR's realization of the importance of trying to engage international attention and revive transnational solidarity networks during the long months of the campaign as a means to put pressure on the government and Electoral Court to allow the referendum to proceed amid all these setbacks. This two-pronged strategy, while revealing, had various degrees of success.

WOLA, for example, maintained interest in the referendum process. However, it was a small organization that had to make difficult decisions about where to spend its limited resources, and Uruguay was largely left out of that strategic calculation. As Eldridge explained, "the focus was so consumed by Central America, that no one was paying attention to the Southern Cone . . . it was just a bandwidth issue."[88] One of the staff members, Virginia Bouvier, did collect extensive information about the process both from the CNPR and other organizations working to overturn the amnesty and from news organizations.[89] Yet, in terms of action, the most significant thing WOLA did during the process was help facilitate Rafael Michelini's visit to the United States in 1988. Michelini was the son of murdered politician Zelmar Michelini. His mother was one of the main organizers of the CNPR. In 1985, Michelini had entered politics and won a seat on the Montevideo City Council. He came to the United States to garner international support for the referendum process, and WOLA held a seminar on the issue and helped connect him to the White House and members of Congress.[90] Despite these efforts, however, his visit received very little press and proved to be one of the few actions WOLA took on the referendum as it focused its energies on other countries and issues during the late 1980s.[91]

Americas Watch was more engaged than WOLA on the referendum issue as the topic of amnesties and accountability grew in importance for the organization. While Americas Watch had had a stronger emphasis on Central America than the Southern Cone since the organization's founding, multiple staff members continued to maintain some engagement with Uruguay during the referendum process. For example, Americas Watch's Executive Director, Aryeh Neier, made public a letter he sent to President Sanguinetti about the organization's opposition to the amnesty law based on international law principles.[92] Further, in 1988 Americas Watch sent two envoys to the country during the referendum process to meet with various human rights groups and report on the difficulties of bringing the referendum to fruition.[93] A press release after Robert Goldman's trip also expressed Americas Watch's belief that the Ley de Caducidad violated Uruguay's obligations under international law to investigate disappearances.[94] These trips resulted in Americas Watch publishing Goldman and Brown's seventy-three-page report, *Challenging Impunity: The Ley de Caducidad and the Referendum Campaign in Uruguay*, which explained Americas Watch's principled opposition to amnesty laws since human rights violators needed to be held accountable for crimes and it was the duty of governments to seek this accountability.[95] Thus, in terms of presence in Uruguay, published reports, and press releases, Americas Watch engaged with the referendum process in various ways.

Perhaps even more importantly for Americas Watch, Uruguay became a critical case study for the organization's board as it debated its stance on emerging justice issues in the region. In many ways, Americas Watch was essential in contributing to the nascent international movement against impunity.[96] Méndez and Goldman, for example, argued cases and submitted reports to the Inter-American Commission on Human Rights throughout the

1980s regarding the right of the victims and their relatives to truth and justice.[97] Uruguay was used as an important argument within the organization for why blanket amnesties should not be upheld and contributed to Americas Watch's stance and thinking on the matter.[98] Despite all these efforts, however, numerous staff members explained that the organization's dominant work was on Central America and only intermittently on Uruguay.[99] While there were sporadic and important efforts, it was never an institutional priority.

Amnesty International offered the most sustained support, even if it was considerably less than during the period of dictatorship. During the 1980s, the organization had once again expanded its mandate, this time working on ending impunity for perpetrators of human rights abuses.[100] Latin America was a particular area of interest, and the organization had been closely tracking developments in Uruguay's investigations into the military's human rights violations since the country's return to democracy. It even sent multiple research missions to the country before Parliament passed the Ley de Caducidad to meet with various stakeholders and report on these investigations.[101] The organization also lobbied Sanguinetti directly to encourage accountability and adherence to international human rights standards while the amnesty law was being debated in Parliament.[102] Once the amnesty law passed, AI issued a statement of concern and mobilized local groups to express its worries over the law and urge investigations into the disappearances.[103] During CNPR's campaign, it issued press statements and urgent actions about the challenges of the verification, such as the arrest of the naval officers who had signed the petition, and denounced the law as violating victims and their relatives' legal redress and the right to the truth.[104] Employing the typical mechanisms that made AI famous—urgent actions, letter-writing campaigns, and press statements—the organization stayed involved in tracking and shining a light on the amnesty battle in Uruguay.

One event in particular brought a great amount of attention to Uruguay's plight. In 1988, there were worldwide celebrations for the fortieth anniversary of the UDHR. AI put on a series of concerts to commemorate the UDHR all over the world, entitled "Human Rights Now." Ending the tour in Argentina in mid-October, a star-studded line-up included artists that ranged from Bruce Springsteen to Tracy Chapman and Sting.[105] At a press conference across the Río de la Plata, Sting held up a sign that said "respect the signatures" right in the middle of the most difficult part of the verification battle.[106] In 1988, Sting was incredibly popular; he received three Grammy nominations and won the Brit Award for Best British Album of the year for *Nothing Like the Sun*.

His support, which received extensive coverage in Uruguay, raised the profile of the issue. *Brecha* argued that Sting's move demonstrated that the international community had not completely lost track of the long verification battle.

In some ways, however, *Brecha's* need to frame Sting's move as proof of continued support demonstrated the extent to which international groups had actually withdrawn engagement with Uruguay during the legal day-to-day battle over signature verification. During this time, many of these groups were focused on more "active" conflicts such as Chile's ongoing struggle against Pinochet or the wars in Central America. WOLA and Americas Watch staff members explicitly admitted this disconnect.[107] In addition, some of the most critical staff members of all three of these organizations who had focused on Uruguay in the late 1970s and early 1980s departed from their ranks by the late 1980s, leaving behind few or even no people with expertise or dedicated focus on Uruguay.[108] Ultimately, these organizations spent more time challenging the narrowly defined human rights abuses that had occurred during the height of Uruguay's dictatorship and were now taking place in other countries, rather than demanding accountability for past human rights violations. Transnational human rights organizations were only in their second decade of prominence and, despite the emergence of discussions over how to deal with impunity, accountability-focused teams or organizations did not proliferate until after the turn of the century.[109] This left Uruguay out of the strategic priorities for many international institutions for much of the referendum battle, particularly during the prolonged fight over signature verification.

The Reagan Administration on Accountability

Just as many international organizations were more focused on Central America, the Reagan administration also paid the most attention to that region of Latin America—but for very different reasons. Reagan saw Central America as key to its strategy of fighting communism, while many human rights groups focused on the violations that Reagan supported or carried out across the region. With its attention focused there, the Reagan administration proved largely ambivalent on accountability in Uruguay as long as efforts did not conflict with broader foreign policy goals.[110] In general, his administration had never endorsed a strong human rights stance toward Southern Cone nations; it had reversed most of Carter's human rights initiatives toward the military regime after Reagan's inauguration and offered support to the

Uruguayan military regime. While Reagan did eventually support a return to electoral rule as part of the administration's shift toward democracy promotion, at best it moderately supported rhetorical moves toward justice and generally saw amnesty as the best avenue to achieve stability and stronger economic ties.[111] Even before the Ley de Caducidad, the administration demonstrated this impulse. In commenting on the 1985 legislative commission that investigated the Gutiérrez Ruiz and Michelini murders, a U.S. State Department report praised the initiative and readily accepted the fact that there had been "no evidence of direct complicity by Uruguayan military or police officials," and, therefore, saw no need for further investigation.[112] Within Uruguay, as Chapter 6 explained, the commission had been largely discredited as a political venture since evidence of Operation Condor directly contradicted the commission's "findings." The Reagan administration clearly accepted the Uruguayan government's minimal efforts as being satisfactory and reason to turn the page.

This sentiment also appeared in debates about the amnesty law. The Reagan administration was not actively involved in public debates over the Ley de Caducidad, although it had quietly supported the amnesty as "the only politically sensible course."[113] Its primary interest in Uruguay centered on its economic stability, cooperation on regional debt issues, and support for U.S. policy in Central America. The administration viewed trials as a potentially disruptive force.[114] The U.S. embassy even cast doubt on the CNPR's legitimacy, repeating a Colorado line that the CNPR had submitted signatures of dead people and implying foul play. Those claims were never proved, and the few examples the government touted as evidence were later shown to be a clerical error by Court employees.[115] However, the fact that the United States was suggesting foul play cast doubt on the CNPR's efforts and demonstrated the U.S. government's position as a quiet supporter of the amnesty.

By the time the debate about the signatures reached a crescendo in 1988, however, even the U.S. ambassador to Uruguay, Malcolm Wilkey, admitted that he had told the Colorado leadership "that they ought to hold the referendum and be done with it." His justification was not rooted in support for accountability, but in the idea that "it would lose and everyone would be rid of the headache."[116] While generally unsupportive of accountability aims, his comments underscore the Reagan administration's priority of democratic stability during this period and its general alliance with the ruling party's line that dominated its strategic calculations toward the country's justice efforts.

The Push for Verification

By October 1988, the Electoral Court was still claiming to verify signatures. It was at that time that the CNPR reached a breaking point. The CNPR realized that in spite of its attempt to counter the Electoral Court's clear partisanship, the Court was not going to change its corrupt process of disqualifying as many signatures as possible. A former judge who resigned from the Court due to his wife's failing health even spoke out against the institution he had been a part of, stating that he was "convinced that the process was being pursued in bad faith."[117] Thus, the CNPR withdrew its delegates to the Court in protest, denouncing its "absolute lack of impartiality," demanding that the current members of the Court resign, and asking the legislature to designate new judges.[118] The PIT-CNT supported the CNPR by calling for a strike and protesting the partiality of the Court.[119] Meanwhile, students temporarily occupied more than forty schools, congregating outside the Court to express their anger at what they termed "a fraud against the people."[120] Nevertheless, the moves had little effect and the Court continued to disqualify or suspend signatures on ambiguous premises.

Finally, in November, after eleven months of verification procedures, the Electoral Court gave a qualified decision on the referendum. It approved 529,110 signatures, which was short of the required 555,701. They argued that of the more than 100,000 rejected signatures, 36,834 were *"en suspenso."* This meant that the signatures were in question but had not been disqualified outright. The Court said it would allow these signatures to be verified and conceded that if the CNPR could verify 22,983 of the 36,834 en suspenso, the Court would approve the referendum. The Court set aside the weekend of December 17 and 18, 1988 to open the registries for verification. Despite the joy of having the opportunity to finally proceed with the referendum, the date was less than three weeks away, and the CNPR had very little time to track down an incredible number of individuals throughout the entire country.

Initially, the CNPR was split on whether to finally put its foot down and take a stand against the Court's onerous procedures by protesting the process, or whether to view the weekend as one last hoop to jump through before finally achieving the referendum. After working for over two years to bring the referendum to fruition, the CNPR made the decision to continue through what the leaders hoped would be the last challenge. As a result, a massive and frenzied campaign ensued to find the individuals whose signatures needed to be verified.[121] The process was not easy. The two main daily papers that were both historically conservative, *El Día* and *El País,* refused to publish the list of names. Instead, they each made the editorial decision to cover their front pages with news of another attempted coup in Argentina, showing violence and unrest as tension mounted between the government and military over possible trials.[122] The pictures only served to further instill fear in Uruguayans about the potential pitfalls that might occur if the referendum succeeded. The Uruguayan Minister of National Defense, former military general Hugo Medina, even explicitly linked Argentina's troubles with the situation in Uruguay during this critical time.[123]

Meanwhile, the Left frantically organized to ratify the signatures through other press venues and on the radio. Leftist papers organized and distributed the names, while two radio stations agreed to broadcast the names around the clock until the referendum.[124] The CNPR also opened seven impromptu offices—mainly any space available where hundreds of volunteers could get together to call and track down names on the list. What made this task more difficult was that 40 percent of those on the list did not have phones, particularly those who lived in the interior parts of the country. Therefore, the CNPR instituted a more expansive method of sending volunteers out in cars or on bicycles to make house visits to track down people and help transport them to the Court's various outposts to verify their names and signatures. The efforts reached a fever pitch when volunteers found out that one signatory was on a fishing trip in the eastern part of the country. The CNPR responded to the news by debating whether someone should get a boat out to locate him on Lake Castillos and bring him in to verify his signature.[125] Other theatrics abounded as well. One woman made her ambulance stop on her way to the hospital for a scheduled cesarean section to sign. Another couple went straight from the church where they had exchanged wedding vows, delaying their reception to affirm their signatures.[126]

The Court's terms of verification gave the Commission until 2 P.M. on Monday, December 19, to submit any affirmed signatures. Over the weekend there had been a hundred tables set up in public schools around the country. Yet, on Monday, the Court allowed only three tables to operate in the entire country: one in Montevideo, one in Colonia, and one in Fray Bentos.[127] Tensions were high. Two buses of Uruguayans crossing from Argentina to the polling site in Fray Bentos (a town just over the border) were stalled by immigration officials and just missed the 2 P.M. deadline.[128] In

Montevideo, the preceding few hours before ratification tables closed saw the streets leading to the Electoral Court lined with referendum supporters to watch signatures come in from all over the country. As people ran up to sign or hand in the verifications, the crowds cheered each person rushing in. Writer Eduardo Galeano subsequently explained that the situation was like a scene straight from the Olympics, as if the crowds had been cheering professional athletes and not heads of neighborhood associations turning in official paperwork.[129]

The CNPR needed 22,983 signatures to be approved to compel a referendum. When the signatures were finally counted, the Court announced that a total of 23,166 had been verified—just over the requisite number. As members of the Court broadcast the final tally, celebrations broke out along the Avenida 18 de Julio in a manner usually reserved for World Cup celebrations. An entire year after the CNPR submitted the original list of signatures, the Court finally accepted that the required number had been reached. With a sense of exhaustion and in some ways relief, the CNPR issued a statement which affirmed that it would now be permitted "to consult directly with the electoral body of the country. It is a triumph root[ed] in the faith of Uruguayans and the consolidation of a democratic system."[130] A few days later, Parliament set April 1989 as the date for the referendum.

Even as they celebrated and remained optimistic about their chances to overturn the law, the pro-referendum movement admitted that it had not expected the verification process to be so difficult.[131] The process, which should have been relatively straightforward and taken only a few months, had dragged on for an entire year. The Court denied and invalidated signatures as politicians launched accusations that the Left was purposefully impugning the good name of the Court because it knew it did not have the support.[132] As such, the campaign had focused its organizing for two full years on the importance of democratic procedures and broad participation in the country's direction, not around the ways that justice for human rights violations was a critical part of achieving peace. The government spread the message that peace could be achieved only through amnesty while the CNPR focused its efforts on challenging the Electoral Court. These factors were all exacerbated by the growing politics of fear about a military uprising. Yet, while Uruguayans watched these developments closely as the country moved into the campaign to vote on the Ley de Caducidad, many activists had also begun to focus their energy on a broader range of issues.

Diverse Human Rights Advocacy and New Movements

While the CNPR had remained focused on validating signatures and campaigning around the importance of democratic engagement throughout this long and arduous year, other civil society actors spent most of their time engaged on a wide array of human rights concerns. Many supported the CNPR's efforts, but the multitude of pressing social and economic issues garnered their attention, and they often used a human rights language to proclaim the urgency of their causes that expanded the term beyond thinking about justice for the military's crimes.[133]

The more expansive invocation of a human rights discourse occurred both in the media and through various organizations. For example, editors from a local paper, *El Telégrafo*, in the interior city of Paysandú published an article that questioned what other human rights concerns had been "forgotten or lost in the face of the complicated deliberations" over the Ley de Caducidad. The editorial went on to argue for a renewed focus on the human right to health, which affected the "most needy in the country."[134] Even SERPAJ, one of the human rights groups most actively involved in the CNPR, had a large enough staff to divide its efforts between supporting the referendum and other concerns. In late 1987, the head of the organization, Luis Pérez Aguirre, spoke at a conference, arguing that "today it takes boldness to believe in human rights, because the integrity of human life is much more than a mere condemnation of torture or of forced disappearances. The integrity of life demands the right to proper nutrition, to education, to a dwelling fit for a human being."[135] In this speech, Pérez Aguirre laid out an expanded vision of SERPAJ's human rights agenda beyond just the impunity battle. Additionally, SERPAJ's annual reports during these years illustrated a larger vision for the organization as it covered other important human rights issues in the country, including nutrition, health, education, and police reform. Only in the last few pages did these reports refer to ongoing but stalled efforts to hold the referendum.[136] As an Americas Watch representative noted after meeting with SERPAJ during one of their trips to the country, the organization was explicitly "concentrating its efforts on expanding human rights (such as shelter, food, and decent wages) . . . while it welcomes attention given to abuses under the military, it is also attempting to change the widespread perception that human rights issues deal only with detentions, tortures, and disappearances."[137]

IELSUR was another organization that added to its scope of work during this period. On the one hand, it continued to work on cases involving the disappeared and tortured. It tried, albeit unsuccessfully, to urge investigations into violations of human rights in the pre-1973 period at a domestic level.[138] Realizing the difficulty of pursuing any legal cases domestically, it filed cases with the Inter-American Commission for Human Rights. By 1988, it succeeded in bringing three cases before the Commission.[139] IELSUR explained that the protracted fight over the amnesty law meant that it was not possible "to do justice" in a domestic forum.[140] In this sense, the organization continued the battle against the crimes of the dictatorship, but the amnesty law forced them to focus on alternative avenues of justice outside Uruguay.

In addition, IELSUR focused some of its efforts toward broader ideas of social justice. IELSUR's magazine articulated this expanded vision of human rights, publishing work by one of its members, Alejandro Artucio, who described a vision that covered a broad range of rights, including individual, collective, political, economic, cultural, and social rights.[141] Evidence of IELSUR's expansive idea of human rights also came in the form of grant applications to the Ford Foundation. Ford had supported IELSUR's early work when it first formed during the end of the dictatorship. In 1987, when IELSUR asked Ford to support new projects in its fight against the amnesty law, IELSUR received a lukewarm response. While the Ford Foundation had long been one of IELSUR's largest funders, by the late 1980s it was less keen to fund projects related to justice for past human rights abuses.[142] Instead, Ford encouraged them to think beyond the original mandate of working with former political prisoners and clarifying the fate of the disappeared. Ford Foundation representatives urged the organization to redirect its energies and activities in the local community and apply for funds on those grounds. As primarily a legal services organization, IELSUR heeded this advice and applied for a grant to work in Montevideo's poor neighborhoods, expanding its scope of human rights to the socioeconomic sphere.[143] The proposal demonstrates the way in which IELSUR broadened its definition of human rights, both as a result of the larger needs in the country within the context of a new democracy, but also at the insistence of a major international funding organization that saw accountability work against the Ley de Caducidad as not worthy of its resources.

In addition to the expansion of various well-established human rights organizations' definitions of human rights, new social movements emerged during this period. Although Uruguay had been a vibrant social democracy throughout the first half of the twentieth century, the dictatorship had completely shut down opportunities and avenues for advocacy. The return to democracy opened up new political opportunities.[144] As activists debated the direction of the nation's reconstituted democracy, new advocacy groups also took the opportunity to engage in political processes and make claims on the state.[145] The precarity of the political direction of the country actually created spaces to have new activists' voices be heard and demand reforms.[146]

For example, Afro-Uruguayans organized a new movement to advocate for rights. As Chapter 2 illustrated, Afro-Uruguayans experienced an added level of repression during the dictatorship, largely related to forced relocation from their homes and removal from the centers of the city and cultural life.[147] After the transition back to democratic rule, a group of younger and more politically left-leaning Afro-Uruguayans organized in response to the plight of those who had been displaced during the dictatorship. The movement was led by people such as Romero Jorge Rodríguez, who had been tortured and in exile in Brazil during the dictatorship, and Beatriz Ramírez, *una desalojada* who had studied the U.S. civil rights movement and the South African anti-apartheid struggle. Indeed, international civil rights and Black liberation movements provided inspiration for activists who began to demand that the government acknowledge the myth of racial democracy and address the effects of discrimination.[148] As such, in 1988 these activists formed Organizaciones Mundo Afro, which functioned as an umbrella for groups with more specific missions, such as the Grupo de Apoyo a la Mujer AfroUruguaya (Support Group for Afro-Uruguayan Women), SOS Racismo, and Movimiento Juvenil Afro, among others.[149] These groups became important venues to advocate for a platform of human rights that included issues of poverty, unemployment, and discrimination. Rodríguez and Ramirez also led the charge to found *Mundo Afro,* a paper that became a mouthpiece for Afro-Uruguayan events and issues. For example, it publicized candombe performances, African art exhibits, and talks. *Mundo Afro* published articles on the history of Afro-Uruguayans and global issues facing African populations from the formation of the Organization of African States to the plight of Afro-Haitians.[150] Free from the constraints of the dictatorship, the emergence of an Afro-Uruguayan rights movement served to address issues including the invisibility of Afro-Uruguayan cultural history and rampant discrimination.[151]

Afro-Uruguayans were not the only group directly targeted during the dictatorship that formed a new movement in the post-military rule era. The dictatorship couched its policies in language that explained it was saving the nation by restoring morality and patriarchal family structures. As a result, it had shut down many of the gay spaces in Uruguay that had surfaced during the 1960s. While the end of the dictatorship allowed for the reemergence of a few gay spaces along the edges of society, the Sanguinetti government was generally conservative and seen as both homophobic and oppressive toward gay culture.[152] One journalist writing at the time mentioned a societal fear of a "gay invasion" and called sex in Uruguay "more subversive than the Tupamaros."[153] These sentiments and oppression permeated society.[154] During this period, police raided bars and gay and lesbian clubs, as well as patrolled areas where young gay men and women were known to be and continued to arrest and detain citizens for "homosexual acts." Some police even bribed the men and women, taking them into custody for their sexual identity and demanding money if they wanted to avoid transfer to jail.[155] In a collection of *testimonios*, gay men recalled being harassed, insulted, and persecuted for their sexual identity.[156]

In response to their treatment during the dictatorship and these continued challenges in the new democratic space, the first gay rights organizations formed, such as the Fundación Escorpio del Uruguay and Homosexuales Unidos.[157] They viewed the transition "as an opportunity to fight for inclusion in the emerging state."[158] Indeed, gay and lesbian rights advocates in Uruguay were part of a broader mass mobilization across the region. As Brazilian historian James Green attests, these activists "challenged societal prejudices, including those held by the Left, with the same language of human rights and democracy that former revolutionaries had adopted to bring down the military regime."[159] For example, Escorpio's founding documents explained their right to have freedom for sexual choice as "our fight in defense of human rights."[160] Meanwhile, Homsexuales Unidos also explained that gay people lived in a society where, as minorities, they were not able to live a life with dignity, respect, or human rights.[161] Thus, they framed their mission as a fight against oppression and the ability to be "homosexual" as a "human right."[162] These efforts were bolstered by the return of many exiles who had left Uruguay during the dictatorship due to being persecuted for their sexuality, and who had witnessed or were even involved in LGBT activism abroad. Many of these returnees had also experienced the freedom to live openly abroad. Upon their return to Uruguay, they suffered under the repressive conditions of gay and lesbian life still prevalent in Uruguay and were motivated to fight back.[163] By establishing groups to protect these harassed youths, the gay rights movement became an important space in which to assert freedom in terms of sexual liberation from continued surveillance after the period of dictatorship. These activists also pushed to include sexuality as part of a broader human rights imperative during the transitional period when the terms of the new democratic society were still being contested.[164]

Finally, women's groups emerged to focus on advocating for their own rights. Gendered advocacy was not new to the post-dictatorship period.[165] During the initial protests against the dictatorship, women in madres groups often led the charge to advocate on behalf of disappeared sons and husbands. When these protests transitioned to the fight against the amnesty law, many of these women then became the public face of and a major source of advocacy in the CNPR. However, important women's groups also formed around the country centered on women's issues, as one manifesto stated, "in response to the lack of freedom and respect for women's rights."[166]

These new feminist organizations were diverse and included research associations, groups of women in unions, and even political parties. For example, GRECMU, as part of the Center for Information and Studies of Uruguay (CIESU), emerged in the latter years of the dictatorship. They began by studying women's participation in the labor force as well as the role of the state in forming public policies that affected women's place in society.[167] In addition, the Women's Commission of Uruguay's national trade union confederation formed immediately following the dictatorship. While trade unions in Uruguay had historically paid little attention to women, men and women had worked side by side to advocate for an end to the dictatorship. Therefore, women won space for their own advocacy in the new democratic environment. Through conferences, new groups, and manifestos, they petitioned for equal pay, nursery schools, and even health care.[168] In 1988, another important group, the Red de Salud de las Mujeres del Uruguay (Network of Women's Health of Uruguay), formed, which added to a growing number of feminist groups to address specific health-related issues for Uruguayan women. Cotidiano Mujer (Everyday Women) was another women's group that launched a campaign to liberalize the nation's abortion policy in the post-dictatorship period. The group's initial efforts sought to create awareness about the risks of clandestine abortions and their dangerous effects on women's health across the country.[169]

These organizations became important social spaces for women beyond just organizing against the dictatorship and focused their attention on topics that specifically affected women in Uruguay.[170] They inspired declarations of women's rights as human rights broadly defined, including through editorials in papers around the country, such as one in *El Telégrafo*. Although relegated to page six, its message was clear: "*¡Las mujeres también tienen derechos!*"

(Women also have rights!) The article then cited the Declaration for the Rights of Women and argued against discrimination and discounting the importance of domestic work.[171] Thus, women across the country, through a variety of means and methods, became social forces outside of formal politics to work on improving conditions for women in society.[172]

All three of these movements emerged in the period immediately following the dictatorship as the referendum battle dragged on in the courts. Their tactics and human rights language evolved in many ways from their advocacy against military rule.[173] Importantly, though, the end of the dictatorship opened up public spaces for such groups in ways that highlighted a range of political agendas and often more future-oriented causes.[174] Their existence demonstrated both the way in which human rights language appeared during this period and the wide scope of concerns within society that existed well beyond a justice framework. While the notion of human rights expanded to include race, sexuality, and gender issues, this also meant that there was less coherence and fewer efforts being made to attain justice for the crimes committed by the dictatorship as these other movements garnered time, attention, and resources from activists.

The Referendum Campaign's Final Stages

By the time the Electoral Court validated the signatures in December 1988 and set the April 1989 date for the referendum, two years had passed since Parliament first approved the Ley de Caducidad. Very few efforts by the CNPR during this period focused on debating justice for the military's actual human rights violations. Instead, the CNPR's campaign centered on affirming democratic institutions, especially throughout 1988 when attention was focused on countering roadblocks imposed by the Electoral Court. Meanwhile, major new rights movements had emerged in Uruguay over this period, other civil society groups worked on reconstituting earlier guarantees of socioeconomic rights that Chapter 6 explored in depth, and transnational groups often refocused their resources on other conflicts.

The CNPR did finally expand its message in those last four months to include an emphasis on justice for past human rights abuses, even while continuing to emphasize a distinctly democratic focus. This work continued through a variety of methods. For example, Uruguayan neighborhood committees revived their work in Montevideo and in the interior. Churches became places

for discussions, volunteers went door to door, and organizers held workshops
to encourage people to vote against the amnesty law. In some of the pamphlets
they distributed, the CNPR emphasized the multitude of crimes committed by
the dictatorship, actively drawing attention to torture, political imprisonment,
and kidnapping. It also explained the importance of "knowing the truth to
build a more just society and ensure the acts would not happen again," rather
than engaging in the "dirty business of hiding the past."[175] Only if the military
were brought to justice, the CNPR argued, would rule of law be restored. The
campaign adopted new slogans, including "we vote for justice." [176] After shying
away for two years from arguments that evoked specific human rights violations, the materials in the last four months actively promoted these concerns
as part of the campaign to vote *verde* (green, the color of the sheet that would
be used to vote to overturn the law).[177]

The overall focus of the CNPR's strategy continued to be a distinctly
democratic appeal, even though the references to the dictatorship's crimes
signaled an important shift during the campaign. It continued to center its
campaign on a future where all individuals would be equal under the law.
For example, the campaign did not just use the slogan "we vote for justice";
it also adopted additional mottos, including "vote green: all are equal before
the law" and "democracy does not have owners: all are equal before the law,"
implying that the military should be judged equally before the justice system
as any ordinary defendant would.[178] Another member of the CNPR, Alberto
Pérez Pérez, explained the importance of overturning the law in terms of
Uruguay's historic commitment to the rule of law. He explained that it was
necessary so that there would be no caste system in Uruguay where "some in
uniform are not judged for their crimes while everyone else is."[179]

While a strategy that focused on democracy had proved effective to gather
a wide range of signatures, it held less appeal during this period. In part, this
was due to Uruguay's stability in the face of Argentina's three attempted coups
during the course of Uruguay's referendum battle. This contrast made Uruguay's transition—where there were no trials but more stability—look more
appealing. However, even arguments for democracy were less compelling in
1989 than two years prior due to impending national elections scheduled for
November. The political parties all launched their national campaigns for
office during debates over the April referendum. While Uruguay was clearly
still struggling with the memory of the dictatorship, it was hardly the only
concern as the economy continued to falter. The November election campaigns became the main focus of the media and many Uruguayans' attention.

In addition, the fact that there were impending elections meant that the country's democracy had strengthened over the past five years. Compared to the 1984 elections, when the military imposed candidate exclusion and censorship, in 1989 there were no longer any proscribed candidates and the press flourished. While the CNPR hoped that the terms of the debate could be focused around strengthening democracy, the government had a strong case to make for Uruguay's growth in this arena both at a domestic level and by regional comparison to places such as Argentina, which had conducted trials but now faced a more unstable political future. Ironically, this progress undercut the campaign's democracy argument.

The campaign also failed to focus on the pain of the dictatorship, choosing instead to focus on an upbeat and happy message in those final months. Following Chile's success with this method in 1988 against Pinochet, the "green vote" pitched a campaign of optimism.[180] Members of the CNPR explained that their movement had transformed "into a movement of hope. . . . We believe that the smile [from campaign posters] expresses that the green vote is a real and authentic smile because we want to build a stronger Uruguay . . . where there are no divisions between the military and civilians."[181] During a last push in late 1988, the CNPR even utilized the phrase "happiness is coming." In early 1989, a rally for the vote displayed a sign which read "*contamos por la alegría.*"[182] Despite using the exact same slogans that had proved effective in Chile, the two situations were drastically different—Chile had been voting against continuing Pinochet's rule, which more closely paralleled Uruguay's 1980 plebiscite than the amnesty referendum. Uruguayans found it difficult to understand why happiness was part of the logic in voting to have trials. As a result, the strategy failed to have the same impact in Uruguay as it did in Chile.

Despite the CNPR's continued calculated decision to focus on democracy over human rights as the center of its outreach strategy, other groups did make the case for human rights as a major reason to overturn the amnesty law—especially in these last months. For example, las Madres y Familiares de Uruguayos Desaparecidos Detenidos founded its group based on advocating against the human rights violations committed by the dictatorship. Unlike the CNPR, its pamphlets continued to focus on this element, explaining that "in this country, there have been many prisoners, many tortured, disappeared, and because we do not want this to happen again: Vote for justice, Vote green."[183] The group also argued that peace was an integral component of justice, evoked the pain of thousands of tortured people, and maintained the injustice of impunity.[184] This strategy marked a stark contrast with the CNPR's discourse, which was more concerned with stressing equality under the law than achieving justice for crimes in the past.

The leftist press was another venue where human rights calculations were front and center in arguments about what was at stake in the vote.[185] *Brecha* was particularly important in these conversations. Mario Benedetti, a prolific poet, novelist, and writer in Uruguay, often wrote during this period about the ethical considerations involved in voting against the amnesty law, including the changing human rights stances of figures such as Sanguinetti, both before and after entering public office.[186] Other journalists were more like Héctor Rodríguez, who had been an early member of the Frente Amplio and spent much of the dictatorship in prison. Rodríguez explicitly described the crimes of the dictatorship. He argued that overturning the amnesty law symbolized the path toward truth, justice, and guaranteeing a future without state terrorism.[187] Although *Brecha* readers were already generally sympathetic to these viewpoints, writers did not shy away from making passionate human rights pleas to the electorate to overturn the amnesty law. Instead of evading the human rights component of the vote, they argued for voting against amnesty in those very terms.

Despite these strong invocations of the 1970s minimalist concept of human rights, the discourse surrounding the national campaign overall set a very different tone. Human rights had been a powerful motivator to pressure the government in the 1970s, and to push for the transition in the early 1980s. During subsequent years, however, the idea of human rights had broadened to include socioeconomic rights and new movements that focused on gender, sexuality, and race. While this expanded discourse demonstrated the strength of a renewed civil society in Uruguay, the term also lost some of the unique power it held during the 1970s to advocate against torture, disappearances, and political imprisonment, or justice for these crimes.

Activists' diverse invocation of human rights was paired with the CNPR's sparse use of the term. The CNPR largely chose to debate the government over the best theory of successful democratic transition and whether it encapsulated turning the page on a painful period in the past or grappling with legacies of abuse. This debate, over whether peace and justice were at odds or inextricably linked to securing democratic peace, came to define the emerging wave of democratization and transitional justice. Uruguay is often left out of global histories of transitional justice because in the immediate aftermath of its neighbors' transitions, other countries made innovative arguments and policy decisions to include justice as a fundamental component of how to achieve lasting democratic peace. For example, Chile employed a truth-telling mechanism, the Rettig Commission, while Argentina published *Nunca Más* and held trials. While both countries' mechanisms were fraught, Uruguay utilized neither until nearly two decades later. Yet, at a fundamental level, referendum debates centered on competing ideas of how to transition to democratic peace. While there were major figures who explicitly argued for impunity, such as General Medina, most other defenders of the Ley de Caducidad such as Sanguinetti and Tarigo explained that the reason to vote against overturning the amnesty law was stability and peace rather than the "dangers'" of justice. Sanguinetti even argued that the choice was over whether society wanted to "consolidate and affirm democratic peace, or return to the past"—referencing the dictatorship.[188] Others, such as representative Victor Valliant, argued that democratic peace could be achieved only if the amnesty law was overturned, so that people could respect the concepts of justice, the law, and the constitution to uphold equality before the law.[189] In his view, justice was the only way to create a more stable peace. These were the very debates that defined the origins of transitional justice, and they were on full display in Uruguay during this period. In this way, Uruguay was very much engaged in these important global and norm-shifting discussions. However, in contrast to many neighboring countries where arguments for peace with justice triumphed, in Uruguay the actors who stressed the incompatibility of peace and justice ultimately won.

The Results

When it was finally announced that the amnesty law would remain in place, the results were somewhat of a surprise, because no one knew what the outcome would be ahead of time. A few days before the election, one poll reported that a full 39 percent of the population was undecided on how they would vote. Whether there was a high degree of indecisiveness or a fear of reporting on intended votes, uncertainty abounded. But on April 16, 1989, with almost a 56 percent majority, the Uruguayan electorate made up its mind. They upheld the amnesty law and culture of impunity.[190] While voters in Montevideo had actually voted by a majority to overturn the law, the interior of the country offered even stronger results in favor of keeping it in place, which ultimately carried the vote and the decision. The government extolled the outcome. Vice President Tarigo declared that the decision had resolved "the last, thorny question from the past."[191]

The results devastated those who had worked so hard on the initiative and who had been optimistic about their chances going into the election. One writer who supported the no vote, Mario Mazzeo, wrote that the country woke up on April 17 in a haze of silence and sadness.[192] Others described activists as being "intensely depressed."[193] The reaffirmation of the amnesty and the protection of military officers from prosecution felt like, as activist and future Frente Amplio representative Felipe Michelini explained, "the ultimate defeat."[194] Another mourned that on April 16 "justice [came] to a standstill . . . we [were] no longer equal under the law."[195] Those who had worked on the campaign remember crying upon hearing the results.[196]

In the days that followed, dozens of letters poured into the CNPR's offices. One letter from Luisa Cuesta, a leader in the Familiares, encapsulated this frustration by explaining that even though they were not alone in the defeat, there "are moments when words cannot describe the anger and the sadness."[197] Others were a bit more defiant. One letter from the Independientes del Barrio Bella Italia, a neighborhood group in northeast Montevideo, outlined its desire to keep fighting. While acknowledging that the majority of Uruguayans had voted for "impunity for the military . . . that committed crimes against humanity during the dictatorship," it ardently argued that the "fight for human rights does not end here, but needs to continue through other means."[198] The group said that the CNPR should issue a call to all the social forces and politicians to defend human rights in the next stage of the fight. The group outlined possible methods, such as transitioning the CNPR into a permanent human rights body, with the neighborhood groups transforming into permanent neighborhood human rights commissions, and pursuing trials for crimes not protected by the law, such as human rights abuses committed before June 27, 1973, which was the earliest date that the amnesty covered.[199]

What is perhaps most notable about the Barrio Bella Italia's letter is its invocation of human rights to explain the importance of the battle. In dozens of other letters that flowed into the CNPR, individuals and groups shared their sadness and disappointment, expressed the hope that they would all stay strong together in the difficult moment, and lamented the fact that the failure of the vote would "impede achieving the truth and preventing justice."[200] Rarely, however, did any other letters explicitly invoke the discourse of human rights, which, as this chapter has shown, mirrors the absence of the discourse from the general campaign. Indeed, the student movement, the PIT, and a housing cooperative movement issued a joint statement that explicitly argued that "the vote does not reflect the consciousness about the atrocities committed by the dictatorship. The people were not voting against justice and for impunity. The population was choosing between two proposals, and they opted for the one with less risk."[201] In this way, these groups seemed to affirm the government's position that people were voting based on fear.

Emilio N. Monti, an election observer invited by Familiares from neighboring Argentina, had a slightly different take. In a report to WOLA about his experience in Montevideo the day the results were announced, Monti explained that "for many, the way in which this plebiscite affects human rights does not seem to be clear."[202] Indeed, between the CNPR's campaign and the increasingly diverse way human rights had come to be invoked in Uruguay during the 1980s, the results of the referendum laid bare the way that human rights had shifted in meaning, impact, and importance from the height of the dictatorship.

Conclusion

For many Uruguayans, the 1989 "referendum results sealed the issue of past human rights violations legally and politically" for decades to come.[203] Sanguinetti claimed that the results of the referendum "completed the transitional process in Uruguay."[204] Indeed, in some ways, concern about the dictatorship's crimes receded into the background as silence prevailed. The international community followed or perhaps contributed to this trend. While prominent, transnational human rights groups had provided support and words of encouragement during the referendum battle, most international organizations found their resources better spent on more active battles in its aftermath. The Ford Foundation, which withdrew all support of projects in Uruguay after the referendum, epitomized this trend. Using the decision letter regarding IELSUR's new proposals as a forum for deciding on a new policy, Ford argued that IELSUR had struggled with how to fit into a democratic context and "establish a clear identity and coherent program strategies in the context of a civilian, constitutional rule." Thus, in early 1990, Ford decided to cease funding "any more human rights projects in Uruguay because of limited resources and the absence of a compelling rationale."[205] Although there continued to be deep struggles over how to deal with the crimes and harms caused by the dictatorship at a national level in Uruguay, Ford perceived a "successful" democratic transition and a return to civilian rule, and devoted its resources elsewhere.

While Ford completely withdrew support, AI, WOLA, and Americas Watch were not as total in their pullback. All three organizations issued statements condemning the amnesty results. However, they also spent much less energy working in the country in subsequent years. Pérez Aguirre expressed frustration with this situation at an international conference later that year, noting that "as soon as the immediate crisis was over, they never heard from INGOs [international NGOs] again."[206] The withdrawal of their attention served to contribute further to the subsequent silence about these issues in the years that followed.

While many scholars have explained the referendum as being the ultimate defeat for human rights, this chapter has analyzed the rather complex role that human rights actually played during the struggle over the Ley de Caducidad. Part of this is tied to the absence of human rights in the CNPR's general campaign strategy. The CNPR made a concerted strategic decision to ensure that the vote was not centered on human rights as such, but rather on reestablishing democratic institutions and discussions of political transitions, which opened up the dialogue about peace versus justice in Uruguay's transitional process. In this way, Uruguay contributed to the critical emerging debates about justice during this period, but the campaign was not ultimately debating a human rights vision.

Second, this period of Uruguay's history reveals the way that human rights as a discourse and organizing principle had dispersed in meaning and assumed a very different set of expectations. The rebirth of civil society had been a critical part of Uruguay's process toward democratic rule, but it also meant that civil society actors had multiple concerns and competing interests. As one letter from a student group explained in reaction to the amnesty referendum's defeat, "We are resolved to fight for this and all our rights—health, teachings, salary, and work."[207] In this way, ASCEEP demonstrated that while it opposed impunity, it also had a broader and more expansive vision of social and economic rights. In addition to the student movement and unions invoking rights talk for more diverse political aims in the 1980s, other movements for women's rights, for racial equality, and for LGBT recognition had emerged during this period. The new mobilization efforts demonstrated how the human rights discourse had expanded well beyond a justice framework. In this way, Uruguayan activists invoked a much broader vision of human rights, in contrast to the minimalist period of the 1970s.

Meanwhile, most transnational human rights groups maintained a focus on active violations in other countries similar to the ones that Uruguayans had suffered a decade earlier.

This research also questions some assumptions about transitional justice. The growing body of transitional justice literature frequently asserts that justice is an integral component of peace and should be an inextricable component of transitions. At the same time, case studies around the world report that many communities are willing to compromise on justice for peace with the promise of other social and economic rights such as education for their children and health care.[208] Other literature by authors such as political scientist Leigh Payne have made the case that the order of transitional justice mechanisms is increasingly important to consider in making claims about justice, especially with respect to the possibility that significant delays in the application of justice might not be a hindrance to successful transitions.[209] Uruguay has rarely been studied as an example of the consequences of delayed justice and the desires of populations during transitional periods.[210] However, from the terms of debate to the overall vote, Uruguay provides a fascinating case that questions the importance of employing justice mechanisms in the immediate transitional period and foretells some of the main debates regarding transitional justice and social and economic rights that emerged more fully in subsequent decades. While the country continues to grapple with accountability for the dictatorship, the strength of its democratic institutions since the return to democracy is rarely in question.

In this way, examining human rights through the lens of the present demonstrates the ways in which the discourse survived the referendum's failure, contributing to a future language for civil society mobilization and influential discourse for advocacy. The language continues to evolve and expand, but these struggles for how to employ human rights to address broader societal problems began during the transitional period. This chapter has helped to explain how the concept of human rights changed and assumed different meanings to various groups of Uruguayans during the path back to democratic rule, based on their own sociopolitical values, experiences, and worldviews. And it is these very same factors that have withstood the referendum's defeat and continue to influence the direction and meaning of human rights discourse in twenty-first-century Uruguay.

Conclusion

I was a young staff member in the Research Unit at the International Center for Transitional Justice (ICTJ) in 2009 when I first learned about another referendum attempt in Uruguay to overturn the Ley de Caducidad.[1] After the 1989 referendum challenge, progress toward accountability had been slow and circuitous in Uruguay, mainly achieved through innovative legal maneuvers meant to circumvent the strict confines of the law.[2] While other accountability measures had emerged in Uruguay, for example, through the state-sponsored truth commission La Comisión Para la Paz in 2003, the domestic battle over the amnesty law continued to stall. However, by 2009, activists believed global and local conditions had shifted enough to justify another referendum attempt. Justice had begun to emerge as an international norm, as demonstrated by an array of international, regional, and national courts and mechanisms to combat impunity.[3] Domestically, Uruguay was one of the most progressive and stable countries in the region. In 2009, the leftist Frente Amplio government had been in power for four years and had earned high approval ratings. Unions, leftist groups, and human rights organizations in Uruguay collected signatures once again to place the law before a popular vote. After securing the requisite number of signatures, the Electoral Court swiftly affirmed the petition and set the referendum date alongside national elections in October of that year. The process lacked the drama of the previous effort.

On the day of the vote, early exit polling results indicated that a majority of Uruguayans had elected to overturn the law, prompting premature celebrations in the streets.[4] Yet, when results were fully counted, this referendum failed too. Only 47.98 percent voted to overturn the law, falling short of the 50 percent majority needed.[5] The results of the national elections compounded the surprise loss. The Frente Amplio Party won another strong majority in Parliament for the second straight election, and in a runoff a month later voters elected José "Pepe" Mujica to the presidency. Mujica had been a victim during the nation's military rule. For being a member of the Tupamaros, he was arrested by the military, and he spent fourteen years in prison—many in isolation—and suffered through numerous torture sessions during a period that spanned almost the entire length of the dictatorship's reign.[6]

In many ways, it was this juxtaposition that first spurred this book's investigation into Uruguay. How could a progressive, democratic, and left-leaning country have voted not once but twice against accountability, especially given the changed geopolitical context?[7] At a time when Uruguay was emerging as a beacon of human rights in the region that would even elect a former guerrilla fighter and victim of the dictatorship to the presidency, why had impunity for past human rights abuses become such an intractable issue?

To answer these questions, this book has looked at an earlier period of Uruguayan and international history, examining the emergence and evolution of human rights and accountability initiatives during Uruguay's experience with dictatorship and democratization from the 1960s through the 1980s. It found that one important avenue to begin understanding these contradictions lies in uncovering various and at times conflicting invocations and prioritizations of human rights definitions. Both activists at the time and scholars ever since have tended to focus their examination of human rights during Uruguay's dictatorship on the most prominent violations committed by the military, mainly disappearances, political imprisonment, and torture. Yet, as this book has shown, during Uruguay's pre- and post-dictatorship experience, activists from a range of movements organized under a rights banner, championing causes that stretched from revolutionary ideals to fair working conditions and minority rights. The apparent coherence of a narrow human rights language at a local and transnational level during the 1970s was brief at best, but did not supplant these other goals. More often than not, activists deployed the rhetoric of human rights to combat the dictatorship's most repressive practices and to garner international support. It was not because there was a full agreement on how to define the term. Before, during, and after military rule, groups across the political spectrum saw a rights language as reflecting the urgency of their diverse projects. While the violence of the dictatorship inspired that relative unity at a global and transnational scale, it is both the promise and peril of human rights that its essential tenets can ultimately be invoked for such varied projects. In many ways, human rights goals were (and are) moving targets, constantly being redefined in contests over economic, political, and social rights.[8]

Part of understanding the constant redefinition of human rights also relies on recovering voices and stories that were silenced during the dictatorship, including those of women, Afro-Uruguayans, LGBT individuals, and Jews. The emergence of new social movements in the post-dictatorship period was in part predicated on their marginalized status that predated the dictatorship in Uruguay's national narrative, as well as on the exclusionary rights framework that created a coherent and minimalist rights narrative during the dictatorship. Much work still remains to be done in incorporating diverse voices into the history of the dictatorship and drawing attention to the experiences of marginalized people based on their ethnoracial identity, sexual orientation, gender, or religion. Yet, starting to reclaim their varied and broader experiences as part of understanding this period in the nation's history offers a critical contribution to the collective memory of Uruguay's military rule and presents a more complex picture of how state violence operated during these dark years. Additionally, it recognizes the long-term costs involved in mobilizing around a limited set of human rights definitions.

A second conclusion offered by this book rests on the idea that human rights improvements do not proceed in a linear, progressive, nor triumphant manner. In the late 1980s, human rights activism flourished in a variety of movements, ranging from women's rights to gay and minority rights; yet, human rights accountability faltered with the referendum movement and many other potential state-sponsored initiatives. This dynamic is ongoing three decades later. Indeed, in 2011, just two years after the second failed referendum vote, the amnesty law was officially overturned by Parliament. The law's annulment followed an Inter-American Court of Human Rights case, *Gelman v. Uruguay*, which found that the amnesty law was in violation of international law and explicitly stated that direct democratic procedures could not be used to determine human rights that were guaranteed under international law.[9] In response, dozens of families who had been waiting decades to see their cases go to trial filed petitions. Yet, even in the decision's aftermath cases have generally encountered stonewalling at a domestic level by both an intransigent judicial branch that has denied cases based on statute of limitations and presidents unwilling to expend political capital on the issue.[10]

These persistent shortcomings in the realm of justice initiatives have transpired within the context of a decade of human rights progress in Uruguay. The same period saw the passage of legislation that largely stemmed from the persistent activism of the new social movements that emerged in the post-dictatorship period. Parliament passed laws protecting abortion, same-sex marriage, and trans rights, and an affirmative action law for Afro-Uruguayans. The country even ranks highest for all of Latin America in

Freedom House's *Freedom in the World* report.[11] The continued accountability setbacks in the long quest for justice in Uruguay mirror the non-teleological nature of human rights that characterized the country's immediate post-dictatorship period and demonstrate how incredible human rights successes in some areas are often paired with obstacles and perceived failures in others.

As this book reveals, a careful reading of Uruguay's experience with accountability also challenges some of the assumptions in the field of transitional justice—particularly if one analyzes what a transition means. In initial understandings of transitional justice, scholars defined the "transition" phase as a short window. This time period was linked to the length of a perceived democratic transition where elections occur, a modicum of rule of law is established, and governance structures are put in place that move society away from an easy reversal to authoritarianism.[12] However, scholars now acknowledge that transitional justice aims cannot all be achieved within that small time frame, and in fact it was "hubris" to ever believe it was a possibility.[13] Political scientist Cath Collins also puts the length of a transition into perspective and is part of a growing group of scholars who argue that the continuing struggle for accountability after the first few transitional years should be delineated and considered a "post-transitional justice" phase.[14] This emerging consensus illustrates the limits of narrowly defining the length of a transition, and Uruguay is one of the earliest cases that demonstrate that democratic stability, and even other rights advances, can be achieved without state-sponsored accountability in its initial phase. This is not meant to question the long-term benefits and value of truth and justice in societies, nor the importance of transitional justice for victims. Instead, Uruguay's experience brings into focus some of the core debates about timing and implementation of justice initiatives.

Indeed, as this book suggests, the very ideas of "democratic" transition and "justice" transition need to be separated since the two processes can operate in different temporalities. A democratic transition can transpire within that initial short time frame, but the transitional justice process should be viewed within a more elastic framework. As the Uruguay case shows, the goals of a transitional justice process can be better pursued when it is delinked from an immediate process of democratic consolidation. From the outset, the struggle for truth and justice must be understood as a decades-long process. While the length of time will differ in each case, the difficult processes of truth-seeking and reconciliation are inherently challenging endeavors that take many years, as evidenced by the case of Uruguay.

Nevertheless, a delicate balance exists in how long the process can be drawn out before it loses all purpose. While modifying the length of a transition in transitional justice is significant, there are other considerations. Pablo de Greiff, the former UN Special Rapporteur on the promotion of truth, justice, reparation and guarantees of non-recurrence, noted that justice cannot be delayed too long, since transitional justice aims to allow victims to benefit from the clarification of facts. This goal is threatened if victims pass away before justice is pursued.[15] In Uruguay, many victims are now at an advanced age, which requires that a careful balance be struck between assuming transitional justice can be achieved in just a few years and then waiting decades for victims to achieve the right to clarification and justice.

Any attempt to achieve this equilibrium needs to grapple with the fact that transitional justice is sometimes assumed to be a technical process, or that the set of transitional justice tools such as trials, truth commissions, memorialization, and reparations exists above politics. As such, most analyses of transitional justice focus on an institutional or legal approach. Instead, it is more helpful to understand transitional justice squarely within a political frame that activists and members of civil society adapt to and maneuver within.[16] Particularly in cases such as Uruguay, which underwent a pacted, or negotiated, transition, political considerations often dominate battles against impunity and the search for truth. As Uruguayan lawyer, former judge, and current head of the National Institute for Human Rights Mariana Mota has explained, "in reality, [the search for justice] has remained and continues to remain mainly in the hands of the victims or the people that suffered violations because the State has not developed a specific policy . . . it has been nothing more than rather weak support for projects carried out mainly by the victims."[17] In this way, transitional justice is perhaps better understood as an aspirational value for opening doors to a long and often winding process that lacks a sense of completion or closure. Even amid the frustration, it becomes a way for discussions of rights, democracy, and justice to become embedded as societal values and discourse. Conclusions or complete justice over a violent and painful past can never be achieved. By releasing transitional justice from a set periodization or time frame, historians, immersed in diverse voices, archives, and sources, have much to add to discussions about the local context and regional and global connections that lead to transitional justice advances and setbacks. This is particularly true in cases in the Southern Cone, where there are four decades of varied experience and pathways pursuing these initiatives.

*   *   *

Human rights discourse has become ubiquitous in the twenty-first century. In the last few years alone, writers and activists in Uruguay have evoked the concept of human rights in the name of the nation's international ground-breaking legalization and regulation of marijuana; LGBTQ rights; and even the country's legal battle over restrictions intended to limit Philip Morris's tobacco advertising.[18] Uruguayan activist Milton Romani Gerner is a perfect example of this trajectory. He fled Uruguay after being persecuted by the dictatorship in 1973 to neighboring Argentina, where he worked on countering the dictatorship for many years out of a room in CELS's offices. He returned to Uruguay in 1985 after Sanguinetti's inauguration and even worked with the CNPR to try to overturn the amnesty law. Yet it was during the post-dictatorship years that he and many others "began to build a defense of human rights that was of a radical democratic conception. It was neither socialist nor anything, but it is this much broader idea that I continue to defend."[19] Indeed, Romani became one of the leaders in forming the nation's drug legalization policy, which he framed consistently from a mental health and human rights perspective, a position that even won him WOLA's 2013 Drugs and Human Rights prize. While during the dictatorship he fought against the military's repressive tools and remained connected to the cause of justice for human rights, he has spent most of the last few decades pushing the bounds of human rights both within Uruguay and at an international level as well.

This ubiquity is perhaps not as new as we might imagine. This book explores Uruguay's human rights history, but also broader encounters with the discourse at both the transnational and local levels. In one analytical sense, human rights connected exiles and activists around a minimalist set of violations during the tumult of the 1970s. As David Kennedy has explained, human rights offered the promise of a "legal vocabulary . . . outside the clash of political interest" to galvanize the international community around stopping the abuses that many Uruguayans were experiencing.[20] On the other hand, human rights were never just a tool to Uruguayans. They gave language to a deeply rooted set of beliefs and visions of social justice that had motivated Uruguayans long before the country's descent into dictatorship. In many respects, while appealing to the notion of an international norm, Uruguayan human rights emerged out of radical politics and leftist traditions during a period of turmoil.[21] Human rights expanded in the 1980s, both embedded in local politics and imagined within a set of social circumstances that recaptured a much broader idea of rights than the narrow violations that characterized advocacy against the dictatorship. Human rights, far from being a stagnant, fixed, or political term, is best understood as a social construct, fluid and reflective of the times and experience in the places it emerges.

Of Light and Struggle examines Uruguay's "long" dictatorship, encompassing both the pre- and post-dictatorship periods. It integrates the country's contributions to both the transnational development of a human rights discourse and transitional justice conversations in historical narratives, to analyze how it differed from the experience of its regional counterparts, and to consider how such variations can shift our analytical perspective on regional and global histories.

When Nelson Rockefeller visited the country in 1969 as an envoy for Richard Nixon, his takeaway was that the country had "international prestige and significance far greater than its small size."[22] While Rockefeller was perhaps most worried about U.S. economic and political interests in the country, he was prescient in his larger vision of the country's importance in the social and political spheres. This idea can be extended to human rights. Through its own trauma and suffering, Uruguay proved to be a major contributor to this critical moment of human rights emergence in the 1970s. However, the country's struggles to implement accountability for violations in the 1980s was balanced against new movements for social and economic rights—a challenge which pointed more broadly to human rights tensions. While Uruguay is often celebrated internationally for its progressive social legislation, its continued impunity reveals that these struggles are ongoing. This paradox of advance and failure speaks to the enduring contradictions that human rights engendered during its emergence, and that continue to plague implementation even in an era of human rights ubiquity.

NOTES

Note to epigraph: Emphasis added. Selection from Letter to Massera, n.d., Folder A: Saludos Liberación, 1984–1985, Box 7, Archivo General de la Universidad, Montevideo, Uruguay (translated by Sofia LeBlanc).

Introduction

1. "Carta desde el Penal de Libertad," *Brecha,* December 18, 1987, 13; William L Wipfler, "In Libertad Prison," *New York Review of Books,* November 19, 1981; Amnesty International, "Uruguay. Conditions In Punta de Rieles Prison," (London: Amnesty International, 1984), AMR 52/28/84; *Memoria de Punta de Rieles en los tiempos del penal de mujeres* (Montevideo, Editorial Vivencias, 2004); David Kennedy, *The Rights of Spring: A Memoir of Innocence Abroad* (Princeton: Princeton University Press, 2009).

2. Alan Riding, "For Freed Leftists in Uruguay, Hidden Terrors," *New York Times,* March 7, 1985, A2.

3. Amnesty International, "Political Imprisonment in Uruguay," AMR/52/BS1/79, Amnesty International Online Archive.

4. Juan Rial, "Makers and Guardians of Fear: Controlled Terror in Uruguay," in *Fear at the Edge: State Terror and Resistance in Latin America,* ed. Juan E. Corradi, Patricia Weiss Fagen, and Manuel A. Garretón Merino (Berkeley: University of California Press, 1992), 90–103.

5. Eduardo Galeano, "The Dictatorship and Its Aftermath: The Secret Wounds," *Contemporary Marxism* 14 (Fall 1986): 16.

6. "Derechos Humanos: Amnistía, ¿y Después?" *Estudiante Libre,* October 1985, Ana María Ferrari Colección, Archivo General de la Universidad, Montevideo, Uruguay [hereinafter AGU].

7. Despite its exclusionary nature, "gay" is employed interchangeably in this book with "LGBT" as it was traditionally employed in Latin America at the time and by other scholars writing on the topic. See Omar Encarnación, "A Latin American Puzzle: Gay Rights Landscapes in Argentina and Brazil," *Human Rights Quarterly* 40 (2018): 194–218. While the author recognizes that LGBTQ+ is now more commonly used as an acronym, "Q" was not added until after the period that this book covers.

8. Martti Koskenniemi, "Foreword," in *Revisiting the Origins of Human Rights,* ed. Pamela Slotte and Miia Halme-Tuomisaari (New York: Cambridge University Press, 2015), xiii.

9. Lynn Hunt, *Inventing Human Rights: A History* (New York: W. W. Norton & Company, 2008); Elizabeth Borgwardt, *A New Deal for the World: America's Vision for Human Rights* (Cambridge: Belknap Press of Harvard University Press, 2005); Mary Ann Glendon, *A World Made New: Eleanor Roosevelt and the Universal Declaration of Human Rights* (New York: Random House, 2001); Eric Weitz, *A World Divided: The Global Struggle for Human Rights in the Age of Nation-States*

(Princeton: Princeton University Press, 2019); Pamela Slotte and Miia Halme-Tuomisaari, eds., *Revisiting the Origins of Human Rights* (New York: Cambridge University Press, 2015).

10. Samuel Moyn, *The Last Utopia: Human Rights in History* (Cambridge: Belknap Press of Harvard University Press, 2010); Jan Eckel and Samuel Moyn, *The Breakthrough: Human Rights in the 1970s* (Philadelphia: University of Pennsylvania Press, 2014); Stefan-Ludwig Hoffmann, "Human Rights and History," *Past and Present* 232, no. 1 (2016): 282; Roland Burke, *Decolonization and the Evolution of International Human Rights* (Philadelphia: University of Pennsylvania Press, 2013); Steven L. B. Jensen, *The Making of International Human Rights: The 1960s, Decolonization, and the Reconstruction of Global Values* (Cambridge: Cambridge University Press, 2016); Sarah Snyder, *From Selma to Moscow: How Human Rights Activists Transformed U.S. Foreign Policy* (New York: Columbia University Press, 2018).

11. For recent and impressive Latin Americanist works on human rights, see Jennifer Adair, *In Search of the Lost Decade: Everyday Rights in Postdictatorship Argentina* (Berkeley: University of California Press, 2020), Patrick Kelly, *Sovereign Emergencies: Latin America and the Making of Global Human Rights Politics* (New York: Cambridge University Press, 2018); Alison Bruey, *Bread, Justice, and Liberty: Grassroots Activism and Human Rights in Pinochet's Chile* (Madison: University of Wisconsin Press, 2018); Luis Van Isschot, *The Social Origins of Human Rights: Protesting Political Violence in Colombia's Oil Capital, 1919–1920* (Madison: University of Wisconsin Press, 2015); Jessica Stites Mor, ed., *Human Rights and Transnational Solidarity in Cold War Latin America* (Madison: University of Wisconsin Press, 2013).

12. Kelly, *Sovereign Emergencies*.

13. Bruey, *Bread,* 11.

14. Winifred Tate, *Counting the Dead: The Culture and Politics of Human Rights Activism in Colombia* (Berkeley: University of California Press, 2007), 4.

15. Among others: Moyn, *Last Utopia*; Kelly, *Sovereign Emergencies;* Edward Cleary, *The Struggle for Human Rights in Latin America* (Westport: Praeger, 1997).

16. Eric Zolov, "Foreword," in *Uruguay 1968: Student Activism from Global Counterculture to Molotov Cocktails,* by Vania Markarian (Berkeley: University of California Press, 2017), ix.

17. Many of these trials and truth commissions were flawed, but they indicated a shift in assumed impunity. Kathryn Sikkink, *The Justice Cascade: How Human Rights Prosecutions Are Changing World Politics* (New York: W. W. Norton & Co, 2011).

18. Author interview with Felipe Michelini, June 14, 2012.

19. Vania Markarian, *Left in Transformation: Uruguayan Exiles and the Latin American Human Rights Network, 1967–1984* (New York: Routledge, 2005); Gabriel Bucheli, et al., *Vivos los llevaron . . . : historia de la lucha de Madres y Familiares de Uruguayos Detenidos Desaparecidos (1976–2005)* (Montevideo: Ediciones Trilce, 2005); Charles Gillespie, *Negotiating Democracy: Politicians and Generals in Uruguay* (New York: Cambridge University Press, 1991); Aldo Marchesi, *El presente de la dictadura: estudios y reflexiones a 30 años del golpe de estado en Uruguay* (Montevideo: Ediciones Trilce, 2004); Marisa Ruiz, *La piedra en el zapato: amnistía y la dictadura uruguaya : la acción de Amnistía Internacional en los sucesos de mayo de 1976 en Buenos Aires* (Montevideo: Universidad de la República, 2006); Diego Sempol, *De los baños a la calle: historia del movimiento lésbico, gay, trans uruguayo (1984–2013)* (Montevideo: Random House Mondadori, 2013); Ana Laura de Giorgi, "A la calle con la cacerola," in *Movimientos de mujeres y lucha feminista en América Latina y el Caribe,* ed. Aline Godois de Castro Tavares et al. (Buenos Aires: CLASCO, 2016), 239–274.

20. Paige Arthur, "How 'Transitions' Reshaped Human Rights: A Conceptual History of Transitional Justice," *Human Rights Quarterly* 31, no. 2 (2009): 321–367; Sikkink, *Justice Cascade*.

21. The recent efforts to produce a truth commission report, as well as overturn the Ley de Caducidad, prompted interesting conversations about reintroducing Uruguay into the transitional justice discussion after two decades of omission. Jo-Marie Burt, Francesca Lessa, and Gabriela Fried Amilivia, "Civil Society and the Resurgent Struggle against Impunity in Uruguay (1986–2012)," *International Journal of Transitional Justice* (March 2013): 1–22; Elin Skaar, "Wavering Courts: From Impunity to Accountability in Uruguay," *Journal of Latin American Studies* 45 (August 2013): 483–512; Francesca Lessa, *Memory and Transitional Justice in Argentina and Uruguay: Against Impunity* (New York: Palgrave Macmillan, 2013). For more about early historiography of Uruguay and transitional justice, see Debbie Sharnak, "Uruguay and the Reconceptualization of Transitional Justice," in *Transitional Justice and Legacies of State Violence in Latin America*, ed. Marcia Esparza and Nina Schneider (Latham: Lexington Books, 2015), 135–153. Larger discussions in the transitional justice literature have also questioned the direct connection of employing transitional justice mechanisms during the immediate transition period. See, for example, Cath Collins, *Post-Transitional Justice: Human Rights Trials in Chile and El Salvador* (University Park: Penn State Press, 2010); Cynthia Horne, "Transitional Justice and Temporal Parameters," *International Journal of Transitional Justice* 14 (2020): 544–565; Paloma Aguilar, "Transitional or Post-transitional Justice," *South European Society and Politics* 13 (2008): 417–433.

22. Scholars have, for example, pointed out the lack of economic justice initiatives, as well as pervasive social and economic realities, in initial transitions. See Dustin Sharp, "Interrogating the Peripheries: The Preoccupations of Fourth Generation Transitional Justice," *Harvard Human Rights Journal* 26 (2013): 149–178; Eilish Rooney and Fionnuala Ní Aoláin, "Transitional Justice from the Margins," *International Journal of Transitional Justice* 12 (2018): 1–8.

23. Sikkink, *Justice Cascade*. For more on setbacks, see Jo-Marie Burt, "The Paradoxes of Accountability: Transitional Justice in Peru," in *The Human Rights Paradox: Universality and Its Discontents*, ed. Steve Stern and Scott Straus (Madison: University of Wisconsin Press, 2014), 148–176; Rebecca Root, *Transitional Justice in Peru* (New York: Palgrave Macmillan, 2012).

24. Conrad Sebastian, *What Is Global History?* (Princeton: Princeton University Press, 2016), 5.

25. As Sebastian charts, there are many types of global history, the "all-in" version of large-scale synthesis of a particular period, a focus on exchange and connection of particular concepts across the globe, or studying particular cases in the context of global transformations—the last being what this book charts mostly closely toward. Ibid., 6–10.

26. Matthew Brown, "The Global History of Latin America," *Journal of Global History* (2015): 365–386; Tanya Harmer and Alberto Martín Álvarez, "Introduction," in *Toward a Global History of Latin America's Revolutionary Left*, ed. Harmer and Álvarez (Gainesville: University of Florida Press, 2021); Aldo Marchesi, "Escribiendo la Guerra Fría Latinoamericana: Entre el Sur "local" y el Norte 'global,'" *Estudos Históricos* 60 (2017): 187–202.

27. It is impossible to account for all international and global voices on this topic—perhaps most notably from European communities that were powerful allies in France and Spain. Markarian's *Left* does a wonderful job of looking at exile communities in Europe, and Pablo Yankelevich, ed., *México, país refugio* (Mexico: INAH, 2002) does this for Mexico.

28. Steve J. Stern and Scott Straus, eds., *The Human Rights Paradox: Universality and Its Discontents* (Madison: University of Wisconsin Press, 2014), 8. Rebecca Atencio, *Memory's Turn: Reckoning with Dictatorship in Brazil* (Madison: University of Wisconsin Press, 2014).

29. Eduardo Canel, "Democratization and the Decline of Urban Social Movements in Uruguay: A Political-Institutional Account," in *The Making of Social Movements in Latin America: Identity, Strategy, and Democracy*, ed. Arturo Escobar and Sonia E. Alvarez (Boulder: Westview Press, 1992), 276-290.

30. "When the War Ends: A Population-Based Survey on Attitudes About Peace, Justice, and Social Reconstruction in Northern Uganda," *Human Rights Center-Berkeley, Payson Center for International Development and the International Center for Transitional Justice* (December 2007).

31. Historians have long debated periodization as a tool that is useful to describe and analyze historical periods, but also very much a matter of interpretation. See Jürgen Osterhammel, *Transformation of the World: A Global History of the Nineteenth Century* (Princeton: Princeton University Press, 2014); Richard Evans, *The Pursuit of Power: Europe 1815-1914* (New York: Viking, 2016), 1.

32. G. M. Trevelyan, *English Social History* (London, 1944), 92.

33. Letter to Massera, nd, Folder A: Saludos Liberación, 1984-1985, Box 7, Massera Colección, AGU.

Chapter 1

1. "Asaltaron el Casino de San Rafael: 42 Millones," *El País*, February 19, 1969, 1, Archivo de Diarios, Palacio Legislativo, Montevideo, Uruguay [hereinafter AD].

2. "Casino: En Pleno día Operaron los Asaltantes," *El País*, February 19, 1969, 6, AD.

3. "Declaración de MLN," *Marcha*, March 7, 1969, 10, Archivos de Centro de Estudios Interdisciplinarios Uruguayos, Montevideo, Uruguay [hereinafter CEIU].

4. "The Robin Hood Guerrillas," *Time*, May 16, 1969, 70.

5. Pablo Brum, *The Robin Hood Guerrillas: The Epic Journey of Uruguay's Tupamaros* (CreateSpace Independent Publishing Platform, 2014), 89.

6. Lindsey Churchill, *Becoming the Tupamaros: Solidarity and Transnational Revolutionaries in Uruguay and the United States* (Nashville: Vanderbilt University Press, 2014), 4.

7. Aldo Marchesi, "Revolution Beyond the Sierra Maestra: The Tupamaros and the Development of a Repertoire of Dissent in the Southern Cone," *The Americas* 70, no. 3 (January 2014): 546-549.

8. Aldo Marchesi and Vania Markarian, "Cinco décadas de estudios sobre la crisis, democracia, y el autoritarismo en Uruguay," *Contemporánea* 3, no. 3 (2012): 231; Clara Aldrighi, *La izquierda armada: ideología, ética e identidad en el MLN-Tupamaros* (Montevideo: Ediciones Trilce, 2001); André Cultelli, *La revolución necesaria, contribución a la autocrítica del MLN Tupamaros* (Buenos Aires: Colihue, 2006); Hebert Gatto, *El cielo por asalta: el Movimiento de Liberación Nacional (Tupamaros) y la izquierda uruguaya (1963-1972)* (Montevideo: Taurus, 2004); José Harari, *Contribución a la historia del ideario del MLN (Tupamaros)* (Montevideo: Editorial MZ, 1986).

9. In 1978, the military published a multivolume explanation of the war against the MLN-T, explaining its connections to other domestic and international seditious groups as a reason to justify their "war" on subversion. See Junta de Comandantes en Jefe, *Las Fuerzas Armadas al pueblo oriental* (Montevideo: República Oriental del Uruguay, 1978).

10. While violence was perpetrated by the Left in many places, it was incomparable to the acts of repressive governments. As historian Stephen Rabe explains, to equate the two "ignores historical chronology and trivializes methodical abuses of the right." Stephen Rabe, *Killing*

Zones: The United States Wages Cold War in Latin America (New York: Oxford University Press, 2012), xxxii; Jeffrey L. Gould, "Solidarity Under Siege: The Latin American Left, 1968," *American Historical Review* 114, no. 2 (April 2009): 348–349; Aldo Marchesi, "¿Guerra' o 'Terrorismo de Estado'? Recuerdos enfrentados sobre el pasado reciente uruguayo," in *Las Conmemoraciones: Las Disputas en las fechas "in-felices,"* ed. Elizabeth Jelin (Madrid: Siglo Veintiuno de España Editores, 2002), 101–146.

11. The reasons for democracy's breakdown have been researched at length by various scholars and can be attributed to a variety of factors. Martin Weinstein, *Uruguay: The Politics of Failure* (Westport: Greenwood Press, 1975); Scott Mainwaring and Aníbal Pérez-Liñán, *Democracies and Dictatorships in Latin America: Emergence, Survival, and Fall* (New York: Cambridge University Press, 2013), 34.

12. Gould, "Solidarity," 348–375.

13. This chapter offers a sampling of diverging visions of social justice prior to the dictatorship—a comprehensive account would take several books.

14. For just a few examples, see Weinstein, *Politics of Failure*, xiii; Lawrence Weschler, *A Miracle, a Universe: Settling Accounts with Torturers* (Chicago: University of Chicago Press, 1998), 92; Martin Weinstein, *Uruguay: Democracy at a Crossroads* (Boulder: Westview Press, 1988), xv; Luis Roniger and Mario Sznajder, "The Legacy of Human Rights Violations and the Collective Identity of Redemocratized Uruguay," *Human Rights Quarterly* 19, no. 1 (February 1997): 57; Gillespie, *Negotiating Democracy*, 19; *Uruguay: Generals Rule* (London: Latin America Bureau, 1980), 22; "Uruguay Succumbs to Military Coup: Congress Abolished as President Points to 'Subversive Threat,'" *Liberation News Service*, June 30, 1973, p9, Box L25, Marshall Bloom Collection, Amherst College Library Archives and Special Collections, Amherst, MA [hereinafter BC].

15. This phrase is attributed to Luis Batlle Berres in 1952. See Ximena Espeche, *La Paradoja Uruguaya: Intelectuales, Latinoamericanismo y Nación a Mediados de Siglo XX* (Bernal: Universidad Nacional de Quilmes Editorial, 2016), 41–42.

16. Uruguay's constitution allows for multiple terms in office as long as they are not consecutive.

17. Michael Goebel, "Gauchos, Gringos and Gallegos: The Assimilation of Italian and Spanish Immigrants in the Making of Modern Uruguay 1880–1930," *Past and Present* 208 (2010): 191.

18. Weinstein, *Politics of Failure*, 20–49; Luis Bértola, "An Overview of the Economic History of Uruguay," *EH.Net Encyclopedia*, ed. Robert Whaples (2008), https://eh.net/encyclopedia/an-overview-of-the-economic-history-of-uruguay-since-the-1870s/; Weinstein, *Democracy at a Crossroads*, 23–25; Christine Ehrick, *The Shield of the Weak: Feminism and the State in Uruguay, 1903–1933* (Albuquerque: University of New Mexico Press, 2005), 70–88; Churchill, *Becoming*, 9.

19. Asunción Lavrín, *Women, Feminism, and Social Change in Argentina, Chile, and Uruguay, 1890–1940* (Lincoln: University of Nebraska Press, 1998), 3.

20. Ibid.; Ehrick, *The Shield of the Weak*; Milton I. Vanger, *The Model Country: José Batlle Y Ordoñez of Uruguay, 1907–1915* (Hanover: University Press of New England, 1980), 173–176, 270.

21. Uruguay's stability stands in contrast to, for example, Argentina, where between 1930 and 1976 nineteen different presidents occupied the presidential palace. Despite the constitution calling for six-year terms, these nineteen presidents averaged only slightly more than two years in office. In Uruguay, the only break from democratic rule in this period was during the

authoritarian Terra regime (1933–1942) after the worldwide economic collapse of 1929. Compared to the Cold War dictatorship, Terra's reign was relatively mild: there was "no torture, no murder, no political prisoners, and little censorship." Alexandra Barahona de Brito, *Human Rights and Democratization in Latin America: Uruguay and Chile* (New York: Oxford University Press, 1997), 18; Paul H. Lewis, *Guerrillas and Generals: The "Dirty War" in Argentina* (Westport: Praeger, 2002), 3; Weinstein, *Democracy at a Crossroads,* 20–22.

22. Vanger, *Model Country.*

23. Uruguay's strong export economy supported his bold ideas only to a certain point. Some of Batlle's more audacious ideas were never implemented. For example, Batlle called for profit-sharing plans in state enterprises for the population and increased taxes on land and inheritances. Particularly because of their potential effect on large landowners and high economic cost, these proposals never made it past the party convention idea stage. Batlle's ideals were thus limited by the political and financial constraints of the era that are at times brushed over in histories of this impressive period. Weinstein, *Democracy at a Crossroads,* 25–27.

24. Fernando Filgueira, "A Century of Social Welfare in Uruguay: Growth to the Limit of the Batllista Social State," *Democracy and Social Policy Series,* The Kellogg Institute (Spring 1995), 3–10.

25. Uruguay had a long-held belief in the use of an international organization to secure global peace and justice, which is not surprising considering its small size. Batlle first supported this idea at the Second Hague Peace Conference in 1907, and Uruguay was also one of the original members of the League of Nations in 1920. Uruguay also proposed an inter-American responsibility for the advancement of human rights in democracy in 1945, known as the Larreta Doctrine. It ultimately failed but demonstrates the deep and long-term thinking about Uruguay on these issues. Carnegie Endowment for International Peace, *Uruguay and the United Nations* (New York: Manhattan Publishing Co., 1958); Tom Long and Max Paul Friedman, "The Promise and Precommitment in Democracy and Human Rights: The Hopeful, Forgotten Failure of the Larreta Doctrine," *Perspectives on Politics* (December 2020): 1088–1103.

26. Kathryn Sikkink, "Latin American Countries as Norm Protagonists of the Idea of International Human Rights," *Global Governance* 20, no. 3 (July–September 2014): 391; Mary Ann Glendon, "The Forgotten Crucible: The Latin American Influence on the Universal Human Rights Idea," *Harvard Human Rights Journal* 16 (Spring 2003): 27–39; Paolo G. Carozza, "From Conquest to Constitutions: Retrieving a Latin American Tradition of the Idea of Human Rights," *Human Rights Quarterly* 25 no. 2 (May 2003): 281–313; Kathryn Sikkink, *Evidence for Hope: Making Human Rights Work in the 21st Century* (Princeton: Princeton University Press, 2017), 57–79.

27. "The Uruguayan Proposal for Intervention in the Affairs of States Through Multilateral Action in Cases of Flagrant Violation of Human Rights or Non-Fulfillment of Freely Contracted Obligations," *Foreign Relations of the United States, Diplomatic Papers, 1945, The American Republics, Volume IX,* documents 126–157; Sikkink, "Latin American Countries," 394–396.

28. Carnegie Endowment for International Peace, *Uruguay and the United Nations*, 28.

29. Janet Lord, "The United Nations High Commissioner for Human Rights: Challenges and Opportunities," *Loyola of Los Angeles International and Comparative Law Review* 17 (1995): 331; Bases of Proposal to Establish a United Nations Attorney-General for Human Rights, Memorandum submitted by Uruguay, 1951, A/C.3/564, United Nations Online Archive.

30. Letter from Uruguay to John Foster Dulles, May 24, 1954, Box 35, Folder 7, Archivo Histórico-Diplomático, Ministerio de Relaciones Exteriores, Montevideo, Uruguay [hereinafter AHD].

31. Sikkink, *Evidence for Hope*, 100, 115–116.

32. Weschler, *A Miracle, A Universe*, 99; Weinstein, *Democracy at a Crossroads*, 35–37.

33. Memo from Mann to Rusk, December 1, 1964, *FRUS, 1964–1968, Volume XXXI, South and Central America; Mexico,* Document 463.

34. Robert Alexander and Eldon Parker, *A History of Organized Labor in Uruguay and Paraguay* (Westport: Praeger, 2005), 46.

35. Espeche, *Paradoja Uruguaya.*

36. Telephone Conversation Between Johnson and Mann, June 11, 1964, *FRUS, 1964–1968, Volume XXXI,* Document 16. Historians debate Mann's legacy. LaFeber credits Mann as a catalyst behind increased U.S. intervention in the region. Walter LaFeber, "Thomas C. Mann and the Devolution of Latin American Policy," in *Behind the Throne: Servants of Power to Imperial Presidents, 1898–1968,* ed. Thomas J. McCormick and Walter LaFeber (Madison: University of Wisconsin Press, 1993), 166–203. Allcock disputes this characterization. Thomas Tunstall Allcock, *Thomas C. Mann: President Johnson, the Cold War, and the Restructuring of Latin American Foreign Policy* (Lexington: University Press of Kentucky, 2018).

37. Memo from Mann to Rusk, December 1, 1964, *FRUS, 1964–1968,* Document 463.

38. "Montar en la sombra la máquina de la dictadura," *Marcha,* December 12, 1965, 5, Biblioteca Nacional, Montevideo, Uruguay [hereinafter BN].

39. Memo from Mann to Rusk, December 1, 1964, *FRUS, 1964–1968,* Document 463.

40. Alexander Edelman, "The Rise and Demise of Uruguay's Second Plural Executive," *Journal of Politics* 31, no. 1 (February 1969): 119–139; Martin Weinstein, "The Decline and Fall of Democracy in Uruguay: Lessons for the Future," in *Repression, Exile, and Democracy: Uruguayan Culture,* ed. Saúl Sosnowski and Louise Popkin (Durham: Duke University Press, 1993), 84.

41. Memo from Oliver to Rusk, August 18, 1967, *FRUS, 1964–1968,* Document 467. Also see Henry Finch, "Uruguay Since 1930," in *Cambridge History of Latin America,* ed. Leslie Bethell (New York: Cambridge University Press, 2008), 213–214.

42. Jeffrey Ryan, "Turning on Their Masters: State Terrorism and Unlearning Democracy in Uruguay," in *When States Kill: Latin America, the U.S. and Technologies of Terror,* ed. Cecilia Menjivar and Néstor Rodriguez (Austin: University of Texas Press, 2005), 280.

43. "Murió el Presidente Gestido," *El País,* December 7, 1967, 1, BN.

44. "Presidente: Datos Biográficos," *El País,* December 7, 1967, 4, BN.

45. Weinstein, "Decline," 84–85.

46. "El Presidente Resolvió Clausurar Época y El Sol," *El País,* December 13, 1967, 5, BN. The OLAS Conference's resolutions from earlier that year had endorsed armed revolutionary struggle. Aldo Marchesi, *Latin America's Radical Left: Rebellion and Cold War in the Global 1960s* (New York: Cambridge University Press, 2017), 86.

47. "Las Libertades Avasalladas," *Marcha,* December 15, 1967, 7, BN.

48. A. J. Langguth, *Hidden Terrors* (New York: Pantheon Books, 1978), 232.

49. Churchill, *Becoming,* 19.

50. Scholars have recently demonstrated how many repressive practices, consolidated under Pacheco, were developed in the earlier parts of the decade as part of Uruguay's anticommunist campaign. Magdalena Broquetas, "Los frentes del anticomunismo. Las derechas en el Uruguay de los tempranos sesenta," *Contemporánea. Historia y problemas del siglo XX* 3:3 (2012), 11–29; Gabriel Bucheli, "Organizaciones 'demócratas' y radicalización anticomunista en Uruguay, 1959–1962," *Contemporánea: Historia y problemas del siglo XX* 3:3 (2012), 31–52.

51. For recent literature on many groups on the Left and their roles in the escalating crisis of this period, see Marchesi and Markarian, "Cinco décadas," 231.

52. Howard Handelman, "Politics and Plebiscites: The Case of Uruguay," *Working Papers of the Latin American Program of the Woodrow Wilson International Center for Scholars*, no. 89 (April 1981), 2.

53. Mauricio Bruno, "Usos y sentidos de la democracia en Uruguay (1955–1989)," GEIPAR, June 2014, p8.

54. Weinstein, "Decline," 85–86.

55. Weinstein, *Politics of Failure*, 50–84; Weinstein, *Democracy at a Crossroads*, 29. This is not the say that the Batllismo model contributed to the full breakdown of democratic rule; the descent into military rule must be attributed to a complex set of factors. However, it is important to see the ways that Batllismo was a contributing factor to the breakdown of democratic rule. Luis Roniger and Mario Sznajder, *The Legacy of Human Rights Violations in the Southern Cone: Argentina, Chile, and Uruguay* (New York: Oxford University Press, 1999), 13.

56. Marchesi, "Revolution Beyond," 535–536.

57. Julio Bordas Martínez, *Tupamaros: Derrota Militar, Metamorfosis Política y Victoria Electoral* (Madrid: Dykinson, 2015), 40–51.

58. Churchill, *Becoming*, 40–41.

59. For an excellent history of the Tupamaros' early years, see Marchesi, *Radical Left*, 45–50.

60. Churchill, *Becoming*, 61.

61. Weschler, *A Miracle, A Universe*, 100–111; Maria Esther Gilio, *The Tupamaros* (London: Secker & Warburg, 1972), 74–80; 117–119; 132–134.

62. "The Tupamaro Manifesto," in *The Tupamaros: Urban Guerrillas in Uruguay*, ed. Alain Labrousse (New York: Penguin, 1973), 157–162.

63. Movimiento de Liberación Nacional, *Documento No. 1*, June 1967, http://www.archivochile.com/America_latina/JCR/MLN_T/tupa_de/tupade0001.pdf. For more on the MLN-T's intellectual ideas, see Gatto, *Cielo*, Chapters 2 and 3.

64. Churchill, *Becoming*, 120; Gabriela Gonzalez-Vaillant, "The Tupamaros: Re-gendering an Ungendered Guerrilla Movement," *International Journal for Masculinity Studies* 10, no. 3–4 (2015): 295–311; Clara Aldrighi, *Memorias de Insurgencia* (Montevideo: Ediciones de la Banda Oriental, 2009), 10.

65. Churchill, *Becoming*, 137.

66. The number of Tupamaros is debated. Estimates vary from several hundred to 5,000 members at their height. Scholars surmise that the lower number likely equates to core members participating in commando operations. Albert Parry, *Terrorism: From Robespierre to Arafat* (New York: Vanguard Press, 1976), 276; Michael Freeman, *Freedom or Security: The Consequences for Democracies Using Emergency Powers to Fight Terror* (Westport: Praeger, 2003), 96–97; Aldrighi, *Memorias*, 13. Women reportedly equaled more than 25 percent of the ranks, which was higher than most other guerrilla groups across the region. Churchill, *Becoming*, 120.

67. Marchesi, *Radical Left*, 56.

68. Churchill, *Becoming*, 41–42.

69. Ibid., 45.

70. Marchesi, "Revolution Beyond," 549–550.

71. Joseph Novitski, "Another Chile in the Making?" *New York Times*, November 28, 1971, E2.

72. Churchill, *Becoming*, 57.

73. Churchill, *Becoming*, 66. There were exceptions to this rule, including when they killed a rural worker, Pascasio Ramón Báez, in order to protect the group from being discovered by authorities.

74. This incident was made famous by Langguth, *Hidden Terrors* which was a commercial book about Dan Mitrione and the CIA's ventures in South America. Mitrione's death was also fictionalized in *State of Siege*, directed by Costa-Gavras (International Films, 1972). Also see Eduardo Galeano, *Memory of Fire* (New York: Pantheon Books, 1988), 208.

75. "Kidnapped U.S. Official Found Slain in Uruguay," *New York Times*, August 11, 1970, 1; "A Murder in Montevideo," *Washington Post*, August 11, 1970, A16; "American Hostage Reported Dead," *The Times: London*, August 10, 1970; David F. Belnap, "Execution of U.S. Aid by Uruguay Guerrillas Reported," *Los Angeles Times*, August 10, 1970, A1; "US Aide Slain in Uruguay," *Boston Globe*, August 11, 1970, 1.

76. "Tupamaros Stage Spectacular Mass Jailbreak as Uruguay Heads Towards Crucial Election," *Liberation News Service*, September 18, 1971, no. 376, GI Press Collection, Wisconsin Historical Society.

77. Clara Aldrighi, *La Intervención de Estados Unidos en Uruguay (1965–1973): El Caso Mitrione* (Montevideo: Trilce, 2007).

78. Gould, "Solidarity," 351, quoting Jay Winter.

79. Héctor Rodríguez, *Unidad sindical y huelga general* (Montevideo: Centro Uruguay Independiente, 1987), 11–25.

80. "Uruguay y sus sindicatos," November 1979, 13, Folder 6, Ponce de León Colección, CEIU.

81. Ingrid Siri, Marta Ponce de Leon, and Salvador Schelotto, *El Pueblo delibera: El Congreso del Pueblo veinte años después* (Montevideo: Centro Uruguay Independiente, 1985), 107–150.

82. Héctor Rodríguez, "Después del Congreso del Pueblo," *Marcha*, August 20, 1965, 6–7; Margaret Randall, "Uruguay: A Woman Remembers," *Social Justice* 42, no. 1 (Spring 2016); José Jorge Martínez, "El Congreso del Pueblo," *Estudios* no. 36 (July–August 1965), 14–21.

83. "De la UGT a la unificación," *Marcha*, September 30, 1966, 12, BN.

84. "Material preparatorio de la Asamblea Nacional de Sindicatos, January 28–29, 1966, in *CNT 1964-1965: Documentos Sindicales* (Montevideo: Centro Uruguay Independiente, 1966), 11–12.

85. Hal Brands, *Latin America's Cold War* (Cambridge: Harvard University Press, 2010), 154; Judith Teichman, *The Politics of Freeing Markets in Latin America: Chile, Argentina, and Mexico* (Chapel Hill: University of North Carolina Press, 2001), 45; Espeche, *Paradoja Uruguaya*, 46.

86. Alexander and Parker, *A History*, 67–69.

87. Martín Gargiulo, "The Uruguayan Labor Movement in the Post-Authoritarian Period," in *Labor Autonomy and the State in Latin America*, ed. Edward Epstein (Boston: Unwin Hyman, 1989), 223–224.

88. Stephen Gregory, *Intellectuals and Left Politics in Uruguay, 1958–2006* (Brighton: Sussex Academic Press, 2009), 41–43.

89. Gould, "Solidarity," 355.

90. As quoted in "Uruguay y Sus Sindicatos," 13.

91. As quoted in Jo Fisher, *Out of the Shadows: Women, Resistance and Politics in South America* (London: Latin American Bureau, 1993), 47.

92. Alexander and Parker, *A History*, 70.

93. *PIT-CNT, un solo movimiento sindical: selección de documentos.* (Montevideo: PIT-CNT, 1985), 103–175.

94. "Bases Programáticas," February 17, 1971, Folder 142, Waksman Colección, CEIU.

95. Victor Bacchetta, "CNT: El Camino y las Perspectivas," *Marcha,* July 2, 1971, 18, BN.

96. *CNT: Declaración de principios, programa y estatutos* (Montevideo: Centro Estudiantes de Derecho, 1967).

97. Mark van Aken, "The Radicalization of the Uruguayan Student Movement," *The Americas* 33, no. 1 (July 1976), 123.

98. Randall, "Remembers," 116.

99. This collaboration began as early as 1919 when student groups argued for university extension classes to take place in the headquarters of labor unions. Van Aken, "Radicalization," 115. From then on, the students supported union activity by helping publicize their complaints and joining strikes, while workers supported the student efforts to gain university reforms. Megan Strom, "Transnational Youth: The Federation of Uruguayan University Students in the Early Cold War, 1941–1958" (PhD diss., University of California, San Diego, 2015), 5.

100. van Aken, "Radicalization," 122.

101. Churchill, *Becoming,* 7.

102. Strom, "Transnational Youth," xix.

103. Ibid., 5–6.

104. Manifiesto de FEUU a la opinión pública, *Jornada,* April 28, 1965; "¡No! A Las Medidas de Seguridad," *Jornada,* October 9, 1965, CEIU.

105. Arthur Liebman, Kenneth Walker, and Myron Glazer, *Latin American University Students: A Six Nation Study* (Cambridge: Harvard University Press, 1972), 136–137.

106. van Aken, "Radicalization," 124.

107. "Editorial: Un momento de definición y lucha," *Jornada,* October 17, 1967.

108. "La autonomía para el pueblo," *Jornada,* August 22, 1968.

109. Vania Markarian, *Uruguay, 1968* (Berkeley: University of California Press, 2017), 140.

110. "Gran Manifestación Estudiantil," *Jornada,* October 1964, CEIU.

111. Markarian, *1968,* 62–63.

112. Gabriela Fried Amilivia, *State Terrorism and the Politics of Memory in Latin America: Transmissions Across the Generations of Post-Dictatorship Uruguay, 1984–2004* (New York: Cambria Press, 2016), 47.

113. Nancy Bermeo, *Ordinary People in Extraordinary Times: The Citizenry and the Breakdown of Democracy* (Princeton: Princeton University Press, 2003), 110–111.

114. Markarian, *1968,* 67.

115. Eduardo Rey Tristán, "Movilización estudiantil e izquierda revolucionara en el Uruguay (1968–1973)," *Revista Complutense de Historia de América* 28 (2002): 185–209.

116. "Jóvenes: Entre la Violencia y a Sociedad Ideal," *Marcha,* June 13, 1969, 12–13, CIEU.

117. "Manifiesto de FEUU," *Jornada,* April, 1965; "Las 'Medidas' se transformaron en dictadura," *Jornada,* October 1965, 1, CEIU.

118. "FEUU: Movilización Popular y Soluciones de Fondo," *El Popular,* June 13, 1973, in *Movimiento estudiantil: resistencia y transición* (Montevideo: Centro Uruguay Independiente, 1988), 14–17.

119. "La Represión en la Universidad," *Militancia,* November 15, 1973, reprinted in *Uruguay y Ahora Qué? Cuadernos de Crisis* no. 4 (1974), p22–3, Folder 4, Álvaro Barros Lémez Colección, CEIU.

120. Convención de la federación de docentes universitarios, "Resolución," July 1972, 47–48, Ana María Ferrari Colección, AGU.

121. With electoral goals over attention-grabbing methods, Markarian notes that many studies of Uruguay in the 1960s overlook the role of communists. Vania Markarian, "To the Beat of the 'The Walrus': Uruguayan Communists and Culture in the Global Sixties," *The Americas* 70, no. 3 (January 2014): 364.

122. Gregory, *Intellectuals*, 36. This equated to 3.6 percent of the total votes cast. The Socialist Party received about 27,000 votes and the Unión Cívica received 35,000 votes.

123. Gerardo Leibner, "Women in Uruguayan Communism: Contradictions and Ambiguities, 1920s–1960s," *Journal of Latin American Studies* (October 2017): 6; Markarian, "Walrus," 368–369; Ana Laura de Giorgi, "La otra nueva ola: Jóvenes mujeres comunistas en el Uruguay de los 60," *Revista Izquierdas* 22 (January 2015): 204–226.

124. Leibner, "Women in Uruguayan Communism," 6.

125. Until the Frente Amplio, the Socialist Party eschewed attempts to create a united party with the PCU. Instead, the Socialist Party advocated for radical reforms to the constitution in the early 1960s, which resulted in decreased support in elections. The party's continued internal battles over how to respond to the nation's problems split the party among various factions. Gregory, *Intellectuals*, 37–41; Wladimir Turiansky, *El Uruguay desde la Izquierda* (Montevideo: Cal y Canto, 1997), 59.

126. Gerardo Leibner, *Camaradas y Compañeros* (Montevideo: Trilce, 2011), 516.

127. "¿Cuánto cuestan al país las medidas de seguridad?," *El Popular*, September 6, 1968, 5; "Ayer se levantaran las medidas," March 16, 1969, 1, David Compora Colección, CEIU; Leibner, *Camaradas y Compañeros*, 521; Wladimir Turiansky, *Los comunistas uruguayos en la historia reciente (1955–1991)* (Montevideo: Fin de Siglo Editorial, 2010), 63, 75.

128. Leibner, *Camaradas y Compañeros*, 589–590.

129. In the 1966 election, 76,750 votes were cast for the PCU, 5.7 percent—the highest since the Cold War began. Ibid., 436.

130. Ibid., 590.

131. Weinstein, *Politics of Failure*, 123.

132. Michael Fox, "Uruguay's Frente Amplio: From Revolution to Dilution," *Upside Down World*, June 2007.

133. Leibner, *Camaradas y Compañeros*, 592.

134. "Constitutive Declaration of the Frente Amplio," reprinted in Chicago Area Group on Latin America Newsletter, June 1971, Folder: CAGLA, Box 072, BC.

135. Julio Castro, "El Frente Amplio," *Cuadernos de Marcha* no. 53 (September 1971): 5.

136. Gregory, *Intellectuals*, 54–58.

137. "Primeras 30 Medidas de Gobierno del Frente Amplio," *Problemas de Desarrollo* 2, no. 9 (1971): 160–168.

138. Castro, "El Frente Amplio," 7.

139. Churchill, *Becoming*, 128.

140. Ibid., 66–67.

141. For example, "La Declaración de Derechos," *El País*, December 10, 1967, and Héctor Rodríguez, "Derechos, Declarados y Conculcados," *Marcha*, December 12, 1969, 6, BN.

142. Eduardo Galeano, "Memoria Viva de Camilo Torres," *Marcha*, December 7, 1967, 24, BN.

143. "Sesión Ordinaria junio 10 1970," Actas de la Cámara de los Senadores, 247–282, Biblioteca del Palacio Legislativo, Montevideo, Uruguay [hereinafter PL].

144. Virginia Martínez, *Los fusilados de abril: Quién mató a los comunistas de la 20?* (Montevideo: Ediciones del Caballo Perdido, 2002), 99.

145. "Del Comité Femenino del Frente Izquierda," *Marcha,* January 7, 1972, 2.

146. Oscar Maggiolo, "Palabras de Inauguración," *Foro Internacional sobre la Vigencia de los Derechos Humanos en América Latina* (Montevideo: UdelaR Departamento de Publicaciones, 1971), 13–14.

147. Jorge Landinelli, "Palabras de Inauguración," *Foro Internacional sobre la Vigencia de los Derechos Humanos en América Latina* (Montevideo: UdelaR Departamento de Publicaciones, 1971), 19–20; "Derechos Humanos," *Ahora,* 20 September 1971, 6.

148. Mario Sambarino, "Derechos Humanos y Desarrollo Soiocultural," *Foro Internacional Sobre la Vigencia de los Derechos Humanos en América Latina* (Montevideo: UdelaR Departamento de Publicaciones, 1971), 51–52.

149. Landinelli, "Palabras"; Alberto Ramón Real, "Los derechos y obligaciones de los individuos y de la comunidad nacional e internacional respecto de ellos," *Foro Internacional sobre la Vigencia de los Derechos Humanos en América Latina* (Montevideo: UdelaR Departamento de Publicaciones, 1971), 39–48.

150. Maggiolo, "Palabras," 15; Georges Pinet, "Palabras de Inauguración," *Foro Internacional sobre la Vigencia de los Derechos Humanos en América Latina* (Montevideo: UdelaR Departamento de Publicaciones, 1971), 23–24.

151. Carlos Martínez Moreno, "Contexto Real Actual de los Derechos Humanos en Uruguay," *Cuadernos de Marcha* 53 (1971): 13–17.

152. Pinet, "Palabras," 24.

153. See documents in Carlos Osorio, ed., National Security Archive Electronic Briefing Book no. 72, June 20, 2002, https://nsarchive2.gwu.edu/NSAEBB/NSAEBB71/; Tanya Harmer, *Allende's Chile and the Inter-American Cold War* (Chapel Hill: University of North Carolina Press, 2011), 126–127.

154. The Colorado Party and more conservative members of the Blanco Party sought to prevent a Ferreira win. Many believed that any votes for Pacheco's bid to amend the constitution were lumped into Bordaberry's total. Weinstein, "Decline," 87–88.

155. Markarian, *Left,* 50.

156. And indeed, many considered it a war. See Carlos Martínez Moreno, "El régimen se va a la guerra," in *Los Días Que Vivimos* (Montevideo: Editorial Giron, 1973), 18.

157. Memo, Rhoads to Ortiz, "Possible Effects of Uruguayan Torture Charges on the AID Public Safety Program," July 1, 1973, National Security Archive Electronic Briefing Book No. 309, http://nsarchive.gwu.edu/NSAEBB/NSAEBB309/.

158. "Decreto de Disolución de las Cámaras," in *Documentos de la Huelga General 1973* (Montevideo: Centro Uruguay Independiente, 1984), 13–15; "June 27, 1973," decrees quoted in "Latin America Update: Uruguay," Washington Office on Latin America, June 1978, Folder WOLA, George Lister Papers, Nettie Lee Benson Latin America Collection, University of Texas at Austin [hereinafter GLP].

159. Henry Finch, "Democratisation in Uruguay," *Third World Quarterly* 7, no. 3 (July 1985): 597; Alexander and Parker, *A History,* 66–67.

160. "Uruguay Security Forces Trap Tupamaro Chief," *Boston Globe,* September 2, 1972, 2.

161. Appendix to Letter, Koeppel to Vasek, July 13, 1984, Committee to Protect Journalists, Folder 4, Álvaro Barros Lémez Colección, CEIU.

162. Gerardo Caetano and José Rilla, *Breve Historia de la Dictadura* (Montevideo: Centro Latinoamericano de Economía Humana, 1991), 16–19; Álvaro Rico et al., eds., *15 Días que Estremecieran al Uruguay: Golpe de Estado y Huelga General* (Montevideo: Editorial Fin de Siglo, 2005).

163. "Declaración del Consejo Directivo Central ante la situación nacional," June 27, 1973, in Álvaro Rico, *La Universidad de la República: Desde el Golpe de Estado a la intervención* (Montevideo: CEIU, 2003), 27.

164. "Uruguay y sus sindicatos," 45; Rico, *15 Días.*

165. "Uruguay y sus sindicatos"; "Decreto de disolución de la CNT," June 30, 1973, in *Documentos de la Huelga General 1973* (Montevideo: Centro Uruguay Independiente, 1984), 22–23.

166. *Marcha,* July 27, 1973, 1, BN.

Chapter 2

1. Press Release, "Amnesty International Launching Worldwide Campaign Against Torture in Uruguay," February 19, 1976, Folder "Uruguay Press Release on CAT," Box 5, David Hawk Files, Amnesty International-USA Collection, Columbia University Archives, New York, NY [hereinafter AIUSA].

2. "Report Documents 22 Cases of Torture Deaths in Uruguay," *Liberation News Service,* March 6, 1976, Box L27, BC.

3. Ibid.

4. Jeri Laber, "Torture and Death in Uruguay," *New York Times,* March 10, 1976, 35; "Uruguay Repression Highlighted," *Irish Times,* February 20, 1976, 5; "The New Torturers," *Observer,* February 22, 1976, 12; "Amnesty Handed Torture Pictures," *Guardian,* March 12, 1976, 2.

5. Aryeh Neier, *The International Human Rights Movement: A History* (Princeton: Princeton University Press, 2012), 188–189; Tom Buchanan, "'The Truth Will Set You Free': The Making of Amnesty International," *Journal of Contemporary History* 37, no. 4 (2002): 575–597; Jonathan Power, *Like Water on Stone: The Story of Amnesty International* (Boston: Northeastern University Press, 2001).

6. Barbara Keys, *Reclaiming American Virtue: The Human Rights Revolution of the 1970s* (Cambridge: Harvard University Press, 2014), 89.

7. David Heaps, "Draft Report on Human Rights," August 1975, Ford Foundation unpublished reports, Report #005643, Box 254, Ford Foundation, Rockefeller Archive Center, Sleepy Hollow, NY [hereinafter RAC].

8. Kelly calls this narrowing "a politics of emergency." Kelly, *Sovereign Emergencies,* 7.

9. Kenneth Cmiel, "The Recent History of Human Rights," *American Historical Review* 109, no. 1 (February 2004): 130. For more on Cold War politics narrowing human rights possibilities, see Carol Anderson, *Eyes Off the Prize* (New York: Cambridge University Press, 2003); David Forsythe, "Human Rights in U.S. Foreign Policy: Retrospect and Prospect," *Political Science Quarterly* 105, no. 3 (Autumn 1990): 435–454.

10. Laber, "Torture."

11. Andrew Tarnowski, "Nobody Is smiling in Uruguay, the 'Torture Chamber of Latin America,'" *The Times: London,* February 8, 1977, 16.

12. This coherence was not universal. Some activists saw human rights as a tool of imperialism and fervently continued to argue in revolutionary terms. An increasing number during these years, though, saw the utility in the strategic use of human rights. Author interview with Milton Romani, May 25, 2020.

13. Cmiel, *Recent History,* 130; Kelly, *Sovereign Emergencies,* 8, 11. Moyn, *Last Utopia,* 213.

14. Terminology for historians of sexuality is an enduring problem. Despite their problematic nature, "gay" and "homosexual" are at times employed interchangeably in this chapter as a shorthand for LGBTQ people, utilizing the language my historical actors did in this period. Encarnación, "Puzzle." Similarly, Afro-Uruguayan or Afro-descendant are relatively recent terms, whereas negro and Black were more often used before the 1980s. This book utilizes the term Afro-Uruguayan most frequently. For more on these terms, see Erica Townsend-Bell, "'We Entered as Blacks and We Left as Afro-Descendants': Tracing the Path to Affirmative Action in Uruguay," *Latin American and Caribbean Ethnic Studies* 16, no. 3 (2021): 237–258.

15. Rajca explores exclusionary language and reproduction of human rights and violence through cultural memories in Brazil—explaining that by some groups being left out of human rights advocacy, minorities can be considered "non-human" and reproduce systems of violence. Andrew Rajca, "Unraveling Normalized Rhetoric of Violence and Human Rights," *Journal of Latin American Cultural Studies* 22, no. 3 (2013): 305–321.

16. Scholars classify these regimes as "bureaucratic-authoritarian," characterized by governments that sought to transform society by combatting perceived subversion and restoring "true" values of the nation. This meant economic neoliberal restructuring simultaneous to the military's counterinsurgency by employing systematic torture and other grave human rights abuses. See, for example, Karen Remmer, *Military Rule in Latin America* (Boulder: Westview Press, 1991); Peter Imbusch et al., "Violence Research in Latin America and the Caribbean: A Literature Review," *International Journal of Conflict and Violence* 5, no. 1 (2011): 87–154.

17. Laura Bolaños, "Uruguay Hacia el Fascismo," *El Universal,* November 12, 1974; "'Depuración' de Marxistas en el Estado y la Educación de Uruguay," *Enseñanza,* nd, Folder 123, Waksman Colección, CEIU.

18. Telegram, "Bordaberry Comments on Role of Armed Forces," January 2, 1975, Wikileaks, https://wikileaks.org/plusd/cables/1975MONTEV00003_b.html.

19. Alexander and Parker, *A History,* 74; Peter Winn, "Dictatorships and the Worlds of Work in the Southern Cone: Argentina, Brazil, and Chile," *International Labor and Working Class History* (Spring 2018): 5.

20. Gargiulo, "Uruguayan Labor Movement," 224.

21. "En Uruguay Tuvieron que Modificar la "Declaración de fe Democrática," *El Día,* November 11, 1974, Folder 123, Waksman Colección, CEIU.

22. "New Arrests of Trade Unionists and University Teachers and Students," December 23, 1974, Folder AMR 52 Americas-Uruguay, Box 6, Executive Director Files 1967–1997, AIUSA.

23. Jeffrey Puryear, "Development Assistance Within Repressive Regimes," June 29, 1979, Box 1, Human Rights and Governance Program, Office of the Program Director, Papers of Shepard Forman, Ford Foundation, RAC.

24. Virginia Martínez, *Tiempos de dictadura: Hechos, Voces, Documentos, La represión y la resistencia día a día* (Montevideo: Ediciones de la Banda Oriental, 2005), 28.

25. Servicio Paz y Justicia, *Uruguay, Nunca Más: Human Rights Violations, 1972–1985,* trans. Elizabeth Hampsten (Philadelphia: Temple University Press, 1992), ix.

26. Abby Goldberg interview with Isabel Trivelli, March 22, 2012. The author wishes to thank Abby Goldberg for sharing her transcripts.

27. J. Patrice McSherry, *Predatory States: Operation Condor and Covert War in Latin America* (New York: Rowman & Littlefield Publishers, 2005); J. Patrice McSherry, "Tracking the Origins of a State Terror Network: Operation Condor," *Latin American Perspectives* 29, no. 1

(January 2002): 38–60; John Dinges, *The Condor Years: How Pinochet and His Allies Brought Terrorism to Three Continents* (New York: The New Press, 2004).

28. "De la Iglesia Católica de Montevideo" and "De las iglesias evangélicas," in *Documentos de la Huelga General* (Montevideo: Centro Uruguay Independiente, 1984), 45–48.

29. "Obispos v Bordaberry," 63–65, reprinted in *Uruguay y Ahora Qué? Cuadernos de Crisis,* no. 4 (1974), Folder 4, Álvaro Barros Lémez Colección, CEIU.

30. Jeffrey Klaiber, *The Church, Dictatorships, and Democracy in Latin America* (New York: Orbis Books, 1998), 113–114. There were some instances of religious leaders speaking out throughout the dictatorship; however, they were frequently met with repression as well. See "Ataques a la Iglesia," *Desde Uruguay,* April 1977, 5–6, in the Uruguay North American Congress on Latin America (NACLA) archive of Americana, Reel 325, Princeton University Library [hereinafter NACLA].

31. Weschler, *A Miracle, A Universe,* 90–92; Galeano, *Memory of Fire,* 231; Martin Anderson, "The Littlest Totalitarian," *The Nation,* March 26, 1983, 358.

32. Nahum Bergstein, *Judío: una experiencia Uruguaya* (Colonia: Editorial Fin de Siglo, 1993), 97–99.

33. Carina Perelli, "Putting Conservatism to Good Use," in *The Women's Movement in Latin America,* ed. Jane Jaquette (Boston: Unwin Hyman, 1989), 101.

34. Rial, "Makers and Guardians," 95.

35. Lawrence Weschler, "Uruguay," in *Dealing with the Past: Truth and Reconciliation in South Africa,* ed. Alex Boraine, Janet Levy, and Ronel Scheffer (Cape Town: IDASA, 1997), 41–42.

36. Langguth, *Hidden Terrors,* 297; Author interview with Jo Marie Griesgraber, December 15, 2017.

37. "M.P.'s in Southern Cone," *Latin America and Caribbean Inside Report* 1, no. 5 (November 1976), Folder Latin America and Caribbean inside Report, Box L5, BC.

38. Louis Bickford, "Human Rights Archives and Research on Historical Memory: Argentina, Chile and Uruguay," a consultancy report prepared for the Andes and Southern Cone Office of the Ford Foundation, November 1998 (on file with author). The author thanks Louis Bickford for sharing this report.

39. Mara Loveman, "High-Risk Collective Action: Defending Human Rights in Chile, Uruguay, and Argentina," *American Journal of Sociology* 104, no. 2 (September 1998): 477–525; Ruiz, *Piedra,* 22.

40. Bickford, "Human Rights Archives."

41. Kelly, *Sovereign Emergencies,* 17.

42. William Michael Schmidli, *The Fate of Freedom Elsewhere: Human Rights and U.S. Cold War Policy Toward Argentina* (Ithaca: Cornell University Press, 2013), 74–75.

43. Author interview with Robert Goldman, March 2, 2020.

44. Markarian, *Left*; Mario Sznajder and Luis Roniger, *The Politics of Exile in Latin America* (New York: Cambridge University Press, 2009), 243.

45. Some exiles, such as Enrique Erro, did continue to wage revolutionary battles. Erro founded the Unión Artigas de Liberación, a group proclaiming total war on the Uruguayan dictatorship. He was arrested in Argentina for violating asylum laws, and after a period in prison he was expelled from the country. Sznajder and Roniger, *Politics,* 245–246; Vania Markarian, "From a Revolutionary Logic to Humanitarian Reasons: Uruguayan Leftists in Exile and Human Rights Transnational Networks," *Cuadernos del CLAEH* 1 (2006).

46. Eckel and Moyn, *Breakthrough*, 2. Particularly, activists protesting the Brazilian dictatorship helped lay the foundation for future activism. James Green, *We Cannot Remain Silent: Opposition to the Brazilian Military Dictatorship in the United States* (Durham: Duke University Press, 2010).

47. Randall, "Remembers," 123.

48. Initially, Allende's Chile was also a refuge for many Uruguayans, especially the Tupamaros. In total, between 1,500 and 3,000 Uruguayans passed through Chile during Allende's presidency. See Tanya Harmer, *Beatriz Allende: A Revolutionary Life in Cold War Latin America* (Chapel Hill: University of North Carolina Press, 2020), 193; Harmer, *Allende's Chile*, 97.

49. Sznadjer and Roniger, *Politics*, 244; Zelmar Michelini, "El refugio en la nueva Argentina," *La Opinión*, September 20, 1973, in *Zelmar Michelini: Artículos periodísticos y ensayos: Tomo VI* (Montevideo: Cámara de Senadores, 1986), 55–56.

50. Cesar di Candia, *Ni Muerte Ni Derrota: Testimonios sobre Zelmar Michelini* (Madrid: Ediciones Atenea, 1987), 184, 230–231; Mauricio Rodríguez, *La voz de todos: Zelmar Michelini: Su Vida* (Montevideo: Fin de Siglo Editorial, 2016), 348; and all of the following: Zelmar Michelini, "Mágicamente, el gobierno uruguayo descubre en su Iglesia al comunismo internacional," *La Opinión,* September 29, 1973, 59–60; Zelmar Michelini, "La torture identifica los regímenes militares del Cono Sur de América," *La Opinión,* December 16, 1973, 76–77; and Zelmar Michelini, "La Ley Kennedy cambiará las relaciones continentales," *La Opinión,* January 3, 1974, 82–83, in *Zelmar Michelini: Artículos periodísticos y ensayos: Tomo VI* (Montevideo: Cámara de Senadores, 1986). For more on Michelini's campaign from Buenos Aires, see Markarian, *Left*, 76–83.

51. "La represión en la Universidad uruguaya," *Militancia*, November 15, 1973, reprinted in *Uruguay y Ahora Qué? Cuadernos de Crisis* no. 4 (1974), 21–22, Folder 4, Álvaro Barros Lémez Colección, CEIU.

52. Mario Benedetti, "Hombre Preso que Mira a Su Hijo," in *Witness* (Buffalo: White Pine Press, 2012), 147.

53. Grupo de Apoyo a la Resistencia Uruguaya, "The Anniversary of the Landing of the '33," *Banda Oriental* 2 (October/November 1974), 10, Reel 325, NACLA.

54. Dinges, *Condor Years,* Chapter 9.

55. Uruguayan exiles fled to Cuba, Italy, Panama, Mexico, Ecuador, Angola, Paris, the United Kingdom, and the United States, among other locales. Ruiz, *Piedra,* 28; Silvia Dutrénit Bielous, ed., *El Uruguay del exilio: Gente, circunstancias, escenarios* (Montevideo: Ediciones Trilce, 2006); Álvaro Rico et al., eds., *El Partido Comunista bajo la dictadura* (Montevideo: Editorial Fin de Siglo, 2021), 388–395.

56. "Amnesty Says Political Prisoners Tortured in Uruguay," Amnesty International News Release, June 25, 1973, Folder AMR 52: Americas–Uruguay 1972–3, Box 6, Executive Director Files Series 5, AIUSA.

57. "Human Rights and Intellectual Freedom," 1975, Folder 293, Box 54, Record Group 3.2, Series 900, RAC.

58. E. J. Kahn, Jr., "The Meddlers," *New Yorker,* August 22, 1970, 46.

59. Stephen Hopgood, *Keepers of the Flame: Understanding Amnesty International* (Ithaca: Cornell University Press, 2006), 80.

60. "Minutes of the IEC," November 28–9, 1970, Folder 413, Amnesty International: International Secretariat Archives, International Institute of Social History Archive, Amsterdam, Netherlands [hereinafter IISH]; Barbara Keys, "Anti-Torture Politics: Amnesty International, the

Greek Junta, and the Origins of the Human Rights 'Boom' in the United States," in *The Human Rights Revolution,* ed. Akira Iriye et al. (New York: Oxford University Press, 2012): 201–221.

61. For tension between AI-USA and the London headquarters, see Keys, *Reclaiming,* Chapter 8, and Sarah Snyder, "Exporting Amnesty International to the United States: Transatlantic Human Rights Activism in the 1960s," *Human Rights Quarterly* 34, no. 3 (August 2012): 779–799.

62. Author interview with David Hawk, June 2, 2016; "Torture," *New Yorker,* May 12, 1973, 31; "Amnesty International Campaign for the Abolition of Torture," December 11, 1972, Folder 61, IISH.

63. Egon Larsen, *A Flame in Barbed Wire: The Story of Amnesty International* (New York: W. W. Norton, 1979), 50–51; Hopgood, *Keepers,* 81–82.

64. "5th United Nations Congress on the Prevention of Crime and the Treatment of Offenders," ND, Folder United Nations, Box 5, David Hawk Files, AIUSA; Carola Stern, "Where Torture Is Being Practiced," April 1973, Folder 64, IISH; "Campaign for the Abolition of Torture," May 14, 1974, Folder 448, IISH.

65. Well before launching CAT, Amnesty recognized the UN's importance. Geneva NGO Conference General Conclusions, January 1968, Folder 41, IISH.

66. Stern, "Where," IISH.

67. Chris Ingelse, *United Nations Committee Against Torture: An Assessment* (Boston: Kluwer Law International, 2001), 68; Press Release, "Fifth United Nations Congress on the Prevention of Crime and Treatment of Offenders Concludes Its Work in Geneva," September 15, 1975, Folder United Nations, Box 5, David Hawk Files, AIUSA; Helena Cook, "The Role of Amnesty International in the Fight Against Torture," in *The International Fight Against Torture,* ed. Antonio Cassese (Germany: Nomos Verlagsgesellschaft, 1991), 172–177.

68. Amnesty International Annual Report 1975–76, 8, Andrew Blane Private Papers [hereinafter Blane Papers].

69. Larsen, *Flame,* 74.

70. International Executive Committee (IEC), September 6–7, 1972, Folder 59, IISH; For more on expansion to Latin America, see IEC minutes and Larsen, *Flame,* 50–58.

71. While Chile's biggest issue was executions and Argentina's disappearances, Uruguay's was torture, which Amnesty was already working on. Author interview with Edy Kaufman, June 22, 2016. Keys also explains that while other organizations addressed many UDHR articles, Amnesty International limited its mandate to torture and political prisoners. Keys, *Reclaiming,* 189. For more on increased attention to Uruguay, see, among others, "Report on Special Actions," Folder 69, IEC, IISH.

72. "Political Imprisonment in Uruguay," 1979, Amnesty International Online Archive, https://www.amnesty.org/en/documents/amr52/013/1979/en/; "Mission to Uruguay and Paraguay," June 12, 1974, and "Report of Mission to Uruguay," April/May 1974, Folder 82, IISH; "Uruguay Campaign Report and Evaluation," August 9, 1976, Folder AMR 52 Americas-Uruguay 1976, Box 6, Executive Director Files 1967–1997, AIUSA.

73. "Action for the GAU Prisoners," December 2, 1975, Folder 453, IISH; "AI Says Gross Violations of Human Rights Have Reached New Peaks," February 12, 1975, Folder, AMR 52 Americas-Uruguay 1974-5, Box 6, Executive Director Files 1967–1997, AIUSA.

74. Author interview with Andrew Blane, June 10, 2016.

75. "Uruguay Campaign," December 1, 1975, Folder 453, IISH.

76. Kaufman interview.

77. Max Holland and Kai Bird, "Siracusa, Our Man in Uruguay," *The Nation,* March 19, 1977.

78. Press Release, "Amnesty International Launching Worldwide Campaign Against Torture in Uruguay," February 19, 1976, Folder Uruguay Press Release on the Campaign Against Torture, Box 5, David Hawk Files, AIUSA.

79. Laber, "Torture"; Jeri Laber, *The Courage of Strangers: Coming of Age with the Human Rights Movement* (New York: Public Affairs, 2002), 73.

80. "Uruguay Campaign Report and Evaluation," AIUSA.

81. Letter from Frank Leichter, May 13, 1976, Folder "ED Files Washington DC Office," Box 5, David Hawk Files, AIUSA.

82. "Uruguay Campaign Report and Evaluation," AIUSA; "Human Rights Groups Reports Repression in South America," *New York Times,* October 31, 1976, 3; "Uruguay Regime Accused of 24 Torture Slayings," *Los Angeles Times,* February 20, 1976, B18; Amnesty International Annual Report 1975–76, p27, Blane Papers.

83. Telegram, Embajada del Uruguay, January 28, 1976, Box 21, Folder 10, AHD; Letter from Ambassador Caldas, March 17, 1976, Folder 5, Box 3, AHD.

84. "AI in Quotes," 1976, 10, Blane Papers.

85. See Howard Handelman, "Uruguayan Journal," July 7, 1976, *Worldview,* Folder Background Press, Box 279, WOLA, Human Rights Archive, Duke University [hereinafter WOLA].

86. "Future Work on Uruguay," January 27, 1977, Folder "ED Files Washington DC Office 1975–80," Box 5, David Hawk Files, AIUSA; for other local press disparaging the campaign, see "Amnesty International vs. Uruguay," *Review of the River Plate,* March 31, 1976, Folder, AMR 52 Americas-Uruguay 1976, Box 6, Executive Director Files 1967–1997, AIUSA.

87. *La Mañana,* 20 febrero 1976, Amnesty International Report 1975–6, Blane Papers. When Amnesty International won the Nobel Peace Prize in 1977, the Uruguayan Minister of Education called the award "a joke in bad taste." See Larsen, *Flame,* 129.

88. Telegram, May 14, 1976, Folder 11 Box 33, AHD. Dinges, *Condor Years,* 120 also notes the military's painting of human rights organizations as "Marxist-Leninst conspiracies … to trick people who are not well informed."

89. Cable, June 22, 1976, Box 21, Folder 10, AHD.

90. Actas de la Comisión Investigadora sobre Secuestro y Asesinato Perpetrados contra los Ex-Legisladores Héctor Gutiérrez Ruiz y Zelmar Michelini, Caja 1, Pieza 1, Acta 3, Archivo del Secretaría de Derechos Humanos para el Pasado Reciente, Montevideo, Uruguay.

91. CIA Report, "Counterterrorism in the Southern Cone," May 9, 1977, Obama Argentina Declassification Project, Tranche II.

92. "Uruguay Campaign Report and Evaluation," AIUSA.

93. Amnesty International 1977 Report, Blane Papers.

94. Hawk interview.

95. "Future Work," AIUSA.

96. Kaufman interview.

97. Vanessa Walker, *Principles in Power: Latin America and the Politics of U.S. Human Rights Diplomacy* (Ithaca: Cornell University Press, 2020), 32–33.

98. Coletta Youngers, *Thirty Years of Advocacy for Human Rights, Democracy and Social Justice* (Washington: Washington Office on Latin America, 2006), 5.

99. Ibid., 2.

100. Tom Quigley, "The Chilean Coup, the Church and the Human Rights Movement," *America Magazine,* February 11, 2002.

101. Juan Raúl Ferreira, *Con la patria en la valija: El exilio, Wilson y los años trágicos* (Montevideo: Linardi y Risso, 2000), 45–59.

102. Author interview with Juan Raúl Ferreira, January 15, 2018.

103. Ibid.; Markarian, *Left*, 123.

104. Juan Raúl Ferreira, "30 Años de WOLA," accessed July 7, 2014, http://www .juanraulferreira.com.uy/30%20A%C3%B1os%20de%20WOLA.pdf.

105. Ferreira interview.

106. Griesgraber interview. Griesgraber also took a trip to Uruguay in August 1977 since Juan Raúl could not travel there. He facilitated her meeting with madres, students, political leaders, and church leaders, among others. See "OAS Hears Testimony," Folder Press Release, Box 282, WOLA.

107. These updates were distributed to several thousand individuals, including people who worked for other NGOs, officials at every level of government, academics, and those involved in religious organizations. Several hundred were also distributed to places in Latin America. William Korey, *Taking on the World's Repressive Regimes: The Ford Foundation's International Human Rights Policies and Practices* (New York: Palgrave Macmillan, 2007), 73–74. See, among many others, Press Releases, "Wola Revela Texto de Trascendente Carta de Vance a Koch Sobre Relaciones con Uruguay," June 13, 1977; "Uruguayan Government Holds Journalist in 'Torture Section' for Exposing Torture Techniques," July 8, 1977; "Uruguayan Government Disappears Prestigious Newsman," October 4, 1977; "Pentagon Criticizes Uruguay on Human Rights," January 25, 1978; all in Folder Press Releases, Box 282, WOLA.

108. Griesgraber interview.

109. Author interview with John Youle, December 5, 2017.

110. U.S. government archives have collections of WOLA bulletins that have highlights and handwritten comments, containing directives for future action and more information. See, for example, Uruguay, June 1, 1976, Department of State Virtual Reading Room [hereinafter DOSVRR].

111. Memo, Proposed Wilson Ferreira Meeting with Christopher, October 29, 1977, DOSVRR.

112. Memo, Deputy, Meeting with Ferreiras, November 19, 1977, DOSVRR.

113. Juan Raúl also attracted criticism for his work. Representative Larry McDonald (D-Georgia) called him "anti-Uruguayan" and accused him of cooperating "with Castroite organizations in the US that serve as the mouthpieces for the Tupamaros and other terrorist groups." *Congressional Record,* July 27, 1977, E4872, Folder 14, Box 21, AHD.

114. Guillermo Waksman also obtained many of WOLA's publications. He spent exile in Mexico and Switzerland, publicizing the information there through other channels and extending WOLA's reach. Folder 26, Waksman Colección, CEIU. The Uruguayan government closely followed WOLA's reports as well, collecting dozens of updates and press releases from the organization in attempts of countering it. Box 21, Folder 14, AHD.

115. "Uruguay and Argentina Held Responsible," February 6, 1976, Folder Press Releases, Box 282, WOLA.

116. Erich Weingärtner, *Human Rights: Solidarities, Networks, and the Ecumenical Movement* (Philippines: Human Rights Desk, National Council of Churches in the Philippines, 1988), 17.

117. Darril Hudson, *The World Council of Churches in International Affairs* (Leighton Buzzard, Bedfordshire, UK: Faith Press, 1977).

118. Patrick William Kelly, "Human Rights and Christian Responsibility," in *Religious Responses to Violence: Human Rights in Latin America Past and Present,* ed. Alexander Wilde

(South Bend: University of Notre Dame Press, 2015), 111; Kelly, *Sovereign Emergencies*, 45, 67–68, 74–77, 217.

119. Weingärtner, *Human Rights*, 17; Charles Harper, *O Acompanhamento: Ecumenical Action for Human Rights in Latin America 1970–1990* (Geneva: WCC Publications, 2006), 2.

120. Harper, *Acompanhamento*, 2.

121. Marjorie Hyer, "World Church Group Urges Uruguay to Restore Rights," *Washington Post*, November 19, 1972, E2; Letter from Epps, September 12, 1972, Folder Uruguay Materials Regarding Liggett Thompson and Stockwell Visit, Box CCIA Country Files South America, Uruguay 1973, World Council of Churches Archive, Geneva, Switzerland [hereinafter WCC].

122. Memo, Niilus to Potter, January 31, 1975, Folder Uruguayan Accusations Against the WCC, Box CCIA Country Files South America, Uruguay 1973, WCC; "Consejo Mundial de Iglesias, instrumento de la guerrilla," *La Mañana*, October 31, 1974.

123. Vanya Walker-Leigh, "Repression in Uruguay," January 23, 1975; WCC Memo, "WCC Urges Uruguay to Correct False, Defamatory Statements," nd; and ICJ, "Supplement to Report on Uruguay of June 17, 1974," Folder Uruguayan Accusations Against the WCC, Box CCIA Country Files South America, Uruguay 1973, WCC; Martínez, *Tiempos de Dictadura*, 48.

124. Carlos Sintado and Manuel Quintero Pérez, *Emilio Castro: A Legacy of Passionate Ecumenism* (Geneva: World Council of Churches Publications, 2018).

125. For issues of GRISUR's newsletter, see Folder 15, Waksman Colección, CEIU.

126. For the best recounting of SIJAU and its politics, see Markarian, *Left*, 134–137. For information about the proceedings of SIJAU in the French Senate, see *Amnesty: Symposium on The State of Emergency and Human Rights in Uruguay* (Paris: SIJAU, 1978).

127. "1976: Año del aislamiento de la dictadura uruguaya," July 1976, Folder 33, Box 11, AHD; Sznadjer and Roniger, *Politics*, 251.

128. Markarian, *Left*, 101. For more on the Toronto group of exiles, the Grupo de Apoyo a las Resistencia Uruguaya, and their publication, *Banda Oriental*, see Reel 325, NACLA. In Toronto, there was also the Comité de Defensa de los Derechos Humanos en Uruguay; see, for example, "Adolfo Wassen Alanis," July 6, 1984, Folder 46, Box 269, AIUSA.

129. "Información," No. 82, April 29, 1978, Folder 15, Waksman Colección, CEIU; "Documentos y Resoluciones," Tendencia Combativa de la CNT del Uruguay en el exilio, 1979, Folder 5, Cores Colección, CEIU; Markarian, *Left*, 101.

130. André Fremd and Germán Kronfeld, *(Des)aparecido: Vida, Obra y Desapración de Eduardo Bleier* (Montevideo: Estuario Editora, 2011), 125–129.

131. Community Action on Latin America, "Statement on CALA's Theory and Practice," nd, Box 1, Folder: CALA's Chile Activities, September 1975–January 1978, Community Action on Latin America, Records 1971–1991, Wisconsin Historical Society, Madison. For more information on Community Action on Latin America on Uruguay, see Box 10, Folder 37; Box 3, Folder 10; Box 3, Folder 4.

132. Margaret E. Keck and Kathryn Sikkink, *Activists Beyond Borders: Advocacy Networks in International Politics* (Ithaca: Cornell University Press, 1998), 97.

133. Korey, *Taking on*, Chapter 1; Peter Bell, "The Ford Foundation as a Transnational Actor," *International Organization* 25, no. 3 (1971): 472. Other scholars note this shift as moving from research to policy studies to "action." F.X. Sutton, "The Ford Foundation's Transatlantic Role and Purposes, 1951–81," *Review (Fernand Braudel Center)* 24, no. 1 (2001): 97.

134. For more on Chile specifically, see Korey, *Taking on*, 25–45; Kelly, *Sovereign Emergencies*, 68–69; Inderjeet Parmar, *Foundations of the American Century: The Ford, Carnegie, and*

Rockefeller Foundations in the Rise of American Power (New York: Columbia University Press, 2012), Chapter 7.

135. Parmar, *Foundations*, 191.

136. Part of these discussions stemmed from McGeorge Bundy's presidency of the foundation and his shift toward "liberal" causes. See Kenneth Cmiel, "The Emergence of Human Rights Politics in the United States," *Journal of American History* 86, no. 3 (December 1999): 1244.

137. "Human Rights and Intellectual Freedom," p36, 1975, Folder 298, Box 54, Record Group 3.2, Series 900, RAC; David Heaps, "Draft Report on Human Rights," 3, August 1975, Box 254, Ford Foundation, RAC.

138. "Human Rights and Intellectual Freedom," 22–23.

139. Heaps, "Draft Report," 5; Korey, *Taking on*, 39–40.

140. Heaps, "Draft Report," 2.

141. Scott Busby, "Making Human Rights Real: A History of the Ford Foundation's Human Rights Program in Latin America and the Caribbean," 1989, p13, Folder 4, Box 18, Series III, Mary E. McClymonth Files, Ford Foundation, RAC.

142. Busbey, "Making"; Korey, *Taking on*, 54–60; Kelly, *Sovereign Emergencies*, 85.

143. Richard Goldstein and Alfred Gellhorn, "Human Rights and the Medical Profession in Uruguay since 1972," August 1982, Ford Foundation Report #015292, Ford Foundation, RAC.

144. Ibid., 4.

145. Ibid.

146. The report also included descriptions of the lack of academic freedom in medical teaching during the dictatorship. Ibid., 5–11.

147. "Final Report to the Agency for International Development-Protection of Human Rights in Selected Latin American Countries," March 1982, Folder 1271, Box 198, Record Group 3.1, Rockefeller Brothers Foundation, RAC.

148. Ibid.

149. Ibid.

150. Steve Stern and Scott Straus, "Embracing Paradox: Human Rights in the Global Age," in *Human Rights Paradox*, 9.

151. Elaine Scarry, *The Body in Pain: The Making and Unmaking of the World* (New York: Oxford University Press, 1987).

152. Abby Goldberg interview with Gabriel Mazzarovich, March 19, 2012.

153. Marisa Bucheli and Rafael Porzecanski, "Racial Inequality in the Uruguayan Labor Market: An Analysis of Wage Differentials Between Afro-Descendants and Whites," *Latin American Politics & Society* 53, no. 2 (Summer 2011): 113–150. Although this book does not address indigenous populations, this mythology dominated strong denials of Uruguay's indigenous populations, where official narratives claimed that indigenous groups were largely exterminated in the colonial period due to diseases, wars, and aggressive campaigns to expel from the land.

154. George Reid Andrews, "Afro-Uruguay," *Black Past*, March 11, 2011, accessed at http://www.blackpast.org/perspectives/afro-uruguay-brief-history; Alex Borucki, *From Shipmates to Soldiers: Emerging Black Identities in the Río de la Plata* (Albuquerque: University of New Mexico Press, 2015).

155. Andrews, "Afro-Uruguay."

156. Tanya Kateri Hernández, *Racial Subordination in Latin America: The Role of the State, Customary Law, and the New Civil Rights Response* (New York: Cambridge University Press, 2013), 20; Mara Loveman, *National Colors: Racial Classification and the State in Latin America*

(New York: Oxford University Press, 2014), 208–209; Felipe Arocena, "Uruguay: un país más diverso que su imaginación: una interpretación a partir del censo de 2011," *Revista de Ciencias Sociales* 33 (2013): 140.

157. Jens Hentschke, "Artiguista, White, Cosmopolitan and Educated: Constructions of Nationhood in Uruguay Textbooks and Related Narratives, 1868–1915," *Journal of Latin American Studies* 44, no. 4 (November 2012): 749.

158. Romero Jorge Rodríguez, *Racismo y derechos humanos en Uruguay* (Montevideo: Ediciones Etnicas: Organizaciones Mundo Afro, 2003).

159. Bucheli and Porzecanski, "Racial Inequality," 116. For more on Afro-Uruguayans in earlier periods of Uruguayan history, see George Reid Andrews, *Blackness in the White Nation: A History of Afro-Uruguay* (Chapel Hill: University of North Carolina Press, 2010); Borucki, *From Shipmates*; Debbie Sharnak, "The Road to Recognition: Afro-Uruguayan Activism and the Struggle for Visibility," in *Narratives of Mass Atrocity*, ed. Sarah Federman and Ronald Niezen (New York: Cambridge University Press, 2022).

160. Bordaberry letter to Kenneth Golby, February 12, 1975, reel 329, NACLA. He also said in the letter that there were "no problems with an indigenous population because there is none." Uruguay also had no question about race in the national census until 2011. Previous estimates placed the Afro-Uruguayan population at approximately 4 percent of the population. In reality, the census revealed 8 percent of Uruguayans self-identified as "afro o negra"—more than double previous guesses, which spoke to the invisibility of the purported "small" Uruguayan population that Bordaberry reinforced with his comments. Arocena, "Un país," 140.

161. Andrews, *Blackness*, 145.

162. The ACSU membership was also generally drawn from a small group of wealthier Afro-Uruguayans. See Entrevistas con Amaro Uriarte and Alicia Equival Rodríguez, in *Triunfadores: Negros Profesionales en el Uruguay*, ed. Pamela Laviñ (Montevideo: Editorial Psicolibros Universitario, 2013), 35 and 41.

163. See, for example, Entrevista con Alejandrina da Luz de los Santos, in *Triunfadores*, 21–22.

164. Vannina Sztainbok, "Imagining the Afro-Uruguayan; *Conventillo*: Belonging and the Fetish of Place and Blackness" (PhD diss., University of Toronto, 2009), 2–3; other descriptions of conventillos explain them as a "a community and culture" for Afro-Uruguayans. Edgardo Ortuño, "Prólogo," in *Mediomundo: Sur, conventillo y después* (Montevideo: Medio&Medio, 2008), 7.

165. "Remodelación del puerto de Montevideo," *El Diario*, December 7, 1978, 4, BN; Victoria Ruetalo, "From Penal Institution to Shopping Mecca: The Economics of Memory and the Case of Punta Carretas," *Cultural Critique* 68 (Winter 2008): 39–40.

166. Andrews, *Blackness*, 142.

167. Lauren Benton, "Reshaping the Urban Core: The Politics of Housing in Authoritarian Uruguay," *Latin American Research Review* 21, no. 2 (1986): 42. Because of this neglect, there had been a series of partial and total collapses; however, as Benton explains, the government applied new eviction edicts "with zeal."

168. "Ultimo candombe en el 'Medio Mundo': por decisión comunal será evacuado el martes," *El Diario*, December 2, 1978, 20, BN.

169. Romero Jorge Rodríguez, "The Afro Populations of America's Southern Cone: Organization, Development, and Culture in Argentina, Bolivia, Paraguay, and Uruguay," in *African Roots/American Cultures: Africa in the Creation of the Americas*, ed. Sheila Walker (Lanham: Rowman & Littlefield Publishers, 2001), 324–325.

170. Rodríguez, *Racismo,* 59; Benton places the number at 2,000. Benton, "Reshaping," 42.

171. Author interview with Beatriz Santos, September 8, 2014. Scholars debate the intent behind the military's intervention in these neighborhoods. Andrews, *Blackness,* 142–144; Sztainbok, "Imagining"; and Rodríguez, "Afro Populations," 324–326.

172. Marvin Lewis, *Afro-Uruguayan Literature: Post-Colonial Perspectives* (Lewisburg: Bucknell University Press, 2003), 124.

173. Benton, "Reshaping," 44–45.

174. Rodriguez, *Racismo,* 59–60.

175. Rodriguez, "Afro Populations."

176. Benton, "Reshaping the Urban Core," 43.

177. During the dictatorship, many popular Uruguayan *candombe* players, such as Alfredo Zitarrosa and Jaime Roos, used the rhythm and spirit of Uruguayan carnival to protest the regime domestically. However, many carnival activities that had often been used as a form of sociopolitical satire were censored and shut down during the dictatorship. Andrews, *Blackness,* 123–124; Abril Trigo, "Candombe and the Reterritorialization of Culture," *Callaloo* 16, no. 3 (Summer 1993): 716–728.

178. Diario de Sesiones de la Cámara de Senadores, 31st Sesión Ordinaria, no. 299 Tomo 509, July 16, 2013, 177–8, Archivo Legislativo, Montevideo, Uruguay [Hereinafter AL]. The three categories on the card were negro, trigueño, o blanco.

179. "El Reino del Neo-Nazismo," *Resumen* 22, March 11, 1979, 39, Folder 4, Álvaro Barros Lémez Colección, CEIU.

180. Martínez, *Tiempos de dictadura,* 47; Håkan Thörn, *Anti-Apartheid and the Emergence of a Global Civil Society* (New York: Palgrave Macmillan, 2006).

181. Report of the United Nations Special Committee Against Apartheid, Supplement no. 22 (A/100222), September 1975, UN Digital Archives.

182. Martínez, *Tiempos de dictadura,* 48.

183. "Uruguai: O regime fascista e a colaboraçã Sul-Africana," *Tempo,* August 5, 1979, 47–48, Digital Arquivo Histórico de Moçambique.

184. In all my reading about international campaigns toward Uruguay, I never read about the displacement of Afro-Uruguayans. The left in Uruguay in the 1960s also failed to acknowledge the racial inequalities in their own nation. Despite expressing solidarity with oppressed African American populations, they failed to acknowledge racial inequality at home, which undoubtedly added to the invisibility of this issue. Churchill, *Becoming,* Chapter 2.

185. Fremd and Kronfeld, *(Des)aparecido,* 15; Miguel Feldman, *Tiempos Difíciles: Inmigrantes judíos en Uruguay 1933–1945* (Montevideo: Departamento de Publicaciones de la Facultad de Humanidades y Ciencias de le Educación de la Universidad de la Republica, 2001).

186. "Sonia Guarneri fue golpeada y tatuada," *El Popular,* April 5, 1969, 1; "Paros de repudio de los textiles," *El Popular,* April 9, 1969, 10; Marchesi, "Revolution Beyond," 539; Randall, "Remembers," 117.

187. "Habla el Gral. Alberto Ballestrino," *Posdata,* January 26, 1996, 18, BN.

188. "El Reino del Neo-Nazismo," *Resumen* 22, March 11, 1979, 39, Folder 4, Álvaro Barros Lémez Colección, CEIU.

189. Fernando Amado, *Mandato de Sangre* (Montevideo: Random House Mondadori, 2012), 150.

190. Marguerite Feitlowitz, *A Lexicon of Terror: Argentina and the Legacies of Torture* (New York: Oxford University Press, 2011), 123. Others in Argentina recount being tortured in front

of portraits of Adolf Hitler and receiving harsher treatment because of their religion. Memo, U.S. Embassy in BA to DOS, August 12, 1976, DOSVRR; Thomas C. Wright, *State Terrorism in Latin America: Chile, Argentina, and International Human Rights* (New York: Rowman & Littlefield Publishers, Inc., 2007), 112–113. There were Nazi influences in Chile also; see, for example, Alan McPherson, *Ghosts of Sheridan Circle: How a Washington Assassination Brought Pinochet's Terror State to Justice* (Chapel Hill: University of North Carolina Press, 2019), 23–25.

191. "Introduction," in *Amnesty: Symposium on the State of Emergency and Human Rights in Uruguay* (Paris: SIJAU, 1978), 7.

192. "Rosencof: 'Le dieron por bolche y por judío,'" *El Espectador,* October 4, 2011, http://www.espectador.com/cultura/223129/rosencof-le-dieron-por-bolche-y-por-judio.

193. Ílan Stavans, "Introduction," in *The Letters That Never Came* by Mauricio Rosencof (Lubbock: Texas Tech University Press, 2014), x and xiii.

194. Author interview with Raquel Nogara, August 1, 2014; SERPAJ, *Uruguay: Nunca Más,* 101; Fremd and Kronfeld, *(Des)parecido,* 98; Aldrighi, *Memorias,* 44; Letter, Juan Raúl Ferreira to Morton Rosenthal, June 6, 1977, https://sitiosdememoria.uy/sites/default/files/2021-06/smdc-uydei-00040.pdf; UN Human Rights Committee, Eduardo Bleier v. Uruguay, March 29, 1982, Communication No. r.7/30, UN Doc Supplemental Number 40 (a/37/40).

195. Fremd and Kronfeld, *(Des)parecido,* 98; Amado, *Mandato de sangre,* 147–151.

196. Nogara interview.

197. Ibid.

198. "Se reorganiza Juventud Nazi en Uruguay," *Nuevo Mundo Israelita,* August 1979, Box 21, Histórico Diplomático-Administrativo, Montevideo, Uruguay [hereinafter ADA].

199. "Más antisemitismo," *Desde Uruguay,* no. 21, November 1978, reel 325, NACLA.

200. "Uruguay: Five Years into the Military Dictatorship and Getting Worse," October 1978, Folder WOLA Publications, Box 282, WOLA.

201. Letter, Rabbi Morton Rosenthal to Ambassador Caldas, January 25, 1980, Box 21, ADA; Press Release, The American Jewish Committee, Folder "Uruguay: April to May 1980," Box 20, RG 59, National Archives and Records Administration [hereinafter NARA].

202. The Delegación de Asociaciones Israelitas Argentinas has been well documented both in Feitlowitz and in Paul Katz, "A New 'Normal': Political Complicity, Exclusionary Violence and the Delegation of Argentine Jewish Associations during the Argentine Dirty War," *International Journal of Transitional Justice* 5 (2011): 366–389.

203. For articles on antisemitism, see, for example, "Fiel lector antisemite," *Semanario Hebreo,* January 6, 1981, and "La policia detuvo a autores de atentados antisemitas," *Semanario Hebreo,* February 26, 1981. But in the hundreds of issues I looked through at the semanario's library in Montevideo, there were no critiques of the regime. Articles tended to focus more on Israel and international Jews, steering clear of contentious Uruguayan politics.

204. Amado, *Mandato,* 153–154. A similar dynamic occurred in Argentina, Feitlowitz, *Lexicon* and Katz, "Political Complicity."

205. Sempol, *De los baños,* 24. It must be noted though that this perspective was rampant throughout the globe dating back to the late nineteenth century. See Laura Belmonte, *The International LGBT Rights Movement* (New York: Bloomsbury Academic, 2021), Chapter 1.

206. Sempol, *De los baños,* 23.

207. Ibid., 27.

208. This law was overturned officially in 2009. "Gays in the Military in Uruguay," *Americas Quarterly,* May 18, 2009, https://www.americasquarterly.org/blog/daily-focus-gays-in-the-military-in-uruguay/.

209. Churchill, *Becoming*, 151.

210. Sempol, *De los baños*, 45.

211. The reason for this lag is that many homosexual prisoners were unwilling to speak out about their experience immediately following the dictatorship. Diego Sempol, "Homosexualidad y cárceles políticas uruguayas. La homofobia como política de Resistencia," *Sexualidad, Salud y Sociedad: Revista Latinoamérica*, no. 4 (2000): 53–79.

212. Nogara interview.

213. Neil Miller, *Out in the World* (New York: Random House, 1993), 219.

214. Carlos Basilio Muñoz, *Uruguay homosexual: culturas, minorías y discriminación desde una sociología de la homosexualidad* (Montevideo: Ediciones Trilce, 1996), 44–45.

215. As quoted in Miller, *Out in the World*, 219.

216. "Testimonios del horror y heroísmo: Eugenio Bentaberry: Comunista y Hombre," *Estudios*, 74 (January 1980), 94; Archivo de Madres y Familiares de Uruguayos Desaparecidos Detenidos Electrónico, Montevideo, Uruguay [hereinafter AMF].

217. Memo, "Visit to Libertad," August 1, 1977, Folder "Human Rights in Uruguay," FCO 7/3359, The National Archives, London, United Kingdom [hereinafter TNA].

218. Sempol, "Homosexualidad y cárceles políticas uruguayas."

219. Nogara interview.

220. Churchill, *Becoming*, 151.

221. "Cárceles: Mas Allá de los Muros," *Marcha*, July 2, 1971, p11, AD.

222. Churchil, *Becoming*, 151.

223. Graciela Sapriza, "Nuestro racismo corriente: Los sustentos ideológicos e institucionales de la discriminación en el Uruguay del siglo XX," cholke.org: un portal sobre la sociedad civil del sur, 2003, www.cholke.org/documentos/sapriza.pdf; Vannina Sztainbok, "From Salsipuedes to Tabaré: Race, Space, and the Uruguayan Subject," *Thamyris/Intersecting* no. 20 (2010), 175–192.

224. Alicia Migdal, "Formación de la Opinión Cultural," in *Cultura(s) y nación en el Uruguay de Fin de Siglo*, ed. Hugo Achugar (Montevideo: FESUR, 1991), 184.

225. Nancy Gates-Madsen, *Trauma, Taboo, and Truth-Telling: Listening to Silences in Postdictatorship Argentina* (Madison: University of Wisconsin Press, 2016), 4.

Chapter 3

1. Memo from the Director of Policy Planning to SecState Vance, January 20, 1978, *FRUS, 1977–1980: Human Rights and Humanitarian Affairs, Volume II*, Document 105.

2. Sikkink, *Evidence for Hope*, 28–29.

3. Samuel Moyn, "The 1970s as a Turning Point in Human Rights History," in *The Breakthrough: Human Rights in the 1970s*, ed. Jan Eckel and Samuel Moyn (Philadelphia: University of Pennsylvania Press, 2014), 13; Moyn, *Last Utopia*, 7–8; Sarah Snyder, "'A Call for U.S. Leadership': Congressional Activism on Human Rights," *Diplomatic History* 37, no. 2 (April 2013): 372–397; David Forsythe, *Human Rights and U.S. Foreign Policy: Congress Reconsidered* (Gainesville: University Presses of Florida, 1988); Snyder, *From Selma*; Barbara Keys, "Congress, Kissinger, and the Origins of Human Rights Diplomacy," *Diplomatic History* 34, no. 5 (November 2010): 823–851; Keys, *Reclaiming*.

4. There is a robust and critical scholarship on Carter's overall foreign policy. Over time, historians have gained a more nuanced and complex perspective on the policy challenges and trade-offs. For a sampling of both perspectives, see Joshua Muravchik, *The Uncertain Crusade: Jimmy Carter and the Dilemmas of Human Rights Policy* (New York: Hamilton Press, 1986);

Erwin C. Hargrove, *Jimmy Carter As President: Leadership and the Politics of Public Good* (Baton Rouge: Louisiana State Press, 1988); Scott Kaufman, *Plans Unraveled: The Foreign Policy of the Carter Administration* (DeKalb: Northern Illinois University Press, 2008); Itai Nartzizenfield Sneh, *The Future Almost Arrived: How Jimmy Carter Failed to Change U.S. Foreign Policy* (New York: Peter Lang Publishing, 2008); Gaddis Smith, *Morality, Reason and Power: American Diplomacy in the Carter Years* (New York: Hill & Wang, 1986); Julian E. Zelizer, *Jimmy Carter* (New York: Times Books, 2010).

5. Mark Bradley, "American Vernaculars: The United States and the Global Human Rights Imagination," *Diplomatic History* 38, no. 1 (January 2014): 14–15.

6. The historiography of U.S. foreign policy with Uruguay is sparse. Arthur Whitaker, *The United States and the Southern Cone: Argentina, Chile and Uruguay* (Cambridge: Harvard University Press, 1976). Uruguay is beginning to receive some scholarly attention from diplomatic historians, but this work focuses on an earlier period in the nation's history: James C. Knarr, *Uruguay and the United States, 1903–1929: Diplomacy in the Progressive Era* (Kent: Kent State University Press, 2012); Pedro Cameselle, "A Forgotten Neighbor: The Challenge of Uruguay-United States Relations during the Era of Franklin Roosevelt, 1929–1945" (PhD diss., Fordham University, 2016).

7. Michael Cangemi, "Ambassador Frank Ortiz and Guatemala's 'Killer President,' 1976–1980," *Diplomatic History* 42, no. 4 (2018): 613–639.

8. Laurien Crump and Susanna Erlandsson, eds., *Margins for Manoeuvre in Cold War Europe: The Influence of Smaller Powers* (New York: Routledge, 2020).

9. Schmidli, *Fate.*

10. For an overview of Nixon-Kissinger relationship historiography, Stephen Rabe, *Kissinger and Latin America: Intervention, Human Rights, and Diplomacy* (Ithaca: Cornell University Press, 2020), 12–13.

11. Cary Reich, *The Life of Nelson A. Rockefeller* (New York: Doubleday, 1996), xix. For more on the overall trip, see Ernest Capello, "Latin America Encounters Nelson Rockefeller," in *Human Rights and Transnational Solidarity in Cold War Latin America*, ed. Jessica Stites Mores (Madison: University of Wisconsin Press, 2013), 48–73. Nixon also directed Kissinger to conduct a "broad study" and review overall U.S. policy toward Latin America in 1969; Kissinger, National Security Study Memorandum 15, February 3, 1969, Nixon Presidential Library Online Archive.

12. Joseph E. Persico, *The Imperial Rockefeller: A Biography of Nelson A. Rockefeller* (New York: Simon and Schuster, 1982), 100.

13. Langguth, *Hidden Terrors*, 158–159.

14. Persico, *Imperial Rockefeller*, 100–101.

15. Langguth, *Hidden Terrors*, 40.

16. Ibid., 224. In addition to the actions of the Office of Public Safety, many Uruguayans were protesting the United States because of the Vietnam War.

17. *Marcha*, June 6, 1969, CEIU; "Uruguay Raiders Burn G.M. Offices," *New York Times*, June 21, 1969, 1.

18. Report from Security Division, June 19, 1969, Folder 83, Record Group III 15 7, Box 10, James Cannon Files, Subseries 2—Latin American Mission, 1969–1970, Rockefeller Archive Center, Sleepy Hollow, New York [hereinafter JCF RAC].

19. Nelson A. Rockefeller, Personal, Series O: Washington, DC; 1969 Latin American Mission, Record Group III 4 O Box 116; Folder 904: Uruguay-NAR Notes, RAC.

20. The same damage now would equate to over $6 million.

21. "Visita de Rockefeller: Piden Suspensión en el Parlamento," *El País,* June 4, 1969, 3, BN; Oscar H. Bruschera, "Una Visita Indeseable," *Marcha,* June 13, 1969, 7, CEIU.

22. "Pacheco no Pedirá que el Enviado Cancele su Visita," *El País,* June 6, 1969, 6, BN; Memo Rockefeller Mission, June 10, 1969, Record Group III 15 7, Folder 83, Box 10, JCF RAC. The same memo was in Uruguay's archives, painstakingly revised in Box 5, Folder 44, AHD; Malcom Browne, "Uruguay Imposes Emergency Rule," *New York Times,* June 25, 1969, 3.

23. Memo Rockefeller Mission, June 10, 1969, Confidential Memo Record Group III 15 7, Folder 83, Box 10, JCF RAC; Juan de Onis, "Rockefeller Shifts Uruguay Talk Site," *New York Times,* June 20, 1969, 1; "Uruguay Violent as Rocky Visits," *Boston Globe,* June 20, 1969, 23.

24. Churchill, *Becoming,* 78–79.

25. United Press International, "Rockefeller Ends Third Latin Trip; He Is 'Heartened,'" *New York Times,* June 23, 1969, 1.

26. Nelson A. Rockefeller, Personal, Series O: Washington, DC, 1969 Latin American Mission, Record Group III. 4 O, Folder 900, Box 116, RAC.

27. "Rockefeller: 'Uruguay Necesita Armas Urgentemente,'" *El País,* November 13, 1969; 3; "Rockefeller Urge Armas Para Uruguay," *El Popular,* November 13, 1969; and José Pedro Aramendia, "La Opinión de Nelson Rockefeller Sobre Uruguay," nd, Box 5, Folder 44, AHD.

28. Persico, *Imperial Rockefeller,* 105–106.

29. "Rocky Clarifies Testimony on Latin America Regimes," *Washington Post,* November 22, 1969, Box 5, Folder 44, AHD.

30. John Lewis Gaddis, *Strategies of Containment: A Critical Appraisal of Postwar American National Security,* revised and expanded (New York: Oxford University Press, 2005), 295–303.

31. Kathryn Sikkink, *Mixed Signals: U.S. Human Rights Policy and Latin America* (Ithaca: Cornell University Press, 2004), 106. For more on the Nixon Doctrine, see Walker, *Principles,* 24.

32. Markarian, *Left,* 45; Uruguay Embassy to DOS, Preliminary Analysis and Strategy Paper- Uruguay, August 25, 1971, Microfiche on Human Rights in Uruguay 1971–1983, DOS, National Security Archive, Washington [hereinafter NSA].

33. Embassy in BA to SecState, Telegram, Uruguayan Situation, August 27, 1971, and Memorandum for Kissinger, November 27, 1971, State Department Subject Numeric files 1970–73, NSA.

34. The Uruguayan Left acknowledged the threat Brazil posed, discussing their fear that Brazil would intervene in the country. "Brasil Amenaza con la Invasión," *Marcha,* July 23, 1971, AD. Writers also published on the close relationship between Bordaberry and Brazil, citing Bordaberry's explanation that the countries closely shared the goal of anti-communism and defending democracy. Reportaje en *La Nación,* July 1973, reprinted in "Bordaberry y Brasil," *Uruguay y Ahora Qué? Cuadernos de Crisis* no. 4 (1974), Folder 4, Álvaro Barros Lémez Colección, CEIU.

35. Chapter 1 describes questions regarding the election's legitimacy. Also see Weinstein, "Decline," 86–89; Carlos Osorio, "Nixon: 'Brazil Helped Rig the Uruguayan Elections,' 1971," June 2002, NSA, http://www2.gwu.edu/~nsarchiv/NSAEBB/NSAEBB71/; Markarian, *Left,* 49.

36. Embassy in Uruguay to SecState, United States and Events in Uruguay, July 2, 1973, NSA http://www.gwu.edu/~nsarchiv/NSAEBB/NSAEBB309/.

37. Embassy in Uruguay to SecState, Memo: Peace Corps, August 1973, NSA.

38. Memo of Siracusa Conversation with Bordaberry, December 26, 1973, NSA, https://nsarchive2.gwu.edu/NSAEBB/NSAEBB309/19731226.pdf

39. William Michael Schmidli, "Institutionalizing Human Rights in U.S. Foreign Policy: U.S.-Argentine Relations, 1976–1980," *Diplomatic History* 35, no. 2 (April 2011): 356.

40. Churchill, *Becoming*, 42; Ryan, "Turning," 282; For more on aid/arms sales/training to Uruguay, see Timothy P. Wickham-Crowley, *Guerrillas and Revolution in Latin America: A Comparative Study of Insurgents and Regimes since 1956* (Princeton: Princeton University Press, 1992), 76; U.S. Overseas Loans and Grants to Uruguay, InsideGov.com, July 18, 1978, http://us-foreign-aid.insidegov.com/l/186/Uruguay.

41. Jeffrey Merritt, "Unilateral Human Rights Intercession: American Practice under Nixon, Ford, and Carter," in *The Diplomacy of Human Rights,* ed. David Newson (Latham: University Press of America, 1986): 44–45.

42. Keys, "Congress, Kissinger," 825.

43. Julian Zelizer, *Arsenal of Democracy: The Politics of National Security—From World War II to the War on Terrorism* (New York: Basic Books, 2010), 276.

44. WOLA wrote the draft of the Harkin Amendment. As Lister wrote, "along with some friends, mainly Quakers [Joe Eldridge, the president of WOLA] put together the Harkin Amendment" and was "one of the authors, and the main stimulator, of the Harkin Amendment." Memo, George Lister to William Rogers, Harkin Amendment, September 16, 1975, Folder 10-W. D. Rogers, Box 12, GLP.

45. Sikkink, *Mixed Signals*, 119.

46. Keys, "Congress, Kissinger," 825.

47. Lars Schoultz, *Human Rights and United States Policy Toward Latin America* (Princeton: Princeton University Press, 1981), 256. For a more sustained view on Ed Koch's role, see Sarah Snyder, "'Ending Our Support for the Dictators': Ed Koch, Uruguay, and Human Rights," *Cold War History* (2020): 1–18.

48. Author interview with Charles Flynn, June 9, 2020.

49. Ibid.

50. Letter, José Pérez Caldas to Juan Carlos Blanco, November 18, 1976, Box 21, Folder 7, AHD; Sikkink, *Mixed Signals*, 73; Schoultz, *Human Rights*, 84; Ruiz, *La piedra*, Chapter 5; Keys, *Reclaiming*, 209.

51. For example, Congressional Record—"Is 'International Security' a Legitimate Justification," April 13, 1976, and *Congressional Record*—"Memo in Support of Amendment to End Military Assistance," May 5, 1976.

52. Snyder, "A Call," 372–373.

53. Fraser noted he was monitoring the situation in Uruguay, which he understood to be "just as serious as the Chilean situation." Letter, Donald Fraser to Lelio Basso, July 9, 1974, Box 149.G.13.7 (B), Donald Fraser Papers, Minnesota Historical Society [hereinafter DFP], 1; Letter, Donald Fraser to Mills Ten Eyck, May 14, 1974, Box 149.G.13.7 (B), DFP.

54. Michael Schmidli interview with Rev. Joe Eldridge, May 4, 2008, as cited in Schmidli, "Institutionalizing," 364.

55. Legislative Update: Latin America, WOLA, September 1975, Folder 7, Box 16, GLP. Similarly, Bishop Armstrong of South Dakota said, "If you think Chile's bad go to Uruguay." Letter, George Lister to William Rogers, March 31, 1976, Folder 10-W. D. Rogers, Box 12, GLP.

56. Memo from George Lister, October 13, 1975, Folder 7, Box 16, GLP.

57. Letter, Fraser to Niall MacDermot, April 11, 1974, Box 149.G.13.7 (B), DFP.

58. "Hearings on Human Rights in Uruguay and Paraguay" (Washington: U.S. Government Printing Office, 1976).

59. Walker, *Principles*, 6.

60. McSherry, *Predatory States.*

61. Ferreira interview; Weschler, *A Miracle, A Universe*, 130.

62. Letter from Lister to Shlaudeman, June 16, 1978, Folder 5, Shlaudeman Box 15, GLP.

63. Ferreira interview.

64. Statement of Wilson Ferreira, "Hearings on Human Rights in Uruguay and Paraguay," 3.

65. Ibid., 8, 28.

66. Ibid., 8.

67. Statement of Dr. Martin Weinstein, "Hearings on Human Rights in Uruguay and Paraguay," 33–34.

68. Statement of Edy Kaufman, "Hearings on Human Rights in Uruguay and Paraguay," 39–41.

69. For more on NGO connections to congressional hearings, see Walker, *Principles*, 38.

70. Lewis Diuguid, "Congress Cuts Uruguay Aid, Rights Violations Are Cited," *Washington Post*, September 20, 1976, A8; Koch received death threats in response to this legislation. The CIA reported that members of the military were extremely irritated with his amendment and that they would have "to send someone to the U.S. to get Congressman Koch"—a threat that was taken very seriously in the aftermath of Chilean Orlando Letelier's assassination in September 1976 on U.S. soil. See Letter, Ed Koch to Ed Levi, October 19, 1976, NSA, http://www.gwu.edu/~nsarchiv/NSAEBB/NSAEBB112/; Dinges, *Condor Years,* Chapter 13.

71. Memo, January 28, 1976, Box 21, Folder 10, AHD.

72. José María Araneo to Don José Pérez Caldes, August 23, 1976, Box 3, Folder 5, AHD.

73. Informe, June 25, 1976, and "Contra Amnistía Internacional," nd, Box 1 Rovira Collection, ADA.

74. Memo, Uruguay Embassy to DOS, "Bordaberry in Bolivia," May 21, 1976, Wikileaks, https://wikileaks.org/plusd/cables/1976MONTEV01805_b.html.

75. There is substantial evidence that Uruguay hired a public relations (PR) firm to counteract the negative press: Sullivan, Sarria & Associate. Memos about payments and instituting new phases of the campaign were found in the government archives. Folder 4, Box 21, AHD. In addition, the author was able to track down and interview a former secretary at the firm, who explained that the PR firm was intimately involved in helping dictatorships in Latin America improve their images in the United States, which she noted was most memorably Anastasio Somoza in Nicaragua under separate auspices, the Nicaragua Government Information Services. While employed in her position, she was unaware of the work the firm did for Uruguay; documents detailing costs confirm that Uruguay similarly used the PR firm, thus further affirming the military government's increased anxiety over the way its nation was being portrayed in the United States. Author interview with Alicia Riley, March 13, 2014.

76. "Ferreira Aldunate: Amnesty Interrumpió su Disertación," *El País*, June 18, 1976, 1, BN. Some papers published his testimony in detail, but also published the response by the Uruguayan government that they were mere "accusations."

77. Handelman, "Politics and Plebiscites," 7–8.

78. Memorandum of Conversation, Uruguayan Foreign Minister's Bilateral Meeting with the Secretary, May 10, 1975, DOSVRR.

79. Memo, Agency Briefing Papers on Major Foreign Policy Issues, August 17, 1974, NSC, Latin American Affairs Staff, Subject Files, Box 11, Ford Presidential Library.

80. Sikkink, *Mixed Signals*, 73.

81. Holland and Bird, "Siracusa," 334.

82. "Adios," *Desde Uruguay,* April 1977, 4, Reel 325, NACLA.

83. Memo, Ernest Siracusa to Assistant Secretary Shlaudeman," July 20, 1976, NSA, https://nsarchive2.gwu.edu/NSAEBB/NSAEBB125/. Dinges also writes about Siracusa's goals in *Condor Years,* 169.

84. Letter, McCloskey to Fraser, October 12, 1975, Folder AMR Americas-Uruguay 1974–1985, Box 6, Executive Director Files 1967-1997, AIUSA.

85. Siracusa to Kissinger, Memorandum, New Initiative in Human Rights, January 20, 1976, DOSVRR.

86. Siracusa to Kissinger, Memorandum, High-Level Military Briefing on Results of Arrests of Communist Party Figures, December 29, 1975, DOSVRR.

87. Hewson Ryan Statement, "Hearings on Human Rights in Uruguay and Paraguay," 111.

88. Letter, Ryan to Koch, June 11, 1976, Box 12, Folder 6, GLP.

89. Ernest Siracusa to Henry Kissinger, Memorandum, Meeting with Foreign Minister, September 11, 1976, DOSVRR; Howard Handelman, "Uruguayan Journal," October 15, 1976, *Worldview,* Folder Background Press, Box 279, WOLA. Handelman also noted that President Méndez called the Democratic Party "the best supporter of subversion and sedition in the world."

90. Siracusa to Kissinger, Memorandum, Meeting with Foreign Minister, September 11, 1976, DOSVRR.

91. Jeremi Suri, *Henry Kissinger and the American Century* (Cambridge: Harvard University Press, 2007), 245–246; Greg Grandin, *Kissinger's Shadow* (New York: Metropolitan Books, 2015), 146–155; Rabe, *Kissinger and Latin America.*

92. Kissinger Speech, "Moral Promise and Practical Needs," *The Department of State Bulletin,* November 15, 1976, Ford Presidential Library Digital Collections.

93. Both in his time in office and while critiquing Carter's administration, Kissinger reinforced this belief. See Memo, Harold Saunders to Warren Christopher, "Comment on Kissinger Article 'Morality and Power,'" October 25, 1977, Folder Human Rights Theory, Box 46, Christopher Papers, National Archives, College Park, Maryland [hereinafter Christopher Papers]. Also see Walker, *Principles,* 57–58.

94. Gaddis, *Strategies of Containment,* 334–342.

95. Keys, *Reclaiming,* 3.

96. Cold warriors utilized a human rights discourse to target the Soviets, whereas liberals tended to foreground human rights as a pathway to restoring American ideals and escaping the bipolar Cold War strictures. Carter sought to bring both groups together during his presidency, without much success. Umberto Tulli, "'Whose rights are human rights?' The Ambiguous Emergence of Human Rights and the Demise of Kissingerism," *Cold War History* 12, no. 4 (November 2012): 573–593.

97. Speech, Jimmy Carter, "Human Rights and Foreign Policy," June 1977, https://usa.usembassy.de/etexts/democrac/55.htm.

98. The North is generally referred to as "wealthy developed countries," broadly located in the Northern Hemisphere. The South is generally understood as "poorer developing countries," broadly located in the Southern Hemisphere. While the roots of the terminology are different, these terms are often used interchangeably in governmental reports with First and Third World nations, and developed and developing countries, respectively.

99. Presidential Review Memorandum/NSC-17, January 26, 1977, *FRUS 1977–1980:* South America; Latin America Region, Volume XXIV, Document 1.

100. Ibid.

101. Richard Fagen, "The Carter Administration and Latin America: Business as Usual?" *Foreign Affairs* (1978), 652; Walker, *Principles*, 64, 79.

102. Jimmy Carter, "Organization of American States Address Before the Permanent Council," April 14, 1977, http://www.presidency.ucsb.edu/ws/index.php?pid=7347.

103. Jimmy Carter, "Rosalyn Carter's Trip to the Caribbean and Latin America: Remarks of the President and Mrs. Carter Prior to Her Departure from Brunswick, Georgia," May 30, 1977, http://www.presidency.ucsb.edu/ws/index.php?pid=7607; Susanna McBee, "'Substantive Talks' Are Slated for Mrs. Carter on Latin Trip," May 25, 1977, *Washington Post*, A24.

104. "Rosalyn Carter's Latin American Trip: Sea Legs for New Policy," *Update Latin America* (May/June 1977), 3–4.

105. Adam Clymer, *Drawing the Line at the Big Ditch: The Panama Canal Treaties and the Rise of the Right* (Lawrence: University Press of Kansas, 2008), 44.

106. Cyrus Vance, *Hard Choices: Critical Years in America's Foreign Policy* (New York: Simon and Schuster, 1983), 156.

107. Clymer, *Big Ditch,* 44.

108. Memo to Warren Christopher, February 28, 1977, Comments on Human Rights Statement, Folder Human Rights, Early Efforts, Box 33, Christopher Papers.

109. Report, David Trask, "A Beacon to the World: Policy on Human Rights, 1977–Present," Office of the Historian March 1980, DOSVRR; Presidential Review Memorandum/NSC 28: Human Rights, July 8, 1977, CREST Documents, Jimmy Carter Presidential Library, Atlanta, Georgia [hereinafter JCL].

110. Walker, *Principles,* 80; 98–100.

111. "Draft Outline for a Human Rights Strategy for the US" and "Guidelines on US Foreign Policy for Human Rights," February 2, 1977, National Security Advisor: Subject File, Box 28, JCL.

112. Holland and Bird, "Siracusa," 335.

113. Youle interview.

114. Ibid.

115. Walker, *Principles,* 97–100; Sikkink, *The Justice Cascade,* 9.

116. Youle interview; Juan Raúl Ferreira, *Vadearás la sangre: Historias del Uruguay de todos* (Montevideo: Linardi y Risso, 2005), 97.

117. Lawrence Pezzullo Oral History, February 24, 1989, *Association for Diplomatic Studies and Training,* https://www.adst.org/OH%20TOCs/Pezzulo,%20Lawrence%20A.toc.pdf?_ga=2 .91837843.82786147.1628799609-136417637.1628799609.

118. Flynn interview. This position was reiterated in a letter from Vance to Koch in June 1977. See Letter, June 3, 1977, Folder Press Releases, Box 282, WOLA.

119. Derian to Pezzullo, March 22, 1978, Record Group 59, Folder Uruguay, Box 5, Bureau of HR and HA Affairs, NARA.

120. Keys, "Congress, Kissinger," 840. Walker explains that advocates from WOLA, Amnesty International, and Americans for Democratic Action lobbied for these measures throughout the Ford administration. Walker, *Principles,* 83–85.

121. Roberta Cohen, "Human Rights Diplomacy: The Carter Administration and the Southern Cone," *Human Rights Quarterly* 4, no. 2 (Spring 1982): 224.

122. Bernard Gwertzman, "Security Links Cited: Assistance Is Reduced for Argentina, Uruguay, and Ethiopia, Vance Says," *New York Times*, February 25, 1977, 1. The Uruguayan

government was outraged when they became aware of the new policy of publicizing the reports. Memo, GOU Protest of Human Rights Report to Congress, March 1977, DOSVRR.

123. Memorandum from Gates to Knoche, Stevens, and Wells, February 3, 1977, *FRUS, 1977–1980: Human Rights and Humanitarian Affairs*, Document 7.

124. Flynn interview.

125. Smith also lays out intradepartment arguments about human rights policy, such as between Derian and Richard Holbroke and Terence Todman. Smith, *Morality*, 51–52; Cohen, "Human Rights Diplomacy;" and "Moral Policeman to the World?" *U.S. News and World Report*, March 14, 1977, 17.

126. Not all groups were supportive of Carter. For example, the Partido por la Victoria del Pueblo (PVP) believed that Carter's human rights policy was a "new imperial maneuver to preserve U.S. hegemony." Markarian, *Left*, 122.

127. Enrique Tarigo, "Carter, El Presidente," February 20, 1977, in *Temas de Nuestro Tiempo, Tomo 1* (Montevideo, Fundación de Cultura Universitaria, 1979): 258–261. Other activists and politicians have written about the hope that Carter imbued, even as a candidate, about the possibility for bringing international attention to Uruguay's plight. See, for example, Yamandú Fau in Di Candia, *Ni Muerte Ni Derrota*, 181.

128. Carta a Terence Todman, August 1, 1977, Folder 14, AMF; Carta a Patricia Derian, September 5, 1978, Folder 14, AMF. Some Argentine mothers and abuelas, part of the much more organized group of Madres de la Plaza de Mayo, also tried to come to Uruguay and plead for help finding their loved ones since the embassy in Montevideo was known to be sympathetic and they thought they would get a better hearing there than in Buenos Aires. Youle interview.

129. Memo of Conversation, OAS, March 7, 1977, National Security Council, Argentina Declassification Project.

130. Graham Hovey, "Panamanian Leader Meets with Carter," *New York Times*, September 7, 1977, 14; "The Canal in Panama," *New York Times*, September 8, 1977, 26; "An Open Letter to President Carter," *Washington Post*, September 7, 1977, A20; WOLA Release, September 8, 1977, Folder 14, Box 21, AHD. Groups also held protests in front of the White House during the meetings, with flyers that read "Carter's Human Rights Policy Unmasked." They argued Carter's reception "of these dictators supports their efforts to legitimize their repressive regimes. It stands in direct contradiction with Carter's public position on human rights." Flyer, Dictators Come to Washington, Folder Human Rights: Latin America, Box 38, Christopher Papers.

131. Jimmy Carter, *White House Diary* (New York: Farrar, Straus and Giroux, 2010), 92–95.

132. Letter, Carter to Méndez, October 31, 1977, Record Group 59, Entry UD-10D, Folder 1977 Uruguay July–December, Box 7, Department of State Human Rights Country Files, NARA.

133. Memo, Brzezinski to Carter, "Nineteen Bilaterals," nd, *FRUS 1977–1980*, South America; Latin America Region, Document 23.

134. Letter to Lister, September 21, 1977, Folder 19, Box 8, GLP.

135. Letter, Caldas to McGovern, September 23, 1977, Folder 14, Box 21, AHD.

136. Walker, *Principles*, 115; Schmidli, *Fate*, 150.

137. Memorandum Prepared in the CIA, March 21, 1977, *FRUS, 1977–1980: Human Rights and Humanitarian Affairs*, Document 25; "Nota Respuesta al Departamento de Estado de los Estados Unidos de Norteamérica con Relación al Informe sobre Derechos Humanos en el Uruguay," nd, 11–12, Folder 4, Álvaro Barros Lémez Colección, CEIU; Memo, Santiago Embassy to DOS, "Visit by Uruguayan Army Chief," August 7, 1980, DOSVRR; Memorandum

Prepared in the CIA, May 11, 1977, *FRUS, 1977–1980: Human Rights and Humanitarian Affairs*, Document 42.

138. Action Memorandum from the Lake to Vance, January 20, 1978, *FRUS, 1977–1980: Human Rights and Humanitarian Affairs,* Document 105.

139. Debbie Sharnak, "Sovereignty and Human Rights: Reexamining Carter's Human Rights Policy Towards the Third World," *Diplomacy & Statecraft* 25, no. 2 (June 2014): 303–330.

140. Paper prepared by the Bureau of Intelligence and Research, Progress and Retrogression in Human Rights in 1977, January 11, 1978, *FRUS, 1977–1980: Human Rights and Humanitarian Affairs,* Document 104.

141. Uruguay Memo on the 34th Commission on Human Rights, 1978, Annex 5, Box 3, Folder 7, AHD

142. Letter, María del Carmen Almeida to Carter, March 29, 1978, and Letter, Cesar Chelala to Mondale, October 3, 1978, White House Central File, Subject File, CO 169 (Uruguay), Executive, 1/20/77-1/20/81, Box CO-65, JCL.

143. Memo, Embassy to DOS, July 17, 1978, DOSVRR. For more on improvements: Memo, Embassy to DOS, September 9, 1978, DOSVRR.

144. Memo, ABA Lawyers Complete Positive Visit, April 1, 1978, DOSVRR. For more on policy discussions over praise and criticism, Memo, Christopher Meeting with Ferreira, November 19, 1977, DOSVRR.

145. "Five Years of Military Rule," June 1978, p7, Folder WOLA Publications, Box 282, WOLA.

146. Letter, Eldridge and Ferreira to Vaky, October 1978, Folder 6, Box 64, GLP.

147. Youle interview.

148. Memo to Mark Schneider, September 13, 1977, Record Group 59, Entry UD-10D, Folder 1977 Uruguay July–December, Box 7, Department of State Human Rights Country Files, NARA.

149. Memo, "Ambassador's Goals and Objectives—Uruguay," February 14, 1978, DOSVRR.

150. Terence Todman Oral History, June 23, 1995, *Association for Diplomatic Studies and Training,* http://adst.org/oral-history/fascinating-figures/being-black-in-a-lily-white-state-department/

151. "National Academy of Sciences Committee on Human Rights: Results of a Visit to Argentina and Uruguay," *National Academy of Sciences,* April 24, 1978, DOSVRR.

152. Airgram, American Embassy to DOS, Human Rights Walk-In Analysis, May 31, 1978, DOSVRR.

153. Memo, "Likely GOU Position at VIII OASGA," May 3, 1978, DOSVRR.

154. Update Latin America: Uruguay, June 1978, Folder 6, Box 16, GLP.

155. Juan de Onis, "Uruguay, Once Shaken by Guerrillas, Asserts Only the Extremists Now Live in Fear," *New York Times,* June 29, 1978, A3.

156. Derian to Pezzullo, March 22, 1978, and Pezzullo to Derian, April 5, 1978, Record Group 59, Folder: Uruguay, Box 5, Bureau of Human Rights and Humanitarian Affairs, NARA.

157. Memorandum from Inderfurth to Brzezinski, December 1, 1978, *FRUS, 1977–1980: Human Rights and Humanitarian Affairs,* Document 172.

158. Critics of Carter's human rights policy claim that he abandoned his human rights platform during the latter part of his administration, especially after crises in Iran and Afghanistan. Carter lessened his criticism, for example, of Argentina during this period to garner favor with the country during the USSR grain embargo. Schmidli, *Fate,* 157; Walker, *Principles,* 200.

159. Salmon to Derian, Weekly Activities Report, July 31, 1979, Folder Weekly Reports 2, 1979 July 5–November 13, Box 1, Carter Years, Patricia Murphy Derian Papers, Duke University [hereinafter PDP].

160. Telegram, "U.S. Opposition to IFI Loans on Human Rights Grounds," January 22, 1980, and Telegram, From Embassy in Montevideo to SecState, January 30, 1980, RG 59, Location UD-06D 25, Folder "Uruguay: January 1980," Box 20, NARA.

161. Memorandum from Vance and Christopher to Carter, March 27, 1978, and Report Prepared by the Interagency Group on Human Rights and Foreign Assistance, April 30, 1978, *FRUS, 1977–1980: Human Rights and Humanitarian Affairs,* Documents 132, 139.

162. Memorandum from Derian and Lake to Christopher, May 16, 1978, *FRUS, 1977–1980: Human Rights and Humanitarian Affairs,* Document, 145.

163. Justin Vaïse, *Neoconservatism: The Biography of a Movement* (Cambridge: Harvard University Press, 2010), 133–134; Keys, *Reclaiming,* 256; Kiron K. Skinner et al., *The Strategy of Campaigning: Lessons from Ronald Reagan and Boris Yeltsin* (Ann Arbor: The University of Michigan Press, 2007), 149; Jay Winik, *On the Brink: The Dramatic Behind-the-Scenes Saga of the Reagan Era and the Men and Women Who Won the Cold War* (New York: Simon & Schuster, 1996), 101.

164. *Country Reports on Human Rights Practices for 1979* (Washington: U.S. Government Printing Office, 1980), 412.

165. Ibid., 413.

166. Telegram, "Uruguay: Charged with Interference Over Human Rights Report," February 14, 1980, RG 59, Location UD-06D 25, Box 20, Folder "Uruguay: January 1980," NARA.

167. Memo, April 17, 1979, 6, Box 1, Folder 1976-1980 Memorabilia-Correspondence, Carter Years, PDP.

168. Ibid.; Mark Bradley, "American Vernaculars," 19.

169. Memo, April 17, 1979, Box 1, Folder 1976–1980 Memorabilia-Correspondence, Carter Years, PDP.

170. Report, David Trask, "A Beacon to the World: Policy on Human Rights, 1977–Present," Office of the Historian March 1980, DOSVRR.

171. Action Memorandum from Lake to Vance, January 20, 1978, *FRUS, 1977–1980: Human Rights and Humanitarian Affairs,* Document 105.

172. Samuel Huntington, *Third Wave: Democratization in the Late Twentieth Century* (Norman: University of Oklahoma Press, 1993), 96.

173. Harkin, Congressional Record, Zelmar Michelini and Héctor Gutiérrez Ruiz, May 22, 1978, House of Representatives.

174. Memo, Tarnoff to Brzezinski, "Human Rights Policy Impact: Latin America," Folder "Human Rights: Latin America," Box 38, Christopher Papers.

175. Walker, *Principles,* 128; Andrew Katz, "Public Opinion and Contradictions of Jimmy Carter's Foreign Policy," *Presidential Studies Quarterly* 30, no. 4 (2000): 662–687.

176. The Carter administration actively cultivated a relationship with men in the military who had "flexibility" to act as "interlocutors" and push a human rights agenda when they had an opportunity. Memo, State Department to Montevideo Embassy, "Acting DCM Conversation with General Raimundez," August 8, 1980, DOSVRR.

177. Edward Schumacher, "Uruguay Brass, Now Tarnished, Begin to Snipe at East Other," *New York Times,* December 28, 1980, E3. Divisions in the military began as early as 1977 when officers began to vie for who would take over after Méndez. Periodically, several purges of

high- and mid-level officers had occurred, which further revealed the divisions. Handelman, "Politics and Plebiscites," 4.

178. Update Latin America: Uruguay, June 1978, Folder 6, Box 16, GLP.

179. Sikkink, *Mixed Signals*, 144–145.

Chapter 4

Note to epigraph: Eduardo Galeano, *Memory of Fire* (New York: Pantheon Books, 1988), 257.

1. Amnesty International, "Uruguay: The Cases of Fourteen Prisoners of Conscience," March 1979, AMR/52/06/9, Amnesty International Online Archive; Don Obderdorfer, "U.S. Links Aid to Human Rights," *Los Angeles Times*, February 25, 1977, B1; *Documentos políticos: La CDU una experiencia unitaria* (Mexico: Ediciones CDU, 1984), 33–34; "International Covenants on Human Rights," United Nations General Assembly, November 1, 1979, A/C.3/34/6.

2. Another important aspect which this chapter does not explore in depth is the internal regime dynamics between the hardliners and reformers, the latter of whom also pushed for the plebiscite to appeal to the democratic history of the country. Gillespie, *Negotiating Democracy*, Chapter 4.

3. Iván Molina and Fabrice Lehoucq, "Political Competition and Electoral Fraud: A Latin American Case Study," *Journal of Interdisciplinary History* 30, No. 2 (Autumn 1999): 199–234; Robert Barros, *Constitutionalism and Dictatorship: Pinochet, the Junta, and the 1980 Constitution* (New York: Cambridge University Press, 2002), 14–15. Literature on plebiscites conducted by totalitarian governments further supports this view. Whereas the act of casting a ballot is considered to be a democratic act, under totalitarian governments there are often no legitimate choices, which means that plebiscites merely function symbolically under the guise of openness to legitimize and reaffirm a regime's power in the international sphere. Matt Qvortrup et al., "Explaining the Paradox of Plebiscites," *Government and Opposition* 55, no. 2 (April 2020): 202–219.

4. Edward Schumacher, "Uruguay's Vote: Exception to the Rule," *New York Times*, December 6, 1980, 3; Stephen A. Rickard et al., "Chile: Human Rights and the Plebiscite," *An Americas Watch Report* (July 1988), 19.

5. Efraín Olivera, "Sigue valiendo la pena," *Si decimos Derechos Humanos . . .* (Montevideo: SERPAJ, 2006).

6. Rarely have historians taken an in-depth look at the dynamics of the plebiscite or its human rights implications; instead, they stress that the vote exemplified Uruguay's strong commitment to its democratic history. Markarian, in *Left*, encompasses this period, but because she focuses on exiles, she spends very little time on the actual plebiscite. Weinstein describes only the basics of the events. Weinstein, *Democracy at a Crossroads*, 74–76. Gillespie focuses more on reasons for the defeat and political parties' revival in his book. Gillespie, *Negotiating Democracy*, 72–76. The most in-depth account is found in Daniel Corbo Longueira, *El Plebiscito Constitucional de 1980: La Derrota del Proyecto Militar Para Legitimar un Régimen Autoritario* (Montevideo: Ediciones Puerta del Sur, 2006), but it is most notable for its primary sources and capturing the voices of the actors involved, whereas this chapter looks at the role of the plebiscite in an emerging human rights discourse.

7. For a comparative analysis of understanding militaries' invocation of human rights and disputed meanings, see João Henrique Roriz, "Clashing Frames: Human Rights and Foreign Policy in the Brazilian Re-Democratization Process," *Revista Brasileira de Política Internacional* 60, no. 1 (2017), and Adair, *Lost Decade*, 22; for more on the co-opting of human rights language by state actors, see Tate, *Counting the Dead*, 4. For a regional analysis of this process in the 1970s

with other countries in the Southern Cone, see Kelly, *Sovereign Emergencies*. More broadly on shifting notions of sovereignty at an international level, see Tom Farer, ed., *Beyond Sovereignty: Collectively Defending Democracy in the Americas* (Baltimore: Johns Hopkins University Press, 1996); Kathryn Sikkink, "Human Rights, Principled Issue-Networks, and Sovereignty in Latin America," *International Organization* 47, no. 3 (Summer 1993): 411–441; Stephen D. Krasner, *Sovereignty: Organized Hypocrisy* (Princeton: Princeton University Press, 1999), 119–120.

8. Mariana Achugar, "Between Remembering and Forgetting: Uruguayan Military Discourse About Human Rights (1976–2004)," *Discourse & Society* 18 (2007): 522; Finch, "Democratisation," 597.

9. Corbo, *El Plebiscito*, 26–28.

10. "Uruguay: Dr. Aparicio Méndez Sworn in as New President of Uruguay," September 1, 1976, Reuters Video Archive.

11. Luis González, "1980–1981: An Unexpected Opening," *Latin American Research Review* 18, no. 3 (1983): 63.

12. Markarian, *Left*, 119–120.

13. Handelman, "Politics and Plebiscites," 4.

14. Robert Goldman, "Voting in Uruguay Will Erase Human Rights," *Los Angeles Times*, November 30, 1980, E3; William L. Wipfler, "Uruguay's Liberty Vote," *New York Times*, November 28, 1980, A27.

15. Patrick Knight, "Military Get Final Word in Uruguay Constitution," *Times of London*, November 8, 1980, 4.

16. Steve J. Stern, *Battling for Hearts and Minds: Memory Struggles in Pinochet's Chile, 1973–1988* (Durham: Duke University Press, 2006), 171–172.

17. Schumacher, "Uruguay's Vote"; Rickard, "Chile: Human Rights and the Plebiscite," 19.

18. Corbo, *El Plebiscito*, 119; in today's currency, $30 million amounts to approximately $86 million. Gillespie, *Negotiating Democracy*, 70.

19. "Ravenna: La Constitución se Ajusta al Proceso de Transición que Viviremos," *El País*, November 19,1980, 10, BN.

20. "Debe Aprobarse," *El País*, November 18, 1980, 14, BN; "Existe Gran Confusión en la Opción por el No," *El País*, November 20, 1980, 6, BN.

21. "Terroristas, Marxistas y Los Que no Quieran a Uruguay Votarían el 'no,'" *El Día*, November 13, 1980, 13, Folder 4, Raúl Jacob Colección, CEIU.

22. Full-page ads appeared in the pages of *El* País, for example on pages 8 and 9, November 26, 1980, BN. Edward Schumacher, "Uruguayans Voting on a Charter Today," *New York Times*, November 30, 1980, 14. For an even bigger collection of these ads, see Folder 4, Raúl Jacob Colección, CEIU. Chile had employed similar "ayer contra hoy" photograph spreads as early as 1975 to try to demonstrate the military's positive impact. Ángeles Donoso Macaya, *The Insubordination of Photography* (Gainesville: University of Florida Press, 2020), 8–9.

23. González, "Unexpected Opening," 70. The newspapers printed long articles explaining why different major public figures were coming out in favor of the "yes" vote. On TV, the military forces also gave lengthy public addresses about the military. See, among others, "La Junta de Comandantes se dirigirá al país el lunes," November 22, 1980, *El País*, 15, BN; "Darracq: El Si Permitirá a los Jóvenes Asumir su Función en la República," *El País*, November 23, 1980, 3, BN; "Callinal: Enamorado de la Paz del Uruguay," November 25, 1980, *El País*, 2, BN.

24. The military's use of the term "democracy" to explain its project began well before the plebiscite. Throughout the 1970s, the military allowed two newspapers, *El Día* and *El País,* to

continue to publish under heavy censorship. In a tightly controlled environment, the military permitted the papers to debate the idea of "new democracy," and grapple with limited understanding of republican or liberal conceptions of the term. Under the government's repression, the papers articulated a new vision for democracy that coexisted with a severe limiting of rights. Gerardo Albistur, "Democracia y Libertad: Un Debate Público en Dictadura (1973–1984)," *Revista Encuentros Latinoamericanos* 6, no. 2 (2012): 397–422; Gerardo Albistur, "La Libertad y la Liberal Republicana: Un Debate entre 'acrecidos' y 'desplazados' durante el régimen cívico-militar," Seminario Permanente de Investigación Sobre Historia Reciente, April 2014, Montevideo, Uruguay. Paul Drake explains that the idea of democracy had developed over two centuries of Latin American history. In earlier versions, some Latin American countries provided a limited or restricted form of democracy, in which citizens had only a minimal level of rights. For example, governments had banned certain political parties and limited free speech. The generals aligned their vision of democracy with this older and restricted version. Despite its anachronistic appeal, almost all contemporary political understandings of democracy rejected this definition on the basis that it was paired with severe censorship, torture, and single-party voting. Political scientist Robert Dahl, for example, argues that at a basic level, democracy must encompass electoral competition, effective civil and political rights, and open state-society relations. Even these elementary tenets of democracy did not exist in the military's invocation of the term. Paul W. Drake, *Between Tyranny and Anarchy: A History of Democracy in Latin America, 1800–2006* (Stanford: Stanford University Press, 2009), 4–5; Robert Alan Dahl, *Polyarchy: Participation and Opposition* (New Haven: Yale University Press, 1971).

25. "El discurso del presidente: La Democracia Liberal," *El Día*, July 30, 1978, 6, BN.

26. "Ravenna," *El País*.

27. "Para confundir e intimidar," *El País*, November 21, 1980, 6, BN.

28. Even with the rise of the UN and UDHR in the 1940s, human rights did not challenge the state system as it did by the 1970s. Moyn, *The Last Utopia*.

29. Kelly, *Sovereign Emergencies*, 6–7.

30. Henrique Roriz, "Clashing Frames," 8.

31. Grupo de Apoyo a la Resistencia Uruguaya, "News from Patria Chica," *Banda Oriental* 3 (December 1974), 9, Reel 325, NACLA.

32. *Generals Rule*, 12; for more on Institutional Act No. 5, see "Report on the Situation of Human Rights in Uruguay," Organization of American States, January 31, 1978, OEA/Ser.L/V/II.32; Edy Kaufman, *Uruguay in Transition: From Civilian to Military Rule* (New Brunswick: Transaction Books, 1979), 117; Corbo, *El Plebiscito*, 42–43.

33. Markarian, *Left*, 98.

34. Guillermo E. Stewart to Michael F. Crowley, October 13, 1977, Box 30, Folder 32, AHD.

35. "Report on the Situation of Human Rights in Uruguay," OAS, 1978.

36. "Debate por la reforma constitucional de 1980." Si-No. Programa, https://www.youtube.com/watch?v=dL2tGaIMpQg

37. Speech by Adolfo Folle Martínez, United Nations General Assembly Official Records, Thirty-Fifth Session, 13th Plenary Meeting, September 26, 1980, A/35/PV.13, p232, and "Texto del Discurso Pronunciado por el Senor Ministro en el XXXV Periodo de Sesiones de la Asamblea General de la Organización de las Naciones Unidas," Box 2, ADA.

38. Similar claims were made by Argentina, Chile, and Brazil in this period. See Henrique Roriz, "Clashing Frames," 9, where Brazil also claimed a "traditional statist position" on human rights in the face of increasing criticism. Kelly, *Sovereign Emergencies*, 138; Adair, *Lost Decade*, 22.

39. Knight, "Military Get," 4.

40. Amnesty International, *Annual Report 1981*, 185, Amnesty International Online Library.

41. Markarian, *Left*.

42. "Declaración Constitutiva de la Convergencia Democrática Uruguaya," Folder 4, Álvaro Barros Lémez Colección, CEIU; "Grupo de Convergencia Democrática en Uruguay," *Aportes* 4 no. 14 (December 1980), 35–36, Folder 4, Waksman Colección, CEIU.

43. Markarian, *Left*, 117–119 notes the CDU did have some detractors among exile groups. However, it still represented the biggest coalition of exiles opposing the military until this point.

44. WOLA, "United Uruguayan Opposition Group Formed," April 22, 1980, Folder 76, Waksman Collection, CEIU.

45. Aureliano Rodríguez Larreta, "Una 'Convergencia Democrática' para Uruguay," *El País*, May 21, 1980, BN.

46. In Uruguay, embassies were guarded to try to prevent people seeking asylum; however, Mexico's embassy was located on Uruguay's most famous and most crowded plaza, Plaza Independencia. This made checking every person impossible. When extra military officers were placed outside the building, the Mexican ambassador issued a formal complaint, and the Uruguayan military was forced to withdraw them. Howard Handelman, "Uruguayan Journal," July 11, 1976, *Worldview*, Folder Background Press, Box 279, WOLA. Juan Raúl Ferreira also praised Mexican officials for receiving Uruguayan exiles during the dictatorship; see Ferreira, *Con la patria*, 33.

47. Pablo Yankelevich, "Memoria y Exilio: Sudamericos En Mexico," in *La Imposibilidad del Olvido: Recorridos de La Memoria En Argentina, Chile, y Uruguay*, ed. Bruno Groppo and Patricia Flier (Argentina: Ediciones al Margen, 2001), 238. Patrick Kelly, similarly, explores how Mexico operated as an asylum for Chilean refugees fleeing Pinochet's dictatorship, in Patrick William Kelly, "The 1973 Chilean Coup and the Origins of Transnational Human Rights Activism," *Journal of Global History* 8, no. 1 (March 2013): 165–186; Mario Sznajder and Luis Roniger, "Political Exile in Latin America," *Latin American Perspectives* 34, no. 4 (2007): 7–30, Yankelevich, *México*.

48. CDU, "En el Plebiscito de Noviembre de 1980 CDU Llama a Votar Por No," in *Documentos políticos: La CDU una experiencia unitaria* (Mexico: Ediciones CDU, 1984), 33–34.

49. Conversely, the CIA found the CDU quite threatening and composed of "disparate elements of the radical left." They accused the organization of "vigorously [seeking] to undermine the regime by attacking its human rights record." "Uruguay: Rough Road Toward Civilian Rule: An Intelligence Assessment," Directorate of Intelligence, August 1983, Virtual CIA Reading Room.

50. Letter from Juan Raúl Ferreira to CDU, 28 julio 1980; Letter from Juan Raúl Ferreira to CDU, May 12, 1980; Informe no. 2, July 29, 1980, Folder 3, "Documentación Interna, Correspondencia, 1981–1983," Luis Echave Colección, CEIU; Handelman, "Politics and Plebiscites," 5.

51. Discurso Wilson Ferreira Aldunate, "Si eres uruguayo," *Aportes* (December 1980), 41–42. Folder 4, Waksman Colección, CEIU.

52. Juan Raúl Ferreira, "Estamos de Acuerdo," in *Documentos políticos: La CDU una experiencia unitaria* (Mexico: Ediciones CDU, 1984), 28–29.

53. Letter, Juan Raúl Ferreira to Lord Eric Averbury, August 1, 1980, Folder 3, "Documentación Interna, Correspondencia, 1980–1983," Luis Echave Colección, CEIU.

54 AI *Annual Report 1981*, 184.

55. Ellen Lutz to All AIUSA Staff, Memo re: Uruguay Special Action, October 31, 1980, Folder Country Files: Americas-Uruguay, Series IV 1.3, Box 17, Membership Mobilization, AIUSA.

56. Letter, Weitz to Derian, November 15, 1980, Record Group 59, Entry P 886, Folder Uruguay, Box 5, Bureau of Human Rights and Humanitarian Affairs, NARA.

57. Letter to Orfila, SecGen of the OAS, November 17, 1980, Folder Commission for Democracy, Box 279, WOLA; Niko Schvarz, "Una gran iniciativa," *El Día* (Mexico), September 13, 1980, 8, Biblioteca Miguel Lerdo de Tejada, Mexico City, Mexico [hereinafter BMLT].

58. Press Release, Latin American Leaders Open First Meeting of Commission for Democracy and Human Rights in Uruguay, November 7, 1980, WOLA, Folder Commission for Democracy, Box 279, WOLA.

59. "Informaciones del Uruguay," *Boletín Socialista Internacional,* October 1980, p. 2, Folder 141, Waksman Colección, CEIU.

60. Memo, From DOS to USSouthCom, "Amparts Article Provokes War College Flare Up," September 30, 1980, DOSVRR.

61. Wipfler, "Uruguay's 'Liberty' Vote."

62. Letter, Socialist International Committee for Latin America and the Caribbean to Muskie, October 17, 1980, Folder 55, Ponce de León Colección, CEIU.

63. Memo, State Department to Montevideo Embassy, "Acting DCM Conversation with General Raimundez," August 8, 1980, DOSVRR.

64. "Siguen registrándose incidentes en la Asamblea Interamericana," *El Informador* (Mexico), November 24, 1980, 1.

65. Organization of American States, "Annual Report 1979–1980," Chapter V Uruguay.

66. Memo, William B. Buffun to Sec Gen Kurt Waldheim, May 3, 1979, "Implementation of Decisions Adopted by the Commission on Human Rights Regarding Ethiopia, Paraguay and Uruguay," Box 24, File 1, Folder: Commission on Human Rights, 1974–1979, UN archive.

67. Commission on Human Rights, Report on the Thirty-Sixth Session, February 4–March 14, 1980, Economic and Social Council official records, 1980, E/1980/13, p83–4. This decision was highly controversial and contested. Secretary General Kurt Waldheim had sent Javier Pérez de Cuéllar, then Under-Secretary General for Special Political Affairs, to Uruguay to investigate human rights abuses. In a glowing report, Pérez de Cuellar whitewashed claims of abuses after going on a highly staged visit by Uruguay's military government. The report was contradicted by various others, including a contemporary visit by the International Commission of the Red Cross, which wrote a scathing report at the same time. As a result, and to the embarrassment of the UN, Pérez de Cuéllar's report was discredited and discounted as Uruguay remained on the blacklist for the UN Human Rights Commission. See Iain Guest, *Behind the Disappearances* (Philadelphia: University of Pennsylvania Press, 1990), 141–145; Markarian, *Left,* 127–131; David Kohut and Olga Vilella, *Historical Dictionary of the Dirty Wars* (New York: Rowman and Littlefield, 2017), 351–352.

68. "Resolution on the Referendum in Uruguay," November 1980, Aeries 347, Box 14, File 4, Folder Uruguay 1980–1984, UN Archive.

69. Others have compared his physical appearance to former Chicago Mayor Richard Daley. See Neil Kritz, *Transitional Justice: How Emerging Democracies Reckon with Former Regimes* (Washington: United States Institute of Peace Press, 1995), 404.

70. Tarigo recounted the difficult approval process in the first edition of *Opinar.* "Por qué no salimos la semana pasada," *Opinar,* November 6, 1980, 1, BN.

71. "Si-No," *Opinar,* November 6, 1980, 2, BN; "Nuestro Primer Editorial," *Opinar,* November 6, 1980, 3, BN; "Uruguay's Military Rulers Challenged by Newspaper," *Boston Globe,* March 10, 1981, 17.

72. Entrevista con Gonzalo Carámbula, November 20, 2015, https://armandolveira
.blogspot.com/2015/11/?fbclid=IwAR00uCMaEi4BZNnMsvVahG2Hz6XXWh8kckM78bOvQ
8zeg8dVTntuHWlHyKI.

73. "Para Hoy, Comenzar," *La Plaza,* November 1979, 1, BN.

74. "Meteorología política: soplan nuevos vientos," *La Plaza,* February 1980, 1, BN.

75. "Marcos Carámbula y la Revista Plaza," *El Espectador,* November 30, 2000.

76. "Debate por la reforma constitucional de 1980." There were three debates in total, but
the one on November 14, 1980, attracted the most interest.

77. There were moments when some of the debaters did raise their voices a bit. Ibid.

78. Ibid.

79. "Una sola voz por el no," *El País,* November 29, 2015, https://www.elpais.com.uy/que
-pasa/sola-voz.html.

80. Schumacher, "Uruguay's Vote: Exception to the Rule."

81. "Si-No," *Opinar,* November 6, 1980, 2, BN.

82. For more on word-of-mouth campaigning, especially in the interior, see Andrés Noguez
Reyes, *San Carlos: Bajo la Dictadura 1973–1985* (Montevideo: Ediciones Trilce, 2013), 200–202.

83. Álvaro Rico et al., eds. *Melodía larga: El partido Comunista bajo la dictadura* (Montevideo: Fin de Siglo, 2021).

84. "Blanco: "El sí ofrece posibilidades de acción partidaria próxima,"" *El País,* November 21, 1980, 1, BN. The debates, on the TV program *El Diálogo,* were covered by the local
papers but were also careful to stress the "yes" side of the debate.

85. Dozens of former politicians were arrested during this time for opposition to the military's project from anywhere of a few hours to several weeks. See "Human Rights and U.S. Policy
in the Multilateral Development Banks," Hearing Before the Subcommittee International Development Institutions and Finance, 97th Congress, First Session, July 21 and 23, 1981 (Washington: U.S. Government Printing Office, 1981), 303–304.

86. "Ante el Próximo Plebiscito Constitucional," November 12, 1980, http://iglesiacatolica
.org.uy//wp-content/uploads/2012/08/Ante-el-proximo-Plebiscito-Constitucional.pdf;   Amy
Edmonds, "Moral Authority and Authoritarianism: The Catholic Church and the Military
Regime in Uruguay," *Journal of Church and State* 56, no. 4 (2013): 656.

87. Wipfler, "Uruguay's Liberty Vote."

88. Markarian, *Left,* 120.

89. Weschler, *A Miracle, A Universe,* 150.

90. Gillespie, *Negotiating Democracy,* 71.

91. "Habla el Gral. Alberto Ballestrino," *Posdata,* January 26, 1996, 26. BN.

92. Corbo, *El Plebiscito,* 202–203.

93. GRISUR, Violaciones de Derechos Humanos en Uruguay: Documentos March 1980–
September 1981, 13, Folder 6, Derechos Humanos Colección, CEIU; Edward Schumacher,
"Uruguay Army Silent on Setback Vote," *New York Times,* December 2, 1980, A3.

94. "Núñez: 'Las FF.AA. o Tienen Apetitos de Poder Como un Todo o Liderando a Nadie,'"
December 1, 1980, *El País,* 3, BN; "Méndez: Gobierno Cumplió y Continua la Reconstrucción,"
El País, December 2, 1980, 1, BN.

95. Carta de Susana Wilson a Carlos Julio Pereyra, December 22, 1980, in *Wilson: Las Cartas del Exilio,* ed. Carlos Julio Pereyra (Montevideo: Ediciones de la Banda Oriental, 2013), 123.

96. "Carta de Uruguay," *Aportes,* December 1980, 3; Folder 4, Waksman Colección, CEIU.

97. "El Pueblo Dijo No," *Opinar,* December 4, 1980, 1, BN.

98. "Qué país, el Uruguay!" *Opinar,* December 4, 1980, 7. BN.

99. "Marcos Carámbula y la Revista Plaza."

100. WOLA, "Uruguay's Military Decisively Repudiated by Plebiscite Vote," December 1, 1980, Folder 6, Derechos Humanos Colección, CEIU.

101. Sikkink, *Mixed Signals,* 57–59; Edward Kennedy, "Beginning Anew in Latin America; The Alianza in Trouble," *Saturday Review of Literature,* October 17, 1970; Snyder, *From Selma,* 122; Kelly, *Sovereign Emergencies,* 200, 216.

102. Juan Raúl Ferreira, *Vadearás la sangre: Historias del Uruguay de todos* (Montevideo: Linardi y Risso, 2005), 50–51; Ferreira, *Con la patria,* 38.

103. Kennedy, "For Democracy in Uruguay," Congressional Record, 96th Congress, Second Session, vol. 126, no. 173, December 9, 1980.

104. Holtzman, "Plebiscite in Uruguay Cause for Celebration," *Congressional Record,* 96th Congress, Second Session, vol. 126, part 24, December 5, 1980.

105. "The Surprising Answer in Uruguay," *New York Times,* December 5, 1980, A30.

106. Ruben Salazar Mallen, "Un triunfo de la democracia," *El Informador,* December 4, 1980, 4.

107. González, "Unexpected Opening," 73.

108. Schumacher, "Uruguay's Vote: Exception to the Rule."; Aparicio Méndez, "Diría Que es Una Derrota Para el Pueblo," *Aportes,* December 1980, 64–65; Folder 4, Waksman Colección, CEIU.

109. Edward Schumacher, "Uruguayan Regime Unbowed by Defeat," *New York Times,* December 7, 1980, 11.

110. Handelman, "Politics and Plebiscites," 9.

111. Gillespie, *Negotiating Democracy,* 70.

112. Anibal Luis Barbagelata, "Y por siempre," *Opinar,* December 26, 1980, 4, BN.

Chapter 5

1. "Uruguay Government Closes Two Opposition Publications," *New York Times,* April 16, 1984, 2.

2. Virginia Martínez, *Los Rusos de San Javier* (Montevideo: Ediciones de la Banda Oriental, 2013), 10.

3. MacLean Gander and Martin Andersen, "The Russians vs. the Generals," *Newsweek,* October 29, 1984, Folder 43, Box 9, Philip Agee Papers, Tamiment Library and Robert F. Wagner Archives, New York University [hereinafter Tamiment].

4. Martin Andersen, "Uruguayan Military Sees Red in Ancestry," *Globe and Mail,* October 3, 1984.

5. Urgent Action, "Death in Custody/Fear of Torture," May 3, 1984, Folder 46, Box 269, AIUSA.

6. *Tribunal Permanente de los Pueblos* (Montevideo: Graphis Ltda, 1990), 167–170.

7. Weinstein, *Democracy at a Crossroads,* 74.

8. "Sin Justicia No Habrá Democracia," September 1984, Madres y familiares, ACEEP y Comisión por la Amnistía y los DDHH, Julio Rügnitz Colección, AGU; "Oremos por el alma de Vladimir Roslik," *Jaque,* April 28, 1984, 2, BN.

9. Gander and Andersen, "The Russians vs. the Generals."

10. Markarian, *Left* has an excellent chapter on this period, which centers her analysis on exiles returning to Uruguay and their important work in building a human rights movement

domestically. My work seeks to build on her strong foundations in recognizing the tensions between emerging human rights groups and the more conciliatory political parties, while also spotlighting emerging tensions with a reemergence of social and economic rights discourse, and the implications of these fraught negotiations on later claims for justice.

11. "La imprescindible libertad de expresión," *Opinar*, December 4, 1980, 3, BN. *Opinar* had a circulation of approximately 11,000.

12. Examples include "Posición de la juventud," *Opinar*, July 30, 1981, 4; Luis Antonio Hierro, "La Apertura está en nosotros," *Opinar*, August 6, 1981, 4; "Libertad de Prensa," *Opinar*, August 13, 1981, 5; "La clausura de 'La Democracia," *Opinar*, September 24, 1981, 3, BN.

13. "Nosotros somos más bien modelos que imitadores de otros," *Opinar*, December 18, 1980, 3, BN.

14. "La Paz se basa en la Justicia," *Opinar*, December 24, 1981, 32, BN. It should be noted that the June 11, 1981 edition mentioned human rights in relation to the United States' foreign policy and the twentieth anniversary of Amnesty International.

15. Edward Schumacher, "Uruguay Editor Is Taking Lead as Army Critic," *New York Times*, May 31, 1981, 11.

16. J. Mastromatteo, "El Arte Como Necesidad," *La Plaza*, January 1980, 14; Luis Elbert, "El Cine Uruguayo Debe Ser Nacional," *La Plaza*, January 1980, 15–16, BN.

17. "Plan Tentativo de Democratización," *La Plaza*, February 1981, 4–5; "Sigamos Hablando con Franqueza," *La Plaza*, July 1981, 1, BN.

18. Luis Pérez Aguirre, "El 'Desconocido' Nobel de la Paz o la Conspiración del Silencio," *La Plaza*, February 1981, 25–26, BN; "Uruguayos Desaparecidos en Argentina," *La Plaza*, August 1981, 12, BN.

19. "Transformar el miedo en libertad," *Aquí*, April 19, 1983, 1, BN.

20. "La libertad de prensa: un tema que preocupa," *Aquí*, April 19, 1983, 7; "Políticos argentinos quieren esclarecer los 'desaparecidos,'" *Aquí*, April 19, 1983, 15, BN.

21. "Una avalancha de críticas sepultó al documento militar," *Aquí*, May 3, 1983, 13; "Enérgica respuesta de madres uruguayos," *Aquí*, May 10, 1983, 13; "Reclaman madres uruguayas," *Aquí*, May 20, 1983, BN.

22. "Jaque y Asamblea," *Aquí*, November 22, 1983, BN.

23. Author interview with Manuel Flores Silva, July 24, 2014. *Jaque* had a circulation of about 16,000.

24. "El País exige una apertura real," *Jaque*, November 18–25, 1983, 1, microfilm 78.717 reel 155, BN.

25. "El hombre prevalecerá," *Jaque*, November 18–25, 1983, 7; "Apoya político e internacional a jornada del PIT," *Jaque*, November 18–25, 1983, 6, microfilm 78.717 reel 155, BN.

26. "Los desaparecidos en Latinoamerica," *Jaque*, December 9, 1983, 6, microfilm 78.717 reel 155, BN.

27. Alejandro Bonasso, "Día Internacional de los Derechos Humanos," *Jaque*, December 16, 1983, 8, microfilm 78.717 reel 155, BN.

28. Although it is not discussed in detail here, one of the other important papers launched during this period was *La Democracia* in July 1981, a paper aligned with the Wilson Ferreira faction of the Blanco Party. Gillespie, *Negotiating Democracy*, 85.

29. There was some resistance within the country prior to the plebiscite. Recently, there have been efforts to recover some of the clandestine work of certain individuals that risked

organizing against incredible odds. Autores Anónimos, *Gol del Pueblo Uruguayo: Crece Desde el Pie*, Chapter 4, PL.

30. Loveman, "High-Risk Collective Action." The Madres began marching in Argentina in April 1977. Donald C. Hodges, *Argentina's "Dirty War": An Intellectual Biography* (Austin: University of Texas Press, 1991), 254. Similarly, SERPAJ had operated in Argentina since 1974, which was before the dictatorship began, although it became a prominent voice of the opposition to the military government in 1977. Chile also had various human rights groups such as the Pro-Peace Committee. Kelly, *Sovereign Emergencies*, 71–74; Sikkink, *Justice Cascade*, 63, 67–68.

31. Loveman, "High-Risk Collective Action"; Interview with Goldman; Markarian, *Left*, 164–165.

32. Anna-Karin Gauding, *Es mejor encender una luz que maldecir la oscuridad: sobre el trabajo de Diakonia por los derechos humanos en América Latina* (Santiago de Chile: Diakonia, 1991), 80.

33. María Delgado, "'So the people can decide': The Experience of the Referendum against the Impunity Law in Uruguay" (November 1999).

34. Before the 1960s, the only organization in the Southern Cone that was explicitly concerned with human rights was the Liga Argentina por los Derechos Humanos. This group emerged in 1937 in response to the political persecution of an earlier Argentine military regime. Loveman, "High-Risk Collective Action," 479.

35. Hereinafter, I refer to the group as either "Madres y Familiares" or simply "Familiares" as other authors do, because members of the group most frequently refer to themselves as "familiares." Bucheli, *Vivos*, 7. For more on their emergence, see Debbie Sharnak, "Uruguay's Long Transitional Decade and a New Era of Gendered Activism," *Journal of Iberian and Latin American Studies* 23, no. 3 (2017): 383–398.

36. Luisa Cuesta Entrevista, February 9, 2004, Folder 2, AMF. The group that eventually became known as Madres y Familiares is actually the integration of three separate groups that emerged in the late 1970s as a result of the search for missing and detained relatives. First, el grupo de madres de uruguayos desaparecidos en Argentina, then los familiares residentes en el país de uruguayos desaparecidos en Uruguay, and finally the Asociación de Familiares de Uruguayos Desaparecidos (AFUDE). Bucheli, *Vivos*, 22.

37. "Breve Historia del Grupo," 1989, Folder 2, AMF.

38. Jean Franco, "Gender, Death, and Resistance," in *Fear at the Edge: State Terror in Latin America*, ed. Juan E. Corradi (Berkeley: University of California Press, 1992), 113. Eventually the government of Argentina did recognize the threat this group posed, and some members were also disappeared including Thelma Jara de Cabezas. Letter, Townsend Friedman to Gerald Whitman, December 5, 1980, DOSVRR.

39. Bucheli, *Vivos*, 26.

40. "Grupo de Madres y Familiares de Uruguayos Detenidos Desaparecidos," nd, Folder 2, AMF.

41. Ibid.

42. "Grupo de Madres y Familiares de Uruguayos Detenidos Desaparecidos," February 1988, p1, Folder 2, AMF.

43. Bucheli, *Vivos*, 28.

44. Ibid.

45. "Grupo de Madres y Familiares de Uruguayos Detenidos Desaparecidos," nd, Folder 2, 2, AMF; the group also received a Peace and Justice award from SERPAJ in December 1982. "Entregaron Premios Paz y Justicia," *Opinar,* December 23, 1982, BN.

46. The larger Familiares group integrated the group in Argentina, as well as Familiares Residentes en el País de Uruguayos Desaparecidos en Uruguay and AFUDE. Bucheli, *Vivos los llevaron,* 22.

47. Agrupación de Familiares de Uruguayos Desaparecidos, "Uruguay Desaparecidos," 1982, p3, Folder 1, AMF.

48. Franco, "Gender, Death," 113.

49. Ibid., 116.

50. Inter-Office Memo, Butler Flora to Dye, January 31, 1980, "Recommendations for 'A' Status: Proposed FY 1980 Activities on Women and Development," 3, Grant 080000635, Reel 3701, Ford Foundation, RAC. It should be noted, however, that women in Uruguay had a very strong presence and advocated for a broad base of rights in the early part of the twentieth century. See Katherine Marino, *Feminism for the Americas: The Making of an International Human Rights Movement* (Chapel Hill: University of North Carolina Press, 2019).

51. For another example of women's increasing role, see "La Mujer y Su Participación," *La Democracia,* August 28, 1981, CEIU.

52. For information on the Argentine's group continued support and collaboration, see "Las madres en Argentina," *Jaque,* December 2, 1983, p4, BN.

53. "Historia del Grupo," 1989, Folder 2, AMF.

54. "Denuncia," 1984, Folder 2, AMF.

55. Minutos, Comite Ejecutivo, February 23, 1987, Archivo de SERPAJ, Montevideo, Uruguay [hereinafter Archivo SERPAJ]. In this memo, the group explained that the sole purpose of Madres y Familiares was the fight for truth and justice, while acknowledging that other groups had more expansive visions.

56. South Africa launched a similar smear campaign against the WCC's work in 1981. See Lauren Frances Turek, *To Bring the Good News to All Nations: Evangelical Influence on Human Rights and U.S. Foreign Policy* (Ithaca: Cornell University Pres, 2020), 167.

57. Weschler, *A Miracle, A Universe,* 154.

58. Monique Brunier a SERPAJ Argentina, 1979, Folder 14, AMF.

59. Carta, Esquivel a Aguirre, June 8, 1981, Archivo SERPAJ.

60. Author interview with Francisco "Pancho" Bustamante, September 11, 2014.

61. Carta, Aguirre a Esquivel, October 25, 1981, Archivo SERPAJ.

62. Luis Pérez Aguirre, "Su Atencion Por Favor . . . " *La Plaza,* August 1981, 25–26, BN.

63. "Honrosa Actitud Distinción," *La Plaza,* August 1981, 29, BN.

64. "Acerca del Servicio Paz y Justicia," *La Plaza,* August 1981, 29–30, BN.

65. Author interview with Efraín Olivera, August 24, 2014.

66. Memo, "Rogamos la Difusión Urgente," December 10, 1981, Archivo SERPAJ; JFB, "La Voz de los que no tienen voz," *La Plaza,* December 1981, 17, BN.

67. Memo, "Breve Informe Pasa el Sr. Adolfo," October 15, 1981, Archivo SERPAJ.

68. Olivera, "Sigue valiendo la pena," 7.

69. "Se agrava la Situación de los Derechos Humanos," *Opinar,* December 23, 1982, Folder 31, Waksman Colección, CEIU; Luis Pérez Aguirre, "El guerrero y la paz," *La Plaza,* March 1982, BN.

70. Entrevista al Padrea Luis Pérez Aguirre, *Dialogo,* June 1983, in *Aportes,* August 1983, 27, Folder 1, Jesus Betancourt Colección, CEIU.

71. "Inció huelga de hambre Adolfo Pérez Esquivel," *Aquí,* May 1983, BN.

72. Weschler, *A Miracle, A Universe,* 155–156; Oscar Mazzeo, *Memorias del Voto Verde* (Montevideo: Rosebud Ediciones, 1999), 10.

73. Louis Bickford, "Human Rights Archives and Research on Historical Memory: Argentina, Chile, and Uruguay," *Latin American Research Review* 35, no. 2 (2000): 178.

74. Author interview with Jorge Pan, August 21, 2014. While many were young, such as Antonio Serrentino, Martin Prat, and Jorge Pan, part of the driving force behind the group was Fernando Uriesto, an older lawyer who had studied human rights and international law at the University of Madrid. Inter-Office Memorandum, Hall to Carmichael, "Delegated Authority Grant," May 20, 1985, Grant 08550674, Reel 5703, Ford Foundation, RAC.

75. Unpublished Report, Margaret Crahan, "Human Rights in Latin America: Report on 11/26/82–12/11/92 trip to Peru, Chile, and Argentina," Report #008234, Box 349, Ford Foundation, RAC.

76. Author interview with Juan Méndez, February 24, 2020.

77. Letter, IELSUR to A. Gridley Hall, November 8, 1984, Grant 08550674, Reel 5703, Ford Foundation, RAC

78. Author interview with Martin Prat, August 19, 2014.

79. Pan interview.

80. "Breve Informe para el Sr. Adolfo Alencastro," October 15, 1981, Archivos de SERPAJ; Hall to Carmichael, "Delegated Authority Grant," RAC. IELSUR's gender dynamics differed from those of the other groups. Familiares was dominated by women; SERPAJ was led by a man but four of the thirteen founding members were women, whereas only one woman was even on the staff of IELSUR, a political scientist and not a lawyer, when the group was primarily a legal organization.

81. Mainwaring and Pérez-Liñán, *Democracies and Dictatorships,* 212.

82. "Actividades del Grupo de Familiares de Desaparecidos en Uruguay," April 1983–March 1984, 5, Folder 1, AMF.

83. Luis Pérez Aguirre, "Año nuevo: entre la frustración y la reconciliación nacional," *La Plaza,* January 1982, 31, BN.

84. Janet Sommerville, "Canadians Speak Out for Threatened Uruguayan Jesuit," *Catholic New Times,* October 3, 1982, 12, Folder 2, Colección Ponce de León-Vilaró, CEIU.

85. "Pérez Esquivel," Folder 31, Colección Waksman, CEIU.

86. Hall to Carmichael, "Delegated Authority Grant," RAC.

87. Renée Jeffery, *Amnesties, Accountability, and Human Rights* (Philadelphia: University of Pennsylvania Press, 2014), 4–5.

88. "Nuestra Intención," Revista de ASU, 1981, volume 1, The Nettie Lee Benson Latin American Collection, University of Texas at Austin [hereinafter Benson].

89. The Lawyers Committee for International Human Rights, "Uruguay: The End of A Nightmare?" (May 1984), 58. The number of reported people who participated varies, with some estimates reaching 150,000 people and 150 unions represented.

90. "El Movimiento sindical uruguayo: un balance del '83 y una visión para el '84 a cargo de su dirigencia," *Aquí,* January 10, 1984, 9, AD.

91. Carlos Llanos, "Libertad, Trabajo, Salario, Amnistía," *Jaque,* December 16, 1983, 14.

92. Alexander and Parker, *A History*, 76.

93. Carlos Llanos, "1o. de Mayo: otro no y van," *Jaque*, April 28, 1984, 10; "Nuestra Intención," and "Quién defiende a los trabajadores orientales?," Revista de ASU, 1981, volume 1, Benson.

94. "Tabajadores, ¡Salud!," *Aquí*, April 24, 1984, 2, AD.

95. "Ensenanza y Dictadura," CNT Uruguay, November 1983, Folder 6, Ponce de León Colección, CEIU.

96. For example, "Sin justicia no habrá democracia!!" nd, Julio Rügnitz Colección, AGU, where ASCEEP joined madres groups and comisión por la amnistía y los DDHH de la Coordinadoras de trabajadores del arte to call for a range of human rights initiatives as part of the transition.

97. "Semana por Derechos Humanos en ASCEEP," *Aquí*, April 24, 1984, 11, AD.

98. "Enseñanza y Dictadura," CNT Uruguay, Novemberr 1983, and "ASCEEP: histórica semana estudiantil," *Convicción*, October 6, 1983, Folder 6, Ponce de León Colección, CEIU; "ASCEEP: apoyo mundial," *Aquí*, January 24, 1984, 7, AD.

99. *Vertiente: Boletín del Frente Independiente Universitario*, no. 3, 1984, Julio Rügnitz Colección, AGU.

100. "Fundamentación de la posición sobre concertación," 1984, Caja 2, Gustavo Olmos Colección, AGU.

101. Enrique Mazzei and Graciela Prat, "El Movimiento Pro-referéndum en Uruguay, 1986–1987," *Ciencias Sociales* 4 (1990), 30.

102. Gabriel Mazzarovich interview with Abby Goldberg, March 19, 2012.

103. Markarian, *Left*, 145–147.

104. Finch, "Democratisation," 598.

105. "Domingo de noche: un pueblo de fiesta," *Opinar*, December 2, 1982, 15, BN.

106. Gillespie, *Negotiating Democracy*, 95.

107. Edward Schumacher, "Uruguay Editor Is Taking Lead as Army Critic," *New York Times*, May 31, 1981, 11.

108. "Monseñor Oscar Arnulfo Romero," *La Plaza*, April 1982, 15–21, BN.

109. "La libertad de todos los presos políticos es una cuestión de principios," *Aportes*, August 1983, 3–4, Folder 1, Jesus Betancourt Colección, CEIU.

110. Patricia Pittman, "Uruguayan Press Still Muzzled," *Buenos Aires Herald*, April 28, 1983, 9; Gillespie, *Negotiating Democracy*, 115.

111. Edward Schumacher, "Uruguay Public Discontent Spurs Crackdown on Dissent," *New York Times*, January 16, 1984, A1.

112. Lawyers Committee, "Nightmare," 5–6.

113. Germán Araujo, "How I run *Radio CX-30*," *Index of Censorship* (May 1984).

114. Letter, Barbara Koeppel to Karel Vasek, July 13, 1984, Folder 4, Álvaro Barros Lémez Colección, CEIU.

115. Letter, Jamie Waterton to Quinton Quayle, "Human Rights," June 12, 1984, Folder Uruguay: Human Rights, FCO 7/5754, TNA.

116. Klaiber, *Church*, 117.

117. Inter-Church Committee, "Human Rights Work Severely Threatened," September 9, 1982, Folder 429.07.15.01.02, Box: Church Reflections, WCC Actions on Uruguay, WCC.

118. "'Paz y Justicia' aclara conceptos," *Aquí*, May 3, 1983, 9, BN.

119. Bickford, "Human Rights Archives," 176–177.

120. Comité de Defensa de los Derechos Humanos en Uruguay, Letter to Supporters, September 7, 1982, Toronto, Canada, Carpeta 26, Waksman Colección, CEIU.

121. Loveman, "High-Risk Collective Action," 506–507, Gauding, *Es mejor,* 87.

122. Barahona de Brito, *Human Rights,* 82.

123. "Manifestación: repercusión sindical," *Aquí,* November 15, 1983, BN.

124. Weschler, *A Miracle, A Universe,* 153.

125. Lawyers Committee, "Nightmare," 58.

126. Memo, Montevideo Embassy to Department of State, "Quarterly Summary of Human Rights Developments in Uruguay," April 1984, DOSVRR; "Tras el decreto contra el PIT", *Aquí,* January 24, 1984, 1, AD.

127. Urgent Action, "Juan Acuna, Health/Legal Concern," March 23, 1983, Folder 46, Box 269, AIUSA.

128. "Informe a Rodney Arismendi," October 5, 1981, Folder 57, Waksman Colección, CEIU.

129. Letter from Ema Julia Massera, March 14, 1982, Box 23, Folder I, Massera Colección, AGU.

130. Amnesty International Report 1982 (London: Amnesty International Publications, 1982); Amnesty International Report 1983 (London: Amnesty International Publications, 1983); Amnesty International Report 1984 (London: Amnesty International Publications, 1984), Amnesty International Online Archives. "Limited Medical Letter Writing Action, Marcos Rivas Borba," October 15, 1984; Urgent Action, "Nuño Pucurull: Health Concern," September 18, 1984; Urgent Action 67/83, "Health/Legal Concern," March 23, 1983, all in Folder 46, Box 269, AIUSA.

131. Press Release, "Over 100 Prominent Civic and Religious Leaders Protest Arms Transfer to Uruguay," September 14, 1981; Press Release, "Uruguayan Authorities Close Opposition Newspaper "Opinar" Arrest Editors," April 15, 1981; Press Release, "WOLA Board Releases Letter of Support for Human Rights Leader," November 1, 1982; Press Release, "Three Senior Citizens and Human Rights: Missing in Uruguay," March 31, 1983; Press Release, "Human Rights Delegation Calls for Release of Uruguayan Politician," July 5, 1984, Folder Press Releases, Box 282, WOLA.

132. Sarah Snyder, *Human Rights Activism and the End of the Cold War: A Transnational History of the Helsinki Network* (New York: Cambridge University Press 2011), Chapter 5. Helsinki Watch focused primarily on Eastern European human rights groups who were subjected to harassment, arrest, or imprisonment for their work. The organization worked to make sure these abuses received international attention, primarily through writing research reports.

133. Neier, *Movement,* 205; Laber, *Courage of Strangers,* 128–130; 168–171; Peter Slezkine, "From Helsinki to Human Rights Watch: How an American Cold War Monitoring Group Became an International Human Rights Institution," *Humanity* 5, no. 3 (Winter 2014): 345–370.

134. Neier, *Movement,* 206–207; Aryeh Neier, *Taking Liberties: Four Decades in the Struggle for Rights* (New York: Public Affairs, 2003), xxvi.

135. Méndez interview; Juan Méndez, *Taking a Stand: The Evolution of Human Rights* (New York: St. Martin's Press, 2011), 92.

136. Interview with Goldman; Neier, *Taking Liberties,* 165–166. For examples of Goldman's extensive work on Uruguay with other organizations prior to joining Americas Watch, see Symposium Memo, Prepared by Robert Goldman, Joaquín Martinez Bjorkman, Jean Louis Weil, Re: Laws and Decrees of the Government of Uruguay which violate UN Conventions and Declarations in the human rights area, February 6, 1978, Folder 26, Waksman Collection, CEIU;

Robert Goldman, "The Uruguayan Regime as It Relates to International Law," in *Symposium on the State of Emergency and Human Rights in Uruguay* (Paris: International Secretariat of Catholic Jurists/International Federation of Human Rights, 1978); Robert Goldman, "Critique of the State Department's 1978 and 1979 Reports on Human Rights Practices in Uruguay," in *Reports on Human Rights Practices for 1979* (New York: Lawyers Committee for International Human Rights, 1980).

137. For her journalism work, see, for example, Patricia Pittman, "Now Uruguayans Fight the Junta," *Nation*, September 17, 1983, 207–208.

138. Author interview with Polly Pittman, May 22, 2020.

139. Report, "Americas Watch 1982–1985," May 1985, Folder Americas Watch Activities 1982–1985, Box 301, Human Rights Watch Collection, Columbia University Archives [hereafter HRW].

140. Ibid. Bob Goldman also published a chapter on Uruguay in Cynthia Brown, ed., *With Friends Like These: The Americas Watch Report on Human Rights & U.S. Policy in Latin America* (New York: Pantheon Books, 1985), 72–91.

141. Méndez interview.

142. Richard Goldstein and Alfred Gellhorn, "Human Rights and the Medical Profession in Uruguay since 1972," August 1982, Ford Foundation Report #015292, Ford Foundation, RAC.

143. Korey, *Taking On*, 61.

144. Inter-Office Memo, Susana Lastarria to William Saint, December 29, 1983, "Final Evaluation," Grant 08550674, Reel 5703, Ford Foundation, RAC.

145. Hall to Carmichael, "Delegated Authority Grant," RAC.

146. While some scholars criticize Carter's waning attention to human rights concerns during the latter half of his presidency, Reagan shifted the emphasis of U.S. human rights policy altogether. Rasmus Sinding Søndergaard, *Reagan, Congress, and Human Rights: Contesting Morality in US Foreign Policy* (New York: Cambridge University Press, 2020); Morris Morley and Chris McGillion, *Reagan and Pinochet: The Struggle over US Policy toward Chile* (New York: Cambridge University Press, 2015), 10; Joe Renouard, *Human Rights in American Foreign Policy* (Philadelphia, University of Pennsylvania Press, 2016), 168; A. Glenn Mower, *Human Rights and American Foreign Policy: The Carter and Reagan Experiences* (New York: Greenwood, 1987); Walker, *Principles*, 205–248. Turek shows the shift to religious freedom as a human right within Reagan's terms in office. Turek, *To Bring*.

147. Jim Mann, *The Rebellion of Ronald Reagan: A History of the End of the Cold War* (New York: Viking, 2009); Brands, *Latin America's Cold War*, 245; Sikkink, *Mixed Signals*, 148–149.

148. Jeanne Kirkpatrick, "Dictatorships and Double Standards," *Commentary* (1979), 34–45. When Kirkpatrick was named as Reagan's U.S. ambassador to the UN, the Uruguayan Foreign Ministry read through her article "Dictatorship and Double Standards," highlighting statements that called for a new approach to foreign policy that was based more on Cold War considerations and supported governments that were threatened by left-wing subversion. Memo, "La América Latina de Reagan," 1980, Box 21, ADA.

149. Brands, *Latin America's Cold War*, 245; Walker, *Principles*, 209–210.

150. Ernest Lefever, "The Rights Standard," *New York Times*, June 24, 1977, 23.

151. Schmidli, *Fate*, 95; Douglas Martin, "Ernest W. Lefever, Rejected as a Reagan Nominee, Dies at 89," *New York Times*, August 5, 2009; "The Case Against Mr. Lefever," *New York Times*, March 2, 1981, A18. For a thorough account of Lefever's nomination debacle, see Sarah Snyder, "The Defeat of Ernest Lefever's Nomination: Keeping Human Rights on the United State Foreign

Policy Agenda," in *Challenging Human Rights on the US Foreign Policy Agenda: America and the World in the Long Twentieth Century*, ed. Bevan Sewell and Scott Lucas (New York: Palgrave, 2011): 136–161.

152. Author interview with Joe Eldridge, January 4, 2018.

153. Judith Miller, "Rebuffed in Senate, Lefever Pulls Out as Rights Nominee," *New York Times*, June 6, 1981, 1.

154. John Ehrman, *The Rise of Neoconservatism: Intellectuals and Foreign Affairs, 1945–1994* (New Haven: Yale University Press, 1995), 158–159.

155. Youle interview.

156. Memo, January 25, 1981, Box 23, Folder 31, AHD.

157. "Derechos Humanos," January 14, 1981, Box 23, Folder 31, AHD.

158. James Nelson Goodsell, "US Policy Tilts Towards Selling Arms to Argentina," *Christian Science Monitor*, March 19, 1981; White House Visits by Foreign Leaders of Argentina, U.S. Department of State Office of the Historian, https://history.state.gov/departmenthistory/visits/argentina.

159. Press Release, "WOLA Survey Notes Deterioration of Human Rights in Latin America after Reagan's First 100 Days," April 23, 1981, Folder Press Releases, Box 282, WOLA.

160. House Congressional Hearings, "Human Rights and U.S. Policy in the Multilateral Development Banks," July 21 and 23, 1981, Serial No. 97-20; Brown, *With Friends*, 87.

161. Press Release, "WOLA Board Releases Letter of Support for Human Rights Leader," November 1, 1982, Folder Press Releases, Box 282, WOLA.

162. Memo, Amestay to Valdés Otero, July 6, 1981, Folder EEUU-ROU DDHH, ADA; Memo, from Uruguayan Embassy in Washington, July 8, 1981, Folder EEUU-ROU DDHH, ADA; "Reagan Reverses Rights Policy," *Chicago Tribune*, July 9, 1981, 2.

163. Memo to the Minister of Foreign Affairs, July 9, 1981, Folder EEUU-ROU DDHH, ADA.

164. Letter to Donald Regan, July 22, 1981, in House Congressional Hearings, "Human Rights and U.S. Policy in the Multilateral Development Banks," July 21 and 23, 1981, Serial No. 97-20, p478–481. Signees included Rep. Gejdenson and Sen. Harkin, among others.

165. House Congressional Resolution 161, July 23, 1981, 97th Congress, 1st Session.

166. Hearings Before the Committee on Foreign Affairs House of Representatives, First Session, "Proposed Transfer of Arms to Uruguay," September 15, 1981. Markarian, *Left*, 158; Brown, *With Friends*, 88.

167. "Statement by Juan R. Ferreira," Subcommittee on Human Rights and International Organizations hearing on Uruguay, Washington, DC, September 15, 1981, Folder 141, Waksman Colección, CEIU.

168. Ibid.

169. Anderson, "The Littlest Totalitarian," *Nation*, 358.

170. Greisgraber interview.

171. "Go Home Kirkpatrick," *La Democracia*, August 14, 1981, 16, Prensa, CEIU.

172. Memo, Secretary's Meeting with Uruguayan Foreign Minister, October 9, 1981, DOSVRR.

173. "Informe del Departamento de Estado de los EEUU sobre la situación de derechos humanos en Uruguay," 1983, Box ROU-EEUU DDHH, ADA.

174. Neier, *Movement*, 172.

175. Press Release, "Three Senior Citizens and Human Rights: Missing in Uruguay," March 31, 1983, Folder Press Releases, Box 282, WOLA; Brown, *With Friends*, 89.

176. House of Representatives, Committee on Foreign Affairs, "International Security and Development Cooperation Act of 1983," H.R. 2992, May 17, 1983, 29. It appears that the $50,000 was approved but the $60,000 was delayed in 1984 until after the elections due to the work of Rep. Gejdenson. "Foreign Assistance Legislation for Fiscal Years 1984–1985, Part 7," Hearings and Markups Before the Subcommittee on Western Hemisphere Affairs of the Committee on Foreign Affairs House of Representatives, March 1, 16, April 12, 13, 1983, p. XIX–XX, 179–181.

177. Memo, Uruguayan embassy in Washington, May 5, 1983, Folder EEUU-ROU DDHH, ADA; Memo, Holly Burkhalter to Americas Watch Executive Committee, March 29, 1983; Memo, Holly Burkhalter to Interested Congressional Aides, "President's FY'84 request for Uruguay," March 21, 1983, Folder General Files: Burkhalter, Holly Correspondence 1984–1984, Box 301, HRW. The same request was made in 1984 for fiscal year 1985, but was rejected by the House of Representatives, Committee on Foreign Affairs, "International Security and Development Cooperation Act of 1984," H.R. 5119, March 21, 1984, p63.

178. Privately, the U.S. government acknowledged that "Uruguay's transition process may be the most problematic of several now underway in South America." "Uruguay: Rough Road Toward Civilian Rule: An Intelligence Assessment," Directorate of Intelligence, August 1983, Virtual CIA Reading Room.

179. U.S. Department of State, "Country Reports on Human Rights Practices for 1982," Report submitted to the Committee on Foreign Relations (Washington: U.S. Government Printing Office, February 1983), 644–651, University of Michigan Libraries; Press Release, "State Department's 1982 Latin American Human Rights Report: The Art of Semi-Fiction," Council on Hemispheric Affairs, February 11, 1983, Princeton University Digital Library, http://pudl.princeton.edu/objects/fx719n453.

180. Lawyers Committee, "Nightmare," 8.

181. Max Holland and Kai Bird, "Shunning a Latin Friend," New York Times, August 1, 1984, A23. Human rights groups such as WOLA tried to convince the Reagan administration to put more pressure on the Uruguayan government to release Ferreira, to no avail. See Folder Press Releases, Box 282, WOLA.

182. Brands, Latin America's Cold War, 246–250; For a broader view of Reagan's democracy promotion articulation, see Thomas Carothers, In the Name of Democracy: U.S. Policy Toward Latin America in the Reagan Years (Berkeley: University of California Press, 1991).

183. Other scholars argue that the United States promotes a model of "low intensity democracy," where there are formal democratic institutions to legitimize rules, but where other structures based on previous authoritarian models limit popular empowerment. See Robert Pee and William Michael Schmidli, "Introduction," in The Reagan Administration, The Cold War, and the Transition to Democracy Promotion, ed. Michael Schmidli and Robert Pee (London: Palgrave Macmillan, 2019), 3; Barry Gills et al., "Low Intensity Democracy," in Low Intensity Democracy: Political Power in the New World Order, ed. Barry Gills et al. (London: Pluto Press, 1993): 3–35.

184. Memo, "Assistant Secretary Enders' Visit to Uruguay," February 17, 1983, DOSVRR.

185. For an in-depth study of the relationship between Reagan and the Uruguayan military during his first term, see Debbie Sharnak, "Reagan and the Waning Years of Uruguay's Military Rule: Democracy Promotion and the Redefinition of Human Rights," in The Reagan Administration, The Cold War, and the Transition to Democracy Promotion, 189–207.

186. Gillespie, Negotiating Democracy, 117.

187. Ibid., 119.

188. Seregni was first imprisoned in 1973 for his participation in a public demonstration after the Uruguayan military shut down Congress. He was released for a time but arrested again in 1976, and he remained in jail until 1984. Letter from José Enrique Díaz, Message to all the Socialists, Social Democrats, and Democratic Parties of the World, September 15, 1978, Folder Socialist Party of Uruguay, Box 91, Collection: Printed Ephemera Collection on Organizations, Tamiment.

189. Urgent Action 154/84, "Legal Concern," June 18, 1984, Folder 46, Box 269, AIUSA; William Columbus Davis, *Warnings from the Far South: Democracy versus Dictatorship in Uruguay, Argentina, and Chile* (Westport: Praeger, 1995), 61.

190. Edward Schumaker, "Is There a Way Out for the Uruguayan Military?" *New York Times*, June 24, 1984, E5.

191. Gillespie, *Negotiating Democracy*, 104.

192. Memo, "Assistant Secretary Enders' Visit to Uruguay," DOSVRR; Finch, "Democratisation in Uruguay," 596.

193. The front page of *Aquí* featured pictures of the protest with thousands of protesters, and the words "el pueblo pidió que se vayan." *Aquí*, 1, November 29, 1983, BN; Finch, "Democratisation," 598.

194. Mazzeo, *Memorias del Voto Verde*, 14–15.

195. Actividades del Grupo de Familiares de Desaparecidos en Uruguay, 1983–1984, Folder 4, Box 1, AMF.

196. Alexander and Parker, *A History*, 77.

197. Lawyers Committee, "Nightmare," 9.

198. Gillespie, *Negotiating Democracy*, 80.

199. Barahona de Brito, *Human Rights*, 82–83.

200. Gillespie, *Negotiating Democracy*, 86. See Table 5.3.

201. Ibid., 160.

202. Ibid.

203. Weschler, *A Miracle, A Universe*, 158.

204. During the legislative debates on the amnesty law, many in the Colorado Party vigorously denied that the topic had been explicitly addressed, stating that it had been sidestepped during negotiations. For example, Manuel Flores Silva, December 20 and 21, 1986, p135, Cámara de Senadores, PL.

205. Gillespie, *Negotiating Democracy*, 175–177.

206. Lessa, *Memory*, 133.

207. *Diario de Sesiones de la Cámara de Senadores*, Tomo 304, December 1986, p116, PL.

208. Gillespie, *Negotiating Democracy*, 13.

Chapter 6

1. William Montalbano, "Uruguay Voting Today After 13-Year Wait," *Los Angeles Times*, November 25, 1984, A8.

2. Alan Riding, "Uruguay to Pick Civilian Leader in Election Today," *New York Times*, November 25, 1984, 1.

3. William Montalbano, "Moderate Takes Lead in Festive Uruguay Vote," *Los Angeles Times*, November 26, 1984, A6.

4. Lessa, *Memory*, 133–134; Weschler, *A Miracle, A Universe*, 166–171, Roniger and Sznajder, *Legacy*, 80; Elin Skaar, *Judicial Independence and Human Rights in Latin America: Violations,*

Politics, and Prosecution (New York: Palgrave Macmillan, 2011), 140; Felipe Michelini, "El largo camino a la verdad," *Revista IIDH* 24 (1996), 161.

5. "El 17 definen las candidaturas a nivel capitalino," *Jaque*, August 10, 1984, 2, BN.

6. Adair, *Lost Decade*, 13.

7. Lessa, *Memory*, 51.

8. Alexandra Barahona de Brito, "Truth, Justice, Memory, and Democratization in the Southern Cone," in *The Politics of Memory: Transitional Justice in Democratizing Societies,* ed. Alexandra Barahona de Brito, Carmen González-Enríquez, and Paloma Aguilar (New York: Oxford University Press, 2001), 127.

9. Finch, "Democratisation," 596.

10. Ibid.

11. Juan Carlos Doyenart, "Debemos construir una nueva democracia," *Aquí,* June 20, 1984, 5, AD.

12. "La transición universitaria," 5, and "La naturaleza de las políticas sociales en el cambio," *Jaque,* September 14, 1984, 14, BN.

13. CONAPRO had multiple working groups, coordinated by an executive board. Decisions were made by consensus although the actual discussions within each working group were confidential. SERPAJ represented the burgeoning human rights movement for the group. CONAPRO sought to build consensus around a basic platform during the time of political precarity between the Naval Club Pact and elections. Lydia Fraile and Gonzalo Falabella, "Tripartism and Economic Reforms in Uruguay and Chile," in *Blunting Neoliberalism: Tripartism and Economic Reforms in the Developing World,* ed. Lydia Fraile (New York: Palgrave Macmillan, 2010), 132.

14. "El arma se llama Concertación Programática Nacional," *Jaque,* September 7, 1984, 1; Finch, "Democratisation," 600–601. CONAPRO was made up entirely of men and it was only after protest by new women's groups that CONAPRO agreed to include a working group on women. Fisher, *Out of the Shadows,* 55–56.

15. Las Familiares note in their internal documents that CONAPRO agreed to clarify the situation of the disappeared and judge those responsible when there was a democratic government. Informe, Historia del Organismo, p3, Folder 2-Informacional Institucional, AMF. Francesca Lessa also notes that CONAPRO declared that "'leaving unpunished' human rights violations constituted a 'serious threat to the power of human rights in the future.'" Lessa, *Memory,* 186.

16. Delgado, "So the people," 12.

17. Ibid.

18. Memorandum, "Evolución de la situación de los derechos humanos en Uruguay desde octubre de 1984 a junio 1986," Grant 08550674, Reel 5703, Ford Foundation, RAC.

19. "El proceso político avanza en medio de grandes interrogantes," *Jaque,* August 10, 1984, 3, BN; "Amnistía General e Irrestricta," *Jaque,* September 21, 1984, 8, BN.

20. "El Frente y Democracia Avanzada," *Al Frente Democracia Avanzada Revista Seminario* 1, no. 2 (November 8, 1984): 3, and PDC, "Por un Uruguay solidario" (August 1984), both in Box 1, Series 1ª, Elections 1984–2004, Princeton University Archives [hereinafter PUA].

21. "Con la IDI al Frente crottogini D'Elia Arana," nd, Folder 48, Waksman Colección, CEIU.

22. "El Frente y Democracia Avanzada," PUA.

23. Point 10 of 12 in "Declaración Constitutiva y Programática de la coalición sublema democracia avanzada," nd, Box 1, Series 1ª, Elections 1984–2004, PUA.

24. "Por un Uruguay solidario," 6, PUA.

25. Sendic had first been arrested in August 1970 for actions associated with the Tupamaros. He escaped in September 1971 and remained a fugitive until he was recaptured in 1972.

26. Finch, "Democratisation," 600. This is not to say that there were not others who were furious at Sendic for supporting the electoral process. However, overall many former Tupamaros did participate in the electoral process, eventually returning to politics under the umbrella of the Frente Amplio, perhaps no one more famous than former Tupamaro José Mujica. For more on the Tupamaros' reintegration into political culture in Uruguay, see Marchesi, *Latin America's Radical Left*, Chapter 5.

27. "Resolución de la Junta Nacional," August 31, 1984, Folder 48, Waksman Colección, CEIU.

28. "Puestos de lucha," IDI, Box 1, Series 1ª, Elections 1984–2004, PUA.

29. Mario Mazzeo, *MPP: origines, ideas, protagonistas* (Montevideo: Ediciones Trilce, 2005), 15–16.

30. Gillespie, *Negotiating Democracy*, 80.

31. Tarigo founded *Opinar* and Silva founded *Jaque*, which are both described in detail in previous chapters.

32. Canel explores how access to structures of political power at times proved to be more important than independent organizing during this period, which weakened some of the human rights vigor during the democratization efforts. Canel, "Democratization."

33. Alan Riding, "Man in the News: Peacemaker for Uruguay," *New York Times*, November 27, 1984, A10.

34. Max Holland and Kai Bird, "Shunning a Latin Friend," A23. Upon Sanguinetti's return to Uruguay, he also began holding well-publicized meetings with the U.S. ambassador; see Brown, ed., *With Friends Like These*, 89.

35. "Sanguinetti Tarigo, Libertad y Cambio," Boletín de información interna no. October 13, 1984, Box 1, Series 1ª, Elections 1984–2004, PUA.

36. They were just two of three former newspaper editors elected to office in 1984, along with Alberto Zumarán who founded *La Democracia*. However, all three of them failed to be reelected in 1989. Flores Silva interview.

37. Juan Pablo Luna, *Segmented Representation: Political Party Strategies in Unequal Democracies* (New York: Oxford University Press, 2014), 86–87.

38. Juan Rial, "Uruguay: Elecciones de 1984: Sistema Electoral y Resultados," *Centro Interamericano de Asesoría y Promoción Electoral* (Costa Rica: Instituto Interamericano de Derechos Humanos, 1986).

39. It should be noted that the entire Parliament, as well as the President and Vice President, were all men.

40. Alan Riding, "Uruguay Installs Civilian President," *New York Times*, March 2, 1985, 1.

41. Bucheli et al., *Vivos Los Llevaron*, 50.

42. Internal Memo, "AI Work on Uruguay Following the Return to Civilian Rule," April 1, 1985, AMR 52/04/85, Folder 15, Box 260, Series IV.I, AIUSA.

43. Jimmy Burns, "Uruguay elects moderate civilian to end military rule," *Christian Science Monitor*, November 28, 1984; Jackson Diehl, "Civilian Inaugurated to Lead Uruguay," *Washington Post*, March 2, 1985, A1; "Rightest Military Rule Ends in Uruguay," *The Day*, March 1, 1985, 29.

44. Alan Riding, "Uruguay's Civilian President to Face Legacy of Army Rule," *New York Times*, March 1, 1985, A8.

45. Lessa, *Memory* 133–134; Weschler, *A Miracle, A Universe*, 166–171, Roniger and Sznajder, *Legacy*, 80.

46. Skaar, *Judicial Independence*, 139.

47. Stephan Haggard and Robert R. Kaufman, *The Political Economy of Democratic Transitions* (Princeton: Princeton University Press, 1995), 212–217; Gargiulo, "Uruguayan Labor Movement," 233–234.

48. "Aportes a la discusión," nd, p4, Julio Rügnitz Colección, AGU.

49. Louise Mallinder, "Uruguay's Evolving Experience of Amnesty and Civil Society's Response," *Working Paper No. 4, Beyond Legalism: Amnesties, Transition, and Conflict Transformation* (Queen's University of Belfast, March 2009), 31. The actual terms of the debate were hotly contested between the three parties with respect to whether blanket amnesty would be passed, or blood crimes would warrant further detention.

50. Lessa, *Memory*, 135.

51. Mariana Achugar, *What We Remember: The Construction of Memory in Military Discourse* (Amsterdam: John Benjamins Publishing, 2008), 79–80. Parliament's first major piece of legislation also ratified the American Convention on Human Rights, which Uruguay had, until this point, avoided. These actions were followed closely by Uruguay signing the UN Convention Against Torture to affirm a new sense of rule of law in the country. "Uruguay no perdonará en el futuro lo que el gobierno quiere perdonar del pasado," *Brecha*, October 31, 1986, 2, AD.

52. "Denuncia," nd, Folder 8, AMF. Sanguinetti had, before his election, also said there would never be an amnesty, a claim that in later years would be used against him. See Memo from Holly to Cynthia, May 15, 1989, Folder Uruguay-Referendum 1987–1989, Box 328, HRW.

53. "Exiliados uruguayos desaparecidos en la República Argentina," *Diario de Sesiones de la Cámara de Representantes* (April 9, 1985), p22–27, CEIU.

54. "Doctor Vladimir Roslik," *Diario de Sesiones de la Cámara de Representantes* (April 16, 1985), p163–167, CEIU.

55. "Denuncia," April 1986, Folder 8, AMF; "Personas Desaparecidas," and "Secuestro y Asesinato perpetrados contra los legisladores," *Diario de Sesiones de la Cámara de Representantes* (April 9, 1985), p59 and 63, CEIU; *Uruguay en la Coyuntura*, July 14 to 21, 1985, no. 18, Folder 32, Waksman Colección, CEIU.

56. "Denuncia," nd, Folder 8, AMF.

57. "Militares indagados," *Uruguay en la Coyuntura*, August 26 to September 1, 1985, Folder 32, Waksman Colección, CEIU.

58. "Uruguay: Legal Action Announced Against Human Rights Abuses," March 29, 1985, Folder Issue Human Rights, Box 279, WOLA.

59. "Sucesos ocurridos el 17 de abril de 1972 en el local de la seccional 20 del Partido comunista," *Diario de Sesiones de la Cámara de Representantes* (April 17, 1985), p191–192, CEIU.

60. Bickford, "Human Rights Archives," 177.

61. Luis Pérez Aguirre, "La Impunidad Asesina a la Democracia por la Espalda," *Brecha*, February 21, 1986, AD.

62. Press Statement, July 16, 1986, Folder "Campaign July," Archivo SERPAJ.

63. Internal Memo, Talking Points for the Radio, nd, Folder "Campaign July," Archivo SERPAJ.

64. "Textos para menciones por Radio," Archivo SERPAJ.

65. Comunicación de prensa, July 16, 1986, Archivo SERPAJ; "Queremos un Uruguay Reconciliado en Paz," nd, Archivo SERPAJ.

66. Letter from Martha Delgado to Mesa Política de Frente Amplio, July 16, 1986, Folder "Campaign July," Archivo SERPAJ.

67. "Informe," Grupo de Madres y Familiares de Uruguayos Detenidos Desaparecidos, 3, Folder 2, AMF.

68. "Semana Mundial del Detenido Desaparecido," May–June 1985, Folder 7: Actividades, AMF.

69. "Acto en la plaza Libertad," *Uruguay en la Coyuntura,* August 26 to September 1, Folder 32, Waksman Colección, CEIU.

70. Inter-Office Memo, A. Gridley Hall to William D. Carmichael, May 20, 1985, "Delegated-authority grant," Grant 08550674, 4389, Ford Foundation, RAC.

71. "Jueces militares no pueden resolver las contiendas de competencia," *Brecha,* February 21, 1986, AD.

72. "Report from IELSUR about Activities June 85/86," nd; Inter-Office Memorandum, Michael Sifter to Jeffrey Puryear, "Final Evaluation and Recommendation for Closing: IELSUR," January 12, 1990, Grant 08550674, Reel 5703, Ford Foundation, RAC.

73. "Delegated-authority grant," RAC.

74. Front Page, *Brecha,* October 8, 1985, 1, AD.

75. "Julio Castro: Persona Buscada," *Brecha,* October 8, 1985, 22, AD.

76. "Juan A. Toledo: de nada sirve reiterar polémicas ya superadas," *Brecha,* October 25, 1985, 9, AD.

77. "Situación Política," *Uruguay en la Coyuntura,* July 29 to August 4, 1985, Folder 32, Waksman Colección, CEIU.

78. Paul G. Buchanan, "Preauthoritarian Institutions and Postauthoritarian Outcomes: Labor Politics in Chile and Uruguay," *Latin American Politics and Society* 50, no. 1 (April 2008): 74.

79. "Ocupación de los lugares de trabajo," *Diario de Sesiones de la Cámara de Representantes* (April 23, 1985), 238, CEIU; Buchanan, "Preauthoritarian Institutions," 74–75.

80. "Nueve de cada diez jubilados en situación de indigencia," *Brecha,* November 22, 1985, 5, AD.

81. "Situación Política," CEIU.

82. Haggard and Kaufman, *Political Economy,* 216–217.

83. "Diálogo nacional: que se acuerde por un ano," *Brecha,* October 11, 1985, p. 3, AD.

84. Alexander and Parker, *A History,* 79–80.

85. G. Waksman, "Acuerdos y desacuerdos," *Brecha,* November 29, 1985, 6, AD.

86. "Ni derechos ni humanos," *Uruguay en la Coyuntura,* August 12 to 18, Folder 32, Waksman Colección, CEIU.

87. This work proved particularly important as the PIT-CNT publicly battled with Sanguinetti over initiatives to improve workers' rights. "La confrontación epistolar abre un necesario debate," *Brecha,* May 16, 1986, 8–9, AD.

88. Weinstein, *Democracy at a Crossroads,* 69–70. Firings also included forced resignations and non-reappointments that extended beyond the university to half of faculty in teacher training schools and 40 to 50 percent of primary and secondary school teachers.

89. "Posición de la AEM Acerca de los Docentes Médicos Militares Durante el Periodo de Dictadura," nd, Ana María Ferrari Colección, AGU.

90. "Derechos Humanos: Amnistía, ¿y Después?" *Estudiante Libre,* October 1985, Ana María Ferrari Colección, AGU.

91. Boletín de la Asociación de Docentes de la Universidad de la República, August 1985, Ana María Ferrari Colección, AGU; "Continuismo o democratización," *Brecha,* November 1, 1985, 6, AD.

92. "Universidad: la política del actual gobierno no difiera de la aplicada por la dictadura," *Brecha,* October 18, 1985; "Ocupación estudiantil," *Brecha,* October 25, 1985, 9, AD.

93. "Derechos Humanos: Amnistía, ¿y Después?," AGU.

94. "Aborto practica con consentimiento de la mujer," *Diario de Sesiones de la Cámara de Representantes* (June 12, 1985); 127–129; 132; 257, CEIU, Montevideo, Uruguay; Reuterswärd's paper also describes that both Colorado and Frente Amplio leaders supported this initial move to liberalize abortion, even though the idea eventually stalled until 2012. Camilla Reuterswärd, "La Libertad de Acción y Conciencia: Cross-Party Alliances and Voting Strategies in Uruguay's Abortion Policy Reform," Paper presented at LASA 2016, New York, NY. For more on the gendered component of Parliament in contrast to organizing groups, see Sharnak, "Uruguay's Long Transitional Decade."

95. Lessa, *Memory,* 136. As Lessa explains, in the first few months the military actually had opposed the idea of an amnesty because they believed the actions they had taken against the population were justified under the logic that they had been involved in a war. This changed in the following months as cases proceeded through civilian courts.

96. Informe, Comisión Investigadora sobre Situación de Personas Desaparecidos y Hechos que la Motivaron, Uruguay Cámara de Representantes, November 1985, Folder Commission of the Disappeared, Box 328, HRW.

97. Ibid., 135; Priscilla B. Hayner, *Unspeakable Truths: Transitional Justice and the Challenge of Truth Commissions* (New York: Routledge, 2010); Skaar, *Judicial Independence,* 141; Aldo Marchesi and Peter Winn, "Uruguay: los tiempos de la memoria," in *No Hay Mañana Sin Ayer,* ed. Peter Winn et al. (Santiago: LOM Ediciones, 2014), 136.

98. "Official Investigations Fail to Establish Fate of the Disappeared," June 1988, Folder Issue "Disappeared," Box 279, WOLA; Amnesty International 1986 Report, 203, Blane Papers; Eduardo Vaerla, "¿Sólo 46 culpables?," *Brecha,* November 9, 1985, 2, AD.

99. Amnesty International 1986 Report, 203, Blane Papers; Internal Memo, "Current investigations into disappearances under the military government in Uruguay," January 8, 1986, Folder, Uruguay/AI, Box 328, HRW.

100. "Denuncia," April 1986, Folder 8, AMF.

101. Hayner, *Unspeakable Truths,* 241; Barahona de Brito, *Human Rights,* 146.

102. Amnesty International 1986 Report, 203, Blane Papers.

103. "Desaparecidos: Durante le Dictadura militar en Uruguay, se cometió genocidio," *Brecha,* October 25, 1985, 2–3, AD; Oscar Bruschera, "El Parlamento debe investigar," *Brecha,* October 25, 1985, 4, AD.

104. "Informe de Actividades Desarrollados," June 1986, Grant 08550674, Reel 5703, Ford Foundation, RAC.

105. Various scholars have outlined the impactful influence of neighboring countries on a nation's democratization process. The relationship between Argentina and Uruguay is particularly clear in this regard. Mainwaring and Pérez-Liñán, *Democracies and Dictatorships.*

106. Lessa, *Memory,* 132.

107. "También sobre Militares Investigaciones y Juicios," *Uruguay en la Coyuntura,* September 22, 1986, Folder 32, Waksman Colección, CEIU.

108. Letter from Thomas Hammarberg to Sanguinetti, July 8, 1986, Folder 15, Box 260, Series IV.I, AIUSA.

109. "Denuncia," April 1986, Folder 8, AMF.
110. Roniger and Sznajder, *Legacy*, 81.
111. El Proyecto de Amnistía ya Está en Parlamento: La transición democrática en la encrucijada," *Uruguay en la Coyuntura*, September 1, 1986, Folder 32, Waksman Colección, CEIU; "Hay votos en el Senado para rechazar la amnistía," *Brecha*, September 19, 1986, 2, AD.
112. "Amnistía de Delitos Cometidos por Funcionarios Militares y Policiales," *Diario de Sesiones de la Cámara de Senadores de la República Oriental del Uruguay*, Tomo 302 (1986), AL. "Challenging Impunity: The Ley de Caducidad and the Referendum Campaign in Uruguay," *An America's Watch Report* (March 1989), 15.
113. Lessa, *Memory*, 136–137.
114. Representation was not equal in Parliament: the Colorados held 40 percent of the seats, the Blancos 33 percent, and the Frente closer to 20 percent.
115. *Diario de Sesiones de la Cámara de Senadores*, Tomo 304, December 1986, 105, AL. The only member of the Colorados to vote against the law was former union leader Victor Vaillant.
116. Flores Silva interview.
117. *Diario de Sesiones de la Cámara de Senadores*, Tomo 304, December 1986, 7, AL.
118. Ibid., 23.
119. "El mayor responsable de la aprobación de la ley es Wilson Ferreira," *Brecha*, December 26, 1986, 6, AD; Barahona de Brito, *Human Rights*, 131.
120. *Diario de Sesiones de la Cámara de Senadores*,11.
121. Ibid., 24.
122. "Frente Amplio opine que se está gestando "una operación política," *El Telégrafo*, December 4, 1986, 3, BN.
123. Barahona de Brito, *Human Rights* 34.
124. *Diario de Sesiones de la Cámara de Senadores*, 15.
125. Manuel Flores Silva is another prime example of a shifting human rights ally. During military rule, he had stood firm against the dictatorship, founded his own paper to provide a voice for his generation to expose human rights abuses, and even worked closely with SERPAJ and the PIT. Once in office, he voted against justice initiatives for those same abuses he had condemned during the earlier period. See Lawrence Weschler, "A Reporter at Large," *New Yorker*, April 10, 1989, 90, and "Apoyo olitico e internacional a jornada del PIT," *Jaque*, November 18–25, 1983, 1, microfilm 78.717 reel 155, BN.
126. Política Nacional, 1986, Caja 2, Gustavo Olmos Colección, AGU.
127. Matilde Rodríguez called Wilson's position "traumatic" and a "personal betrayal." Marisa Ruiz interview with Matilde Rodríguez, 1999 (copy on file with author). The author wishes to thank Marisa for providing her with the transcript of this interview. Also see Weschler, *A Miracle, A Universe*, 170–171; "El mayor responsable de la aprobación de la ley es Wilson Ferreira," *Brecha*, December 26, 1986, 6, AD; Barahona de Brito, *Human Rights*, 131; Sikkink, *Justice Cascade*, 62; Marchesi et al., ed., *Ley de Caducidad: Un Tema Inconcluso*, 52–32, 197. He also argued for this position in various articles in *La Democracia*, the Blanco newspaper.
128. He died in 1988 and therefore was unable to run for president in 1989.
129. Author interview with Joe Eldridge, June 2, 2020.
130. "Junta de Generales decide que los militares no comparezcan," *El Telégrafo*, December 18, 1986, 1, BN.
131. "Uruguay Approves a Military Amnesty," *New York Times*, December 23, 1986, A3.

132. Ley 15848, Funcionarios Militares y Policiales, Palacio Legislativo, https://www.impo.com.uy/bases/leyes/15848-1986

133. Luis Roniger and Mario Sznajder, "Legacy of Human Rights Violations," 63.

134. "Fue la opción entre la guerra o la paz," *El Telégrafo*, December 30, 1986, 1, BN.

135. Mazzeo, *Memorias*, 20.

136. Ferreira interview.

137. Araújo was one of the most outspoken opponents of the amnesty law, and days later he was impeached and removed from office. Opponents accused him of inciting the crowds who reacted with outrage to the law. "Pedirán desafuera de Araújo por promover incidentes de anoche," *El Día*, December 22, 1986, 5, AD.

138. David Ransom, "Uruguay after Dictatorship," *New Internationalist*, September 1987, 114.

139. "Coacción y Amenazas en Domicilios de Lideres Políticos y de Jefes Militares," *El País*, December 22, 1986, 1, AD.

140. Number varied wildly in the newspapers the next day over how many protesters were at the Palacio. *El País* reported that the number "did not exceed 1500." while *El Día* estimated the number to be about 300. "Grave Disturbio en Palacio, Varios Diputados Lesionados," *El País*, December 22, 1986, 1; "Hubo heridos en graves disturbios en Parlamento," *El Día*, December 22, 1986, 7, AD.

141. "Hubo heridos en graves disturbios en Parlamento," *El Día*, December 22, 1986, 7; "El Olvido Imposible," *Brecha*, December 26, 1986, AD. All but one were released within twenty-four hours.

142. Antonio Pereira, "Análisis de los informativos televisivos durante el proceso de aprobación de la ley de caducidad," *Cuadernos de Historia* (2012): 125–149.

143. Steve J. Stern, *Remembering Pinochet's Chile: On the Eve of London 1998* (Durham: Duke University Press, 2006), 369.

144. Aracely Fernández Conze, "Qué nos aporta el caso uruguayo a los estudios sobre las transiciones a la democracia del Cono Sur latinoamericano en los 80?" Seminario de Historia Reciente, September 2014, Montevideo, Uruguay.

Chapter 7

1. "Plantearan plebiscite por DDHH," *El Día*, December 24, 1986, 9, AD; Centro Uruguay Independiente, *Referéndum* (Montevideo: CUI, 1987), 65.

2. Their husbands were Zelmar Michelini and Hector Gutiérrez Rodríguez, who had been murdered in Argentina in 1976. Gatti's daughter, son-in-law, and granddaughter were abducted and disappeared in Argentina the same year. They had been founding members of the PVP. Her granddaughter was eventually found in 1992, having been given to and adopted by an Argentine secret service officer's family. "Por un referéndum contra la impunidad," *Brecha*, December 26, 1986, 12, AD.

3. Referendums have a long and storied history in Uruguay as part of the nation's strong democratic roots, where many public issues have been submitted to votes. For more, see Monica Barczak, "Representation by Consultation? The Rise of Direct Democracy in Latin America," *Latin America Politics and Society* 43, no. 3 (Autumn 2001): 37–59.

4. 41.30 percent voted to overturn it, 1.45 percent voted blank, and 1.3 percent had their votes annulled.

5. Literature focuses on the valiant efforts by the Commission in the face of difficult domestic and international conditions, while also stressing the fear aspect. Burt, Lessa, and Fried

Amilivia, "Civil Society"; Delgado, "So the people can decide"; Rial, "Makers and Guardians"; Mallinder, "Uruguay's Evolving Experience," 53–55.

6. Adair, *Lost Decade*, 4. While Adair talks about this phenomenon in the Argentine context, it applies to Uruguayan rights dynamics as well.

7. Morley and McGillion, *Reagan and Pinochet*; Schmidli, *Fate*, 190.

8. The term "transitional justice" didn't exist until Ruti Teitel coined it in 1991, but the ideas, debates, and origins behind it often date back to the Southern Cone transitions in the 1980s. Uruguay was initially part of emerging discussions regarding transitions to democracy, but as the field of transitional justice cohered in the 1990s, it increasingly became left out of early histories due to the absence of any state-sponsored mechanisms until the early 2000s. For a much longer discussion on this topic and longer bibliography, see Sharnak, "Uruguay and the Reconceptualization of Transitional Justice."

9. For students, see "ADUR ante el Referendum," *Boletin* 6 (May 1987): 2, Ana María Ferrari Colección, AGU. This is not to say that arguments for the expansion of human rights diminished during this period; in fact, the fierce debate about human rights in other contexts continued. For example, *Brecha* explained the need to widen the understanding of human rights, arguing for the system of human rights to include not just political and civil rights, but also economic, social, and cultural rights to realize a more complete and complex social justice vision. Oscar López Goldaracena, "La educación, aporte para la causa de los derechos humanos," *Brecha*, May 22, 1987, 30, AD.

10. "La dignidad no caduca," *Enfoque*, June 1987, 23, Ana Laura Mello Colección, AGU.

11. "Este es un acto de la dignidad uruguaya," *Brecha*, December 26, 1986, 7, AD.

12. "Confirmaron presencia de la viuda del exlegislador Gutiérrez Ruiz," *El Telégrafo*, February 1, 1987, 3, BN.

13. Delgado, "'So the people can decide,'" 16; Mario Mazzeo, *MPP: orígenes, ideas, y protagonistas* (Montevideo: Ediciones Trilce, 2005), 41–42.

14. Roniger and Sznajder, *Legacy*, 67; Pereira, "Análisis," 126.

15. Most of the politicians who joined the campaign were from the Frente Amplio; however, several Blancos and one Colorado, Victor Vaillant, did as well. Lessa, *Memory*, 138; Diego Sempol, "A la sombra de una impunidad perenne: El movimiento de derechos humanos y la ley de caducidad," in *Ley de Caducidad: Un Tema Inconcluso*, ed. Aldo Marchesi et al. (Montevideo: Ediciones Trilce, 2013), 106.

16. Ruiz interview with Rodríguez; Sempol, "A la sombra," 107.

17. Nagora interview.

18. Susan Francheschet, Jennifer Piscopo, and Gwynn Thomas, "Supermadres, Maternal Legacies, and Women's Political Participation in Contemporary Latin America," *Journal of Latin American Studies* 48, no. 1 (February 2016): 2.

19. Ruiz interview with Rodríguez. It should be noted though that Uruguay had a history of more radical feminism. See Marino, *Feminism*; Christine Ehrick, "*Madrinas* and Missionaries: Uruguay and the Pan-American Women's Movement," *Gender & History* 10, no. 3 (November 1998): 406–424; Christine Ehrick, *Radio and the Gendered Soundscape: Women and Broadcasting in Argentina and Uruguay, 1930–1950* (New York: Cambridge University Press, 2016); Ehrick, *Shield*. Women were also in the Tupamaros in relatively high numbers (despite the group's somewhat weak viewpoints about women's liberation because of its supposed association with bourgeois middle-class values), and the PVP. Churchill, *Becoming*, especially Chapter 4. The point here is that this issue brought out a broader gendered engagement.

20. Women utilized experience they had gained during the activism against the dictatorship. Delgado, "'So the people can decide,'" 31–33.

21. Ibid., 32.

22. Marisa Ruiz, *Ciudadanas en tiempos de incertidumbre* (Montevideo: Doble Clic, 2010), 82–83.

23. Delgado, "'So the people can decide,'" 32; Ruiz interview with Rodríguez.

24. Ruiz interview with Rodríguez.

25. Memo, Comité Ejecutivo, March 4, 1987, Archivo SERPAJ.

26. Ruiz interview with Rodríguez.

27. "Sesiones del 18 de diciembre al 23 de diciembre," *Diario de Sesiones de la Cámara de Senadores de la República Oriental del Uruguay*, 7–8, AL.

28. Wilson Ferreira Aldunate, "Costo y recompense de la grandeza," *La Democracia*, December 31, 1986, 3, CEIU.

29. "Sanguinetti destacó clima de libertad y seguridad en el país," *El Dia*, December 24, 1986, 9, AD.

30. Ibid.

31. See more statements to this effect in articles such as "Aquí, el camino es firmar contra la impunidad," *Brecha*, April 24, 1987, 22, AD; "En materia de justicia, estamos lejos de una solución a la argentina," *Brecha*, May 8, 1987, 7, AD; "Se prepara acto por Zelmar y Tobo," May 8, 1987, *Brecha*, 8, AD.

32. "Llamiento a un referéndum Contra la Ley de Impunidad," January 28, 1987, Folder 35, Archivo SERPAJ. José Artigas is often considered to be the founding father of Uruguay.

33. Ibid.

34. Autoadhesivos, "Yo Firmo," Archivo SERPAJ.

35. Enrique Mazzei and Graciela Prat, "El Movimiento Pro-Referéndum en Uruguay, 1986–1987," *Revista Ciencias Sociales* 4 (1990): 29–33, Facultad Ciencias Sociales, Montevideo, Uruguay.

36. Boletín Interno No. 1, 12 enero 1987, Compaña Pro Referéndum Contra la Ley de Impunidad, Folder, Publicación Periódica, Archivo SERPAJ; "Acto central de campaña tuvo lugar en Plaza Independencia," and "Inician campaña para recolección de firmas," *El Telégrafo*, February 23, 1987, 1, BN.

37. "El Referéndum Moviliza a Una Ciudad," *Brecha*, March 20, 1987, 3, AD.

38. Ibid., 4–5, AD.

39. Delgado, "'So the people can decide.'"

40. Nagora interview.

41. Memo, "Uruguay: Amnesty International's Concerns on 'Disappearances' Following Legislation Granting Immunity from Prosecution to Alleged Violators of Human Rights," February 2, 1987, Folder 15, Box 260, AIUSA.

42. Letter, PEN to Julia Sanguinetti, July 6, 1987, Folder Uruguay 1987–1988 General, Box 328; and Letter, American Watch Aryeh Neier to Julio Sanguinetti, June 4, 1987, Folder: Amnesties/Justice 1987–1988, Box 331, HRW.

43. Flyer, "Uruguayo," Date 1985–1990, Box 1, Folder 120, Archive of Latin American and Caribbean Ephemera, PUA.

44. "Consideraciones de la Comisión de la campana de recolecciones de firmas," April 6, 1987, Archivo SERPAJ.

45. "Textos Radios 15," nd, Archivo SERPAJ.

46. "Sin ánimo de revancha: la democracia no se consolida ignorando los crímenes," *Brecha*, March 20, 1987, 8, AD.

47. "Editorial. El momento exige grandeza," *Mate Amargo*, February 2, 1989, 4.

48. The idea of forgetting as a positive policy has, over time, been expanded on by scholars. For example, see Mark Freeman, *Necessary Evils: Amnesties and the Search for Justice* (New York: Cambridge University Press, 2009).

49. Álvaro de Giorgi, "Las defensas blanca y colorada de la ley: entre el mal menor y el 'broche de oro' de la 'restauración modelo,'" in *Ley de Caducidad Un Tema Inconcluso: Momentos, Actores, y Argumentos (1986–2013)*, ed. Aldo Marchesi (Montevideo: Ediciones Trilce, 2013), 40.

50. Ibid.

51. Deborah Norden, *Military Rebellion in Argentina* (Lincoln: University of Nebraska Press, 1996), 129.

52. Some of those working for the referendum also received death threats in Uruguay, including well-known members such as Senator Carlos Julio Pereyra, municipal leader Rodolfo Nin Noyoa, and the president of the Commission, Jaime Castells. "Campana de amenazas contra el referéndum y necesidad de que se adopten medidas para garantizar el proceso del plebiscite," (June 10, 1987), p707, *Diario de Sesiones de la Cámara de Representantes,* Tomo 628, May–June 1987, AL.

53. de Giorgi, "Defensas."

54. Politicians also attacked the individuals behind the pro-referendum movement, stating that those promoting the referendum were the same as those who were in the Tupamaros and union strikes of the 1960s and 1970s that launched the country into violence and provoked the coup. De Giorgi, "Defensas," 40.

55. "6350008," *Brecha*, December 18, 1987, 4, AD.

56. The requisite 25 percent amounted to 555,701 signatures, so the CNPR collected well over that number, reaching more than 28.5 percent of the population.

57. Aficha, December 17, 1987, Archivo SERPAJ.

58. "6350008," *Brecha*, December 18, 1987, 4, AD.

59. Press Statement, "Proclama," December 17, 1987, Archivo SERPAJ.

60. There were, however, reports of intimidation which led to people asking to have their names taken off the registry. Handwritten Notes from Convo with Luis Pérez Aguirre, June 25, 1987, Folder Uruguay 1987/1988, Box 328, HRW.

61. Daniel Gianelli, "Algunas Reflexiones y comentarios al concluir la recolección de firmas por el referéndum," *Búsqueda*, December 17, 1987, 3, AD.

62. "Referéndum: La Cuenta Final," *Brecha*, January 8, 1988, AD.

63. Weschler, *A Miracle, A Universe,* 179.

64. Ibid., 182; "Ejemplos de Firmas no numerados por la corte," 1988, E05, Archivo SER-PAJ; Mazzeo, *MPP,* 54.

65. Pereyra was a National Party politician and 1971 running mate of Wilson Ferreira. He remained in Uruguay during the dictatorship and led the underground resistance domestically against the dictatorship. He was then elected as a senator again in 1984. Eduardo Alonso, *Clandestinos: Blancos y colorados frente a la dictadura 1973–1985* (Montevideo: Ediciones de la Banda Oriental 2012).

66. Weschler, *A Miracle, A Universe,* 219; Memo, Polly Pittman to Cynthia Brown, "Uruguay: ratification of signatures," December 24, 1988, Folder Uruguay 1987/1988, Box 328, HRW. These transcription errors by the court employees were actually not uncommon and none of

these people were ever given the opportunity to ratify their signatures in the subsequent year; Eduardo Galeano, "Sign on the Invisible Line," *Nation,* March 27, 1989, 411.

67. Author interview with Jo-Marie Burt, July 12, 2020.

68. Norden, *Military Rebellion,* 130–131.

69. Weschler, *A Miracle, A Universe* 179; "Los sucesos argentinos y los comentarios de políticos uruguayos," *Búsqueda,* January 21, 1988, 5, AD; "Instructivo Ante Pasible Ingreso a Nuestro País," *El País,* January 19, 1988, 4, AD.

70. "Silbermann: destino incierto; Retamoso: tribunal de honor," *Brecha,* September 20, 1988, 5, AD.

71. "Naval Officers Released but Concern Continues About Virtual Impunity of Human Rights Violators," October 29, 1988, Box 328, Folder "Uruguay AW Delegation 1988," HRW.

72. "A la opinión pública," CNPR, 1988, Archivo SERPAJ.

73. "Al Pueblo Uruguayo," January 28, 1988, Archivo SERPAJ.

74. "Ud. Debe saber por qué se pretende ahora descartar firmas," Archivo SERPAJ.

75. "El Plebiscite debe realizarse este año," June 15, 1988, unnamed clipping in folder, Archivo SERPAJ.

76. Jo-Marie Burt, "The Current Status of the Campaign for the Referendum on the 'Ley de Caducidad' in Uruguay," August 31, 1988, updated October 1988, Folder Plebiscite Campaign, Box 279, WOLA. During the rally, Burt notes that the organizers stressed that the purpose was first "to return to the democratic principles that Uruguayans have enjoyed for nearly a hundred years." She also notes that they also included justice for human rights violations and never having to relive the dark moments of the dictatorship. Yet, in stressing that the purpose was not vengeance, the democratic aspect was stressed first even under a broader mandate.

77. "Alerta a la Opinión Publica," Archivo SERPAJ.

78. Cynthia Brown was one of the first employees at the organization in 1982, and she was assigned in the late 1980s as the Uruguay researcher.

79. Memo, Brown to Goldman, "Uruguay Mission," November 24, 1988, Folder "Uruguay AW Delegation, 1988," Box 328, HRW.

80. Joe Eldridge interview, January 4, 2018.

81. These were not the sole international groups that focused on Uruguay's referendum process. For example, others provided periodic spotlights on activity to support the referendum. For example, the *Comisión de Apoyo Pro-Referendum* (Commission in Support of the Uruguayan Referendum) appeared in Toronto, which published newsletters on the evolving situation. See, for example, "Referendum for Peace and Justice in Uruguay," February 1989, Folder Plebiscite Campaign, Box 279, WOLA. There was a similar solidarity group, the Comisión de Nueva York y Nueva Jersey Pro-Referéndum in Uruguay, that sought to support the referendum efforts. See Letter, Carlos Varela to Ginny Bouvier, June 5, 1987, Folder Uruguay Razias, Box 280, WOLA.

82. Letter from Luis Pérez Aguirre, nd, Folder Issue Referendum, Box 280, WOLA; Handwritten Notes from Convo with Luis Pérez Aguirre, June 25, 1987, Folder Uruguay 1987/1988, Box 328, HRW.

83. Letter, Luis Pérez Aguirre to Ginny Bouvier, August 31, 1988, Folder Issue Referendum, Box 280, WOLA.

84. "Uruguayan Parliament Granted Impunity for Torturers," February 9, 1987, Comité de Defensa de los Derechos Humanos en Uruguay (Toronto), Folder Issue Referendum, Box 280, WOLA.

85. While there were numerous letters from international groups in the archives, this quote is from "A People's Campaign for Justice and Human Rights in Uruguay," nd, Comisión de Nueva York y Nueva Jersey Pro-Referendum en el Uruguay, p5, Folder Issue Referendum, Box 280, WOLA.

86. For example, the Comisión pro-referendum de Nueva York y Nueva Jersey set up a table in Jackson Heights, Queens. "Convocatoria," nd, Folder Issue Referendum, Box 280, WOLA.

87. Markarian, *Left*; Kelly, *Sovereign Emergencies*, 11; Alison Brysk, *Speaking Rights to Power: Constructing Political Will* (New York: Oxford University Press, 2013).

88. Joe Eldridge interview, June 2, 2020. Alex Wilde also explained that WOLA was engaged most with influencing U.S. foreign policy, which focused on Central America much more than South America during this period, so "we worked heavily on Central America." Author interview with Alex Wilde, June 4, 2020.

89. The WOLA archive has hundreds of pages about Uruguay even in the late 1980s when WOLA focused its attentions elsewhere. For example, Letter, Pérez Aguirre to Bouvier, August 31, 1988, and Letter from Madres y Familiares, October 1986, Folder Issue Referendum, Box 280, WOLA.

90. Press Release, "Rafael Michelini Discusses Uruguayan Democracy," July 16, 1988, Folder Issue Referendum, Box 280, WOLA. Michelini actually ended his 1988 trip to the United States by going to the Democratic National Convention in Atlanta as Edward Kennedy's guest. As earlier chapters discuss, Kennedy had long been a supporter of human rights in Uruguay.

91. To the extent that WOLA was working on the Southern Cone, it focused on Stroessner in Paraguay. The other major areas during this time were Central America, a new initiative on the War on Drugs, and human rights in Mexico. Wilde interview.

92. Americas Watch Letter to Sanguinetti, June 4, 1987, Folder Uruguay 1987/1988, Box 328, HRW.

93. One trip consisted of Cynthia Brown and Polly Pittman, the other of Bob Goldman and Giorgio Solimano. Goldman interview; Memo, "Uruguay Mission," HRW; Memo from Polly to Cynthia, December 24, 1988, "Uruguay: Ratification of signatures," Folder: Uruguay 1987/1988, Box 328, HRW.

94. Press Release by Bob Goldman, December 9, 1988, Folder Uruguay AW Delegation, 1988, Box 328, HRW; "Draft *New York Times* Op-Ed on Uruguay," Folder Uruguay 1987/1988, Box 328, HRW. Americas Watch also drafted an op-ed that they sought to publish in the *New York Times* about their visit and urging the Bush/Quayle administration to signal their support that the military respect the popular will of referendum despite threats that were emerging. I was unable to find any evidence that it was published. However, the effort demonstrates the multifaceted attempt by Americas Watch to publicize information about the referendum in the United States and lobby the Bush administration to support it. The George H. W. Bush administration was considerably less focused on Latin American issues than previous presidents (with the exception of Panama) and therefore tended to leave human rights issues in Latin America to the State Department. See Sikkink, *Mixed Signals*, 182–183. Andrew Natsios and Andrew Card Jr., *Transforming Our World: President George H.W. Bush and American Foreign Policy* (Lanham: Rowman & Littlefield, 2021) barely mentions Latin America at all.

95. Robert Goldman and Cynthia Brown, *Challenging Impunity: The Ley de Caducidad and the Referendum Campaign in Uruguay,* Americas Watch Committee, 1989.

96. For more on Americas Watch's contributions to this emerging movement, see Arthur, "How Transitions," 326.

97. Neier, *Movement*, 201–209; Méndez interview. Méndez noted Americas Watch played a large role in the *Velásquez Rodríguez v. Honduras* case that developed the obligation to investigate, prosecute, and punish those responsible for crimes against humanity. Méndez argued the case and Americas Watch helped raise the money to pay for witnesses to come to the court and to develop evidentiary material based on forensic reports. Juan E. Méndez and Javier Mariezcurrena, "Accountability for Past Human Rights Violations: Contributions of the Inter-American Organs of Protection," *Social Justice* 26, no. 4 (Winter 1999): 84–106; Méndez, *Taking a Stand*, 144–146.

98. Memo, "Uruguay Mission," HRW.

99. Interviews with Pittman, Méndez, and Goldman.

100. Hopgood, *Keepers*, 102.

101. AI Memo, Sebastian Brett to José Zalaquett, Uruguay Mission Briefing, March 10, 1986, Folder Uruguay AW Delegation 1988, Box 323, HRW; Memo from AI Americas Research Department, August 4, 1986, Folder 15, Box 250, Series IV.1.6, AIUSA.

102. Letter, Secretary General Thomas Hammarberg to President Julio María Sanguinetti, July 8, 1986, Folder 15, Box 250, Series IV.1.6, AIUSA.

103. Internal Memo on AI's Concerns of Disappearances, February 2, 1987, AMR 52/01/87, Folder 15, Box 250, Series IV.1.6, AIUSA.

104. Amnesty International, "Naval Officers released but concern continues about virtual impunity of human rights violators," AMR 52/03/88, October 29, 1988, Folder Plebiscite Campaign, Box 279, WOLA. The organization also distributed a report on failed investigations by military prosecutors and the challenges of the amnesty to further remedies, Amnesty International, "Official Investigations Fail to Establish Fate of the 'Disappeared,'" AMR/52/01/88, June 1988, Folder Uruguay AW 1988 Delegation, Box 328, HRW.

105. William Michael Schmidli, "Rockin' to Free the World?: Amnesty International's Benefit Concert Tours, 1968–1988," *Diplomatic History* (2021): 1–26.

106. "Levantate y Pelea," *Brecha*, October 21, 1988, 2, AD.

107. Pittman, Eldridge, Wilde, Juan Méndez, and Goldman interviews.

108. At WOLA, Juan Raúl Ferreira had returned to Uruguay, Eldridge had left the organization to live in Honduras, and Kathryn Sikkink, who worked at WOLA on Argentina and Uruguay in the late 1970s and early 1980s, had left as well. At Americas Watch, Polly Pittman was working only sporadically on Uruguay and became much more focused on Paraguay, which still had a dictatorship. At AI, Edy Kaufman's sabbatical at the International Secretariat in London was over as well and there was significant staff turnover from the 1970s.

109. Sikkink, *Justice Cascade*; Arthur, "How Transitions." Although Arthur and Sikkink point to the 1990s as the origins of real international momentum around transitional justice, specific organizations, such as the International Center for Transitional Justice, were not founded until 2001, and the first UN report on transitional justice was published in 2004. Also see Sandrine Lefranc and Frédéric Vairel, "The Emergency of Transitional Justice as a Professional International Practice," in *Dealing with Wars and Dictatorships: Legal Concepts and Categories in Action*, ed. Loira Israël and Guillaume Mouralis (New York: Springer: 2004), 235–252.

110. Carothers, *In the Name*, 117.

111. Sikkink, *Mixed Signals*, 149. The CIA also painted human rights groups as radical leftist groups seeking to "agitate for justice" and to "take advantage of the withdrawal of the military from power to pressure the new government to ensure 'the guilty will be punished.'" CIA Memo,

"Identification, Political Goals, and Anticipated Initiatives of Leftist Human Rights Organizations Operating in Uruguay," April 16, 1985, Virtual CIA Reading Room.

112. Uruguay, Country report on human rights practices, report submitted to the committee on foreign affairs, U.S. House of Representatives, 1987, 625, Washington: U.S. Government Printing Office.

113. Goldman and Brown, *Challenging Impunity,* 44.

114. Memo from State Department, December 19, 1985, Folder Uruguay/Kennedy Material, Box 328, HRW Collection; "Uruguay: Challenges to Democracy: An Intelligence Assessment," Directorate of Intelligence, January 1986, Virtual CIA Reading Room.

115. Memo, "Uruguay Mission," HRW.

116. Memo, Cynthia Brown, "Uruguay Trip Notes," November 2–4, 1988, Folder "Uruguay AW Delegation, 1988," Box 328, HRW.

117. Ibid.

118. "La Corte Electoral contra la voluntad popular," *Brecha,* October 21, 1988, AD.

119. Ibid.

120. "Resistir el fraude," *Brecha,* October 28, 1988, 4, AD.

121. Roniger and Sznajder, *Legacy,* 84. In fact, the Electoral Court did not publicize the list, but rather only released the list of names in an obscure daily, *Diario Oficial.* The names were organized by voting credential number and not even by name, making it more difficult to parse through the list. Memo, Pittman to Brown, "Uruguay: ratification of signatures," December 24, 1988, Folder Uruguay 1987/1988, Box 328, HRW.

122. "Uruguay: ratification of signatures," HRW; Norden, *Military Rebellion,* 130–133. This was the Villa Martelli uprising and was seen as having an even higher level of support among the military numbering approximately 1,000.

123. "Medina: de Derogarse ley caducidad no habrá anulación de los casos," *El País,* 5 diciembre 1988, 7, AD.

124. "Uruguay: ratification of signatures," HRW. The papers included *La República, La Hora, Brecha,* and *Mate Amargo.* The radio stations were CC 30 and CX44.

125. Weschler, *A Miracle, A Universe,* 223–226. This incident is also recounted in "Uruguay: ratification of signatures," HRW.

126. Samuel Blixen, "Referendum to overturn military amnesty will test limits of Uruguayan Democracy," *Latinamerica Press,* February 23, 1989, Folder Plebiscite Campaign, Box 279, WOLA.

127. "Uruguay: ratification of signatures," HRW. The two in the interior were in areas accessible to people coming back from Argentina who sought to ratify their signatures.

128. "Uruguay: ratification of signatures," HRW. It is possible that this was not an accident, as a congressman opposed to the referendum, Ruben Diaz (a Colorado) was in Fray Bentos for this last day of verification and is linked to the fact that those 82 signatures were never ratified.

129. Weschler, *A Miracle, A Universe,* 227.

130. "Universidad y Ley de Caducidad," *Boletín de Asociación de Docentes de la República,* marzo 1989, 4, Ana María Ferrari, AGU.

131. Memo, Cynthia Brown, "Uruguay Trip Notes," November 2–4, 1988, Folder, "Uruguay AW Delegation, 1988," Box 328, HRW; Burt interview.

132. Vice President Tarigo made these claims to representatives of Americas Watch. "Uruguay Trip Notes," HRW.

133. In terms of support for the CNPR, for example, the PIT-CNT labor union issued a pamphlet arguing forcefully for the Court to allow a referendum based on democratic and human rights grounds. "Las firmas están a votar contra la impunidad," PIT-CNT, Archivo SER-PAJ. The PIT-CNT also was critical in helping collect signatures. Matilde Rodríguez suggests that almost 100,000 signatures resulted from their efforts. Ruiz interview with Rodríguez.

134. "Proyecto llamado a tener trascendente proyección," *El Telégrafo,* January 4, 1987, 3, BN.

135. Luis Pérez Aguirre, "The Violation of Human Rights as an Instrument of the National Security Doctrine," 1st Conference on Human Rights in Latin America, November 1987, 1–2, Box 2, Massera Colección, AGU. This issue was expanded upon in late 1988 in the SERPAJ newsletter, which explained that not all violence was characterized by bloody encounters, but structural violence also helped create hunger and poverty within Uruguay that needed to be addressed. Francisco Bustamante, "La violencia tiene padres conocidos," *Paz y Justicia* (August–September 1988), 4, Box Paz y Justicia Sumario de DD.HH, Archivo SERPAJ.

136. "Informe: Derechos Humanos en Uruguay/1988," *SERPAJ,* Archivo SERPAJ.

137. Notes from Trip, Kern to Brown, March 7, 1988, Folder Uruguay General 1987–1988, Box 328, HRW.

138. "Piden a jueces investigar violaciones a los derechos humanes de antes de 1973," *El Telégrafo,* March 6, 1987, 3, BN.

139. Pan Interview; "Acciones legales contra la impunidad del terrorismo de estado," *Revista de IELSUR,* December 1987, Folder Uruguay AW 1988 Delegation, Box 328, HRW.

140. "Uruguay Trip Notes," HRW.

141. Alejandro Artucio, "Los Derechos Humanos y Las Organizaciones no Gubernamen-tales," *Revista de IELSUR,* July 1988, Folder Uruguay/1988 General, Box 328, HRW. Artucio was an Uruguayan lawyer who spent much of the dictatorship in exile in Europe after having been arrested early in the dictatorship for trying to defend political prisoners. In Europe, he was a legal advisor for the International Commission of Jurists and had long advocated for a broader vision of human rights. See Alejandro Artucio, "Violations of Economic and Social Rights of Political Prisoners," in *Amnesty: symposium on the state of emergency and human rights in Uruguay* (Paris: SIJAU, 1978).

142. Letter from Antonio Serrentino Sabella to Ford Office, September 9, 1987, Grant 08550674, Reel 5703, Ford Foundation, RAC.

143. Inter-Office Memorandum, Michael Sifter to Jeffrey Puryear, "Final Evaluation and Recommendation for Closing IELSUR," January 12, 1990, Grant 08550674, Ford Foundation, RAC.

144. For more on the sociological theory behind political opportunities in tumultuous times, see Sidney Tarrow, *Power in Movement: Social Movements, Collective Action and Politics* (New York: Cambridge University Press, 1994).

145. Loveman, *National Colors,* 265–267.

146. "Otro verano sin negoción salarial," *Brecha,* January 15, 1988; "Un derecho que se cas-tiga," *Brecha,* 12, AD; Hugo Rodríguez, "El cascoteado derecho a la educación," *Brecha,* November 25, 1988, 16, AD.

147. Andrews, *Blackness,* 144.

148. George Reid Andrews, *Afro-Latin America 1800–2000* (New York: Oxford University Press, 2004), 183; Paulina Alberto, *Terms of Inclusion: Black Intellectuals in Twentieth Century Brazil* (Chapel Hill: University of North Carolina Press, 2011). Other countries in

the region also witnessed a surge in Afro-descendent activism in the transitional period. See, for example, Eduardo Elena, "Argentina in Black and White," in *Rethinking Race in Modern Argentina*, ed. Paulina Alberto and Eduardo Elena (New York: Cambridge University Press, 2016), 202.

149. Author interview with Romero Jorge Rodríguez, October 9, 2014; Rodríguez, *Racismo y Derechos Humanos*; Sztainbok, *Imagining*.

150. *Mundo Afro*, 1, no. 2 (November 1988), Schomburg Research Center, New York Public Library.

151. Mónica Olaza, "Afrodescendencia y restauración democrática en Uruguay: ¿Una nueva visión de ciudadanía?" *Revista de Ciencias Sociales* 30, no. 40 (January–June 2017): 63–82.

152. Sempol, *De los baños*, 58.

153. "El himno nacional de carajo," *Jaque*, 3 no. 145, October 1, 1986, 27.

154. Nogara interview.

155. Gerardo quote in Diego Sempol, "Violencia Policial y Democracia en Disputa," *Estudos Sociologia, Recife* 2, no. 23 (2017), 247.

156. Ettore Pierri and Luciana Possamay, *Hablan los otros* (Montevideo: Proyección, 1987), 14.

157. Sempol, *De los baños*, 61–65; Miller, *Out in the World*, 219; Muñoz, *Uruguay homosexual*, 45.

158. Churchill, *Becoming*, 152.

159. James Green, "(Homo)sexuality, Human Rights, and Revolution in Latin America," in *Human Rights and Revolution*, ed. Jeffrey Wasserstrom, Lynn Hunt, and Marilyn Young (Lanham: Rowman and Littlefield, 2000), 140.

160. Grupo Escorpio, "Boletín Número 2 del Grupo Escorpio," Archivo Sociedades en Movimiento [hereinafter ASM], https://asm.udelar.edu.uy/items/show/282.

161. Homosexuales Unidos, "Descubriéndonos," Año I Número 1, June 1989, ASM, https://asm.udelar.edu.uy/items/show/295.

162. Homosexuales Unidos, "Aquí estamos," November 1990, ASM, https://asm.udelar.edu.uy/items/show/885.

163. Sempol, "Violencia," 268.

164. Ibid., 264.

165. In fact, strong Uruguayan feminist movements dated back to the early nineteenth century that focused on broad social and economic rights. Marino, *Feminism*.

166. Comisión de Mujeres Uruguayas (CMU), "Mujer y política," June 1986, ASM, https://asm.udelar.edu.uy/items/show/290.

167. By the late 1980s, CIESU was run by women and also started to study social movements as political actors who did not exist during the dictatorship. See Notes from Trip, Kern to Brown, HRW. Inter-Office Memo, Lastarria to Saint, December 29, 1983, "Final Evaluation," Grant 08550674, Reel 5703, Ford Foundation, RAC.

168. Comisión de Mujeres Uruguayas (CMU), "Mujer y política," June 1986, ASM, https://asm.udelar.edu.uy/items/show/290; Fisher, *Out of the Shadows*, 45.

169. Reuterswärd, "Libertad de Acción."

170. Ines Pousadela, "The Women's Movement in Uruguay: A Decades-Long Struggle for Legal Abortion," *Crossroads Initiative, Society for Participatory Research*, 2012.

171. María Pueblo, "¡Las mujeres también tienen derechos!" *El Telégrafo*, January 18, 1987, 6, BN.

172. These diverse feminist groups also participated in larger debates and advocacy in the region. See Pilar Fernández, "Crecimiento, contradicción, y desafíos del feminismo," *Brecha*, December 11, 1987, AD.

173. Mainwaring and Pérez-Liñán, *Democracies and Dictatorships in Latin America*, 227.

174. Atencio, *Memory's Turn*, 12.

175. "Ciudadano," pamphlet by CNPR, 1989, E05, Archivo SERPAJ. In talks in the interior of the country, the CNPR emphasized that political prisoners had been in jail without having committed a single crime. "Queremos que la justiciar actúe, como corresponde en un estado de derecho," *El Telégrafo*, April 3, 1989, 3, BN.

176. Carpeta de autoadhesivos, 1989, Archivo SERPAJ; Material Gráfico, 1989, Archivo SERPAJ.

177. "16 de abril: su voto decide," pamphlet by CNPR, 1989, E05, Archivo SERPAJ.

178. Carpeta de autoadhesivos, 1989, Archivo SERPAJ; Material Gráfico, 1989, Archivo SERPAJ.

179. "Lo que rechazamos es la división del país en castas," *El Telégrafo*, April 7, 1989, 1, BN.

180. Memo from Holly to Cynthia, May 15, 1989, Folder Uruguay-Referendum 1987–1989, Box 328, HRW; "Sempol, "A la sombra de una impunidad perenne," 111; Taylor C. Boas, "Voting for Democracy: Campaign Effects in Chile's Democratic Transition," *Latin American Politics and Society* 57, no. 2 (2015): 67–90.

181. "El referéndum trasciende cintillos partidarios," *El Telégrafo*, April 11, 1989, 3, BN.

182. Materials Graficos, 1988–1989; Archivo SERPAJ.

183. Madres y Familiares, "16 Razones para votar por la justicia el 16 de abril," 1989, Archivo SERPAJ.

184. Ibid.

185. For others, see, for instance, Marchesi, *Latin America's Radical Left*, 212–213.

186. Mario Benedetti, "Cuando al gobierno se le mueve el quepis," *Brecha*, January 13, 1989, 7, AD.

187. Héctor Rodríguez, "Igualdad ante la ley y la democracia sin tutela," *Brecha*, January 20, 1989, 5, AD.

188. "Sanguinetti: construir un futuro en paz y no volver atrás "el reloj de la historia,"" *El Telégrafo*, January 22, 1989, 3, BN. The official line coming from Sanguinetti's administration was also that the vote was a partisan issue, and those who voted for him in office should vote against verde as well. Party politics are strong in Uruguay and this inevitably had an impact as well. Emilio N. Monti, "Montevideo, Uruguay," nd, Folder, "Law Modifications," Box 279, WOLA.

189. "No puedo decir que va a ganar el voto verde, digo que quiero que ganar," *El Telégrafo*, March 16, 1989, 3, BN.

190. In Uruguay, about half of the entire population lives in the capital, Montevideo, whereas the rest of the population is spread out among the rest of the "departments." When the results were announced, the papers reported that in Montevideo the population had voted with a 55.4 percent majority to overturn the law. However, in the rest of the country, 67.4 percent voted to keep it intact. Clearly, this resulted in the amnesty law being upheld, but the difference in approval rates exposes an interesting divide between the capital and the remainder of the country. "Escrutinio para armar," *Brecha*, April 21, 1989, 6, AD. The country's *Nunca Más* report establishes that 75 percent of those tortured were from Montevideo. While it is not true to say that people in the interior did not feel the repression—they most certainly did—the dictatorship was experienced differently there. SERPAJ, *Uruguay: Nunca Más*, 324–336. More research on the

campaign and divide between Montevideo and the interior is needed. See, among others, Debbie Sharnak, "Justice for Whom?: Debating the 1986 Amnesty Law in Urban versus Rural Uruguay," Paper presented at LASA 2019, Boston, MA, and Emilia Abin and Emmanuel Martínez, "Rituales ruraloides en la transición a la democracia," in *Al Retorno a la Democracia: otras miradas,* ed. Álvaro de Giorgi and Carlos Demasi (Montevideo: Fin de Siglo Editorial, 2016): 141–168.

191. Shirley Christian, "Uruguay Votes to Retain Amnesty for the Military," *New York Times,* April 17, 1989, A6.

192. Mazzeo, *MPP,* 25.

193. Memo from Holly to Cynthia, May 15, 1989, Folder Uruguay-Referendum 1987–1989, Box 328, HRW.

194. Michelini interview.

195. "Uruguay Ponders Justice of Amnesty," *Globe and Mail,* April 18, 1989.

196. Nagora interview. Everyone I talked to about the defeat spoke in similarly devastated terms. Jo-Marie Burt remembered that it was like "mourning a death." Burt interview.

197. Letter, from Luisa Cuesta a Madres, April 18, 1989, Folder 11, AMF.

198. Letter, Independientes del Barrio Bella Italia to the National Pro-Referendum Commission, April 20, 1989, Folder: Cartas, Archivo SERPAJ.

199. Ibid.

200. This particular quote came from a letter from Jamie Pérez, writing on behalf of the Communist Party in Uruguay, but dozens of other letters also reflected these concerns without specifically mentioning human rights. Letter, Pérez to Comisión Nacional Pro-referéndum, April 20, 1989, Folder Cartas, Archivo SERPAJ. Other letters came in from ASCEEP, the Frente Amplio, the Asociación de Bancarios del Uruguay, and Alberto Pérez Pérez (a constitutional law scholar), among others. A group of "people that worked in different places" for the "green vote" also mentioned that the fight needed to continue for "equality under the law and respect for human rights," but they were the only other mention of human rights. Letter to Commission, April 20, 1989, Folder Cartas, Archivo SERPAJ. Similar letters were found in Folder 13, AMF.

201. "No acatar la impunidad," May 1, 1989, Julio Rügnitz Colección, AGU.

202. Emilio N. Monti, "Montevideo, Uruguay," nd, Folder "Law Modifications," Box 279, WOLA.

203. Burt, Lessa, and Amilivia, "Civil Society," 313.

204. Julio María Sanguinetti, "Present at the Transition," in *The Global Resurgence of Democracy,* ed. Larry Diamond and Marc F. Plattner (Baltimore: Johns Hopkins University Press, 1993), 59.

205. Inter-Office Memorandum, Michael Sifter to Jeffrey Puryear, "Final Evaluation and Recommendation for Closing: IELSUR," January 12, 1990, Grant 08550674, Reel 5703, Ford Foundation, RAC.

206. Letter, Anderson to Neier, June 20, 1989, Folder HRW/General 1989, HRW.

207. "No Acatar la impunidad," May 1, 1989, Julio Rügnitz Colección, AGU.

208. "When the War Ends," Human Rights Center-Berkeley, Payson Center for International Development and the International Center for Transitional Justice (December 2007).

209. Tricia Olsen, Leigh Payne, and Andrew Reiter, *Transitional Justice in Balance: Comparing Processes, Weighing Efficacy* (Washington: United States Institute of Peace, 2010). These claims for justice include not just trials but also truth commissions and memorialization—all of which did not occur in Uruguay until after the turn of the century. For instance, the Peace

Commission's report was published in 2003, and the first big memorial, *Memorial de los Desa-parecidos*, was inaugurated in 2001.

210. For recent research on this topic, see the dissertation of Mariana Mendes, "Delayed Transitional Justice: Timing and Cross-Country Variation in Spain, Brazil, and Uruguay" (PhD diss., European University Institute, 2019).

Conclusion

1. "Lanzan campana electoral para anular la Ley de Caducidad en Uruguay," *EFE News Service,* July 30, 2009; "Transitions Newsletter," *ICTJ,* November 2009, accessed at ictj.org/sites /default/files/ICTJ-Global-Newsletter-November-2009-English.pdf.

2. Lawrence Weschler, "Prologue," in *Uruguay: Nunca Más* (Philadelphia: Temple University Press, 1992), xxv; Skaar, "Wavering Courts." In addition to the truth commission, lawyers had pursued cases at the Inter-American Commission on Human Rights and domestically by circumventing the amnesty law through pursuing crimes that fell outside the 1973–1985 time frame or by targeting civilian offenders who were not protected under the military-only amnesty.

3. Sikkink, *Justice Cascade.*

4. "Sondeos a pie de urna apuntan que Ley de Caducidad será anulada en Uruguay," *EFE News Service,* October 25, 2009.

5. For some of the possible reasons for failure, see Lessa, *Memory,* 152–153.

6. Mujica was shot six times by police before being captured the first time of three times. He escaped from imprisonment twice. For his third imprisonment, he had a much longer jail stay—which almost broke him. He "howled at noises that weren't there and obsessed over procuring a tiny portable toilet for his cell." Eve Fairbanks, "Jose Mujica Was Every Liberal's Dream President. He Was Too Good to Be True," *Pulitzer Center,* February 6, 2015, http://pulitzercenter .org/reporting/south-america-uruguay-president-popular-politics-liberal-disappointment.

7. Robert Goldman, among other legal scholars, supports an emerging legal standard about minority rights and referendum: "You can't subject something like amnesty to a popular referendum. Human rights law is not majoritarian law. [The majority] can't take away the right to remedy, the right to truth, all of that, from a single person. It's not the way it works." Goldman interview. See also Daniel Lewis, *Direct Democracy and Minority Rights: A Critical Assessment of the Tyranny of the Majority in American States* (London: Routledge, 2013).

8. I come to this term from Greta de Jong, *You Can't Eat Freedom* (Chapel Hill: University of North Carolina Press, 2016), 1, and her own discussion of Barbara Fields. Just as freedom was a moving target, so were human rights.

9. Gelman v. Uruguay, Inter-American Court of Human Rights, Judgment of February 24, 2011 (Merits and Reparations), 84, 88. Robert Goldman also made this argument as early as the 1980s, filing cases that argued human rights law "is not majoritarian law. Ninety-nine percent can't take away the right to remedy, the right to truth." Goldman interview.

10. For more on this issue, see Debbie Sharnak and Francesca Parente, "Uruguay and the Inter-American Court of Human Rights: Ten Years Post-Gelman," Paper presented at LASA 2022, Virtual.

11. Freedom House, *Freedom in the World 2020,* accessed at https://freedomhouse.org /explore-the-map?type=fiw&year=2020; https://freedomhouse.org/sites/default/files/2020-02 /FIW_2020_REPORT_BOOKLET_Final.pdf

12. Kritz, *Transitional Justice*; and Ruti Teitel, *Transitional Justice* (New York: Oxford University Press, 2000).

13. Harvey M. Weinstein, "Editorial Note: The Myth of Closure, the Illusion of Reconciliation: Final Thoughts on Five Years as Co-Editor-in-Chief," *International Journal of Transitional Justice* 5, no. 1 (March 2011): 2.

14. Collins, *Post-Transitional Justice*; Aguilar, "Transitional or Post-Transitional Justice?" Other scholars focus on terms such as delayed justice or postponed justice. Jon Elster, ed., *Retribution and Reparation in the Transition to Democracy* (New York: Cambridge University Press, 2006); Skaar, *Judicial Independence*, 2; Iosif Kovras, *Grassroots Activism and the Evolution of Transitional Justice: The Families of the Disappeared* (New York: Cambridge University Press, 2017).

15. United Nations Office of the High Commission for Human Rights, "Observaciones preliminares del Relator Especial para la promoción de la verdad, la justicia, la reparación, y las garantías de no repetición al final de su visita oficial a la República Oriental del Uruguay," http://www.ohchr.org/SP/NewsEvents/Pages/DisplayNews.aspx?NewsID=13849&LangID=S.

16. For more on the political nature of transitional justice, see Leslie Vinjamuri and Jack Snyder, "Law and Politics in Transitional Justice," *Annual Review of Political Science* 18 (2015): 303–327.

17. Author interview with Mariana Mota, January 17, 2018.

18. Andra Lenart, United Nations General Assembly Special Session 2016, accessed June 16, 2016, https://twitter.com/andraslenart/status/722496422495588352; "Uruguay: en una primera etapa, serán 50 las farmacias que vendan marihuana legal," accessed June 16, 2016, http://miradaprofesional.com/ampliarpagina.php?npag=3&id=1744; Dignity Initiative, accessed June 2, 2016, https://twitter.com/InfoDignity/status/738390772131737601; "Guía para sistema libre de homofobia," *La Republica*, accessed June 10, 2016, http://www.republica.com.uy/guia-para-sistema-libre-de-homofobia/571010/.

19. Romani interview.

20. David Kennedy, "The International Human Rights Movement: Part of the Problem?" *Harvard Human Rights Journal* 15 (Spring 2002), 116–117.

21. Tate looks at a similar set of tensions in Colombia. Tate, *Counting the Dead*, 134.

22. Uruguay Country Analysis and Strategic Report, Folder 1354, Box 166, Rockefeller Papers, RAC.

SELECTED SOURCES AND BIBLIOGRAPHY

For a complete bibliography of sources used in this book, please go to
http://www.debbiesharnak.com

Manuscripts and Archival Collections

Archives and Specialized Collections in Latin America

Archivo de Diarios, Palacio Legislativo, Montevideo, Uruguay (AD)
Archivo Diplomático-Administrativo, Montevideo, Uruguay (ADA)
Archivo General de la Universidad, Montevideo, Uruguay (AGU)
    Ana María Ferrari Colección
    Massera Colección
    Ana Laura Mello Colección
    Gustavo Olmos Colección
    Julio Rügnitz Colección
Archivo Histórico- Diplomático, Ministerio de Relaciones Exteriores, Montevideo, Uruguay (AHD)
Archivo Legislativo, Montevideo, Uruguay (AL)
Archivo de Madres y Familiares de Uruguayos Detenidos Desaparecidos, Montevideo, Uruguay (AMF)
Archivo del Secretaría de Derechos Humanos para el Pasado Reciente, Montevideo, Uruguay
Archivo de Servicio Paz y Justicia, Montevideo, Uruguay (Archivo SERPAJ)
Biblioteca Miguel Lerdo Tejada, Mexico City, Mexico (BMLT)
Biblioteca Nacional, Montevideo, Uruguay (BN)
Biblioteca del Palacio Legislativo, Montevideo, Uruguay (PL)
Centro de Documentación e Investigación de la Cultura de Izquierdas, Buenos Aires, Argentina
Centro de Fotografía de Montevideo
Centro de Estudios Interdisciplinarios Uruguayos, Montevideo, Uruguay (CEIU)
    Álvaro Barros Lémez Colección
    Cores Colección
    David Compora Colección
    Derechos Humanos Colección
    Jesus Betancourt Colección
    Luis Echave Colección
    Ponce de León Colección
    Prensa
    Raúl Jacob Colección
    Waksman Colección

Archives and Specialized Collections in the United States and Europe

Columbia University Archives, New York, NY
  Amnesty International-USA Collection (AIUSA)
  Human Rights Watch Collection (HRW)
Carter Presidential Library, Atlanta, GA (JCL)
Donald Fraser Papers, Minnesota Historical Society, St. Paul, MN (DFP)
Ford Presidential Library, Ann Arbor, MI
Nettie Lee Benson Latin America Collection, University of Texas at Austin Archives (Benson)
  George Lister Papers (GLP)
Human Rights Archives, Duke University, Durham, NC
  Patricia Derian Papers (PDP)
  Washington Office on Latin America Collection (WOLA)
International Institute of Social History, Amsterdam, the Netherlands (IISH)
Rockefeller Archives Center, Sleepy Hollow, NY (RAC)
  Ford Foundation Archive
  James Cannon Files (JCF RAC)
  Nelson Rockefeller Papers
Manuscripts and Archives at Yale University, New Haven, CT
Marshall Bloom Collection, Amherst College Library Archives and Special Collections, Amherst, MA (BC)
National Archives and Records Administration, College Park, MD (NARA)
  Warrren Christopher Papers (Christopher Papers)
National Archives, United Kingdom, London, UK (TNA)
National Security Archive, Washington, DC (NSA)
Reagan Presidential Library, Simi Valley, CA
Princeton University Archives, Princeton, NJ (PUA)
  North American Congress on Latin America (NACLA)
  Archive of Latin American and Caribbean Ephemera
Schomburg Center for Research in Black Culture, New York, NY
Tamiment Library, New York University, New York, NY (Tamiment)
  Philip Agee Papers
  Printed Ephemera Collection on Organizations
United Nations Archives and Documents, New York, NY (UN)
Wisconsin Historical Society, Madison, WI
World Council of Churches Archives, Geneva, Switzerland (WCC)

Online Archives
Archivo Chile, Centro de Estudios Miguel Enriquez, Online
Archivo Sociedades en Movimiento (Uruguay) (ASM)
Argentina Declassification Project
Amnesty International Online Archive
Department of State Virtual Reading Room (DOSVRR)
Nixon Presidential Library Online Archive
Reuters Video Archive
United Nations Online Archive
Virtual CIA Reading Room
Wikileaks

Private Papers
Blane, Andrew. New York, NY.
Flynn, Charles. Davidson, NC.
Nogara, Raquel. Montevideo, Uruguay.

Interviews
Blane, Andrew. June 10, 2016, Email. June 17, 2016, New York, NY.
Burt, Jo-Marie. July 12, 2020. Phone.
Bustamante, Francisco "Pancho". September 11, 2014. Montevideo, Uruguay.
Eldridge, Joe. January 4, 2018. Washington, DC.
Eldridge, Joe. June 2, 2020. Phone.
Ferreira, Juan Raúl. January 15, 2018. Montevideo, Uruguay.
Flores Silva, Manuel. July 24, 2014. Montevideo, Uruguay.
Flynn, Charles. June 9, 2020. Phone.
Goldman, Robert. March 2, 2020. Phone.
Griesgraber, Jo Marie. December 15, 2017. Phone.
Hawk, David. June 2, 2016. Phone.
Kaufman, Edy. June 22, 2016. Phone.
Mazzarovich, Gabriel. March 19, 2012. Montevideo, Uruguay. Interview with Abby Goldberg.
Méndez, Juan. February 24, 2020. Washington, DC.
Michelini, Felipe. June 14, 2012. Montevideo, Uruguay.
Mota, Mariana. January 17, 2018. Montevideo, Uruguay.
Nagora, Raquel. August 1, 2014. Montevideo, Uruguay.
Olivera, Efraín. August 24, 2014. Montevideo, Uruguay.
Pan y Pan, Jorge. August 21, 2014. Montevideo, Uruguay.
Pittman, Patricia. May 22, 2020. Zoom.
Prat, Martin. August 19, 2014. Montevideo, Uruguay.
Riley, Alicia. March 13, 2014. Phone.
Rodríguez Larreta, Matilde. March 3, 1999. Monteivdeo, Uruguay. Interview with Marisa Ruiz.
Rodríguez, Romero Jorge. October 9, 2014. Montevideo, Uruguay.
Romani, Milton. May 25, 2020. Zoom.
Santos, Beatriz. September 8, 2014. Montevideo, Uruguay.
Tiscornia, Jorge. November 28, 2015. Montevideo, Uruguay.
Trivelli, Isabel. March 22, 2012. Montevideo, Uruguay. Interview with Abby Goldberg.
Weschler, Lawrence. October 9, 2014. Email.
Wilde, Alex. June 4, 2020. Phone.
Youle, John. December 5, 2017. Phone.

Published Reports, Documents, Memoirs
Amnesty: Symposium on The State of Emergency and Human Rights in Uruguay. Paris: SIJAU, 1978.
Association for Diplomatic Studies and Training Oral Histories
 Pezzulo, Lawrence. February 24, 2989, https://www.adst.org/OH%20TOCs/Pezzulo,%20 Lawrence%20A.toc.pdf?_ga=2.91837843.82786147.1628799609-136417637.1628799609.
 Todman, Terrance. June 23, 1995. http://adst.org/oral-history/fascinating-figures/being -black-in-a-lily-white-state-department/
Brown, Cynthia, ed. *With Friends Like These: The Americas Watch Report on Human Rights and U.S. Policy in Latin America.* New York: Pantheon Books, 1985.

Carter, Jimmy. *White House Diary*. New York: Farrar, Straus and Giroux, 2010.

Centro Uruguay Independiente. *Referéndum*. Montevideo: CUI, 1987.

Country Reports on Human Rights Practices for 1979. Washington: U.S. Government Printing Office, 1980.

PIT-CNT: un solo movimiento sindical: selección de documentos. Montevideo: PIT-CNT, 1985.

CNT 1964-1965: Documentos Sindicales. Montevideo: Centro Uruguay Independiente, 1966.

CNT: Declaración de principios, programa y estatutos. Montevideo: Centro Estudiantes de Derecho, 1967.

Department of State Bulletin. Washington: Office of Public Communication, 1945.

di Candia, Cesar. *Ni Muerte Ni Derrota: Testimonios sobre Zelmar Michelini*. Madrid: Ediciones Atenea, 1987.

Documentos de la Huelga General. Montevideo: Centro Uruguay Independiente, 1984.

Documentos políticos: La CDU una experiencia unitaria. Mexico: Ediciones CDU, 1984.

Foreign Relations of the United States (FRUS) volumes
    FRUS, 1964–1968, Volume XXXI, South and Central America; Mexico
    FRUS, 1977–1980: Human Rights and Humanitarian Affairs, Volume II

Foro Internacional sobre la Vigencia de los Derechos Humanos en América Latina. Montevideo: Universidad de la República Departamento De Publicaciones, 1971.

Goldman, Robert, and Cynthia Brown. *Challenging Impunity: The Ley de Caducidad and the Referendum Campaign in Uruguay*. Americas Watch Committee, 1989."Hearings on Human Rights in Uruguay and Paraguay." Washington: U.S. Government Printing Office, 1976.

Hudson, Darril. *The World Council of Churches in International Affairs*. Great Britain: Faith Press, 1977.

"Human Rights and U.S. Policy in the Multilateral Development Banks." Hearing before the Subcommittee International Development Institutions and Finance, 97th Congress, First Session, July 21 and 23, 1981. Washington: U.S. Government Printing Office, 1981.

Junta de Comandantes en Jefe. *Las Fuerzas Armadas al pueblo oriental*. Montevideo: República Oriental del Uruguay, 1978.

Laber, Jeri. *The Courage of Strangers: Coming of Age with the Human Rights Movement*. New York: Public Affairs, 2002.

The Lawyers Committee for International Human Rights. "Uruguay: The End of a Nightmare?" May 1984.

Martínez Moreno, Carlos. *Los Días Que Vivimos* Montevideo: Editorial Giron, 1973.

Mazzeo, Omar. *Memorias del Voto Verde*. Montevideo: Rosebud Ediciones, 1999.

Memoria de Punta de Rieles en los tiempos del penal de mujeres. Montevideo, Editorial Vivencias, 2004.

Méndez, Juan. *Taking a Stand: The Evolution of Human Rights*. New York: St. Martin's Press, 2011.

Movimiento estudiantil: resistencia y transición. Montevideo: Centro Uruguay Independiente, 1988.

Neier, Aryeh. *The International Human Rights Movement: A History*. Princeton: Princeton University Press, 2012.

Neier, Aryeh. *Taking Liberties: Four Decades in the Struggle for Rights*. New York: Public Affairs, 2003.

Olivera, Efraín. "Sigue valiendo la pena." *Si decimos Derechos Humanos . . .* Montevideo: SERPAJ, 2006.

Organization of American States. "Annual Report 1979–1980." Chapter V Uruguay, http://www .cidh.org/annualrep/79.80eng/chap.5.htm.

Pereyra, Carlos Julio, ed. *Wilson: Las Cartas del Exilio*. Montevideo: Ediciones de la Banda Oriental, 2013.

"Primeras 30 Medidas de Gobierno del Frente Amplio." *Problemas de Desarrollo* 2, no. 9 (1971): 160–168.

"Report on the Situation of Human Rights in Uruguay." Organization of American States, 1978.

Rial, Juan. "Uruguay: Elecciones de 1984: Sistema Electoral y Resultados." In *Centro Interamericano de Asesoría y Promoción Electoral*. Costa Rica: Instituto Interamericano de Derechos Humanos, 1986.

Rickard, Stephen A. et al. "Chile: Human Rights and the Plebiscite." In *An Americas Watch Report*. July 1988.

Sanguinetti, Julio María. "Present at the Transition." In *The Global Resurgence of Democracy*, edited by Larry Diamond and Marc F. Plattner, 53–60. Baltimore: Johns Hopkins University Press, 1993.

Servicio Paz y Justicia. *Uruguay, Nunca Más: Human Rights Violations, 1972–1985*, translated by Elizabeth Hampsten. Philadelphia: Temple University Press, 1992.

Symposium on the State of Emergency and Human Rights in Uruguay. Paris: International Secretariat of Catholic Jurists/International Federation of Human Rights, 1978.

Tarigo, Enrique. *Temas de Nuestro Tiempo, Tomo I*. Montevideo: Fundación de Cultura Universitaria, 1979.

Torture in Greece: The First Torturers' Trial 1975. Amnesty International Publications, 1977.

Tribunal Permanente de los Pueblos. Montevideo: Graphis Ltda, 1990.

"The Tupamaro Manifesto." In *The Tupamaros: Urban Guerrillas in Uruguay*, edited by Alain Labrousse, 157–162. New York: Penguin, 1973.

Uruguay. Country Report on Human Rights Practices. Report Submitted to the Committee on Foreign Affairs, U.S. House of Representatives. Washington: U.S. Government Printing Office, 1987.

Uruguay: Generals Rule. London: Latin America Bureau, 1980.

U.S. Congress. House Committee on International Relations. *Human Rights in Uruguay and Paraguay, Hearings Before the Subcommittee on International Relations*. 94th Congress, 2d sess., 1976.

U.S. Department of State. "Country Reports on Human Rights Practices for 1982." Report Submitted to the Committee on Foreign Relations. Washington: U.S. Government Printing Office, February 1983.

Vance, Cyrus. *Hard Choices: Critical Years in America's Foreign Policy*. New York: Simon and Schuster, 1983.

"When the War Ends: A Population-Based Survey on Attitudes About Peace, Justice and Social Reconstruction in Northern Uganda." Human Rights Center-Berkeley, Payson Center for International Development and the International Center for Transitional Justice. December 2007.

Weingärtner, Erich. *Human Rights: Solidarities, Networks, and the Ecumenical Movement*. Philippines: Human Rights Desk, National Council of Churches in the Philippines, 1988.

Zelmar Michelini: Artículos Periodisticos y Ensanyo, Tomo VI. Montevideo: Cámara de Senadores, 1986.

INDEX

ACKNOWLEDGMENTS

Writing, according to the author Mavis Gallant, "is like a love affair: the best part is the beginning." I do not wholly disagree. For while it was perhaps easier to start this book, to see it actually come to fruition, I have relied on a lengthy list of people. It is hard to know how properly to convey such an overwhelming feeling of gratitude. While no words can properly express my thanks, the list below acknowledges just some of the incredible people who made this book possible.

First and foremost, thank you to the amazing activists and policy makers who spoke with me about their experiences fighting for various ideas of human rights and accountability in Uruguay. Some are named on my interview list, though many are not. Countless individuals spent time with me on Zoom, met me at cafés, or welcomed me into their homes for maté, conversation, and difficult discussions of the past. I am indebted to them for their time and efforts. Their resilience is an inspiration. I only hope to have done a semblance of justice to their experiences.

I also owe a debt of gratitude to the mentors who guided me at various stages of my education, dating back to my undergraduate years at Vassar College. Katherine Hite's passion for Latin American human rights struggles ignited my own interest in the field. Robert Brigham introduced me to a love of history that first semester in Poughkeepsie, and every year since, he has helped me grapple with questions of the past, policy, and how history can be our best teacher. In graduate school at the University of Wisconsin-Madison, Jeremi Suri supported my initial investigation into Carter's foreign policy, and has championed my work through an energetic dialogue from Austin in the years since. Jennifer Ratner-Rosenhagen, Florencia Mallon, Scott Status, and especially Steve Stern taught me how to be a historian, providing patience, support, and guidance that made me a better writer, thinker, and scholar. Leslie Abadie was incomparable for her support in navigating both Wisconsin's bureaucracy and life as a graduate student.

At the University of Wisconsin-Madison, I also found an unparalleled intellectual community among my peers. Simon Balto, Jake Blanc, Alison Brady, Vaneesa Cook, Genevieve Dorais, Katherine Eade, Tamara Feinstein, Julie Gibbings, Jessica Kirstein, Johanna Lanner-Cusin, Elena McGrath, Valeria Navarro-Rosenblatt, Campbell Scriber, Nicholas Strohl, and Bridgette Werner are just some of the remarkable individuals who shared their work, energy, and ideas with me over the years. Bridgette, in particular, provided invaluable feedback on my chapters throughout my writing and produced the book's stellar index. Aliza Luft and I formed our interdisciplinary friendship on the Madison campus; I am so grateful that our bond and research exchanges extended well beyond Bascom Hill. Special recognition goes to Rachel Gross, Christine Lamberson, and Britt Tevis, whose support started with cheese curds and bike rides, but stretched to our post-PhD writing group, which has been a heroic source of motivation and friendship. Somehow, we scheduled writing group meetings even as our time zone differences spanned three continents. Britt deserves particular credit for reading every chapter in this book, I would venture to guess, no less than three times, and for supporting this project and me even in my darkest moments of not being able to see the forest for the trees. I am deeply grateful that history introduced me to all these scholars and allowed me to learn from their passion and intellect along the way.

After Wisconsin, I am grateful for support from other institutions, including Michelle D'Amico and Vera Jelinek at NYU's Center for Global Affairs for providing an intellectual home when I lived in New York City. Amazing scholars and friends also surrounded me at the History and Literature Program at Harvard University. Particular thanks go to Lauren Kaminsky, Jenni Brady, Paul Adler, Jordan Brower, Paul Edwards, Reed Gochberg, Ernest Hartwell, Rebecca Kastleman, Marina Magloire, Ugur Pece, Emily Pope-Obeda, Mark Sanchez, and Duncan White. I could not have asked for better scholars to teach with and learn from. Also at Harvard, Kirsten Weld's formidable Boston Area Latin America Research Group provided me with especially helpful comments on my Introduction and included me in an exchange of ideas on various Tuesday evenings at the David Rockefeller Center for Latin American Studies. I am also grateful for the meticulous research work done by Ariette Escobar over two different semesters during my time as a lecturer.

Much appreciation also goes to my colleagues at Rowan University, especially my fellow historians. Members of my department have been especially gracious, supporting my research, extending their friendship, and providing valuable feedback on chapters in our Works in Progress sessions. College of Humanities and Social Science Dean Nawal Ammar and Associate Dean Cory Blake have also been especially supportive in seeing this book completed. Rowan is home to outstanding students, some of whom provided research support in the latter stages of this book, including Ryn Seu, for her work on my bibliography, and SirMichael Cianci, who offered amazing transcription support and research during some of the toughest months of the COVID pandemic. Special thanks at Rowan goes to my writing group for many conversations at Dawn to Dusk with Emily Blanck, Jody Manning, Jennifer Rich, Chanelle Rose, and especially Stephen Hague, whose incredible edits and feedback provide a model for the type of colleague I aspire to be.

In my broader intellectual community, particular gratitude extends to Jennifer Adair, Jeannette Estruth, Paul Katz, Rachel Nolan, Karin Rosemblatt, Sarah Snyder, and Marisa Tramontano for their various contributions, conversations, and encouragement in this project. Sarah was particularly valiant in sharing research with me from Amnesty International. In addition, I am indebted to the "Women Who (Try To) Write" group, who met so many mornings on Zoom to figure out how to cope with motherhood, the patriarchy, and academia, all while getting writing done. We are all indebted to our fearless leader, Sheyda Jahanbani, but special thanks go to other women in the trenches, including Jennie Miller, Poornima Paidipaty, Marta Vicente, and Vanessa Walker. While I must thank Vanessa for bringing me into this group, my gratitude to her extends back to when I was deciding where to go to graduate school. She has never been too busy to offer her time for a conversation, an extra set of eyes on my writing, or a voice of support. Her deep and cogent grappling with the complexity of rights is an example of the scholarship I hope to produce, and her support of more junior scholars offers a standard for the academic I want to be.

During my time in Uruguay, in 2012, 2014, and 2018, my support network spanned far outside the archives. Uruguayan scholars provided me immeasurable support and help. Aldo Marchesi sponsored my Fulbright application to travel to Uruguay and then helped me in every subsequent stage of researching, writing, and editing. In addition, Vania Markarian, Jaime Yaffé, Mercedes Altuna, and many other scholars of the Seminario de Investigación en Historia Reciente provided me with a vibrant intellectual environment and community. I also had the good fortune of connecting with Francesca Lessa, Pedro Cameselle, Megan Strom, Carolina de Robertis, Pamela Harris, and Samuel Brandt, all of whom were also scholars from abroad working on

Uruguayan history. Our ongoing conversations and exchanges through the years have proved enormously beneficial.

This book also would not have been possible without the financial support of various institutions. The History Department and Latin American, Caribbean, & Iberian Studies Program at the University of Wisconsin-Madison provided financial support to allow me to travel to archives around the Americas. The Rockefeller Foundation and the Fulbright Organization supported critical stages of my research. Patricia Vargas at Fulbright-Uruguay must be especially recognized for her gallant efforts on behalf of the scholars working in the country. In the revision stages of the book, I am also grateful to the Society for Historians of American Foreign Relations for making additional research possible. Harvard and Rowan Universities also provided critical research funds for me to conduct archival work and fieldwork.

In *The Devil in the White City,* Erik Larson writes, "To me every trip to a library or archive is like a small detective story. There are always little moments of such trips when the past flares to life, like a match in the darkness." I had many similar experiences and have dozens of archivists around the world to thank for them. For assistance in finding those magical historian moments, I thank Lucas Buresch, Laura Bálsamo, Mariah Leavitt, Graham Stinnett, Magdalena Figueredo, Jose Tejera, Carlos Osorio, Pamela Graham, Patrick Stawski, and Albert Nason, among many others. Thank you as well to Diana Ávila Hernández for her work in the Mexican archives and Oluwaseun Otosede Williams for his research in the WCC archives in Geneva. I am also indebted to Nancy Piñeiro and Daniela Steppes who helped me transcribe the many interviews I conducted and shared a passion for social justice.

I am also so grateful to the team at Penn Press, particularly to series editor Chris Dietrich, who offered valuable feedback on my writing. I am also deeply indebted to Bob Lockhart, whose excitement about this project, expertise, patience, editing, and long conversations strengthened my chapters in every conceivable way.

Last but certainly not least, I thank my family. I have the most amazing sister, brother-in-law, and nieces: Barbara Sharnak and Nathan, Jeri, and Casey Blouin, who bring me so much joy and have offered me unending support. This book, though, is dedicated to my parents, Diane and Larry Sharnak, who instilled in me the intellectual curiosity to even begin this endeavor and championed my work throughout with pep talks and love. It would take another book to put my thanks into words. I am also so grateful to my partner, Joshua Duboff, who is truly a partner in every sense of the word. If I can agree with Gallant that the best part of writing is the beginning, the same cannot be said about our love affair, which has only gotten better every day I have been with him. I feel so fortunate to have his support in life's journey, and in helping me finish this book. This book is also for my daughters, Maya and Gabby, who undoubtedly delayed its publication, but in every way have been *vale la pena*. I hope they learn from the activists within these pages, and I am so grateful to them for bringing such enormous amounts of love and happiness to my life each day.

To my community of scholars, friends, and family, I owe my deepest thanks and acknowledge the vast debts I doubt I ever can repay. This book is the result of their contributions and love along the way.

CPSIA information can be obtained
at www.ICGtesting.com
Printed in the USA
JSHW011704230223
38131JS00002B/4/J